Economic Diversification
in the Gulf States

Public Expenditure and
Non-Oil Economic Growth
in Bahrain, Oman and Qatar

Gulf Studies at Gerlach Press

The Gulf Region: Economic Development and Diversification (4 vols set)
Ed. by L. Luciani, S. Hertog, E. Woertz and R. Youngs
ISBN 9783940924001, 2012

The GCC in the Global Economy
Ed. by Richard Youngs
ISBN 9783940924018, 2012

Resources Blessed: Diversification and the Gulf Development Model
Ed. by Giacomo Luciani
ISBN 9783940924025, 2012

GCC Financial Markets: The World's New Money Centers
Ed. by Eckart Woertz
ISBN 9783940924032, 2012

National Employment, Migration and Education in the GCC
Ed. by Steffen Hertog
ISBN 9783940924049, 2012

Asia-Gulf Economic Relations in the 21st Century: The Local to Global Transformation
Ed. by Tim Niblock with Monica Malik
ISBN 9783940924100, 2013

A New Gulf Security Architecture: Prospects and Challenges for an Asian Role
Ed. by Ranjit Gupta, Abubaker Bagader, Talmiz Ahmad and N. Janardhan
ISBN 9783940924360, 2014

Gulf Charities and Islamic Philanthropy in the 'Age of Terror' and Beyond
Ed. by Robert Lacey and Jonathan Benthall
ISBN 9783940924322, 2014

State-Society Relations in the Arab Gulf States
Ed. by Mazhar Al-Zoby and Birol Baskan
ISBN 9783940924384, 2014

Political Economy of Energy Reform: The Clean Energy-Fossil Fuel Balance in the Gulf
Ed. by Giacomo Luciani and Rabia Ferroukhi
ISBN 9783940924407, 2014

The Silent Revolution: The Arab Spring and the Gulf States
Ed. by May Seikaly and Khawla Mattar
ISBN 9783940924346, 2014

Security Dynamics of East Asia in the Gulf Region
Ed. by Tim Niblock with Yang Guang
ISBN 9783940924483, 2014

Islamic Finance: Political Economy, Performance and Risk
Ed. by Mehmet Asutay and 'Abdullah Turkistani
ISBN 9783940924124, 3 vols set, 2015

Employment and Career Motivation in the Arab Gulf States: The Rentier Mentality Revisited
Ed. by Annika Kropf and Mohamed Ramady
ISBN 9783940924605, 2015

The Changing Energy Landscape in the Gulf: Strategic Implications
Ed. by Gawdat Bahgat
ISBN 9783940924643, 2015

Sustainable Development Challenges in the Arab States of the Gulf
Ed. by David Bryde, Yusra Mouzughi and Turki Al Rasheed
ISBN 9783940924629, 2015

The United States and the Gulf: Shifting Pressures, Strategies and Alignments
Ed. by Steven W. Hook and Tim Niblock
ISBN 9783940924667, 2015

Africa and the Gulf Region: Blurred Boundaries and Shifting Ties
Ed. by Rogaia Mustafa Abusharaf and Dale F. Eickelman
ISBN 9783940924704, 2015

Rebuilding Yemen: Political, Economic and Social Challenges
Ed. by Noel Brehony and Saud Al-Sarhan
ISBN 9783940924681, 2015

Science and Technology Development in the Gulf States: Economic Diversification through Regional Collaboration
Ed. by Afreen Siddiqi and Laura Diaz Anadon
ISBN 9783959940023, 2016

Higher Education Investment in the Arab States of the Gulf: Strategies for Excellence and Diversity
Ed. by Dale F. Eickelman and Rogaia Mustafa Abusharaf
ISBN 9783959940122, 2016

Iran's Relations with the Arab States of the Gulf: Common Interests over Historic Rivalry
Ed. by Maaike Warnaar, Luciano Zaccara and Paul Aarts
ISBN 9783959940047, 2016

Egypt and the Gulf: A Renewed Regional Policy Alliance
Ed. by Robert Mason
ISBN 9783959940061, 2016

Intellectual Property Rights: Development and Enforcement in the Arab States of the Gulf
Ed. by David Price and Alhanoof AlDebasi
ISBN 9783959940108, 2016

The Arab States of the Gulf and BRICS: New Strategic Partnerships in Geopolitcs and Economics
Ed. by Tim Niblock, Alejandra Galindo and Degang Sun
ISBN 9783959940085, 2016

The Arms Trade, Military Services and the Security Market in the Gulf States: Trends and Implications
Ed. by David B. Des Roches and Dania Thafer
ISBN 9783959940160, 2016

Strategies of Knowledge Transfer for Economic Diversification in the Arab States of the Gulf
Ed. by Rasmus Gjedssø Bertelsen, Neema Noori and Jean-Marc Rickli
ISBN 9783959940146, 2018

Yemen and the Gulf States: The Making of a Crisis
Ed. by Helen Lackner and Daniel Martin Varisco
ISBN 9783959940306, 2018

Conflict Resolution and Creation of a Security Community in the Gulf Region
Ed. by Tim Niblock with Talmiz Ahmad and Degang Sun
ISBN 9783959940368, 2018

The Future of Labour Market Reform in the Gulf States: Towards a Multi-Disciplinary, Evidence-Based and Practical Understanding
Ed. by David B. Jones and Sofiane Sahraoui
ISBN 9783959940344, 2018

Cihat Battaloğlu
Political Reforms in Qatar: From Authoritarianism to Political Grey Zone
ISBN 9783959940429, 2018

Yesenn El-Radhi

Economic Diversification in the Gulf States

Public Expenditure and Non-Oil Economic Growth in Bahrain, Oman and Qatar

Gerlach Press

First published 2018
by Gerlach Press
Berlin, Germany
www.gerlach-press.de

Cover Design: Frauke Schön, Hamburg
Printed and bound in Germany

British Library Cataloguing in Publication Data.
A catalogue record for this book is available from the British Library.

Bibliographic data available from Deutsche Nationalbibliothek
http://d-nb.info/1155492358

ISBN: 978-3-95994-052-8 (hardcover volume)
ISBN: 978-3-95994-053-5 (eBook)

To the memory of my father

Contents

List of Tables viii

List of Figures ix

List of Abbreviations xi

Acknowledgments xiii

Introduction 1

I Public Expenditure and Long-Run Economic Growth: General Insights 11

1 Causes of Long-Run Economic Growth 13
- 1.1 Causes of Long-Run Economic Growth in Economic Theory 13
- 1.2 The Convergence Hypothesis 24
- 1.3 Searching for Correlates of Growth in a World of Model Uncertainty 31

2 Does Public Expenditure Cause Economic Growth? 45
- 2.1 Public Expenditure in Models of Economic Growth 45
- 2.2 Empirical Evidence Capital and Current Expenditure . . . 51
- 2.3 Empirical Evidence Education and Health Expenditure . . 55

II Exploring the Links Between Public Expenditure and Non-Oil Economic Growth in Bahrain, Oman and Qatar 61

3 The Impact of Public Expenditure on Non-Oil GDP and on Labour Productivity: An Econometric Analysis 63
- 3.1 Introduction 63

3.2 Current Status of Research . . . 67
3.3 Data . . . 72
3.4 Econometric Methodology . . . 77
3.5 Empirical Results . . . 99
3.6 Conclusion . . . 120

4 Bahrain: Non-Oil Development Efforts in a Semi-Rich Oil Rentier Economy 125
4.1 Overview . . . 125
4.2 Public Expenditure . . . 128
4.3 Non-Oil GDP . . . 135
4.4 Labour Productivity . . . 144

5 Oman: A Late Non-Oil Economic Blooming Caused by Rising Public Oil Rents 153
5.1 Overview . . . 153
5.2 Public Expenditure . . . 156
5.3 Non-Oil GDP . . . 166
5.4 Labour Productivity . . . 175

6 Qatar: Big Push Non-Oil Investment by Qatar Inc. 189
6.1 Overview . . . 189
6.2 Public Expenditure . . . 192
6.3 Non-Oil GDP . . . 202
6.4 Labour Productivity . . . 211

III The Impact of Public Expenditure on Potential Sources of Non-Oil Economic Growth 221

7 Public Expenditure and Private Sector Investment 223
7.1 Introduction . . . 223
7.2 The Economic Roles of the Public and Private Sectors . . . 225
7.3 Crowding-In or Crowding-Out - An Econometric Analysis . 236
7.4 The Impact of Investment on Non-Oil Economic Growth Dynamics . . . 251

8 Public Expenditure and Labour Productivity 261
8.1 Introduction . . . 261
8.2 Labour Productivity Developments in International Perspective . . . 263
8.3 Public Expenditure and Human Capital . . . 267

8.4 Public Expenditure and Structural Change 278

Conclusion **291**

References **301**

Appendix A: Data Sources and Definition of Variables **337**

Appendix B: Econometric Results Chapter 3 **349**

Appendix C: Robustness Checks Chapter 3 **361**
Change Variable Order Orthogonalised Impulse Responses 361
Robustness Check: Time Series in Current Prices 365
Robustness Check: Private Sector Non-Oil GDP 376

Appendix D: Econometric Results and Robustness Checks Chapter 7 **385**
Econometric Results Chapter 7 385
Robustness Check: Time Series in Current Prices 394

List of Tables

1.1 High Growth and Low Growth Countries 1960-2009 26
1.2 Empirically Relevant Correlates of Economic Growth 38

3.1 Oil and Gas Exports GCC Countries 1980-2013 66
3.2 Oil and Gas Public Revenues GCC Countries 1997-2013 . . 66
3.3 Time Span of Variables 74
3.4 Overview - Order of Integration 100
3.5 Overview - Number of Cointegration Relations 102
3.6 VECM - Final Specification 105
3.7 Granger Causality Tests 112

4.1 Bahrain - Average Annual Growth Rates Public Expenditure, Non-Oil GDP and Labour Productivity 1979-2013 . . 126
4.2 Bahrain - Education, Health, and Infrastructure Indicators 1950-2013 132
4.3 Bahrain - Composition & Size of Public Expenditure 1976-2013 134
4.4 Bahrain - Levels Public Expenditure, Non-Oil GDP and Labour Productivity 1979-2013 138
4.5 Bahrain - Indicators of Economic Activity 1979-2013 140
4.6 Bahrain - Gross Value Added by Economic Activity 1976-2013 142
4.7 Bahrain - Total Employment Census Years 1971-2010 . . . 148
4.8 Bahrain - Employment by Sector and Nationality Census Years 1971-2010 150
4.9 Bahrain - Sectoral Employment Shares Bahraini and Non-Bahraini Nationals 1971-2010 151

5.1 Oman - Average Annual Growth Rates Public Expenditure, Non-Oil GDP and Labour Productivity 1979-2013 154
5.2 Oman - Education, Health, and Infrastructure Indicators 1950-2013 160
5.3 Oman - Composition & Size of Public Expenditure 1976-2013 162

5.4 Oman - Levels Public Expenditure, Non-Oil GDP and Labour Productivity 1979-2013 168
5.5 Oman - Indicators of Economic Activity 1979-2013 170
5.6 Oman - Gross Value Added by Economic Activity 1967-2013 172
5.7 Oman - Average Annual Growth Rates Capital Intensity and Labour Productivity 1979-2013 178
5.8 Oman - Overview Employment 1975-2010 180
5.9 Oman - Employment by Sector and Nationality 1975-2010 . 182
5.10 Oman - Sectoral Employment Shares Omani and Non-Omani Nationals 1975-2010 184

6.1 Qatar - Average Annual Growth Rates Public Expenditure, Non-Oil GDP and Labour Productivity 1980-2013 190
6.2 Qatar - Education, Health, and Infrastructure Indicators 1950-2013 196
6.3 Qatar - Composition & Size of Public Expenditure 1976-2013 198
6.4 Qatar - Levels Public Expenditure, Non-Oil GDP and Labour Productivity 1979-2013 204
6.5 Qatar - Indicators of Economic Activity 1979-2013 206
6.6 Qatar - Gross Value Added by Economic Activity 1975-2013 208
6.7 Qatar - Total Employment Census Years 1970-2010 214
6.8 Qatar - Employment by Sector and Nationality Census Years 1970-2010 216
6.9 Qatar - Sectoral Employment Shares Qatari and Non-Qatari Nationals 1970-2010 218

7.1 Indicators Private Sector Investment Bahrain, Oman and Qatar 1979-2013 228
7.2 Government Shareholdings in the Five Largest Publicly Listed Companies 234
7.3 Overview - Cointegration and Causality Analysis 246
7.4 Overview - Cointegration and Causality Analysis (Current Prices) 247
7.5 Total Gross Fixed Capital Formation 1975-2013 252
7.6 Main Export Goods 1980-2010 254
7.7 Industrial Electricity Prices and Energy Use 256
7.8 Main Employment Sectors Census Years 258

8.1 CAGR Non-Oil GVA per Worker, Labour Force, and Aggregate Non-Oil GVA 1980-2013 266

8.2 Public Education and Health Expenditures GCC and Comparator Countries 1980-2013 272
8.3 Education and Health Indicators GCC and Comparator Countries 1980-2013 274
8.4 TIMSS 2011 Test Scores GCC and Comparator Countries . 276
8.5 Sectoral Structure Employment of Nationals in Census Years 284
8.6 Sectoral Structure Employment of Non-Nationals in Census Years 286
8.7 Wages Public and Private Sectors Bahrain and Oman . . . 288
8.8 Wages and Work Hours Public and Private Sector Qatar (2013) 288

A1 Data Sources - Total, Capital, and Current Expenditure . . 338
A2 Ministries and Public Agencies included in Education and Health Expenditure 340
A3 Data Sources - Education Expenditure 341
A4 Data Sources - Health Expenditure 342
A5 Data Sources - Labour Force 344
A6 Data Sources - Domestic Credit to Private Sector & Households 346
A7 Data Sources - Gross Fixed Capital Formation Private Sector 348
B1 Unit Root Tests: ADF Test 350
B2 Unit Root Tests: KPSS Test 351
B3 Unit Root Tests: ADF-GLS Test 352
B4 Unit Root Tests: Unit Root Test with Structural Break . . 353
B5 Cointegration Tests: Bahrain 354
B6 Cointegration Tests: Oman 355
B7 Cointegration Tests: Qatar 356
B8 Zero Restriction Tests 357
B9 Stability Tests 359
C1 Overview - Order of Integration (Current Prices) 365
C2 Unit Root Tests: ADF Test 366
C3 Unit Root Tests: KPSS Test 367
C4 Unit Root Tests: ADF-GLS Test 368
C5 Unit Root Tests: Unit Root Test with Structural Break . . 369
C6 Overview - Number of Cointegration Relations (Full Samples) 370
C7 Cointegration Tests: Bahrain (Current Prices) 371
C8 Cointegration Tests: Qatar (Current Prices) 373
C9 Zero Restriction Tests (Current Prices) 374
C10 Stability Tests (Current Prices) 375
C11 Overview - Order of Integration (Private Sector) 376
C12 Unit Root Tests: ADF Test 377
C13 Unit Root Tests: KPSS Test 378

C14 Unit Root Tests: ADF-GLS Test 379
C15 Unit Root Tests: Unit Root Test with Structural Break . . 380
C16 Overview - Number of Cointegration Relations 381
C17 Cointegration Tests: Bahrain (Private Sector) 382
C18 Zero Restriction Tests (Private Sector) 383
C19 Stability Tests (Private Sector) 383
C20 VECM - Final Specification (Private Sector) 384
C21 Granger Causality Tests (Private Sector) 384
D1 Overview - Order of Integration 385
D2 Unit Root Tests: ADF Test 386
D3 Unit Root Tests: KPSS Test 387
D4 Unit Root Tests: ADF-GLS Test 388
D5 Unit Root Tests: Unit Root Test with Structural Break . . 389
D6 Cointegration Tests: Bahrain, Oman and Qatar 390
D7 Zero Restriction Tests 391
D8 Stability Tests 392
D9 VECM - Final Specification 393
D10 Granger Causality Tests 393
D11 Overview - Order of Integration 394
D12 Unit Root Tests: ADF Test 395
D13 Unit Root Tests: KPSS Test 396
D14 Unit Root Tests: ADF-GLS Test 397
D15 Unit Root Tests: Unit Root Test with Structural Break . . 398
D16 Cointegration Tests: Bahrain 399
D17 Zero Restriction Tests 400
D18 Stability Tests 400
D19 VECM - Final Specification 401
D20 Granger Causality Tests 401

List of Figures

1 Public Expenditure, Non-Oil GDP and Labour Productivity 1979-2013 . . . 5

3.1 Impulse Response Analysis Bahrain & Oman . . . 108
3.2 Impulse Response Analysis Qatar I . . . 109
3.3 Impulse Response Analysis Qatar II . . . 110
3.4 Impulse Response Analysis Bahrain (Private Sector) . . . 119

4.1 Bahrain - Oil Prices and Total Expenditure 1960-2013 . . . 130
4.2 Bahrain - Labour Productivity, Aggregate Non-Oil GDP and Labour Force 1979-2013 . . . 146

5.1 Oman - Oil Prices and Total Expenditure 1967-2013 . . . 158
5.2 Oman - Labour Productivity, Aggregate Non-Oil GDP and Labour Force 1979-2013 . . . 176

6.1 Qatar - Oil Prices and Total Expenditure 1967-2013 . . . 194
6.2 Qatar - Labour Productivity, Aggregate Non-Oil GDP and Labour Force 1979-2013 . . . 212

7.1 Public Expenditure and Private Gross Fixed Capital Formation . . . 239
7.2 Public Expenditure and Domestic Credit to Private Sector . 240
7.3 Impulse Responses Cointegrated Variables . . . 249
7.4 Impulse Responses Cointegrated Variables (Current Prices) 250

8.1 Non-Oil GVA per Worker 1980-2013 . . . 268

C1 Impulse Responses Bahrain & Oman (Modified Variable Order) . . . 362
C2 Impulse Responses Qatar I (Modified Variable Order) . . . 363
C3 Impulse Responses Qatar II (Modified Variable Order) . . . 364

List of Abbreviations

ALBA	Aluminium Bahrain
BAPCO	Bahrain Petroleum Company
BATELCO	Bahrain Telecommunications Company
BH	Kingdom of Bahrain
BP	British Petroleum
CAGR	Compound Annual Growth Rate
CPI	Consumer Price Index
CSIS	Center For Strategic & International Studies
EIA	Energy Information Administration
GCC	Gulf Cooperation Council
GDP	Gross Domestic Product
GFCF	Gross Fixed Capital Formation
GPIC	Gulf Petrochemical Industries Company
GVA	Gross Value Added
IMF	International Monetary Fund
IBRD	International Bank for Reconstruction and Development
LNG	Liquified Natural Gas
MEED	Middle East Economic Digest
OM	Sultanate of Oman
PDO	Petroleum Development Oman
QA	State of Qatar
QP	Qatar Petroleum
UN-ECWA	United Nations, Economic Commission for Western Asia
UN-IDO	United Nations, Industrial Development Organization
USGS	U.S. Geological Survey
VECM	Vector Error Correction Model

Acknowledgments

This book is based on my doctoral dissertation at Friedrich-Alexander-Universität Erlangen-Nürnberg. Writing a doctoral dissertation is a long and laborious process. Over the course of this process, I have accumulated huge intellectual and emotional debts. Firstly, I would like to express my sincere gratitude to my advisors Prof. Dr. Sefik Alp Bahadir and Prof. Jürgen Kähler, Ph.D. for providing me with the opportunity to complete my doctoral dissertation at Friedrich-Alexander-Universität Erlangen-Nürnberg as an external student. Their guidance and comments were essential for shaping the final version of this book.

I also benefitted substantially from my former employer DZ Bank AG since it enabled me to turn my full-time job as a country risk analyst into a part-time-position for a total of five years. This allowed me to devote sufficient time to the research and writing of my doctoral dissertation. I would also like to thank the helpful staff at the Arab World Documentation Unit (University of Exeter) and at the German National Library of Economics in Kiel and Hamburg. These libraries have been very valuable sources for official publications from the Arab Gulf countries.

Most of all, I would like to thank my wife Annika. Her understanding and support in difficult times have made the completion of my dissertation and everything else so much easier. Annika and our two daughters Amelie and Sophia have given me a better life than I could have ever imagined. Finally, my deep gratitude goes to my parents for everything they have done for me. I dedicate this book to the memory of my father who was a source of love and inspiration for me and my sister Ischtar.

Introduction

The Topic and the Aim of the Book

Public expenditure shaped the economic development patterns in the six member countries of the Gulf Cooperation Council (GCC; Bahrain, Kuwait, Oman, Qatar, Saudi Arabia, United Arab Emirates). The start of oil production provided GCC governments with large inflows of oil export earnings. These inflows allowed GCC governments for strong increases of public expenditure levels over the following decades which altered local economies in various aspects.

Prior to the start of oil production in the early-to-mid-20th century, economic activities in the pre-industrial societies on the Arabian Peninsula primarily consisted of trade, fishing and pearl diving. In addition, modern day infrastructure as well as public health and education services were virtually non-existent. This all changed with the start of oil production and, even more so, with the strong increase of oil prices during the years of the first oil price boom (1974-1985). A substantial expansion of public education and health services contributed to a large improvement of socio-economic development levels. In addition, oil wealth gave rise to a very important role of GCC governments in production and employment patterns. While the trade balances and the fiscal accounts of the GCC countries continue to be dominated by oil and gas export revenues, all GCC economies witnessed strongly rising levels of economic activity outside the oil and gas sector over the last decades.

This book examines in more detail the impact of public expenditure on non-oil economic growth in the three GCC countries Bahrain, Oman and Qatar since the late 1970s. While the academic literature highlighted different roles of public expenditure within the political economies of the GCC countries, very little empirical research has so far analysed the overall impact of public expenditure on non-oil economic growth dynamics. This book aims to fill this gap by elaborating the country-specific characteristics of the links between public expenditure and non-oil economic growth in Bahrain, Oman and Qatar against the background of economic growth theory.

The perspectives on the economic and political roles of public expenditure in the GCC countries are not uniform across different strands of the academic literature. Proponents of *rentier state theory* such as Luciani (1990) and Beblawi (1990) do not attribute public expenditure an important role for fostering the development of non-oil economies. As GCC governments command over sizeable external oil rents, they are presumed to have only little incentives for pursuing a developmental economic policy. This link between oil wealth and an unambitious economic policy is based on the funding structure of rentier states. Large external oil rents increase both the financial and political autonomy of governments as it frees them from the need for taxation. As a result, rentier states are seen to be much less compelled to promote the growth of productive economic activities and, hence, taxable earnings than states which depend on taxes from the domestic economy.

Instead, rentier state theory regards public expenditure in the GCC countries primarily as a tool for political patronage. In this view, the strong increases of public expenditure levels over the last decades served as a means for enhancing the political legitimacy of GCC governments. This perspective typically relates to the build-up of extensive welfare systems for local populations in the GCC countries since the mid-1970s and to a strong expansion of public sector employment, most notably, during years of high oil price levels (1974-1985, 2002-2013). Accordingly, Luciani (1990) singles out the allocation of external oil and gas rents as the main economic policy task of rentier states *(Allocation States)*.

More recently, several authors have criticised the focus of rentier state theory on the allocative aspects of economic policy and public expenditure patterns in the GCC countries as being too narrow (e.g. Gray 2011; Hertog 2010, 2012a; Luciani 2012). While acknowledging that a rentier state perspective helps to explain certain aspects of public expenditure patterns such as the GCC countries' high public wage bills, these authors emphasise that GCC governments promoted the economic development of non-oil sectors through a much more active economic policy stance than envisaged by rentier state theory. Along the lines of *developmental state theory*, these authors ascribe GCC governments a very important role for the strong increases of production capacities across several non-oil sectors. Hertog (2010, 2012a) points to the successful business expansions of several state-owned companies in different non-oil sectors of the GCC countries. In a departure from earlier work, Luciani (2012) singles out large-scale public investments in infrastructure and in the production capacities of state-owned companies as important economic policy tools of GCC governments for an increasing economic diversification towards non-oil economic activities.

This book contributes to the discussion about a potential developmental role of public expenditure in the GCC countries by analysing the impact of public expenditure on non-oil economic growth in Bahrain, Oman and Qatar. The underlying question in this regard is whether different categories of public expenditure promoted the diversification of GCC economies by raising the relative importance of non-oil sectors vis-a-vis the oil and gas sector over the last decades. In order to gain a more comprehensive understanding of the link between public expenditure and non-oil economic growth, this book examines not only if public expenditure has been an important driver of overall non-oil economic growth but also how public expenditure impacted different sources of non-oil economic growth such as economy-wide investment or productivity levels. By identifying the channels through which public expenditure tends to impact non-oil economic growth, this book aims to shed light on the efficiency of public expenditure for raising the growth potential of non-oil economies in Bahrain, Oman and Qatar.

Empirical research on the relationship between public expenditure and non-oil economic growth in the GCC countries has so far been limited to an econometric analysis of Fasano and Wang (2001) who find a positive long-term link between current expenditure and non-oil GDP levels in five GCC countries during the period 1980-1999. This book departs from the approach of Fasano and Wang (2001) as it examines not only the impact of public expenditure on the overall size of non-oil economies but also elaborates how public expenditure shaped non-oil economic growth dynamics in Bahrain, Oman and Qatar. Building on a newly compiled dataset of different public expenditure categories (capital, education, health), the effects of public expenditure both on non-oil GDP and on labour productivity development patterns are explored through an econometric analysis and detailed country studies. This, in turn, helps to clarify whether a potential growth-enhancing impact of public expenditure is related to increases of labour productivity.

The focus on labour productivity developments arises from economic growth theory which regards increases in productivity as a more sustainable source of economic growth than an accumulation of factor inputs (e.g. labour, physical capital). Endogenous growth models such as Barro (1990) ascribe a potential growth-enhancing impact of certain public expenditure categories (e.g. infrastructure, education, health) to increases in productivity. In this view, public spending might raise the productivity of economic activities and, hence, long-term economic growth prospects by removing infrastructure bottlenecks, promoting the development of skill-intensive industries or by improving the educational level and the health status of the country's workforce.

In contrast, public expenditure in Bahrain, Oman and Qatar does not appear to have fostered non-oil economic growth primarily through increases in economy-wide productivity levels. The upswing of public expenditure levels over the last decades gave rise to a rapid modernization of public infrastructure, the build-up of large production capacities in several non-oil sectors as well as to considerable improvements of the health status and the educational level of local populations. This, however, was not accompanied by sustained increases in labour productivity levels.

As can be seen from figure 1, the labour productivity indicator non-oil GDP per worker and aggregate non-oil GDP levels exhibited strongly diverging trends in all three countries during the last decades. While the levels of total public expenditure and aggregate non-oil GDP increased strongly since the late 1970s, labour productivity levels witnessed either an overall decrease (Bahrain, Qatar) or much smaller increases than non-oil GDP levels (Oman) over the same time period. Hence, the strong increases in non-oil GDP levels were largely driven by an increasing size and not by a rising productivity of the factor input labour. This factor input-driven growth dynamic is particularly pronounced during periods of high public investment levels such as the 2000s.

This book aims to analyse whether different categories of public expenditure strengthened the input-driven growth dynamics within the non-oil economies of Bahrain, Oman and Qatar. For this purpose, it examines if public expenditure impacted the development patterns of non-oil GDP and labour productivity levels in strongly differing ways. In addition to explor-

Figure 1: Public Expenditure, Non-Oil GDP and Labour Productivity 1979-2013

(Index, 1979=100)

(a) Bahrain

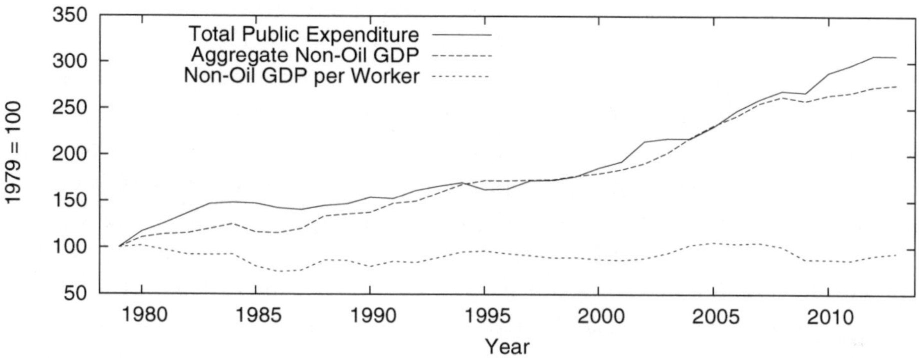

(b) Oman

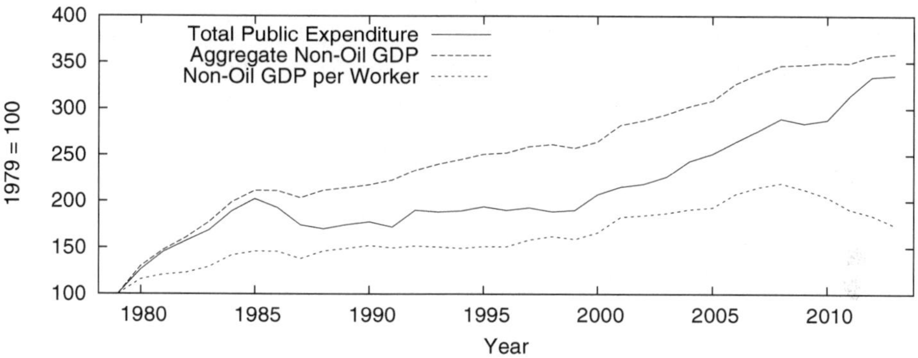

(c) Qatar

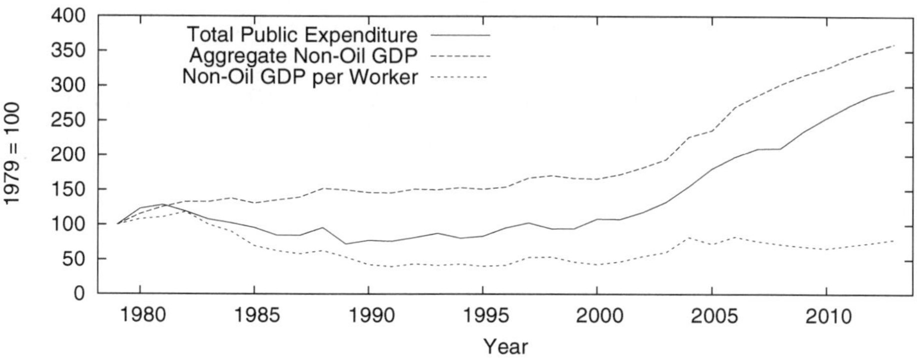

Notes: Times series in logarithms and in constant prices.

Sources: Appendix A.

ing the direct impact of public expenditure on non-oil economic growth dynamics, this empirical analysis also elaborates how public expenditure influenced other potential growth drivers such as private sector investment activity.

The rationale for an important role of public expenditure in igniting input-driven non-oil growth dynamics can be based on two arguments. First, large-scale public investments projects fostered a substantial expansion of non-oil GDP levels but did not lead to a rising importance of skill-intensive non-oil economic activities. While public investments in the economic infrastructure (e.g. build-up of wholesale ports, economic cities) stimulated a substantial upswing of investments by both public and private sector companies, a large part of these investments falls upon non-oil sectors which either exhibit a high capital intensity (petrochemicals, aluminium) or a high dependency on low-skilled, mostly, foreign labour (construction, trade). Second, the strong expansion of public sector employment over the last decades diminished the incentives of nationals for seeking employment outside the public sector and, hence, impeded a structural change in employment patterns towards skill-intensive economic activities. Therefore, the high public wage bills of GCC governments might be singled out as an important factor why large public investments in the human and physical capital stock of local economies did not translate into sustained increases of labour productivity.

The Structure of the Book

This book is organised in three parts. Part one provides a background to the subsequent empirical analysis by presenting general findings of the economic growth literature on the causes of economic growth (chapter 1) and on a potential growth-enhancing impact of certain categories of public expenditure (chapter 2). Part two turns to the country-specific links between public expenditure and non-oil economic growth in Bahrain, Oman and Qatar and elaborates in which way different categories of public expenditure (capital, education, health) impacted non-oil GDP and labour productivity developments in these three countries since the 1970s. This empirical analysis takes the form of an econometric analysis (chapter 3) and country studies of Bahrain (chapter 4), Oman (chapter 5) and Qatar (chapter 6). Building on the empirical findings in part two, part three highlights important country-specific characteristics of the links between public expenditure and non-oil economic growth in Bahrain, Oman and

Qatar. For this purpose, part three analyses in more detail how public expenditure impacts potential drivers of non-oil economic growth such as private sector investment activity (chapter 7) and labour productivity developments (chapter 8).

Chapter 1 starts by reviewing different causes of economic growth emphasised by successive strands of economic growth theory. While successive strands of economic growth theory agree upon the importance of increases in productivity as the primary source of economic growth, they reveal marked differences in the understanding on which factors cause increases in economy-wide productivity levels. In addition, this chapter highlights the empirical findings on potential drivers of economic growth. This includes a discussion about methodological problems inherent to econometric analyses of economic growth determinants. Here, testing the empirical validity of a proposed single determinant of growth is complicated by an interdependence of many factors in a macroeconomic context like economic growth. General statements about the relevance of a single cause of growth are often impeded by a difficulty to control for reverse causality dynamics between economic growth and this proposed determinant as well as for a potential impact of other unobserved factors on the relationship between both variables.

Chapter 2 lays out the theoretical concepts and the empirical evidence for a potential growth-enhancing impact of different public expenditure categories (infrastructure, education, health). Endogenous growth models such as Barro (1990) link the overall impact of increases in public expenditure on long-run economic growth to the evolution of the private capital stock. In these models, increases in potentially growth-enhancing public expenditure categories (infrastructure, education, health) exert two opposing effects on private capital formation and, following, on long-run economic growth. On the one hand, a higher public provisioning level of infrastructure, education or health services might enhance the production capabilities of economic agents and, as a result, stimulate private sector investment activity (crowding-in effect). On the other hand, increases in public expenditure might limit the resources available for private sector capital formation if higher public spending levels are financed by increases in taxes or by rising public borrowing levels in the financial sector (crowding-out effect). Empirical results reveal that the impact of public spending on infrastructure, education and health on long-term economic growth exhibits a substantial cross-country heterogeneity. In this regard, the empirical literature points particularly to institutional characteristics of an economy as an important determinant of the effectiveness of public expenditure for raising long-term economic growth prospects.

Chapter 3 clarifies the country-specific effects of public expenditure on non-oil economic growth dynamics in Bahrain, Oman and Qatar. Drawing on cointegration and causality analysis, this chapter examines whether different categories of public expenditure (capital, education, health) exert a statistically significant positive impact on non-oil GDP and labour productivity levels in Bahrain, Oman and Qatar. In a first step, the existence of long-term links between different categories of public expenditure and non-oil GDP as well as labour productivity levels is scrutinised through cointegration analysis. In case the existence of a long-term link has been confirmed, the mutual impacts between cointegrated variables are simulated through impulse response analysis. In addition, the direction of causality between these variables is investigated by Granger causality tests.

Thereupon, three country studies (chapters 4-6) put the econometric results into context by analysing the long-term development patterns of public expenditure, non-oil GDP and labour productivity levels in Bahrain, Oman and Qatar. These country studies examine in more detail which categories of public expenditure drove the overall increase of public spending levels over the last decades. In addition, the country studies investigate how different categories of public expenditure (investment, education, health, public wage bill) impacted potential drivers of non-oil GDP and labour productivity developments such as the countries' socio-economic development levels, private and public sector production capacities in different non-oil sectors as well as the overall size and the sectoral composition of employment. By revealing the impact of public expenditure on these different growth factors, the country studies aim to elaborate to what extent public expenditure contributed to the strong divergence of non-oil GDP and labour productivity development patterns in all three countries.

Chapter 7 investigates the impact of public expenditure on private sector investment activity in Bahrain, Oman and Qatar. The link between public expenditure and private sector investment in these three countries differs from that in most other countries since public expenditure in the GCC countries is largely funded by external oil and gas rents and not by taxes on domestic households and private business. As increases in public expenditure do not necessitate rising taxes on the private sector, public expenditure in the GCC countries might be presumed to exhibit a lower tendency to crowd-out private sector investment than public expenditure in countries which depend on tax revenues. For gaining a more accurate understanding of the interplay between public expenditure and private investment, chapter 7 examines the econometric evidence for crowding-out and crowding-in effects of public expenditure on private sector investment levels. In addition, this chapter explores to what extent public and private sector investment activity contributed to the factor input-driven non-oil growth dynamics by elaborating which non-oil sectors typically benefitted from large upswings of public and private sector investment activity.

Chapter 8 examines in more detail why increases in labour productivity constitute only a minor source of non-oil economic growth in Bahrain, Oman and Qatar. This chapter starts by putting labour productivity developments in Bahrain, Oman and Qatar in an international perspective. Thereupon, it analyses whether public expenditure patterns have impeded sustained increases of labour productivity. For this purpose, chapter 8 explores the impact of public expenditure on two potential drivers of increases in labour productivity (human capital, structural change). As seen above, the importance of human capital for increases in economy-wide productivity levels is strongly emphasised by different endogenous growth models which regard the educational level and the health status of a country's workforce as crucial determinants for long-term productivity developments. Apart from increases in human capital, productivity levels might also benefit from structural changes in employment and production patterns if the latter reallocate the factor inputs labour and physical capital from low-productivity to high-productivity sectors.

Part I

Public Expenditure and Long-Run Economic Growth: General Insights

Chapter 1

Causes of Long-Run Economic Growth

1.1 Causes of Long-Run Economic Growth in Economic Theory

Economic thinking about the causes of long-run economic growth has changed considerably since Robert Solow (1956) published his article "A Contribution to the Theory of Economic Growth" which is widely regarded as the starting point of modern economic growth theory. Since then, successive strands of economic theory proposed differing causes of long-run growth. While not being mutually exclusive, these differing causes reveal marked differences in the understanding of successive theories about the crucial factors in an economic growth process.

The main insight of neoclassical growth theory (section 1.1.1) is that long-run growth cannot be sustained by a mere accumulation of the factor inputs labour and physical capital since the growth impact of, say, continued high levels of investment in the stock of physical capital is set to dwindle eventually. Instead, long-run economic growth ultimately depends on *increases in productivity*, or alternatively, technological change.

Building on this, endogenous growth theory (section 1.1.2) went further and explicitly examined the economic processes which impact productivity developments in an economy such as deliberate R&D efforts by companies or technology spillover effects across industries or countries. In contrast to neoclassical growth models, technological change in these models is determined endogenously by the decisions of economic agents in an economy.

Here, endogenous growth theory has particularly focussed on the drivers of an *endogenous technological change* such as the level of human capital in an economy or a potential complementarity between human capital and technology.

Following, more recent strands of economic growth theory like the institutions view (section 1.1.3) elaborated the impact of socio-political factors on economic growth. In this view, the occurrence of an endogenous technological change depends on underlying *fundamental causes of growth* such as the institutional characteristics of an economy.

1.1.1 Increases in Productivity

Modern economic growth theory goes back to the contributions of Solow (1956) and Swan (1956) which by now have become known as *neoclassical growth theory*. The main conclusion of the neoclassical growth model is that sustained growth of per capita output is solely caused by technological change, i.e. increases in productivity but not by high levels of investment in the stock of physical capital.[1]

Consider a Cobb-Douglas production function

$$Y(t) = (A(t)L(t))^{1-\alpha}K(t)^{\alpha} \quad \text{with} \quad 0 < \alpha < 1 \tag{1.1}$$

where $Y(t)$ denotes the aggregate output Y of an economy at time instant t within a continuous time setting. A is a productivity parameter which reflects the current state of technology in the economy, L is the labour force and K is the stock of physical capital. The production function exhibits constant returns to scale

$$\lambda Y(t) = (\lambda A(t)L(t))^{1-\alpha}(\lambda K(t))^{\alpha} \quad \text{for all} \quad \lambda > 0 \tag{1.2}$$

as well as positive and diminishing returns to the factor inputs $L(t)$ and $K(t)$

$$\begin{aligned} \frac{\partial Y}{\partial K} > 0, \quad \frac{\partial^2 Y}{\partial K^2} < 0 \\ \frac{\partial Y}{\partial L} > 0, \quad \frac{\partial^2 Y}{\partial L^2} < 0 \end{aligned} \tag{1.3}$$

[1] The following description of the neoclassical growth model broadly follows the lines of Acemoglu (2009:47-67).

which, as will be seen below, are crucial assumptions of the neoclassical growth model.

In each time instant t, the productivity parameter $A(t)$ and the labour force $L(t)$ rise by the constant rates g and n, respectively:

$$A(t) = A(0)e^{gt} \text{ with } \frac{\dot{A}(t)}{A(t)} = g \tag{1.4}$$
$$L(t) = L(0)e^{nt} \text{ with } \frac{\dot{L}(t)}{L(t)} = n$$

With regard to the evolution of the capital stock $K(t)$, a constant share s of the aggregate output $Y(t)$ is not consumed but saved and invested in the stock of physical capital $K(t)$. Since the capital stock depreciates by the constant rate δ, net investment in the capital stock is given by

$$\dot{K}(t) = sY(t) - \delta K(t) \tag{1.5}$$

Beyond, it is assumed that technological progress takes a *labour-augmenting* form, i.e. it raises the productivity of the factor input labour.[2] In order to obtain neoclassical growth dynamics in units of *effective labour*, $A(t)L(t)$, we first define

$$\hat{k}(t) \equiv \frac{K(t)}{A(t)L(t)} \tag{1.6}$$

as the capital stock per unit of effective labour and

$$\hat{y}(t) \equiv \frac{Y(t)}{A(t)L(t)} \tag{1.7}$$

[2]The labour-augmenting form of technological progress goes back to Harrod (1942) who defines a technological innovation as neutral if the relative factor input shares, $(K \times F_K)/(L \times F_L)$, do not change for a given capital-output ratio. Alternative definitions for the neutrality of technological innovations have been provided by Hicks (1932) who defines a technological innovation as neutral if the ratio of the marginal products does not change for a given capital-labour ratio and by Solow (1960) who sees neutrality as given if the relative factor input shares, $(L \times F_L)/(K \times F_K)$, do not change for a given labour-output ratio *(capital-augmenting technological progress).* In case of a Cobb-Douglas function, the assumption of labour-augmenting technological change is less stringent. Since the elasticity of substitution between capital and labour equals unity in a Cobb-Douglas production function, any change in the ratio of the factor inputs K/L will be matched by a proportional change in the ratio of the marginal products F_L/F_K. As a result, the Cobb-Douglas production function is consistent with all three definitions for the neutrality of technological innovations. (Barro and Sala-i-Martin 2004:51-53)

as output per unit of effective labour which, in turn, is determined by $\hat{y}(t) = \hat{k}(t)^{\alpha}$.

Differantiating equation (1.6) with respect to time yields

$$\frac{\dot{\hat{k}}(t)}{\hat{k}(t)} = \frac{\dot{K}(t)}{K(t)} - g - n \tag{1.8}$$

Now, substituting for $\dot{K}(t)$ from (1.5) into (1.8) leads to

$$\frac{\dot{k}(t)}{\hat{k}(t)} = s\frac{Y(t)}{K(t)} - g - n - \delta \tag{1.9}$$

with

$$\frac{Y(t)}{K(t)} = \frac{Y(t)}{A(t)L(t)}\frac{A(t)L(t)}{K(t)} \equiv \frac{\hat{y}(t)}{\hat{k}(t)} \tag{1.10}$$

By rearranging (1.9), we obtain net investment per unit of effective labour

$$\dot{\hat{k}}(t) = s\hat{y}(t) - (g + n + \delta)\hat{k}(t) \tag{1.11}$$

where the capital stock per unit of effective labour, $\hat{k}(t)$, decreases both through the depreciation rate δ as well as through increases in the stock of effective labour, $A(t)L(t)$. Hence, the *effective depreciation rate* equals $(g + n + \delta)$.

Equation (1.11) shows that sustained growth of per capita output within the neoclassical growth model cannot be achieved merely by high levels of investment in the stock of physical capital. Here, the capital stock per unit of effective labour, $\hat{k}(t)$, increases only as long as $\dot{\hat{k}}(t) > 0$. However, since a rising capital stock leads to a diminishing return to capital, output per unit of effective labour, $\hat{y}(t) = \hat{k}(t)^{\alpha}$, will not grow as fast as $\hat{k}(t)$. As a result, the economy converges to a *steady state* where

$$s\hat{y}(t) = (n + g + \delta)\hat{k}(t) \tag{1.12}$$

A constant capital stock per unit of effective labour, $\hat{k}$, implies a constant *effective capital-labour ratio*, $K(t)/A(t)L(t)$, in the steady state. Here, the aggregate capital stock $K(t)$ expands by the same rate $n+g$ as the effective amount of labour $A(t)L(t)$ and, as a result of constant returns to scale, so does aggregate output $Y(t)$. Accordingly, the long-run growth rates of the per capita variables $k \equiv K(t)/L(t)$ and $y \equiv Y(t)/L(t)$ in the steady state are given by the exogenous rate of technological change g.

A permanent increase of the saving rate s to $\acute{s}$ will temporarily raise the capital stock per unit of effective labour, $\hat{k}$, and, following, $\hat{y}$. Yet, given diminishing returns to capital, the growth impact of a higher level of investment will eventually fizzle out and $\hat{k}$ and $\hat{y}$ will converge to a new steady state. Likewise, cross-country differences in the depreciation rate δ, the population growth rate n and the initial level of technology A_0 do have an impact on the level but not on the long-term growth rate of per capita output $y(t)$ in the respective economy.

1.1.2 Endogenous Technological Change

The strong emphasis of neoclassical growth theory on the importance of increases in productivity is widely accepted within the economic growth literature. However, the neoclassical growth model does not provide insights into the economic factors which might influence long-term productivity developments since increases of the productivity parameter $A(t)$ in equation (1.1) are driven entirely by the exogenous and, hence, unexplained growth rate g.

Due to a lack of economic explanations for productivity increases, research interest in the causes of long-term economic growth ebbed until Romer (1986) developed the first economic growth model which explains sustained growth of per capita output through endogenous variables. This influential paper, in turn, sparked the voluminous literature of *endogenous growth theory*.

Endogenous technological change in the Romer (1986) model is driven by spillover effects from the accumulation of knowledge. As a result of spillover effects, investments by one economic agent enhance the production capabilities of other economic agents as well. These positive externalities, in turn, offset the growth slowing effect of diminishing returns to factor inputs.

Aggregate output Y in the Romer model is generated by n different companies. The factor inputs physical capital and labour are assumed to be in fixed supply and are not explicitly modeled. Instead, output y of a representative company i, y_i, depends on the private stock of firm-specific knowledge in the respective company k_i and on the aggregate level of public knowledge within an economy K.

$$y_i = k_i^\alpha K^\beta \tag{1.13}$$

The factor input knowledge has different characteristics than the factor inputs labour and physical capital. First, contrary to physical capital, the stock of knowledge is assumed not to depreciate. Second, the factor input knowledge resembles a public good since it is non-rival and non-excludable.[3] As a result of non-excludability, private knowledge k_i of the n different companies spills over to the stock of public knowledge K which is defined as

$$K = \sum_{i=1}^{n} k_i \tag{1.14}$$

Due to non-rivalry of public knowledge, every company has the ability to utilise K for the production of y_i. Hence, there exists a positive externality for each company.

With regard to the investment behaviour of the n different companies, Romer reduces the complexity of the model by assuming that consumers and producers are identical. Hence, each consumer (or producer) faces an intertemporal choice between consumption and investment. Consider a representative consumer i with a two period time horizon who possesses an initial endowment e_i which can either be used for consumption in period 1, c_{i1}, or for investing into the build-up of private knowledge, k_i. The stock of private knowledge k_i, in turn, allows for the production of output, y_i, and, following, consumption in the second period, c_{i2}.[4]

The allocation of e_i depends on the intertemporal utility function $U(c_{i1}, c_{i2})$ of the representative consumer. Maximising $U(c_{i1}, c_{i2})$ subject to the budget constraints $c_{i1} = e_i - k_i$ and $c_{i2} = y_i$ leads to the first order optimality

---

[3] The assumption that knowledge or technology is non-excludable has been relaxed in later models of endogenous growth. For example, research efforts of single companies are awarded with monopoly rents as a result of patents in an endogenous growth model by Romer (1990).

[4] Romer (1986) presents his model both within a two period and an infinite time horizon. For the sake of brevity, I focus on the two period version of the model. Note that Romer does not account for a rate of time preference in the two period model.

condition[5]

$$\frac{\frac{\partial U}{\partial c_{i1}}}{\frac{\partial U}{\partial c_{i2}}} = \alpha k_i^{\alpha-1} K^{\beta} \tag{1.15}$$

In the private optimum (1.15), the marginal rate of substitution in consumption equals the marginal product of k_i. Hence, when optimising the intertemporal allocation of the initial endowment e_i, the representative consumer considers only the *private return* of an investment in his private stock of knowledge k_i. Instead, he does not internalise the spillover effect of his private investment k_i on the stock of public knowledge K.[6]

Similar to the factor inputs physical capital and labour in the neoclassical growth model, the private stock of firm-specific knowledge k_i exhibits positive and diminishing returns. However, the crucial implication of the Romer (1986) model is that diminishing private returns of the factor input k_i may be outweighed by positive externalities from a rising stock of public knowledge K with the latter resulting from higher stocks of private knowledge k_i in the n different companies.

Therefore, the *social* return to the factor input knowledge may be constant (if $\alpha + \beta = 1$) or even increasing (if $\alpha + \beta > 1$).[7] Despite diminishing private returns to k_i, output per company y_i in (1.13) might rise by the same rate ($\alpha + \beta = 1$) or by a higher rate ($\alpha + \beta > 1$) as the stock of private knowledge k_i. In contrast to the neoclassical growth model, long-term per capita economic growth may be accelerated by an increase in the savings rate as the latter translates into higher levels of investment and, following, knowledge spillovers.

By broadening the range of factor inputs in the production process, Romer (1986) showed that it is the endogenous investment decisions of economic agents which matter for the long-term development of technology and,

---

[5]The Langrange function is given by $\mathcal{L} = U(c_{i1}, c_{i2}) + \lambda_1(e_i - c_{i1} - k_i) + \lambda_2(k_i^{\alpha} K^{\beta} - c_{i2})$. Substitution in the three partial derivatives $\frac{\partial U}{\partial c_{i1}} - \lambda_1 = 0$, $\frac{\partial U}{\partial c_{i2}} - \lambda_2 = 0$ and $-\lambda_1 + \lambda_2 \alpha k_i^{\alpha-1} K^{\beta} = 0$ yields equation (1.15).

[6]Since this spillover effect is not internalised by the representative consumer, the level of investment in the private optimum (1.15) is below the level required in a Pareto optimum. In a Pareto optimum, a higher level of investment would be induced by the higher marginal product of k_i: $\alpha k_i^{\alpha-1} K^{\beta} + \beta k_i^{\alpha} K^{\beta-1}$.

[7]The Romer (1986) model exhibits increasing social returns to knowledge ($\alpha + \beta > 1$). For preventing growth rates of y_i becoming too large, Romer assumed the existence of an upper bound for the investment in k_i.

hence, long-term growth of per capita output. Emphasising the endogeneity of technology, Romer (1994:12) postulates that "technological advance comes from things that people do".

While technological progress in the Romer model merely results from unintended knowledge spillovers of private investments, subsequent papers in the endogenous growth literature modeled improvements in technology as a result of deliberate research and development (R&D) activities from companies (*innovation based growth*). Endogenous technological change in innovation based growth models takes two forms. In the *expanding variety models*, product innovations raise the number of products which, in turn, leads to a higher economy-wide technology level as a result of the increase in the division of labour (e.g. Romer 1987, 1990). Instead, *Schumpeterian growth models* emphasise the process of creative destruction with older products being replaced by new improved product versions (e.g. Aghion and Howitt 1992; Grossman and Helpmann 1991).

Since the level of technology is determined endogenously by economic agents, endogenous growth theory particularly focussed on the role of human capital for long-run economic growth (e.g. Lucas 1988; Azariadis and Drazen 1990; Caballe and Santos 1993). A further research focus was the impact of structural features in an economy (market structure, competition, antitrust policy and intellectual property regime) on the incentives of economic agents to invest into the accumulation of factor inputs (e.g. Aghion and Howitt 1998:205-232; Aghion et al. 2001; Lai 1998; Scotchmer 2004).

In contrast to developed countries, endogenous technological change in developing countries often does not result from the innovation of new technologies but from the successful adoption or imitation of technologies existing in technologically leading economies. Therefore, research on long-run growth in developing countries examined the factors affecting the *diffusion of technology*. Here, the economic literature particularly emphasised the roles of foreign trade (e.g. Coe and Helpmann 1995; Keller 2002; Lumenga-Neso et al. 2005) and of foreign direct investment (e.g. Borensztein et al. 1998; Xu 2000; Fosfuri et al. 2001) as potential transmission channels for the diffusion of technology.

The speed of technology diffusion, however, is seen to depend on a range of country-specific characteristics. Models of international technology diffusion particularly highlighted the domestic level of human capital as a decisive factor for a country's ability to adopt foreign technologies (e.g. Benhabib and Spiegel 2005). Similarly, Howitt (2000) points to the level of domestic R&D activity as an important determinant of a country's absorptive capacity for technology spillovers. Instead, Parente and Prescott (1994) focus on legal or political barriers to technology adoption.

Another factor which might impede a technology importing country from fully exploiting the benefits of new innovations is *directed technical change*, i.e. a bias of new innovations towards certain factors of production. Technological innovations are usually designed in a way that optimises the prevailing production factors and conditions in a specific sector or country. Hence, large mismatches between a technology innovating and a technology importing country with regard to the factor endowments capital and labour (Basu and Weil 1998) or the skill-set of the workforce (Acemoglu and Zilibotti 2001) might render a technological innovation inappropriate for a technology importing country.

1.1.3 Fundamental Causes of Growth

Some recent strands of the economic growth literature have criticised the focus of endogenous growth theory on human capital and technology as being too narrow. While acknowledging a high complementarity between technology and human capital as well as a potential growth-enhancing effect of a high stock of human capital, these theories deem accumulation of technology, human or physical capital only as mechanics or *proximate causes of economic growth.*

In this view, the incentives of an economic agent to invest into the accumulation of factor inputs might vary across economies due to different characteristics of the respective societies. Hence, triggering of these growth mechanics depends on underlying *fundamental causes of economic growth.* Acemoglu et al. (2005:388) illustrate the difference between proximate and fundamental causes of growth by citing North and Thomas (1973:2): "The factors we have listed (innovation, economies of scale, education, capital accumulation, etc.) are not causes of growth; they *are* growth" (italics in original).

The most prominent fundamental explanation of long-run economic growth is the *institutions view* which holds that strongly diverging income levels between countries can be traced back to different institutional set-ups. Other fundamental explanations for diverging economic development levels across countries refer to geographical or socio-cultural differences.

The hypothesis that institutions are a fundamental cause for the long-term economic development of countries goes back to North (1989, 1990) and has more recently been put forward by Acemoglu et al. (2001, 2002, 2003, 2005).[8] The institutions view employs a very broad notion of institutions which incorporates aspects of the political, social and economical organisation of a society. For example, North (1990:3) defines institutions as "the rules of the game in a society or, more formally, [as] the humanly devised constraints that shape human interaction".

The reason why *institutions matter* for the long-term growth prospects of an economy is the existence of transaction costs.[9] In contrast to a Walrasian general equilibrium model, North assumes that the production costs of an economic agent who engages into the exchange of goods comprise not only the costs of the factor inputs but also transaction costs.

The latter arise as the exchange parties both need to gather information about the goods to be exchanged (*measurement costs*) and have to monitor and enforce the exchange of goods (*enforcement costs*). High transaction costs entail a low productivity in the economy since they deter economic agents from engaging in the exchange of goods and, as a result, inhibit the division of labour and increased specialisation within the economy. Hence, the purpose of institutions is to lower transaction costs by providing well-specified rules, safeguarding property rights and enforcing contracts or as North (1989:1324) puts it by "provid[ing] certainty in human interaction".

The importance of property rights and enforcement of contracts for long-run economic growth are typically emphasised.[10] Yet, the institutions view does not spell out specific embodiments of institutional set-ups. Instead,

---

[8] The work of North is part of the large *new institutional economics* (NIE) literature. A common assumption of all proponents of NIE is the existence of transaction costs. The branches of research in NIE are very diverse (e.g. principal agent theory, property rights theory, public choice theory, transaction cost theory). Since the role of institutions for the long-term economic development cannot be considered the preeminent research focus of NIE, I do not use the rather broad term NIE in this regard.

[9] The concept of transaction costs goes back to Coase (1937). He defines transaction costs as the cost of participating in a market exchange or rather as the "cost of using the price mechanism" (Coase 1937:390).

[10] See, for example, North (1990:54): "The inability of societies to develop effective, low-cost enforcements of contracts is the most important source of both historical stagnation and contemporary underdevelopment in the Third World."

the basic principle of this line of thought can be summarised by stating that institutional set-ups are conducive to economic growth if they exhibit a high degree of inclusiveness in the sense that they do not erect political, social and economic barriers for a broad cross-section of society to engage in economic activities. In addition to rule of law, low entry barriers for new companies and the absence of arbitrary taxation are particularly highlighted as features of economic institutions favourable to economic growth.

As to political institutions, the institutions view stresses the necessity of checks and balances in political decision making processes.[11] The emphasis on political constraints on governments or ruling elites emanates from a political economy perspective on the evolution of institutions. Here, the choice of a particular design of economic institutions is assumed to influence the distribution of economic rents in an economy. This, in turn, causes a conflict of interest between different groups competing for these economic rents. Ultimately, the choice of a particular design of economic institutions depends on the political power of the different groups. A high concentration of political power might lead to economic institutions which are favourable only to a small group and provide no incentive for the vast majority of the population to engage in economic activities such as accumulation of technology, physical or human capital.

This political economy perspective on the evolution of institutions is related to the hypothesis that *institutional change is path dependent*. In this view, current institutional outcomes are not only driven by current conditions in an economy but also by past institutional outcomes. Past events have an enduring influence on the current state. Hence, there is no natural tendency for economic institutions to evolve towards the single outcome of a Pareto optimal institutional framework. Instead, economic institutions which are not Pareto optimal may persist if the status quo is preserved by mutually self-reinforcing processes (e.g. interplay between distribution of political power and economic rents).

The most established fundamental explanation which relates diverging long-term growth rates to geographical differences is the *disease burden* approach. It postulates that low productivity and dismal growth prospects in

[11]This broad notion of institutions is exemplified in Acemoglu et al. (2001). When examining the impact of institutions in former European colonies on long-run economic growth, Acemoglu et al. (2001) supplement their main variable for measuring institutional quality ("average protection against expropriation risk") by two variables on political institutions ("constraints on executive"; "democracy").

certain regions of the world are due to the prevalence of infectious diseases such as Malaria or Aids (e.g. Bloom et al. 1998; Gallup and Sachs 2001).

Another fundamental explanation stresses the importance of religion for long-term economic development. This line of thought goes back to the sociologist Max Weber (1930) who ascribed the surge of economic activity in the industrial revolution primarily to a prevalence of a protestant work ethic in different Western European countries. In a similar vein, Barro and McClearly (2003) relate economic growth to the extent of religious beliefs in a society.

With regard to the low rates of economic growth in most Sub-Saharan African countries, Easterly and Levine (1997) and Alesina et al. (2003) provide a socio-cultural fundamental explanation as they link a high level of ethnolinguistic heterogeneity with low economic development prospects. In this view, a high ethnolinguistic heterogeneity potentially leads to a higher ethnic polarisation. This polarisation, in turn, might induce induce rent seeking behaviour within an economy and inhibit a social consensus about the provision of public goods.

1.2 The Convergence Hypothesis

Empirical research analysed cross-country growth data extensively for identifying important factors of economic growth. A longstanding topic in this line of research has been the question whether a country's current output level impacts its subsequent rates of economic growth lastingly. Interest in this topic has been sparked by the convergence hypothesis which states that economies with low initial levels of per capita output exhibit higher transitional rates of economic growth (*catch-up growth*) than economies with high initial output levels until the output levels of the former economy converge to those of the latter. For testing the empirical validity of the convergence hypothesis, economic research examined whether cross-country growth patterns point to a convergence or a divergence of output levels globally.

The convergence hypothesis is based on two different concepts: *capital deepening* and *technology transfer*. The emphasis on capital deepening, i.e. an increase in the per capita capital stock, k, or, alternatively, a rise in capital-labour ratio, K/L, as the main driver of catch-up growth in developing countries goes back to neoclassical growth theory. More specifically, the neoclassical growth model assumes the existence of positive and diminishing returns to the factor inputs labour and physical capital (equation (1.3) in section 1.1.1). This assumption implies the farther an economy's per capita capital stock, k, is below its steady state level, the higher is the marginal product for a given net investment into the stock of physical capital, Δk, and, following, the transitional growth rate of per capita output, y.

Since early development stages of economies are typically characterised by low levels of physical capital, an economy's growth rate during this period is hypothesised to be higher than in more mature development stages when the capital stock has already approached its steady state level. Under the condition of similar steady state determinants in the respective economies (e.g. saving or investment ratio, population growth rate), diminishing returns to physical capital eventually lead to a convergence of output levels across economies.

In contrast to neoclassical growth theory, the conclusions of endogenous growth theory about convergence are not uniform. Early endogenous growth models such as Romer (1986), Lucas (1988) or Rebelo (1991) do not predict a convergence of per capita output levels across economies since these models employ constant or even, as Romer (1986), increasing returns to the factor inputs.

Instead, some later models of endogenous growth allow for a convergence of output levels through technology transfer (e.g. Eaton and Kortum 1996; Keller 1996; Barro and Sala-i-Martin 1997). Building on what has been first described by Gerschenkron (1962) as an advantage of economic backwardness, these models assume adoption of existing technology to be less difficult than innovation of new technology. As a result, technology transfer potentially enables developing countries to reduce their distance to the *world technology frontier*.

In contrast to the emphasis on investment levels and population growth rates in the capital deepening concept, models of technology transfer typically point to the absorptive capacity and, particularly, the level of human capital in a technology importing country as a crucial condition for a convergence of output levels across countries. Romer (1993) refers to these two different convergence concepts as *object gaps* and *idea gaps*, respectively.

Results from different empirical techniques do not permit general conclusions about the validity of the convergence hypothesis. In part, a lack of

Table 1.1: High Growth and Low Growth Countries 1960-2009

Country	GDP 1960	GDP 2009	Average Growth
High Growth Countries:			
Equatorial Guinea[1]	582	22,008	7.7%
Taiwan	1,836	28,716	5.8%
Botswana	578	8,868	5.7%
Republic of Korea	1,804	25,048	5.5%
Singapore	4,307	47,313	5.0%
Hong Kong	3,346	36,293	5.0%
China	846	7,431	4.5%
Thailand	974	7,799	4.3%
Malaysia	1,489	11,309	4.2%
Romania	1,507	9,742	3.9%
Low Growth Countries:			
Zambia	1,807	1,765	-0.1%
Togo	764	733	-0.1%
Madagascar	841	753	-0.2%
Nicaragua	2,576	2,190	-0.3%
Guinea	984	823	-0.4%
Zimbabwe	176	143	-0.4%
Haiti	1,894	1,444	-0.6%
Niger	750	534	-0.7%
Central African Republic	1,072	647	-1.0%
DR Congo	1,098	231	-3.1%
Memo:			
Japan	6,101	31,980	3.4%
United Kingdom	12,860	33,410	2.0%
United States	15,458	41,147	2.0%

Source: Penn World Table 7.0 (Heston et al. 2011)
Notes: GDP 1960 and GDP 2009 refer to the levels of GDP per capita in the years 1960 and 2009, respectively. GDP levels are PPP adjusted and expressed in constant 2005 international dollar prices. Average growth denotes the average annual growth rate of GDP per capita levels between 1960 and 2009. Rankings in the table are based on 111 countries. Due to missing data for the GDP per capita values in 1960 all six GCC countries are not included in this table.
[1] Equatorial Guinea can be considered a special case since its high growth between 1960 and 2009 is almost entirely attributable to a strong upswing in oil production after the discovery of large offshore oil reserves in 1995. In contrast, the country's GDP per capita value stood at 631 international dollars in 1994, implying an average annual growth rate of 0.2% between 1960 and 1994.

clarity may be ascribed to methodological difficulties inherent in empirical research on the convergence hypothesis. Beyond, cross-country growth patterns are simply too diverse to allow for an unanimous finding of either convergence or divergence.

On the one hand, empirical results support the notion of a weak form of convergence since convergence of output levels takes place in case countries share a lot of common characteristics (*convergence clubs*). On the other hand, empirical evidence shows a clear pattern of divergence in output levels particularly between highly developed and least developed countries.

A strong heterogeneity in economic growth patterns is also emphasised by the differing growth trajectories of developing countries in table 1.1. For example, Taiwan and the Republic of Korea on the one hand as well as Zambia and Haiti on the other hand have all been on a similar economic development level back in 1960 and, yet, experienced strongly diverging rates of economic growth between 1960 and 2009.

Empirical work on the convergence hypothesis was primarily triggered by Barro (1991), Barro and Sala-i-Martin (1992a) and Mankiw et al. (1992).[12] These papers test the empirical validity of the convergence hypothesis through a cross-sectional growth regression of the following form:

$$g_i = \pi + y_{i,0}\beta + X_i\gamma + \epsilon_i \tag{1.16}$$

where g_i is the average growth rate of real per capita output g in country i during a fixed time period,[13] π is a constant, $y_{i,0}$ is the initial level of per capita income in country i at the start of this time period, X_i is a vector of additional variables and ϵ_i is the error term.

Convergence within a cross-section of countries requires the initial level of per capita income $y_{i,0}$ to be negatively related to the average growth rate g_i. Hence, the existence of convergence is confirmed if $\beta < 0$. If this negative relationship is found to be statistically significant without the inclusion

[12] An earlier contribution is Baumol (1986) who finds evidence of (unconditional) convergence for a group of 16 countries between 1870-1979. Yet, contrary to later papers on convergence, Baumol's research relies on the data set from Maddison (1982) which includes only 16 OECD countries. A much broader data set for cross-country growth observations become only available with the publication of the Penn World Tables by Summers and Heston (1988, 1991).

[13] Mankiw et al. (1992) utilise the cumulative growth of per capita output in country i, Δy_i, during the entire time period as the dependent variable which, of course, does not alter the implications for the parameter β in (1.16).

of any additional variables in the X_i vector, *unconditional convergence* is given. In case $\beta < 0$ depends on the existence of additional variables in the X_i vector, the country sample exhibits *conditional convergence*.

The empirical results of the above mentioned cross-sectional tests support the existence of conditional convergence. Barro (1991) finds evidence for convergence in a sample of 98 countries during the period 1960-1985 once he controls for a set of country-specific factors, most notably human capital, in the X_i vector.[14] Hence, one may conclude that only countries which exhibited a sufficiently high level of human capital at the start of the sample period have been able to catch up to the income levels of richer countries. Drawing on the same data sample as Barro (1991), Mankiw et al. (1992) obtain a statistically significant negative coefficient for β when conditioning on a proxy for human capital (secondary school enrollment rate) and on two determinants of per capita output levels in the neoclassical growth model (investment ratio, population growth rate).

Empirical evidence of unconditional convergence is typically limited to subsamples of countries or regions which share a lot of structural characteristics such as OECD countries (Mankiw et al. 1992) or different states in the U.S. (Barro and Sala-i-Martin 1992a). Instead, tests for unconditional convergence in a broad cross section of countries do not yield meaningful findings about the existence of convergence or divergence. For example, Mankiw et al. (1992) obtain a slightly positive estimate for β and, hence, an indication for global divergence, when testing for unconditional convergence in the above mentioned sample of 98 countries. Yet, this growth regression has very little explanatory power since its adjusted R^2 stands at a mere 0.03

The empirical results derived from cross-sectional growth regressions have been criticised on a number of grounds. Most importantly, Islam (1995) and Caselli et al. (1996) pointed out that the very strong homogeneity assumptions on the respective countries in cross-sectional regressions might lead to an omitted variable bias and, as a result, to inconsistent estimates.

[14] For lack of better measures, Barro (1991) utilises the 1960 primary and secondary school enrollment rates as proxies for human capital in the respective countries. An obvious objection is that these measures rather reflect investments in human capital than the quality of the human capital stock in 1960. Other conditioning variables in the X_i vector include the average ratio of real government consumption to real GDP, the number of revolutions and coups per year, the number of assassinations per million population per year and a measure for price distortions (deviation of the purchasing power parity value for the investment deflator from the sample mean in 1960), all of which are estimated to have negative coefficients.

Therefore, both papers employ panel-data methods to account for country-specific heterogeneity when analysing cross-country growth patterns. For example, Islam (1995) allows for country-specific constants, π_i, in his panel estimates which might proxy for different initial levels of the technology parameter A_0 or other individual effects. Panel-data approaches confirm the existence of conditional convergence but obtain much higher rates of annual convergence than cross-sectional regressions.[15]

Yet, the weak spot of these panel data approaches is their conceptual ambiguity with regard to a convergence of output levels across countries. To a lesser extent, this criticism applies as well to cross sectional growth regressions which utilise conditioning variables. As a result of the inclusion of conditioning variables in the X_i vector and, even more so, through country-specific constants, π_i, each country approaches an *individual steady state.*

Hence, by allowing for heterogeneity in the parameters, one also obtains heterogenous steady state output levels. As a result of this heterogeneity, a statistically significant negative coefficient for β primarily indicates that countries exhibit catch-up growth towards their individual steady states and not towards the steady state output levels of other countries. Given the high speed of convergence estimates, panel data approaches suggest that countries are usually near their individual steady states. Hence, persistent differences in the output levels across countries need to be explained by different steady state levels.

In view of the methodological shortcomings of both cross-sectional and panel data regressions, Quah (1993, 1996, 1997) proposes an intertempo-

---

[15]Despite differing sets of countries and conditioning variables, Mankiw et al. (1992) and Barro and Sala-i-Martin (1992a) unanimously find convergence rates of around 2% per year. Accordingly, it takes a country 35 years to eliminate 50% of the initial output gap. Instead, the estimated annual rates of convergence in Islam (1995) range between 3.8% (sample of 79 countries) and 9.1% (22 OECD countries). Caselli et al. (1996) suggest an annual rate of 10.0% (90 countries) which translates into a duration of only 7 years for closing 50% of the initial gap. When applying cross sectional regressions, Islam (1995) finds annual convergence rates in the range of 1.1%-1.9% for his country samples. Islam (1995:1147) and Caselli et al. (1996:367) ascribe the much lower rates of convergence in cross-sectional approaches to an omitted variable bias. The omitted variable initial level of technology, A_0, is likely to be positively correlated with the explanatory variable initial income, $y_{i,0}$. This, in turn, leads to an upward bias in the estimation of the coefficient β. In cross-sectional approaches, the implied annual convergence rate λ is derived through the following equation: $\lambda = (-1/t) \times ln(1+\beta)$, where t denotes the number of years during the time period under investigation. Thus, an upward bias in the estimate for β translates into a downward bias in the implied annual convergence rate λ.

ral analysis of the worldwide distribution of per capita output levels as an alternative approach for examining the convergence hypothesis. More precisely, Quah utilises the evolution of the distribution's shape over time as well as estimates of the intra-distribution dynamics as empirical evidence for the long-term development of cross-country differences in output levels.

Since Quah focusses on relative differences, per capita output values of countries are divided by the world average of this figure in the respective year. Drawing on the data set from Summers and Heston (1991), he estimates the densities of per capita output levels between 1961 and 1988 through a Gaussian kernel.[16]

Similar to the results of cross-sectional growth regressions, the long-term evolution of the distribution's shape does not indicate a uniform trend of either convergence or divergence. In part, the convergence hypothesis is confirmed insofar as the concentration of rich countries in the upper tail of the distribution is increasing. Yet, the distribution as a whole shows signs of polarisation with more countries clustering together either in the upper or in the lower tail of the distribution. Quah (1997:28) refers to this finding as "emerging twin peaks" in the distribution of per capita output levels.

The finding of a stronger polarisation is confirmed by Quah's more formal estimates of the intra-distribution dynamics. In Quah (1993), the cross-sectional distribution is divided by 5 (and, alternatively, 4) quantiles into different groups of relative output levels. When estimating the probabilities for individual countries to migrate between these groups by means of Markov chains, he finds the highest levels of persistence in the lower and upper tails of the distribution. This finding is not due to the arbitrary choice of the number of quantiles since Quah (1997) obtains similar results when utilising a continuous stochastic kernel estimation approach.

With regard to the output gap between highly developed and least developed countries, there is strong evidence for a continued divergence of output levels. For example, Pritchett (1997) shows that the ratio of GDP per capita levels between the richest and the poorest countries has been increasing both between 1870-1960 as well as between 1960-1990.

---

[16] A comprehensive overview about kernel density estimation is given by Cameron and Trivedi (2009:298-306).

1.3 Searching for Correlates of Growth in a World of Model Uncertainty

The previous section showed that catch-up growth is not a general feature of developing countries but remains, instead, confined to certain countries. This, in turn, makes the search for the determinants which enable a developing country to catch up to the income levels of developed countries even more important. Numerous empirical studies examined potential determinants of growth and pointed to strong empirical links between economic growth and a range of factors such as macroeconomic stability (Fischer 1993), political stability (Alesina et al. 1996), absence of corruption (Mauro 1995), high levels of investment (De Long and Summers 1991), school enrollment rates (Barro 1991), life expectancy levels (Bloom et al. 1998) and trade openness (Sachs and Warner 1995).

Yet, as will be seen below, the existence of statistically significant links between economic growth and these factors does not necessarily imply that improvements of the latter factors in any given country constitute a sufficient condition for accelerating economic growth in the respective economy. Instead, tests on the empirical validity of a single potential determinant of growth are complicated by an interdependence of many factors in an macroeconomic context like economic growth. Here, general statements about the relevance of a single potential cause of growth are often impeded by a difficulty to control for reverse causality dynamics between economic growth and this proposed determinant as well as for a potential impact of other factors on the relationship between both variables.

Typically, the above mentioned empirical links between economic growth and a potential determinant of growth are derived from a cross-sectional growth regression of the following form:

$$g_i = \pi + +x_i\beta + Z_i\gamma + \epsilon_i \tag{1.17}$$

where g_i is the average rate of per capita economic growth g in country i during a certain time period, π is a constant, x_i is the potential determinant of growth, Z_i is a vector of control variables and ϵ_i is an error term. Empirical evidence for a link between economic growth g_i and a potential determinant of growth x_i is given by a statistically significant coefficient estimate for β.

However, drawing general conclusions about the relevancy of a potential growth determinant x_i from empirical results obtained in a cross-country regression such as equation (1.17) is hindered by three problems. Due to a potential endogeneity of the explanatory variable x_i, it is unclear whether the β estimate describes the impact of x_i on the dependent variable g_i or merely a partial correlation between both variables (section 1.3.1).

In addition to a lack of clarity with regard to the direction of causality, the search for potential growth determinants is complicated by uncertainty about the adequate specification of the regression in equation (1.17) *(model uncertainty)*. Brock and Durlauf (2001) emphasise two types of model uncertainty: *theory uncertainty* and *heterogeneity uncertainty.*

Theory uncertainty refers to the question which additional explanatory variables should be included in the Z_i vector within equation (1.17) in order to control for any effects on economic growth which are unrelated to x_i (section 1.3.2). Heterogeneity uncertainty exists since it is not known a priori whether results from cross-sectional growth regression are applicable to a broad cross-section of countries or only to more homogenous sub-groups of countries (section 1.3.3).

1.3.1 Causality or Correlation

Causal inference in a cross-country growth regression such as equation (1.17) is complicated by a potential endogeneity of explanatory variables. Endogeneity problems in growth regressions arise primarily as a result of *simultaneity* and *omitted variables.*[17] In these cases it is misleading to interpret the coefficient estimate for β as measuring a causal effect of x_i on the dependent variable g_i.

Simultaneity problems emerge when a dependent variable g_i and an explanatory variable x_i mutually impact each other during one time period, for example, as a result of reverse causality between both variables. In view of a potentially strong interrelation of many explanatory variables

[17] Another potential source of endogeneity is a *measurement error* in the dependent or the explanatory variables. Note that the definition of endogeneity in an econometric sense differs from the definition in other branches of economics. In a non-econometric context, an explanatory variable x_i is defined to be endogenous within a certain model if it is explained or determined by other (observable) variables of that model. In econometrics, endogeneity of x_i is given by $Cov(x_i; \epsilon_i) \neq 0$, i.e. x_i is correlated to a factor which is not picked up by any of the explanatory variables but by the error term ϵ_i as a result of unobservability or inadequate measurement. For an overview of endogeneity in an econometric context refer to Woolridge (2010:53-55).

(e.g. schooling levels, investment levels, trade openness, life expectancy) with economic growth this problem is particularly relevant in growth regressions. For example, higher levels of investment may both be the source as well as the outcome of higher rates of economic growth. Given this reverse causality problem, pinpointing the direction of causality is often not possible.

Furthermore, the explanatory and the dependent variables may both be determined by an omitted variable which is not included in the regression. Sticking with the example given above, the high levels of investment and economic growth might in fact primarily be driven by an unobserved factor such as institutional or political characteristics of the economy. In general, ruling out any unobserved factors in growth regressions is difficult both in view of the heterogeneity of cross-country growth observations as well as the complexity of economic activity subsumed in macroeconomic aggregates such as economic growth.

In summary, isolating the extent of changes in the explanatory variable x_i that are not driven by unobserved factors or by reverse causality dynamics with the dependent variable g_i is often not possible in a cross-country growth regression such as equation (1.17). Yet, measurability of such an exogenous change in x_i (with all other observed and unobserved factors remaining unchanged) is a precondition for determining the causal effect of the potential growth determinant x_i on the dependent variable economic growth g_i. Therefore, in light of prevalent simultaneity and omitted variables problems, the economic growth literature refers to the β estimate in equation (1.17) primarily as measuring a *partial correlation* and not a causal effect between x_i and g_i.[18]

In addition, given the lack of clarity about cause and effect, an explanatory

[18] A word of caution is necessary about the consistency of the coefficient estimates for β and γ in (1.17). Cross-country growth regressions are typically estimated with the ordinary least squares (OLS) estimation method. As discussed earlier, OLS delivers only consistent coefficient estimates if the explanatory variables are not endogenous (in an econometric sense) and, hence, not correlated with the error term ϵ_i, i.e. $Cov(x_i; \epsilon_i) = 0$ and $Cov(Z_i; \epsilon_i) = 0$. Potential endogeneity in form of a simultaneity bias is often addressed by choosing a value of the explanatory variable at the beginning of the time period under investigation (e.g. secondary school enrollment rate in 1960), thus, avoiding reverse causality with the dependent variable (e.g. average per capita economic growth 1960-1990). The problem of an omitted variable bias in a cross-sectional framework is more difficult to come by but might be somewhat alleviated by the use of proxy variables (e.g. regional dummies) which pick up part of the effects from unobserved factors.

variable x_i is often simply deemed to be a *correlate of growth* and not a determinant of growth. While being uninformative about cause and effect between two variables, the sign of a partial correlation can help to restrict the range of possible causal statements (Wacziarg 2002:909). A negative partial correlation between, say, corruption and economic growth does not shed light on the direction of causality between both variables. Yet, the negative sign of the partial correlation makes the statement that increases in corruption might foster economic growth implausible.

In macroeconomic set-ups like cross-country growth regressions, the instrumental variable estimation method is currently the only approach which allows for an assessment of the causal effect of x_i on the dependent variable, g_i.[19] In this approach, the exogenous variation in an endogenous explanatory variable x_i is partly identified by the help of an instrumental variable z_i which satisfies three conditions.

First, an instrumental variable z_i needs to exhibit a strong partial correlation with the endogenous explanatory variable x_i. Second, z_i must not exert a direct effect on the dependent variable economic growth *(exclusion restriction)*. Third, the instrumental variable z_i must not be correlated with any unobserved factors captured by the error term ϵ_i in a cross-country growth regression, i.e. $Cov(z_i;\epsilon_i) = 0$ *(exogeneity restriction)*.[20]

Given the difficulty of finding valid instrumental variables which satisfy these three conditions in a growth regression context, the instrumental variable approach has so far only been applied to a few potential determinants growth. A prominent example is Acemoglu et al. (2001) who detect

[19]Development economists such as Banerjee et al. (2007) have increasingly adopted *randomised controlled trials* to study the impact of specific policies in microeconomic development issues (e.g. immunisation rates, educational quality in schools). Obviously, controlled experiments are not a feasible approach for examining causality in macroeconomic questions such as the determinants of economic growth.

[20]In case x_i is the only endogenous explanatory variable in equation (1.17), the instrumental variable estimation method proceeds in the following two steps. First, the fitted values of x_i, $\hat{x_i}$, are obtained in a reduced from equation: $x_i = Z_i\delta + z_i\theta + u_i$ where Z_i is a vector of the exogenous explanatory variables from (1.17) and z_i is the instrumental variable. For z_i to qualify as an instrumental variable for x_i, its coefficient estimate must be non-zero, $\theta \neq 0$. Since x_i is regressed only on exogenous variables in the reduced from equation, the fitted values $\hat{x_i}$ describe a form of exogenous variation in the explanatory variable x_i. In a second step, $\hat{x_i}$ replaces x_i in (1.17): $g_i = \pi + +\hat{x_i}\beta + Z_i\gamma + \epsilon_i$. In contrast to x_i, the fitted values $\hat{x_i}$ are not endogenous. Therefore, the β estimate for $\hat{x_i}$ can be interpreted as measuring a causal effect from $\hat{x_i}$ on g_i. See also Woolridge (2010:89-96).

a causal effect of institutional quality on economic growth when utilising the differences in European settler mortality rates in former colonies as an instrumental variable for the quality of institutions.

Here, the authors presume that higher settler mortality rates in former European colonies have led to the set-up of more extractive institutions since the settlers were unlikely to settle permanently in a disease environment which was not favourable to them. The main purpose of institutions in these countries was not safeguarding the participation of different groups of settlers in economic activities, but, instead, a transfer of resources from the colony to the coloniser.

The authors find a negative correlation between settler mortality rates and current institutional quality. In addition, the instrumental variable can reasonably be assumed to satisfy the exclusion and the exogeneity restrictions since mortality rates of European settlers in former centuries are unlikely, first, to exert a direct impact on current GDP levels and, second, to be related to any unobserved factors which might impact these current GDP levels. When utilising this instrumental variable for identifying a form of exogenous variation in the quality of current institutions, the authors find a positive impact of this variation on current GDP levels. As a result, Acemoglu et al. (2001) conclude that improvements of institutional quality cause economic growth.

1.3.2 Theory Uncertainty

The challenge of including appropriate explanatory variables in a cross-country growth regression such as equation (1.17) is compounded by a plethora of potential growth determinants. In a review of the empirical growth literature, Durlauf et al. (2005:652-659) list 43 conceptually distinct categories of potential growth determinants. Overall, they find 145 different variables which have been employed as regressors in cross-country growth regressions.

In addition, many of these variables are not mutually exclusive because the validity of one growth theory does not necessarily falsify another. Brock and Durlauf (2001:234) refer to this as the "open-endedness of theories". For example, empirical evidence for a statistically significant relationship between economic growth and variables for institutional quality does not imply that other potential growth determinants such as the level of human capital or investments in the stock of physical capital are of minor importance.

The abundance of potential growth determinants is in stark contrast to a limited number of cross-country growth observations. For example, the Penn World Tables 7.0 (Heston et al. 2011) which are currently the most comprehensive database in this regard, contain time series on economic growth for only 111 countries during the period 1960-2009. Hence, simply including a large number of potential growth determinants in a cross-country growth regression and assessing the importance of individual determinants by the significance levels of the respective regressors is not a feasible strategy since this approach would lead to problems of overfitting and, accordingly, a low statistical power of the model.[21]

Different approaches have been proposed for examining the relevance of individual variables in explaining cross-country growth patterns. A first such attempt was undertaken by Levine and Renelt (1992) which apply a variant of *extreme bound analysis* for determining the explanatory power of 19 different variables frequently used in the empirical growth literature.[22] In their view, a variable is only empirically relevant if the partial correlation between economic growth and the particular variable is robust to changes in the set of additional explanatory variables in a cross-country growth regression of the following form

$$g_i = \pi + +x_i\beta + I_i\gamma + Z_i\delta + \epsilon_i \qquad (1.18)$$

where g_i is the average per capita GDP growth rate g in country i between 1960-1989, π is a constant, x_i is the variable of interest, I_i is a vector of variables which are included in all regressions (investment share of GDP, real GDP per capita level in 1960, population growth rate, secondary-school enrollment rate in 1960), Z_i is a vector of up to 3 additional explanatory variables and ϵ_i is an error term.

For each of the 19 different variables, the authors compute regression results for all possible combinations of the additional explanatory variables in the Z_i vector. Hence, each variable x_i is related to a multitude of coefficient estimates for β. A particular variable x_i is labelled robust only if the highest and the lowest coefficient estimate for β are statistically significant

[21] Even cross-sectional growth regressions which draw on a large country sample such as Barro (1991) employ at most 9 different explanatory variables in each regression specification.

[22] Extreme bound analysis goes back to the work of Leamer (1983, 1985).

and of the same sign.

The empirical results of Levine and Renelt (1992) ascribe a low explanatory power to most variables typically employed in growth regressions. As can be seen in table 1.2, only three variables from the I_i vector (investment share of GDP, real GDP per capita in 1960, secondary-school enrollment rate in 1960) meet the robustness criteria from Levine and Renelt (1992) and are therefore deemed empirically relevant in explaining cross-country growth patterns. Instead, the authors conclude that all others variables do not exert an independent influence on economic growth since their partial correlations are not robust to the inclusion of other explanatory variables in the Z_i vector.

The robustness criteria of Levine and Renelt (1992) have been criticised, among others, by Sala-i-Martin (1997) and Temple (1999a) as overly restrictive in a growth regression context. The approach of Levine and Renelt (1992) implies that a variable is labelled non-robust once the sign of its coefficient estimate changes in a single regression even if this particular regression might be characterised by a low goodness of fit. Yet, unstable coefficient estimates for a regressor cannot unambiguously be ascribed to a low explanatory power of the particular variable but might also be due to multicollinearity between the respective variable and other variables included in a growth regression. This ambiguity about the sources of a coefficient's unstableness is particularly acute in growth regressions given the high degree of correlation and, hence, potential multicollinearity between some explanatory variables.

An alternative approach was pioneered by Fernandez et al. (2001) and Sala-i-Martin et al. (2004). Both papers utilise *Bayesian Model Averaging* for evaluating the relevance of different explanatory variables. The general idea in this framework is running growth regressions such as equation (1.17) for every possible combination from a pool of explanatory variables. Thereupon, the relevance of each explanatory variable is deduced from analysing the goodness of fit of the regression models which included this particular variable.[23]

[23] In contrast to Levine and Renelt (1992) which included four key variables in all specifications of (1.18), Fernandez et al. (2001) and Sala-i-Martin et al. (2004) allow for model specifications with all possible sub-sets of variables. Thus, k different variables lead to a model space $\mathcal{M}$ of 2^k possible regression models. Since the number of different variables in Fernandez et al. (2001) and Sala-i-Martin et al. (2004) stands at 41 and 67, respectively, estimation of all possible model specifications is computationally not

Table 1.2: Empirically Relevant Correlates of Economic Growth

Variable	Estimate β	Relevance Criterion
Levine and Renelt (1992):		*Robust PC:*
Total Investment (% of GDP)	0.17490	Yes
GDP per capita in 1960	-0.00350	Yes
Secondary School Enrollment Rate in 1960	0.03170	Yes
Sala-i-Martin et al. (2004):		*PIP:*
East Asia Dummy Variable	0.02181	0.823
Primary School Enrollment Rate in 1960	0.02685	0.796
Price Level Investment Goods 1960s	-0.00008	0.774
GDP per capita in 1960 (log)	-0.00854	0.685
Fraction of Tropical Area (% of total land)	-0.01476	0.563
Population Density in Coastal Areas 1960s	0.00001	0.428
Malaria Prevalence in 1960s	-0.01570	0.252
Life Expectancy in 1960	0.00081	0.209
Fraction Confucian in 1960 (% population)	0.05443	0.206
Africa Dummy Variable	-0.01471	0.154
Latin America Dummy Variable	-0.01276	0.149
Fraction GDP in Mining	0.03882	0.124
Former Spanish Colony Dummy Variable	-0.01072	0.123
Openness Trade 1950-1994 (Number of Years)	0.01221	0.119
Fraction Muslim in 1960 (% population)	0.01263	0.114
Fraction Buddhist in 1960 (% population)	0.02167	0.108
Ethnolinguistic Fractionalisation	-0.01128	0.105
Government Consumption 1960s (% of GDP)	-0.04417	0.104

Notes: Levine and Renelt's (1992) estimates of β refer to a specification of equation (1.18) which comprises only the variables from the I_i vector. Estimates of β in Sala-i-Martin et al. (2004) are given by the posterior means of the respective variables in equation (1.21). In Levine and Renelt (1992), a variable is only deemed relevant if the partial correlation (PC) between economic growth and the particular variable is robust to changes in the set of additional explanatory variables in equation (1.18). The relevance criterion in Sala-i-Martin et al. (2004) is given by: posterior inclusion probability (PIP) $\geq$ 10.4% (prior inclusion probability). The dependent variables are the average rates of real per capita GDP growth between 1960-1989 (Levine and Renelt 1992) and 1960-1996 (Sala-i-Martin et al. 2004), respectively. The data sets comprise 101 countries (Levine and Renelt 1992) and 88 countries (Sala-i-Martin et al. 2004), respectively. Fernandez et al. (2001) publish only the PIP but not the posterior means of the respective variables which is why their results are not mentioned in this table.

Formally, the explanatory power of each regression model m_j is assessed by the *posterior model probability*, $p(m_j \mid D)$, i.d. the conditional probability that m_j is the correct model specification given the available information from the data set D. Thereupon, the relevance of a particular variable is evaluated by its *posterior inclusion probability* (PIP) which denotes the sum of the posterior model probabilities of all models which include this variable.

By application of the Bayes' theorem, Sala-i-Martin et al. (2004) derive the posterior model probability for a model m_j through

$$p(m_j \mid D) = p(m_j) \cdot \omega(j) \tag{1.19}$$

$$\text{with } \omega(j) = \frac{T^{-k_j/2} \cdot SSE_j^{-T/2}}{\sum_{i=1}^{2K} p(m_i) T^{-k_i/2} \cdot SSE_i^{-T/2}}$$

where SSE_j is the sum of squared errors for model m_j, k_j is the number of regressors in model m_j, T is the number of observations, K is the total number of potential regressors and $p(m_j)$ is the prior model probability for model m_j. The ratio $\omega(j)$ measures the goodness of fit of model m_j in relation to the goodness of fit of all possible models.[24]

In view of the large number of models, fully specifying a prior model probability $p(m_j)$ for each model is not feasible. Instead, Sala-i-Martin et al. (2004) derive the prior model probability $p(m_j)$ for a model m_j by

$$p(m_j) = \left(\frac{\bar{k}}{K}\right)^{k_j} \left(1 - \frac{\bar{k}}{K}\right)^{K-k_j} \tag{1.20}$$

where $\bar{k}$ is the expected size of the model, K is the total number of potential regressors and k_j is the number of regressors in model m_j. For lowering the prior model probabilities of models with a large number of regressors,

feasible. Therefore, both papers reduce the computational burden through application of algorithms such as the MC^3 methodology by Madigan and York (1995) which simulates a sample from the model space $\mathcal{M}$.

[24]Equation (1.19) is a variant of the Bayes theorem, $p(m_j \mid D) = p(m_j)p(D \mid m_j)/p(D)$, where $p(D)$ has been substituted by $\sum_{j=1}^{n} p(D \mid m_j)p(m_j)$ using the law of total probability. Note that a model m_j with a large number of regressors k gets penalised through the term $T^{-k_j/2}$ in the respective marginal likelihood of the model, $p(D \mid m_j)$.

Sala-i-Martin et al. (2004) set $\bar{k} = 7$ in their estimates.[25]

The prior probability of being included in a growth regression is the same for every explanatory variable and is given by $\bar{k}/K$. Since $K = 67$, this translates into a *prior inclusion probability* of $7/67 = 0.104$ for every explanatory variable. Building on this, the authors deem an explanatory variable only empirically relevant if its posterior inclusion probability $\geq 10.4\%$ (prior inclusion probability). Overall, they find 18 variables which meet this relevance criterion (see table 1.2)

After determining the empirically most relevant variables, Sala-i-Martin et al. (2004) estimate the impact of the different explanatory variables on the dependent variable economic growth. Here, the β estimate for each explanatory variable x_i is given by the *posterior mean*, $E(\beta \mid D)$, which is a weighted average of the respective β estimates in the different model specifications:

$$E(\beta \mid D) = \frac{\sum_{j=1}^{2^K} p(m_j \mid D)}{PIP_{xi}} \hat{\beta}_j \tag{1.21}$$

where $\hat{\beta}_j$ denotes the estimate of β in model m_j *(posterior mean conditional on model j)*, $p(m_j \mid D)$ is the posterior model probability of model m_j and PIP_{xi} is the posterior inclusion probability of the respective explanatory variable x_i. In case an explanatory variable x_i is not included in a particular model specification m_j, its coefficient estimate equals zero, $\hat{\beta}_j = 0$.

The empirical results of Sala-i-Martin et al. (2004) differ from Levine and Renelt (1992) in two major aspects. First, the list of Sala-i-Martin et al. (2004) does not include a variable which proxies for the investment in the stock of physical capital.[26] This is in stark contrast to the very high β estimate for the variable "Total Investment (% of GDP)" in Levine and Renelt (1992) and, thus, illustrates the difficulty of drawing general conclusions about the relevance of a particular variable in growth regressions.

Second, the results of Sala-i-Martin et al. (2004) point to a much broader

[25] Setting $\bar{k} = 7$ discriminates the prior model probabilities in favour of models with a low number of regressors. Given $K = 67$, equal prior model probabilities for every model specification m_j would require $\bar{k} = 33.5$ in (1.20). In contrast, Fernandez et al. (2001) assume an equal prior model probability for every model specification, $p(m_j) = 2^{-K}$.

[26] Sala-i-Martin (2004:827) state that the variable "Total Investment (% of GDP)" became insignificant in their results once the variable "Average Price Level Investment Goods 1960s" had been added to the pool of explanatory variables.

set of potential growth determinants than Levine and Renelt (1992) and are therefore much more informative than the latter with regard to the partial correlation between economic growth and a range of macroeconomic and socioeconomic factors.

However, their results also demonstrate that even Bayesian model averaging approaches to cross-country growth regressions do not necessarily take us very far in identifying the underlying factors associated with high levels of economic growth in certain countries. For example, their results indicate a high empirical relevance of the variables "East Asia Dummy Variable" (highest posterior inclusion probability) and "Fraction Confucian" (highest β estimate). In view of the high rates of economic growth in East Asian countries during recent decades, both results are not surprising and, thus, one may be tempted to ascribe this superior growth performance primarily to regional or religious characteristics of these countries.

Yet, given the (relative) stableness of both variables during recent centuries, this approach fails to explain why these countries exhibited a low level of economic development back in 1960. Instead, both variables seem to pick up country-specific effects of unobserved factors which are not adequately captured by other existing explanatory variables.

For the time being, it is unlikely that this omitted variable problem can simply be overcome by more detailed cross-country data since many factors which might potentially impact economic growth (e.g. institutional quality, effectiveness of economic policy, human capital of workforce) are difficult to quantify. This applies particularly to developing countries given the limited availability of accurate data for most of these countries. Therefore, it is safe to say that for getting a better grasp of the factors robustly related to economic growth in certain countries one needs to go beyond cross-country growth regressions and explore potential determinants of growth in detailed case studies of the respective economies.

1.3.3 Heterogeneity Uncertainty

An obvious candidate for allowing potential parameter heterogeneity in growth regressions are panel data approaches which account for unobserved country-specific characteristics through a fixed effect estimator.[27] Yet, this

[27] In contrast to fixed effect estimation, a random effect estimator approach does not allow for correlation between the unobserved individual effect, c_i, and the observed explanatory variables, $x_{i,t}$. This orthogonality assumption between unobserved country-

approach is often not applicable because it relies on variation in the time dimension of the variables for uncovering parameters. Many variables in growth regressions exhibit no or only slow variation in the time dimension (e.g. political regime, institutional or geographical characteristics, human capital proxies). In these cases, one typically depends on cross-sectional variation of the variables for estimating coefficients.

An alternative approach is followed by Liu and Stengos (1999). For examining potential cross-country heterogeneity with regard to the impact of schooling levels (as a proxy variable for human capital) and initial output levels on economic growth rates, the authors utilise a semiparametric specification of a cross-country growth regression.

In contrast to a parametric specification such as equation (1.17), the semiparametric approach of Liu and Stengos (1999) allows for greater estimation flexibility since it permits non-linear relationships between the dependend variable $g_{i,t}$ and the nonparametric regressors $School_{i,t}$ and $y_{i,0}$. Drawing on pooled cross-section data for 86 countries averaged over the 1960s, the 1970s and the 1980s, the authors estimate a semiparametric *partially linear regression model*:

$$g_{i,t} = X_{i,t}\beta + g_1(School_{i,t}) + g_2(y_{i,0}) + \epsilon_i \qquad (1.22)$$

where $g_{i,t}$ is the average rate of per capita output growth g in country i during a particular decade (1960s, 1970s or 1980s), $X_{i,t}$ contains the parametric model components (decade dummies, population growth rate, investment ratio), $y_{i,0}$ is the initial level of per capita output in the year 1960 and $School_{i,t}$ is the enrollment rate in secondary schools. In contrast to the parametric model components in $X_{i,t}$, the estimated impact of the variables $School_{i,t}$ and $y_{i,0}$ is not quantified by a constant coefficient but by estimates of the unknown functions $g_1(\cdot)$ and $g_2(\cdot)$.

The model estimates of Liu and Stengos (1999) reveal a non-linear impact of schooling and initial output levels on economic growth.[28] For example, the

specific characteristics and explanatory variables is unlikely to hold in a cross-country growth regression context. Therefore, panel data growth regressions such as Islam (1995) typically utilise fixed effect estimators. For a discussion of the appropriateness of fixed effect estimators in growth regressions see also Durlauf et al. (2005:628-630).

[28] Liu and Stengos (1999) derive the estimates for the parameter β and the unknown functions $g_1(\cdot)$ and $g_2(\cdot)$ in two steps. First, they obtain a $\sqrt{n}$-consistent estimator $\hat{\beta}$ for the parameter β by applying an estimation method from Robinson (1988). Second, they rearrange equation (1.22) to $g_{i,t} - X_{i,t}\hat{\beta} = g_1(School_{i,t}) + g_2(y_{i,t0}) + \epsilon_i + X_{i,t}(\beta - \hat{\beta})$ where

positive effect of $g_1(School_{i,t})$ on the dependend variable $g_{i,t}$ is much higher for secondary enrollment rates ranging between 15% and 75% than for values of $School_{i,t}$ outside this range. Furthermore, the value of $g_2(y_{i,0})$ turns only negative for initial output levels exceeding 1,800 US-Dollar. Hence, a tendency for a convergence of output levels is only confirmed for countries in the middle and upper ranges of output levels.

Durlauf et al. (2001) examine parameter heterogeneity through a *varying coefficient model.* Here, the parameters of the cross-country growth regression are country-specific since they vary as functions of a country's initial output level. The authors find evidence of significant parameter heterogeneity in particular among poorer economies. For example, the coefficients for the variables population growth and secondary school enrollment rate are relatively stable only for countries whose per capita GDP level exceeded 944 US-Dollar in 1960. The coefficients estimates for physical capital are unstable throughout the entire sample indicating strong cross-country differences in the impact of physical capital investment on economic growth.

Given the strong empirical evidence for parameter heterogeneity one may conclude that any empirical analysis which fails to capture cross-country heterogeneity is likely to lead to misleading inferences about correlates of economic growth. Yet, controlling for heterogeneity in a broad cross-section of countries is complicated by the fact that many country-specific characteristics are difficult to quantify (e.g. institutional quality, socio-economic factors). Therefore, Brock and Durlauf (2001:243) suggest to confine empirical analyses of correlates of economic growth to sub-groups of countries which can be plausibly assumed to be similar in various aspects.

$\epsilon_i + X_{i,t}(\beta - \hat{\beta})$ is the composite error term. Thereupon, they estimate the functions $g_1(School_{i,t})$ and $g_2(y_{i,t0})$ through a kernel procedure developed by Linton and Nielsen (1995). A comprehensive treatment of different estimation techniques for the parametric and the nonparametric components in partially linear regression models is given in Li and Racine (2006:222-230).

Chapter 2

Does Public Expenditure Cause Economic Growth?

2.1 Public Expenditure in Models of Economic Growth

The long-term link between economic growth and different types of public expenditure had not been a major research focus in the economic growth literature until the first writings of endogenous growth theory gained traction by the end of the 1980s. Research interest in this subject was sparked by endogenous growth models which allow for a potential long-term impact of investments in human or physical capital on economic growth. Here, the stronger focus on the long-term impact of investments also led researchers to examine long-term effects of different kinds of government expenditure (e.g. public infrastructure, education spending) on the growth potential of an economy.

The first endogenous growth model which analyses the long-term link between public expenditure and economic growth was published by Barro (1990). In this model, increases in public expenditure exert two opposing effects on private capital formation and, following, on long-run economic growth. On the one hand, public investments in infrastructure or a higher public provisioning level of education and health services might enhance the production capabilities of economic agents and, as a result, potentially raise the profitability of private investment *(crowding-in effect)*. On the other hand, a higher level of public expenditure might limit the resources available for private capital formation *(crowding-out effect)*.

In contrast to endogenous growth theory, neoclassical growth theory does not assign a prominent role to government expenditure for explaining long-run economic growth. As seen above, the long-term rate of economic growth in the neoclassical growth model is solely determined by exogenous increases of productivity. In this view, governments which aim to alter the rates of population growth or of capital accumulation in an economy through different kinds of public expenditure may only impact transitory growth rates but not the long-term rate of economic growth in the steady state.[1]

By conceptualising a potential impact of certain public expenditure categories on the long-run productive capacity of an economy, endogenous growth theory changed the perspective on the long-term link between public expenditure and economic growth. Prior to that, the level of government expenditure was primarily seen as a result and not as a cause of economic development. This is best exemplified by *Wagner's law* which was named after the German economist Adolph Wagner (1890). Wagner's law of increasing state activity postulates that higher per capita income levels are accompanied by a rising demand for different kinds of government services such as the provision of law and order, social security as well as cultural services. Here, the income elasticity of the demand for these government services is assumed to be greater than unity. As a result, the relative importance of the provision of government services and, hence, public spending, within an economy is set to grow for higher economic development levels (Diamond 1977; Musgrave and Peacock 1967).

While public expenditure was not deemed ineffective, economic thinking typically confined the impact of public expenditure to social welfare objectives and to short-term economic stabilisation policies. An example for the former is the importance of public expenditure for a Pareto-optimal provisioning level of public goods. As shown by Samuelson (1954, 1955), a decentralised private provision leads to an under-provisioning of the public good and, as a result, does not maximise the utility functions of economic agents. This market failure may be overcome by a public provision of public goods and, hence, a certain level of public expenditure and taxation.

In addition, following the adoption of Keynesian ideas into macroeconomic thinking in the aftermath of the 1930's Great Depression, government ex-

[1] An example for the neoclassical view on the relationship between public expenditure and economic growth is Arrow and Kurz (1970) since public spending impacts economic growth only temporarily in their model. Devarajan et al. (1996:315)

penditure was considered an important economic policy tool for stabilising strong fluctuations in aggregate demand. While most economists nowadays advocate a less active fiscal policy than during the heyday of the neoclassical synthesis in the 1960s, the notion that government expenditure exerts a short-term impact on aggregate demand remains widely accepted. Yet, consistent with the conclusions of neoclassical growth theory, both the social welfare and the economic stabilisation perspectives do not explicitly relate government expenditure to the long-term productive capacity of an economy.

The link between public expenditure and long-run economic growth was first formalised by Barro (1990). In his endogenous growth model, he distinguishes between productive and non-productive types of public expenditure. The criterion for the productiveness of a certain type of public expenditure is the latter's impact on the production function of an economic agent. Here, a particular kind of government expenditure is only defined to be productive if it can reasonably assumed to be a factor input in the production function which enhances the production capabilities of an economic agent. Thus, productive government expenditures need to exhibit complementarity to other factor inputs of the production function.

In contrast, government expenditure which impacts only the utility function but not the production function of an economic agent is deemed unproductive. Hence, compared to the demand-side perspective on government expenditures with regard to economic stabilisation policies, the Barro (1990) model attaches a much greater importance to the composition of public expenditure.

The presumptions about the potential productiveness of different types of public expenditure are not uniform across different models. For example, Barro (1990) ascribes a potential growth-enhancing effect only to capital expenditure whereas current expenditure is assumed to be unproductive. This is in line with contributions by Aschauer (1989a, 1989b) which emphasise the important role of public infrastructure for long-term productivity developments within an economy.[2] Later models go beyond the capital-current expenditure dichotomy and examine the expenditure-growth nexus with regard to different functional categories of public expenditure such as public education expenditure (e.g. Glomm and Ravikumar 1992; Eckstein

[2] Aschauer (1989a:193) defines "core infrastructure" to include transportation facilities (roads, railways, airports), water and sanitation systems, and energy production.

and Zilcha 1994; Blankenau 2005) and, to a lesser extent, public health expenditure (e.g. Hosoya 2003; Agenor 2008).

The rationale for at least a partial role of the government in the provision of certain factor inputs rests on the assumption that public and private factor inputs are not close substitutes. In this reasoning, government intervention is necessitated if a private provision of a factor input does not result in a Pareto-optimal provisioning level as a result of market failures. Typically, publicly provided factor inputs comprise not only public goods (e.g. institutional quality) but also factor inputs like education or infrastructure which might be considered private goods since they are (to some extent) rival and excludable. With regard to a public role in education, it can be argued that positive externalities of the factor input education cause its private provisioning level to be to low. In case of infrastructure services, a competitive equilibrium between different private producers might be inhibited by natural monopoly conditions in the production of these services.[3]

The long-term impact of an increase in productive public expenditure on economic growth is not uniform and depends on the long-term evolution of the private capital stock. Here, an increase in public expenditure exerts two opposing effects on private capital formation. On the one hand, an increase of productive public spending raises the profitability of private investment as a result of the complementarity between public and private factor inputs. This rise in the profitability of private investment might, in turn, induce higher private capital formation *(crowding-in effect)*. On the other hand, a higher level of public spending limits the resources available

[3]The positive externalities assumption for the factor input education presumes that an economic agent benefits not only from an increase in his own level of education but also from higher levels of education of other economic agents. As discussed earlier with regard to the factor input knowledge in the Romer (1986) model (see section 1.1.2), an economic agent does not internalise positive externalities of his investment decision on other economic agents when optimising the level of his investment into factor inputs. Therefore, the private optimum of the economic agent is below the Pareto-optimum. This market failure can be corrected by lowering the marginal cost of an investment into the factor input education, for example through public subsidies, hence, inducing a higher level of investment by economic agents. Natural monopoly conditions in the provision of infrastructure services emanate from economies of scale in the production of these services. Most infrastructure services require huge initial investments. Since the cost structure of infrastructure providers is dominated by such fixed costs, an increase in production leads to a decline in average production costs and, following, a cost advantage over competitors. Generally, the lack of a competitive equilibrium in the provision of infrastructure services has either led to public provisioning or to price regulation by the government in case of private provisioning.

for private capital formation since increased spending levels need to be financed by higher taxes *(crowding-out effect).*

Rising levels of productive public expenditure increase long-run economic growth only if the crowding-in effect outweighs the crowding-out effect. As a result of diminishing returns to public factor inputs, the net impact of higher public spending on economic growth is more likely to be positive for lower levels of public expenditure. This can be illustrated by the production function of a representative economic agent which, following Barro and Sala-i-Martin (1992b), is given by

$$y = k^{1-\alpha} g^{\alpha} \text{ with } 0 < \alpha < 1 \tag{2.1}$$

where y is the per capita output of a representative economic agent, k is his per capita stock of private capital and g the per capita quantity of (productive) public expenditures.[4] The production functions exhibits constant returns to scale but positive and diminishing returns to the factor inputs k and g.

In a Cobb-Douglas production function such as equation (2.1), the elasticity of substitution between the factor inputs g and k equals unity. Therefore, complementarity is given in the sense that an increase (decrease) in the ratio of public and private factor inputs, g/k, leads to a proportional increase (decrease) in the ratio between the marginal products of private and public factor inputs, $(\partial y/\partial k)/(\partial y/\partial g)$.

The government expenditure g is financed contemporaneously by a proportional tax at the rate of τ:[5]

$$g = \tau y = \tau k^{1-\alpha} g^{\alpha} \tag{2.2}$$

[4]The per capita specification of public expenditure, g, presumes that the public factor input is rival and excludable and, hence, a private good. Alternatively, public expenditure might be modeled as a public good in a production function: $y = k^{1-\alpha}G^{\alpha}$. Here, the aggregate quantity of public factor inputs, G, is utilised in a non-rival manner by different economic agents. Both model specifications do not lead to qualitatively different conclusions. The Pareto optimal size of public expenditure in the public good model specification is not given by (2.5) but by: $G/Y = \alpha$, where Y denotes aggregate output. See also Barro and Sala-i-Martin (1992b:649-650)

[5]Allowing for intertemporal financing of public expenditure through the inclusion of a financial sector in the model does not remove the incidence of crowding-out effects. In this case, private investment will be crowded out by a higher public demand for borrowing on financial markets since the latter leads either to higher interest rates or, in case of administered interest rates, to a stronger incidence of credit rationing towards the private sector. Agenor and Moreno-Dodson (2006:10)

As mentioned above, a rise in productive public spending has only a positive impact on long-run economic growth if it induces higher private capital formation. Here, the level of private investment is determined by an economic agent who utilises per capita output, y, either for consumption, c, or for investment in the private capital stock, Δk, i.e. $y = c + \Delta k$. When choosing the level of Δk, the economic agent decides upon per capita output in the future time period. With g exogenously given, the choice of the level of investment in the private capital stock, Δk, depends on the after tax marginal product of k:

$$\frac{\partial y}{\partial k} = (1-\alpha)k^{-\alpha}g^{\alpha}(1-\tau) \tag{2.3}$$

As can be seen in equation (2.3), an exogenous increase in the level of public expenditure g has two opposing effects on the after-tax marginal product of k, $\partial y/\partial k$, and, hence, private capital formation. One the one hand, the crowding-in effect of a higher level of public spending g raises the profitability of private investment through g^{α}. One the other hand, the accompanying higher level of taxation crowds out private investment through $(1-\tau)$. While $(1-\tau)$ impacts $\partial y/\partial k$ linearly, the crowding-in effect of g^{α} is stronger for lower values of g as a result of diminishing returns to factor inputs. Hence, the crowding-in effect is more likely to outweigh the crowding-out effect for lower levels of public expenditure.

The Pareto optimum is given by the level of public expenditure where the crowding-in and the crowding out effects offset each other. Barro (1990) determines such a Pareto optimum for the level of public expenditure by the *productive efficiency condition*: $\partial y/\partial g = 1 = g$. This condition implies that the marginal product of government spending, $\partial y/\partial g$, must equal 1 in the Pareto optimum since each unit of additional spending needs to be financed by one unit of tax revenue, $g = \tau y$. Substituting equation (2.1) into the following productive efficiency condition

$$\frac{\partial y}{\partial g} = \alpha k^{1-\alpha}g^{\alpha-1} = 1 \tag{2.4}$$

yields the Pareto optimal level of productive public expenditure:

$$\frac{g}{y} = \alpha \tag{2.5}$$

Hence, increases in productive public expenditure have a positive impact on long-run economic growth as long as the level of public expenditure within an economy is below the Pareto optimum, $g/y < \alpha$. In contrast, the crowding-out effect is set to outweigh the crowding-in effect for levels of public expenditure above the Pareto optimum, $g/y > \alpha$. It is important to point out, that the Pareto optimal size of government expenditure is not uniform across different economies but is determined by the (relative) productiveness of public and private factor inputs in an economy which are indicated by the values for α and $1 - \alpha$, respectively in equation (2.1). Hence, the higher the productiveness of public expenditure, the higher the Pareto optimal size of public expenditure and taxation.

2.2 Empirical Evidence Capital and Current Expenditure

Empirical research on the impact of capital expenditure on economic growth allows for two main conclusions. On the one hand, capital expenditure has been shown to cause economic growth in different countries. On the other hand, this growth-enhancing impact of capital expenditure is far from being a general finding across countries. Instead, the empirical literature reveals substantial cross-country heterogeneity in the relationship between capital expenditure and economic growth particularly in developing countries.

This heterogeneity can be attributed to the finding that the macroeconomic outcome of higher capital expenditure depends upon multiple factors. Here, the empirical literature points particularly to institutional characteristics of an economy as an important determinant of the effectiveness of capital expenditure. Furthermore, a lack of clarity can also be ascribed to methodological problems such as the difficulty to control for a potential endogeneity of public expenditure with regard to economic growth.

Cross-country empirical evidence about the effects of current expenditure on economic growth is largely limited to results from cross-sectional growth regressions. While most partial correlations between different categories of public expenditure and economic growth are found not to be statistically significant in cross-sectional growth regressions, the few statistically robust links can be considered consistent with the conclusions of the Barro (1990) model. For example, Barro (1991) and Landau (1986) find a negative association between the level of current expenditure (excluding education and defence expenditure) and economic growth.

As to capital expenditure, Easterly and Rebelo (1993) detect a positive partial correlation between the level of capital expenditure (in transport and communication) and economic growth. Yet, these statistically significant links should at best be seen as offering weak support for the Barro (1990) model given the above discussed difficulties to control for potential biases of the coefficient estimates in a cross-sectional regression set-up such as equation (1.17) in section 1.3 (e.g. reverse causality dynamics, impact of omitted variables, multicollinearity).[6]

The most popular estimation methods for gauging the impact of public capital on economic growth are the production function approach and vector error correction models (VECM). The production function approach has been put forward by Aschauer (1989a). In this approach, the stock of public capital is modeled as a separate factor input in the aggregate production function of an economy. This, in turn, allows for an estimation of the output elasticity with regard to this factor input. Consider a production function

$$Y_t = A_t\, L_t^{\alpha}\, K_t^{\beta}\, G_t^{\gamma} \;\text{ with }\; \alpha + \beta + \gamma = 1 \tag{2.6}$$

where Y_t is aggregate output Y in an economy in period t, A is a productivity parameter, L is the labour force, K is the stock of private capital and G is the stock of public capital.

Rewriting equation (2.6) in units of private capital and taking natural logarithms yields the basic regression set-up of Aschauer (1989a):[7]

$$ln\frac{Y_t}{K_t} = ln\, A_t + \alpha\, ln\frac{L_t}{K_t} + \gamma\, ln\frac{G_t}{K_t} + \epsilon_t \tag{2.7}$$

[6]The study of Devarajan et al. (1996) is often cited as counter-evidence to the aforementioned results from cross-sectional regressions in the economic growth literature. In a sample of 43 developing countries, Devarajan et al. (1996) find that increases in the share of current expenditure at total expenditure exhibit a positive association with economic growth while the share of capital expenditure at total expenditure is found to be negatively correlated with economic growth. The authors attribute these findings to the adverse effects of overprovisioning of public capital on economic growth. The results of Devarajan et al. (1996) are not directly comparable to the above mentioned cross-sectional studies since Devarajan et al. focus only on the composition of expenditure and not on the level of public expenditure as measured by the share of public expenditure at GDP. Nevertheless, the results of Devarajan et al. (1996) offer empirical evidence against overly simplistic conclusions with regard to the potential productiveness of current and capital expenditure.

[7]In his regression set-up Aschauer (1989a), proxies lnA_t by a constant and a time trend. In addition, he employs a capacity utilisation rate as a control variable for business cycle effects.

A measure of the elasticity of output with regard to public capital is given by the estimate of the coefficient γ in equation (2.7). When utilising annual data for the United States in the period 1949-1985, Aschauer (1989a) obtains a γ estimate of 0.39. Accordingly, a 1% rise in the ratio between public and private capital raises output per unit of private capital by 0.39%. This large impact of public capital on economic growth is confirmed by the results of Munnell (1990) who estimates the output elasticity of public capital to be in the range of 0.31-0.39%.

The work of Aschauer (1989a) and Munnell (1990) has been criticised among others by Gramlich (1994) and Sturm and de Haan (1995). In particular, the latter papers point to a failure of Aschauer (1989a) and Munnell (1990) to control for methodological problems related to a potential endogeneity of public capital (e.g. reverse causality dynamics between economic growth and public capital, omitted variable bias). As discussed earlier, any conclusion about causal links requires an explicit analysis of the direction of causality between the respective variables. In addition, they question the consistency of both estimates because Aschauer (1989a) and Munnell (1990) utilise time series in levels and, hence, potentially non-stationary data, for deriving ordinary least squares (OLS) estimates of the output elasticity.

Fernald (1999) addresses the latter concern by first differencing the data.[8] In addition, he examines the direction of causality between public capital and economic growth by drawing on a disaggregated data set. For a panel of 29 different industries of the US economy, Fernald (1999) utilises a production function such as equation (2.6) where public capital, G, is proxied by the stock of government roads.[9] When applying a growth accounting procedure to these 29 sectoral production functions, he finds that higher growth

[8] When reestimating the Aschauer (1989a) model with first differences of the respective time series, and hence, stationary data, Sturm and de Haan (1995) obtain no clear statistical evidence for a link between public capital and economic growth. Fernald (1999:633) ascribes this to a lack of sufficient information in the aggregate data utilised by Sturm and de Haan. For a detailed description of the characteristics of stationary and non-stationary data, the concept of cointegration, the vector error correction model (VECM) estimation method as well as Granger causality tests please refer to section 3.4.

[9] The use of non-monetary indicators as a proxy for public capital has primarily been motivated by the observation that monetary indicators might overstate the actual size of public capital in an economy. Typically, monetary indicators for the public capital stock are constructed on the basis of accumulated capital expenditure flows. Yet, as shown by Pritchett (1996), the level of capital expenditure might strongly exceed the value of public capital created as a result of inefficiencies in project implementation. Romp and de Haan (2005:47-48)

rates in the stock of government roads are associated with higher rates of total factor productivity growth particularly in those industries which utilise more vehicles. Fernald argues that this link between above-average productivity growth in vehicle-intensive industries and road-building can be interpreted as an evidence for causation running from public capital to productivity since, otherwise, productivity growth should be independent of an industry's vehicle intensity.

While confirming a causal effect of public capital on productivity developments in the US economy, the results of Fernald (1999) also suggest that this effect is not linear because the impact of public road-building on economy-wide productivity developments is much stronger for the period 1953-1973 than during 1974-1989. He ascribes the high impact of public capital on productivity in the former period to the building of an interstate highway network during the 1950s and 1960s. In Fernald's (1999:632) view, public capital led to a one-time increase in the level of productivity during the first period while the returns to the factor input public capital decreased strongly in the second period. Fernald (1999:630) summarises his findings by stating that "building one [interstate highway] network may have a very high rate of return; but building a second network may have a very low marginal return."

The finding that infrastructure may potentially cause economic growth is also confirmed by cross-country empirical studies which employ the VECM estimation method. Kamps (2005) confirms a growth-enhancing impact of the public capital stock in a sample of 22 OECD countries. Cross-country evidence on the impact of public capital in developing countries is more mixed and is largely limited to the work of Canning and Pedroni (2008). The authors examine the direction of causality between growth and infrastructure through Granger causality tests after finding evidence of cointegration relationships between GDP per capita levels and three physical measures of infrastructure (kilometers of paved roads, kilowatts of electricity generating capacity, number of telephones). With regard to the impact of these infrastructure measures on GDP per capita, Canning and Pedroni (2008) detect a strong heterogeneity across countries since the statistically significant long-run effects of an increasing stock of infrastructure are found to be positive in some countries while being negative in other countries. As a result of this wide dispersion, the authors cannot reject the null hypothesis that the *average* impact of infrastructure on GDP per capita levels is zero across countries.

The incidence of a growth-enhancing impact of additional infrastructure is on average somewhat higher in developed countries than in developing countries which might be considered a striking result given the fact that the stock of infrastructure in developed countries is typically higher than in developing countries. For example, the impact of the indicator "kilometers of paved roads" on GDP per capita is predominately positive in a panel of 12 OCED countries while exhibiting a large degree of heterogeneity in a panel of 30 non-OECD countries. Here, the median impact in the latter panel is close to zero.

In line with the predictions of the Barro (1990) model, Cannning and Pedroni (2008) ascribe the negative long-run effects of infrastructure on economic growth to an above-optimum level of capital expenditure in the respective countries. In this view, overspending on infrastructure drains resources from other potentially growth-enhancing expenditure categories such as public education spending.

An alternative explanation is proposed by Gwartney et al. (2006) and Haque and Kneller (2008) who relate the efficiency of capital expenditure to the institutional characteristics of an economy. The empirical results of Haque and Kneller (2008) suggest that the level of corruption in an economy affects capital expenditure in two ways. First, a higher level of corruption raises the level of capital expenditure. In this regard, Haque and Kneller (2008:4) argue that the large-scale construction nature of most infrastructure projects makes bribes easier to collect which, in turn, leads to a bias towards capital expenditure in economies characterised by high corruption. Second, the productiveness of capital expenditure is lowered by corruption. In a sample of 66 countries, the authors find that public investment exerts a statistically significant positive impact on long-run economic growth only in these countries where the level of corruption is below a certain threshold.

2.3 Empirical Evidence Education and Health Expenditure

Apart from capital expenditure, economic theory also highlightes a potential growth-enhancing impact of higher public outlays on education and health. Empirical analyses of education and health expenditures utilise breakdowns of total public expenditure by function. Instead, breakdowns of public expenditure by economic type into capital and current spending categories are not conducive for testing the impact of education and health expenditures since the latter contain both capital expenditures (e.g. new buildings) as well as current expenditures (e.g. wages and salaries).

The hypothesis that public spending on education and health has a positive impact on long-run economic growth can be based on several grounds. For example, a higher educational level might well increase a country's absorptive capacity for technology spillovers. Furthermore, the productivity of a country's workforce may reasonably be assumed to be impacted by the latter's health status. Yet, while a growth-enhancing impact of improvements in the educational level and the health status is confirmed in most microeconomic empirical studies, the macroeconomic empirical evidence is mixed.

Most microeconomic empirical studies approximate the economic return to investments in the educational level by a wage regression proposed by Mincer (1974). In this (cross-sectional) approach, the current levels of individual wage earnings are regressed on the number of respective schooling years. This, in turn, yields an estimate of the economic return to each additional year of schooling. The Mincer wage regression is given by

$$ln\, w_i = \pi + S_i\beta + E_i\gamma + E_i^2\delta + \epsilon_i \tag{2.8}$$

where ln is the natural logarithm, w_i is the wage w of person i, π is a constant, S is the number of completed schooling years, E is the number of (after school) years of work experience and ϵ_i is an error term.[10] An estimate of the (marginal) return to one additional year of schooling is given by the coefficient β. Surveys of the returns to schooling in different countries (e.g. Psacharopoulos 1994; Psacharopoulos and Patrinos 2004) find the β estimates primarily to be in the range of 5%-15%. On average, the returns to schooling are higher in developing countries than in developed countries. In addition, when allowing for different schooling levels in equation (2.8), the return to one year of primary education typically exceeds the returns to secondary or tertiary education. Both findings might be interpreted as an indication for positive and diminishing returns to the factor input education.

Likewise, microeconomic empirical studies highlight the importance of an

[10] Mincer (1974) assumes that the number of schooling years S impacts the natural logarithm of wage earnings $ln\, w$ linearly. Instead, the positive impact of additional years of work experience E is set to decrease over time since the latter variable is specified by a quadratic function in equation (2.8). For a discussion about alternative specifications of the Mincer wage regression refer to Murphy and Welch (1990) and Lemieux (2006).

improved health status for productivity developments in developing countries. In this regard, randomised controlled trials as well as observational studies point particularly to nutritional status as an important determinant of individual work capacity (e.g. Thomas and Frankenberg 2002; Alderman et al. 2005).

In contrast, macroeconomic studies yield much more ambiguous findings about the links between investments in education or health and economic growth. This ambiguity is highlighted by the fact that different approaches for examining the importance of education and health for economic growth lead to conflicting results. With regard to education, a positive link between public education expenditure and economic growth is confirmed by the results of Bose et al. (2007). In a sample of 30 developing countries, the authors find that education expenditure is the only sectoral public expenditure category which exhibits a positive statistical association with economic growth. In addition, the studies of Levine and Renelt (1992) and Sala-i-Martin et al. (2004) highlight a strong positive correlation between school enrollment rates and economic growth as can be seen on table 1.2 in section 1.3.2.[11]

However, empirical studies which utilise other indicators for the educational level within an economy do not confirm a growth-enhancing impact of investments in education. Benhabib and Spiegel (1994) utilise the number of average schooling years in the labor force as a proxy variable for the educational level in an economy. Pritchett (2001) calculates a measure of educational capital by valueing average schooling years in an economy with estimates from Mincer wage regressions on returns to schooling years. When applying a growth accounting framework, both papers do not find evidence for a positive statistical association between per capita GDP growth and increases in their measures of education. In contrast, most of their regression specifications yield a negative, though statistically insignificant, coefficient estimate for their education proxy variables.

[11]The results of Levine and Renelt (1992) and Sala-i-Martin et al. (2004) primarily indicate a strong link between the initial level of school enrollment and subsequent growth rates since both papers utilise enrollment rates from the beginning of their sample periods. High initial school enrollment levels, in turn, may not only be the result of high levels of investments into education but might also be driven by other factors such as the effectiveness of public expenditure. With regard to the effectiveness of public education expenditure, Gupta et al. (2002) obtain a robust link between increased levels of public education expenditure and primary and secondary enrollment rates in a sample of 50 developing countries. In contrast, the statistical association between increased levels of public health expenditure and indicators of health status (e.g. mortality rates) is weaker.

Temple (1999b) shows that the empirical results of Benhabib and Spiegel (1994) are driven by statistical outliers in the latter's sample of 78 countries. When excluding 14 countries from the original Benhabib and Spiegel (1994) country sample, Temple (1999b) finds a positive and statistically significant correlation between increases in average schooling levels and economic growth for the remaining 64 countries. The empirical results of Temple (1999b) need to be interpreted cautiously given the selection bias inherent in his approach of simply eliminating statistical outliers. However, the results of Temple (1999b) point to a strong heterogeneity across countries with regard to the relationship between investments in education and economic growth.[12]

Hanushek and Wößmann (2007) criticise the focus of existing empirical research on quantitative education measures (e.g. level of public education expenditure, enrollment ratios, average number of schooling years). In their view, economic growth is primarily related to the quality of education within an economy. The quality of education, in turn, is argued to depend not only on the quantity of funds invested but also on a range of institutional characteristics of the educational system (e.g. existence of school performance measures, degree of local decision making). Therefore, Hanushek and Wößmann (2007) recommend the use of measures on educational outcomes (e.g. results from international student performance tests) as proxy variables for the educational level within an economy.

With regard to the nexus between quality of education and economic growth, Hanushek and Kimko (2000) find a statistically significant positive correlation between a country's rate of economic growth and its international test score on student achievements in mathematics and science. Since the quality of education in any given country can reasonably assumed to be endogenous to the respective country's rates of economic growth, Hanushek and Kimko (2000) focus on the earning levels of immigrants in the US for examining the direction of causality. With regard to immigrants which were schooled in their home countries, Hanushek and Kimko (2000) detect that the home country's test score has a positive impact on the earning levels

[12] Another explanation for the missing link between increases in average schooling levels and economic growth in the Benhabib and Spiegel (1994) paper is provided by Krueger and Lindahl (2001). The latter ascribe the lack of a statistically significant positive link to substantial measurement error in the cross-country education data source of Benhabib and Spiegel (1994) i.e. the average year of schooling estimates by Kyriacou (1991). Here, the strong incidence of statistical noise in the explanatory variable data is argued to cause a downward bias in the latter's coefficient estimate towards zero *(attenuation bias).*

of immigrants in the US. In contrast, when comparing the earning levels of immigrants which were schooled in the US, the authors find no such earning advantage of immigrants from countries with higher test scores. Therefore, Hanushek and Kimko (2000) conclude that a high educational quality of a country's labor force causes economic growth.

Similar to investments in education, the macroeconomic empirical literature does not agree on whether substantial improvements in the health status of a population spur economic growth. Bloom et al. (2004) examine the impact of life expectancy on economic growth through a production function approach along the lines of equation (2.6). Here, economic growth is assumed to depend on the three factor inputs physical capital, labour and human capital. The factor input human capital, in turn, is determined by the levels of education, work experience and health status in a country's work force. With regard to health status, the authors utilise life expectancy data as a proxy variable.[13] The results of Bloom et al. (2004) point to a large impact of health on economic growth. A one year increase in average life expectancy is estimated to raise aggregate output by 4%. In contrast, their results do not indicate a strong link between economic growth and the levels of education or work experience since the latter's coefficient estimates are not statistically significant.

The findings of Bloom et al. (2004) are disputed by Weil (2007:1271). He ascribes their large coefficient estimate for the variable life expectancy to a failure of Bloom et al. (2004) to control both for an omitted variable bias as well as for reverse causality dynamics between life expectancy and economic growth. Acemoglu and Johnson (2007) address the potential endogeneity of the variable life expectancy by applying an instrumental variable approach. They utilise the strong increase in life expectancy following the widespread introduction of medical innovations starting in the 1940s *(epidemiological transition)* as a source for an exogenous variation in the variable life expectancy. The empirical results of Acemoglu and Johnson (2007) show that increases in life expectancy have a large impact on population growth, but no statistically significant effect on aggregate GDP. Moreover, their results point to declines of GDP per capita particularly in those countries which exhibited large increases in life expectancy.

Hence, while being confirmed by some macroeconomic studies, the over-

---

[13] In order to avoid a potential non-stationarity of the time series, Bloom et al. (2004) draw on the first differences of the variables when estimating the production function.

all empirical evidence for a growth-enhancing impact of investments in education or health is much weaker in the macroeconomic literature than in microeconomic empirical approaches *(micro-macro paradox)*. This disparity between macroeconomic and microeconomic results has primarily been ascribed to the fact that macroeconomic outcomes of investments in education or health depend on a much broader range of factors than microeconomic outcomes. For example, Pritchett (2001) emphasises that certain structural features of an economy have an impact on the macroeconomic return of such investments. In line with the institutions view, he argues that the potential growth-enhancing impact of these investments might be strongly lowered in case the higher stock of human capital is allocated to socially non-productive activities as a result of distorted incentives within an economy (e.g. rent seeking). In that case, higher individual skills are employed to activities which are individually remunerative but socially counterproductive. Here, the investment in human capital exerts a negative externality which is only captured by macroeconomic but not by microeconomic empirical studies.

Similarly, Acemoglu and Johnson (2007:926) hold that microeconomic results potentially overstate the economy-wide impact of investments in human capital since the former do not incorporate general equilibrium effects. Given the complementarity between factor inputs, the impact of investments in human capital on economic growth is higher if these investments are accompanied by increases in other factor inputs (e.g. physical capital, infrastructure). Yet, in case the other factor inputs remain unaltered, the marginal return to the increased stock of human capital diminishes as a result of general equilibrium effects. As an example for such diminishing returns, the economic literature often alludes to a surplus of skilled labour in the public sectors of some developing countries which results from the respective government's role as an employer of last resort particularly with regard to university graduates (e.g. Gelb et al. 1991).

Part II

Exploring the Links Between Public Expenditure and Non-Oil Economic Growth in Bahrain, Oman and Qatar

Chapter 3

The Impact of Public Expenditure on Non-Oil GDP and on Labour Productivity: An Econometric Analysis

3.1 Introduction

Public expenditure appears as an obvious economic policy tool for raising the long-term economic growth prospects in the six member countries (Bahrain, Kuwait, Oman, Qatar, Saudi Arabia, and the United Arab Emirates) of the Gulf Cooperation Council (GCC). Large external rents from public oil and gas exports have provided the governments of all six GCC countries with sizeable financial funds over the last decades. Among other things, these export earnings allowed for large public investments in the countries' infrastructure (e.g. roads, electricity production, airports) and in the provisioning level of education and health services.

Different models of economic growth ascribe a potential growth-enhancing impact to public expenditure categories which aim at raising the stock of public infrastructure, the educational level and the health status of local populations. Yet, the long-term link between economic growth and these categories of public expenditure exhibits substantial cross-country heterogeneity (chapter 2). Therefore, the following analysis explores the country-specific characteristics of the long-term link between public expenditure and non-oil economic growth in Bahrain, Oman and Qatar since the late 1970s.

Before turning to the long-term relationship between public expenditure and non-oil economic growth, a word is due on the importance of the oil and gas sector within the GCC economies. With a combined share at global proven crude oil and natural gas reserves of 29.9% and 20.3%, respectively, the GCC countries are prime examples for resource-rich countries (BP 2012). While the level of resource endowment varies between individual countries, the production of crude oil and, to a lesser extent, natural gas continues to play an important role in all GCC economies. This is particularly evident with regard to the trade balances and the fiscal accounts of the GCC states which are both dominated by oil and gas export revenues (tables 3.1 and 3.2).

In view of the long-term depletion of oil and gas reserves, however, a stronger importance of the non-oil economy has been a long held goal of economic policy in the GCC countries. Yet, increasing the long-run growth potential of non-oil economies appears as a complex economic policy task. Triggering broad-based non-oil economic growth depends on a very different set of economic conditions than launching the production of crude oil or natural gas. A crucial condition for oil and gas production is the availability of modern production technologies. Even in case of technological constraints within the domestic economy, a country might well advance the exploitation of its oil and gas reserves by drawing on foreign operators (e.g. multinational companies). Here, the oil and gas sector is likely to attract foreign operators to a greater extent than is the case with most other economic sectors. This, in turn, lowers the technological barriers to economic growth within the oil and gas sector.

In contrast to the exploitation of oil and gas reserves, the potential triggers of sustained non-oil economic growth are less obvious. Instead, the non-oil economies in the GCC countries face challenges similar to those typically described in the economic growth literature. Given the absence of natural resources, long-term economic growth in the non-oil sectors can be seen to rely largely on increases in the productive capacity within the domestic economies. These increases in productive capacity, in turn, might necessitate wide-ranging improvements of various economic factors (e.g. modernisation public infrastructure, improvement of educational level). Devising an appropriate non-oil growth strategy for a particular country is further complicated by the empirical observation that the relative importance of these economic factors is highly country-specific. While the economic growth literature has proposed various potential growth factors, empirical research typically points to the difficulty of drawing general conclusions about the relevance of a certain factor (section 1.3).

In the following econometric analysis, I aim to examine whether different categories of public expenditure have exerted a positive long-term impact on non-oil economic growth in the GCC countries. Due to data limitations, this analysis is confined to Bahrain, Oman and Qatar. In terms of measures for non-oil economic growth, I draw on changes in the non-oil GDP levels of the respective economies. Here, non-oil GDP levels are a much more appropriate measure for non-oil economic growth than overall GDP levels since the latter are strongly impacted by changes in the annual oil and gas output levels.

In addition to aggregate non-oil GDP levels, I also examine the impact of public expenditure on labour productivity developments in the non-oil economy. This helps to clarify whether a potential growth-enhancing impact of public expenditure originates from an accumulation of factor inputs or from increases in productivity. As already discussed in section 1.1, economic growth theory regards improvements in economy-wide productivity levels as a more sustainable source of long-run economic growth than a mere accumulation of factor inputs.

The following chapter starts by reviewing the current status of research (section 3.2). Existing econometric analyses confirmed the existence of long-run relationships between public expenditure and non-oil GDP levels in the GCC countries but are inconclusive about the direction of causality between these variables. Furthermore, these econometric studies only examined the link between current and capital expenditure and aggregate non-oil GDP levels.

For deepening the understanding of the public expenditure-economic growth nexus in the GCC countries, I draw on a broader data set which has been newly compiled for this work (section 3.3). In addition to capital and current expenditure, this data set also includes time series for public education and health expenditure. Moreover, I examine the impact of these different categories of public expenditure not only on aggregate non-oil GDP growth

Table 3.1: Oil and Gas Exports GCC Countries 1980-2013

In percent of total exports[1]

Period	Bahrain	Kuwait	Oman	Qatar	Saudi Arabia	UAE
1980-1989	84.7	88.0	91.8	72.9	90.9	72.8
1990-1999	67.0	92.6[2]	79.6	78.7	89.0	64.4[3]
2000-2013	75.9	92.7	75.6	89.3	88.1	53.8[3]

Sources: IMF, *World Economic Outlook Database*, *International Financial Statistics*, *Direction of Trade Statistics*, *Country Reports*; Ministry of National Economy Oman, *Statistical Yearbook, various issues*; BH/MFNE (1991)
[1] Total exports include re-exports.
[2] Does not include export figures for the year 1991.
[3] The important role of oil exports for the UAE economy is somewhat attenuated by the growing size of re-exports from the Jebel Ali Free Zone in Dubai (UAE) during the recent two decades. According to estimates by IMF (2003:102), re-exports accounted for 30.0% of total UAE exports during the period 1997-2000.

Table 3.2: Oil and Gas Public Revenues GCC Countries 1997-2013

In percent of total public revenues[1]

Period	Bahrain	Kuwait	Oman	Qatar	Saudi Arabia	UAE
1997-2001	65.8[2]	64.5	76.3	68.5	73.8	55.3
2002-2007	74.3	74.6	82.3	65.0	85.0	72.8
2008-2013	86.1	82.7	86.5	59.9	89.9	77.3

Sources: IMF, *Country Reports*, *Public Information Notices*
Note: Official government finance statistics in the GCC countries do not comprise data on investment income from sovereign wealth funds. In addition, officially disclosed public revenues from oil and gas exports typically do not entail export revenues which have been transferred to sovereign wealth funds during the respective fiscal year. The table above draws on IMF government finance data which incorporate estimates of investment income. Unfortunately, these time series are publicly available only since the mid-1990s.
[1] Total revenues include IMF estimates of investment income by sovereign wealth funds.
[2] Does not include revenue figures for the years 1997 and 1998.

but also on labour productivity developments in these countries.

In terms of the econometric methodology (section 3.4), I utilise cointegration analysis for checking the existence of long-run relationships between different variables. Here, a particular focus will be on controlling for a small sample bias of popular cointegration tests such as the Johansen trace test towards indicating more long-run relationships between different variables than suggested by asymptotic theory. This problem typically arises in most empirical work on the GCC countries since many time series are only available on an annual basis. In case the existence of a long-term link has been confirmed, the mutual impacts between cointegrated variables are simulated through impulse response analysis. In addition, the direction of causality between the variables is investigated by Granger causality tests. The empirical results are reported in section 3.5. Section 3.6 concludes.

3.2 Current Status of Research

Empirical research on the relationship between economic growth and public expenditure in the GCC countries is limited to a few studies. These papers adopted either a production function approach or time series methods such as vector autoregressive (VAR) models or vector error correction models (VECM) for analysing a potential growth-enhancing impact of public expenditure.

In general, the empirical results from these studies do not lend support to the notion of a strong impact of public expenditure on economic growth. However, existing research points to different characteristics of the growth-expenditure nexus depending on whether the empirical studies utilise non-oil GDP or total GDP as a variable for economic growth. Empirical studies which analyse the direction of causality between public expenditure and total GDP, typically show that public spending patterns in the GCC countries are not the cause but rather the effect of real GDP growth rates. Instead, the empirical results of Fasano and Wang (2001), which is the only study focussing on non-oil GDP, provide much less clarity about cause and effect between public expenditure and long-term economic growth.

Aly and Strazicich (2000) adopt a production function approach for analysing the effectiveness of public expenditure in the GCC countries. In a regression set-up similar to equation (2.7), the authors examine the statistical association between real GDP growth rates in five different GCC countries

(Bahrain, Kuwait, Oman, Saudi Arabia, and United Arab Emirates) and changes of the three production factors labour, physical capital, and current public expenditure over the period 1970-1992.[1]

For gauging the appropriateness of the size of public spending in the GCC countries, Aly and Strazicich (2000) derive estimates of the marginal return to the production factor current expenditure. This approach is based on Barro's (1990) productive efficiency condition which postulates that the marginal return of government spending equals one in a Pareto optimum (see equation 2.4). Given the well established assumption of diminishing returns to individual production factor inputs, the Barro condition implies that government services are over-provided (under-provided) if the marginal return to government spending is smaller (greater) than one.

Since Aly and Strazicich (2000) obtain marginal return estimates in a range between 0.11 and 0.89, they conclude that the size of current spending in these five GCC countries is larger than optimal. However, the consistency of these marginal return estimates might well be questioned on the grounds of an omitted variable bias and a simultaneity bias. In addition, the approach of Aly and Strazicich (2000) measures only the statistical association between GDP growth and contemporaneous changes in the production factors and, hence, does not account for a potential long-term relationship between different variables. Given these methodological difficulties in obtaining consistent empirical estimates for the marginal return to public expenditure, the results of Aly and Strazicich (2000) need to be interpreted cautiously.

As discussed earlier, production function regression set-ups like equation (2.7) are not adequate for statistical inference about the direction of causality between dependent and independent variables. Due to a potential endogeneity of production factors, empirical results from this approach cannot be interpreted as measuring causal effects between economic growth and public expenditure. In contrast, time series methods like VAR or VECM do not exhibit this methodological drawback since they allow for an application of Granger causality tests.

Most VAR or VECM analyses which examine the relationship between

[1] In contrast to the regression set-up of Aschauer (1989a) in equation (2.7), Aly and Strazicich (2000) utilise first differences of the data. Note that Aly and Srazicich's (2000) analysis of the effectiveness of the production factor current expenditure is based on an estimate of the latter's marginal return and not, as in (2.7), on an estimate of the output elasticity.

government expenditure and economic growth in the GCC countries utilise total GDP growth rates as a measure for economic growth. These studies offer strong empirical support for the existence of unidirectional causality patterns running from GDP to public expenditure. This finding is robust to the choice of country or different model specifications. For example, the empirical results of Ghali (1997) and Al-Khulaifi (2012) both show that GDP growth predicts changes in public expenditure, but not vice versa. Here, Ghali (1997) builds on a bivariate VAR model for the growth rate of real per capita GDP and the share of total government spending in GDP in Saudi Arabia during the period 1960-1996. The empirical results from Al-Khulaifi (2012) stem from a bivariate VECM analysis of the level of total GDP (in real terms) and the level of total expenditure (in real terms) in Qatar for the years 1980-2011. Similar results are obtained by Al-Faris (2002) in a VECM approach for the six GCC countries in the period 1970-1997.[2] Except for Bahrain where causality is found to be bi-directional, Granger causality runs solely from real GDP per capita to the share of public expenditure in GDP in his country sample.

Yet, it can be argued that utilising total GDP data is not adequate for exploring the link between non-oil GDP and public expenditure. The oil and the non-oil sectors in the GCC economies display very diverse structural characteristics particularly with regard to their development stages as well as their importance for GCC fiscal accounts. Here, the above described strong empirical evidence for economic growth causing public spending patterns need not necessarily apply to all sectors in the GCC economies. Instead, causality patterns between public expenditure and non-oil sectors might well be concealed by the dominant role of the oil and the gas sectors in GCC economies.[3]

As to the GCC oil sectors, a tendency for causation to run from real GDP growth in the oil sector to public expenditure can be presumed for two reasons. First, the annual production volume and, hence, real GDP growth rates in the GCC oil sectors are influenced by a range of exogenous factors (e.g. OPEC quotas, life span of oil fields). While public (capital) expen-

[2]Since Al-Faris (2002) does not mention any of his data sources, the extent of comparability between his empirical results and other empirical studies about the GCC countries cannot be assessed.

[3]According to official national accounts country data (sourced from UN Data), the average share of the oil and gas sectors at nominal GDP in the GCC economies during 1980-2010 ranges between a minimum of 22% in Bahrain and a maximum of 46% in Qatar.

diture potentially impacts annual oil production through an expansion of output capacity, this causal impact of public expenditure is attenuated by the presence of the above mentioned exogenous factors.

Second, the fiscal stance of the GCC economies depends largely on developments in the oil and gas sectors (see table 3.2). Here, upswings in oil and gas export revenues as a result of increases in annual production volumes might well precede a higher level of public spending. As shown by Fasano and Wang (2002), the six GCC countries adopted a pro-cyclical fiscal policy during the period 1975-2000 in the sense that total revenues tended to cause total expenditure.

The presumption that the oil and the non-oil sectors exhibit different causality patterns with public expenditure is strengthened by the results of Fasano and Wang (2001) which is the only empirical study examining the long-term relationship between non-oil economic growth and public expenditure in the GCC countries.[4] In contrast to the above mentioned empirical studies, Fasano and Wang (2001) do not find clear evidence for an unidirectional causality link between economic growth and public expenditure. When drawing on time series for non-oil GDP, current and capital expenditures in five GCC countries (Bahrain, Oman, Qatar, Saudi Arabia, and United Arab Emirates) during the period 1980-1999, the authors find evidence of a cointegration relationship in each country between non-oil GDP and capital and current expenditures. In all countries but Saudi Arabia, non-oil GDP is negatively related to capital expenditure and positively related to current expenditure over the long run.

With regard to causality patterns, the empirical results of Fasano and Wang (2001) can be considered somewhat vague since they do not indicate clear causality patterns between the respective public expenditure variables and non-oil GDP. Fasano and Wang (2001) tentatively conclude that changes in the long-run equilibrium relationship between the three variables are primarily caused by adjustments in capital expenditure. The authors ascribe

[4]Treichel (1999) is another empirical study focussing on the interrelation between non-oil GDP as well as capital and current expenditures in Oman during 1981-1997. His analysis is based on an OLS regression with the real growth rate of non-oil GDP as the dependent variable and the contemporaneous real growth rates of capital and current expenditure as independent variables. The empirical results reveal a statistically significant positive correlation between non-oil economic growth and both public expenditure categories. However, as discussed earlier, contemporaneous correlations from OLS regressions are not informative about long-term causality patterns between the different variables.

the negative long-term relationship between non-oil GDP and capital expenditure to crowding out effects of the latter, but offer no explanation for the positive long-term link between non-oil GDP and current expenditure.

The empirical approach of Fasano and Wang (2001) suffers from methodological shortcomings. In particular, the explanatory power of causality analysis might be enhanced by the application of zero restriction tests. Fasano and Wang (2001) estimate the long-run cointegration vector for the three variables without applying further specification tests. After finding evidence for the existence of one cointegration relationship, the authors implicitly assume all three variables to be part of that cointegration relationship. The resulting estimates of the cointegration vector exhibit several coefficients with low t-statistics. The presence of potentially redundant variables in a trivariate framework complicates causality analysis. In a trivariate framework such as in Fasano and Wang (2001), the causal relationship between between two variables cannot be examined directly because this approach would only take into account the direct causal links between both variables but no indirect linkages through the third variable. Here, testing for the exclusion of variables from the cointegration vector through zero restriction tests potentially facilitates a more thorough examination of the main causality patterns.

Another methodological shortcoming of Fasano and Wang (2001) is the failure to control for a small sample bias of cointegration tests. The authors employ the standard Johansen trace test and find evidence for the existence of long-cointegration relationships in every country examined. This finding might be questioned on the grounds of the small sample bias since the empirical analysis of Fasano and Wang (2001) is based only on 20 annual observations for each country.

Furthermore, additional insights about the expenditure-growth nexus in the GCC countries might also be gained by drawing on a larger data set. On the one hand, this includes an expanded set of variables as will be discussed at greater length in the next section. On the other hand, the empirical analysis would also benefit from a longer time span of the respective variables. A longer time span does not only facilitate more consistent estimates of the long-run cointegration relationship but permits also the application of stability tests (e.g. Chow breakpoint test). The latter tests, in turn, allow for an assessment whether the long-run cointegration relationship has undergone a structural change.

3.3 Data

Empirical work on the potential impact of public expenditure on non-oil economic growth in the GCC countries has so far been limited to examining the interrelation between current and capital expenditure and aggregate non-oil GDP. For gaining a more comprehensive understanding of the effects of public expenditures in the GCC countries, I extend existing research in two important aspects. First, in addition to current and capital expenditure, I also examine the potential growth-enhancing effects of education and health expenditure. Second, I elaborate the impact of public expenditure not only on aggregate non-oil GDP growth but also on labour productivity developments in the non-oil sectors. Due to a lack of more accurate data, I utilise non-oil GDP per worker as a proxy for labour productivity developments.

As has been discussed in section 2.1, a high level of capital expenditure is often warranted on the grounds that the growth potential of an economy presumably benefits from removing infrastructure bottlenecks. Similarly, public education and health expenditures have been ascribed a productivity facilitating impact as they potentially raise the human capital and the working ability within an economy. In contrast, high levels of current expenditure are typically seen as being detrimental for economic growth.

This is in stark contrast to the empirical findings of Fasano and Wang (2001) who detect a positive long-term cointegration relationship between non-oil GDP and current expenditure in most GCC countries. A possible explanation for the empirical finding of Fasano and Wang (2001) might be that education and health expenditure are partly included in current expenditure. As discussed earlier, functional categories of public spending such as education or health expenditure consist of current (e.g. wages) and capital expenditure (e.g. new buildings). Here, drawing on breakdowns of public expenditure both by economic type and by function might shed more light on the specific type of public spending categories which have exerted a growth-enhancing impact. When analysing the effects of education and health spending, respectively, I employ control variables (non-education expenditure, non-health expenditure) to account for the potential impact of the remainder of public spending.

Databases of multilateral organisations such as the IMF's Government Financial Statistics do not include consistent time series on public expenditure in the GCC countries. However, all GCC countries continue to publish final accounts for government finances in miscellaneous official publications (e.g. statistical yearbooks, statistical bulletins of central banks and ministries of finance) since the 1970s. Financial information in these publications have been compiled, validated and used to construct time series of government expenditures. Breakdowns of government expenditure by economic type into capital and current spending are published in most official publications. With regard to public spending on education and health, I utilise overall expenditures of the respective ministries and government agencies. For a detailed description of the variables and the data sources please refer to tables A1-A5 in the appendix.

Data availability of public expenditure time series is a limiting factor for the scope of the empirical analysis. Bahrain, Oman and Qatar are the only member countries of the Gulf Cooperation Council where available data allows for a breakdown of expenditure both by economic type and by function. In the case of Kuwait, econometric testing procedures are impeded by missing data in the years 1990-1992 as a result of the Iraqi invasion. Time series of public education and health expenditure are not available for Saudi-Arabia and the United Arab Emirates since both countries publish neither breakdowns of public expenditure by function nor actual expenditure data of individual ministries or public agencies. As a result, the empirical analysis comprises only Bahrain, Oman and Qatar.

In addition to an analysis of the effects of public education and health expenditure, the characteristics of the expenditure-growth nexus might be further clarified by examining the impact of public expenditure not only on aggregate non-oil GDP but also on productivity developments in the GCC countries. This helps to distinguish whether public expenditure has potentially impacted economic growth by an accumulation of factor inputs or by increases in productivity. As already emphasised by Solow (1956), gains in productivity can be seen as a more sustainable source of growth than a mere accumulation of factor inputs (capital, labour).

Productivity indicators aim to capture the efficiency with which factor inputs such as labour and capital are deployed within an economy. For doing so, productivity indicators typically relate a measure of output (e.g. gross output, gross value added) to a measure of factor inputs. Here, one can distinguish between indicators which relate output to a single factor input (e.g. labour productivity, capital productivity) or to multiple factor inputs (e.g. growth accounting analysis).

Table 3.3: Time Span of Variables

Variable	Bahrain	Oman	Qatar
Total Expenditure	1979-2013	1979-2013	1979-2013
Current Expenditure	1979-2013	1979-2013	1979-2013
Capital Expenditure	1979-2013	1979-2013	1979-2013
Education Expenditure	1979-2013	1979-2013	1979-2013
Non-Education Expenditure	1979-2013	1979-2013	1979-2013
Health Expenditure	1979-2013	1979-2013	1979-2013
Non-Health Expenditure	1979-2013	1979-2013	1979-2013
Non-Oil GDP	1979-2013	1979-2013	1979-2013
Non-Oil GDP per Worker	1979-2013	1979-2013	1979-2013

Given their ease of measurement, the utilisation of single factor productivity indicators such as labour productivity is particularly appropriate in case of a scarcity of reliable data. The main drawback of single factor productivity measures is a lack of clarity with regard to the sources of growth. For example, an increase of the labour productivity measure non-oil GDP per worker might be driven by a rising stock of physical capital per worker, an increase in the human capital of the labour force or any other labour productivity enhancing development within the economy (e.g. technological change, institutional changes). Since labour productivity measures do not account for shifts in the endowment of physical capital, changes in labour productivity cannot unambiguously be ascribed to productivity related developments within an economy (e.g. change human capital workforce, technological change).

In contrast, multi factor productivity measures such as growth accounting aim to pinpoint the growth contributions of all factor inputs. In a standard growth accounting setting, output growth is decomposed into growth contributions of the two factor inputs capital and labour and a residual ("Total Factor Productivity"; TFP). More elaborate approaches do not only account for changes in quantity but also for shifts in the quality of these two factor inputs through appropriate measures for human capital and the quality of physical capital. The TFP-residual, in turn, can best be understood as an approximate measure of the efficiency with which all factor inputs are deployed within an economy. Hence, positive residuals indicate rising efficiency levels within an economy.

Since the TFP-residual, however, is also affected by several non-efficiency related factors (e.g. measurement errors in time series and factor input shares, impact omitted variables), the explanatory power of this residual is very sensitive to data quality. The utilisation of flawed time series might strongly aggravate the measurement error problem and render the TFP-residual meaningless. Even though a growth accounting framework is conceptually superior to labour productivity measures, implementation of the former in empirical work is often impeded by a lack of consistent time series for all factor inputs (OECD 2001; Barro 1999).

In view of the existing data, I deem labour productivity the most appropriate indicator for measuring productivity developments in the non-oil sectors of the GCC countries. Instead, the utilisation of more comprehensive multiple factor productivity indicators is constrained by a lack of data. For example, a growth accounting analysis of non-oil GDP growth is not feasible because time series of the factor inputs labour and capital are not available separately for the oil and the non-oil sectors.

In addition, a growth accounting approach which draws on overall GDP growth and aggregate factor inputs is not suitable for analysing productivity developments in the GCC economies. Overall GDP growth in the GCC countries is heavily influenced by changes in the annual output level of the oil and gas sector. These output changes are often not accompanied by changes in the factor inputs. This applies in particular to the factor input labour since oil and gas production is not labour intensive. A considerable change in oil output as a result of an altered OPEC quota might therefore impact the TFP-residual strongly and lead to a distorted view on productivity developments.

With regard to single factor productivity measures, labour productivity can be seen as a more accurate indicator of productivity developments in the non-oil sectors than capital productivity. As already mentioned, time series of the factor inputs labour and physical capital are not available separately for the non-oil sectors. Given the high capital-intensity of oil and gas production it seems reasonable to assume that a substantial fraction of the GCC countries' total capital stocks falls upon the oil and gas sectors. In contrast, census year figures show that the oil and gas sector accounts only for a very small share of the overall labour force. Therefore, relating output to the overall labour force appears as a much less distorted measure of productivity developments in the non-oil economy than relating output to the country's total capital stock.

Unfortunately, more elaborate labour productivity indicators such non-oil GDP per hour worked cannot be calculated for the GCC countries since data on the total hours worked within the economies is absent. Instead, labour productivity developments will be measured by the indicator non-oil GDP per worker. Labour force data emanates from the sources displayed in table A5 in the appendix. The indicator non-oil GDP per worker is certainly less comprehensive than some of the other productivity measures described above. However, since it disentangles growth contributions of the factor input labour from other sources of growth it sheds more light on the way public spending potentially affects non-oil GDP growth.

For precluding a distortionary effect of changes in the price level, I utilise public expenditure and non-oil GDP time series in constant prices. In my view, drawing on time series measured in current prices is particularly misleading with regard to the growth contribution of the manufacturing sector since the nominal value added in most manufacturing industries in the GCC countries is strongly influenced by oil price developments (e.g. refining, petrochemicals).

While being in principle preferable to an analysis of time series in current prices, the empirical analysis of time series in constant prices is complicated by a shortage of data in the GCC countries. GDP time series which are measured in constant prices of one single base year are not available for the entire sample period. In addition, GDP deflator data is only published on an aggregate level for total GDP developments and not for the value added in individual industries. Here, the only price variables available are the total GDP deflator and the consumer price index (CPI) of the respective countries.

With the exception of the manufacturing sector, I deem the CPI a better deflator for nominal public expenditure and nominal value added in non-oil sectors than the GDP deflator since the latter is strongly impacted by price changes in the oil and gas sector. Given the above mentioned correlation between the prices of crude oil and many GCC manufacturing products, the nominal value added in the manufacturing sector is deflated by the GDP deflator. Due to a lack of CPI or GDP deflator data, no empirical analysis of time series in constant prices is possible for Qatar prior to the year 1979.

In order to control for potential measurement errors induced by the deflating procedure outlined above, I also conduct a cointegration analysis for the time series in current prices as a robustness check. To avoid heteroscedasticity, all variables have been transformed to logarithms.

3.4 Econometric Methodology

For examining the long-term link between different categories of public expenditure and non-oil economic growth in Bahrain, Oman and Qatar, I rely on cointegration analysis. A cointegration approach is suitable for analysing the long-run relationship between time series because it examines whether the levels of different non-stationary variables move together over a long-run time horizon.

In case different variables are found to follow a common stochastic trend and, hence, to be cointegrated, estimates of this cointegration relationship are obtained in a vector error correction model (VECM). Similar to other time series methods like vector autoregressive (VAR) models, these VECM estimates allow for an examination of the direction of causality between the different variables of the model through Granger causality tests.

With regard to long-run causality patterns, VECM estimates are preferable to VAR models since the former are based on a broader set of information from the underlying data. In contrast to VAR models, VECM estimates take into account not only stationary first differences but also long-run movements between the non-stationary levels of the respective variables.

The concept of cointegration analysis has been applied to the expenditure-growth nexus in the GCC countries by Fasano and Wang (2001), Al-Faris (2002) and Al-Khulaifi (2012). However, the empirical analyses in these papers exhibit several methodological shortcomings which I aim to address by the econometric methodology employed in this work.

This methodological section starts with a short review of the properties of stationary and non-stationary time series which serves as a background for the econometric concepts adopted in the following empirical analysis (section 3.4.1). Thereupon, I present four different unit root tests which are utilised for determining the order of integration of the different variables (section 3.4.2). Unit root test results determine which variables may be utilised for cointegration analysis since the latter approach is only applicable to variables which are integrated of the same order.

While the above mentioned papers apply only the ADF test, I deem it necessary to cross-check the results from the ADF test with results from other unit root tests. The power of the ADF test in determining the order of integration has been shown to be low in the presence of a structural break or a high degree of persistence of the respective time series. In view of the high dependency of GCC fiscal accounts on oil export revenues, I consider both cases relevant for the GCC countries. Given the prolonged periods of both high and low world market prices for oil during the last four decades, GCC public expenditure patterns might well be characterised by structural breaks or a high degree of persistence as a result of long periods of either high or low spending levels.

With regard to cointegration analysis (section 3.4.3), existing research does not control for a small sample bias of cointegration tests. Sample sizes of GDP and public expenditure data in the GCC countries are typically small since most time series are only available on an annual basis for a comparatively short time period. In particular, the Johansen trace test which is the most common cointegration test in empirical work exhibits a small sample bias towards indicating more cointegration relationships than suggested by asymptotic theory. In order to avoid asserting non-valid cointegration relationships, this bias will addressed through employing a small sample correction factor for the Johansen trace test. Furthermore, the existence of cointegration relationships will not only be examined by the Johansen trace test but also by the Saikkonen and Lütkepohl test since the latter test exhibits better small sample properties.

In contrast to the approaches adopted in existing research, I draw on zero restriction tests and on Chow breakpoint tests for specifying the final VECM estimates of the long-run cointegration relationships. Zero restriction tests examine whether single variables can be excluded from the cointegration vector. This, in turn, leads to a better grasp of the key elements in a long-run cointegration relationship. Chow breakpoint tests scrutinise the stability of a cointegration relationship over the full sample period.

The final VECM specifications are utilised for simulating the mutual impacts of cointegrated variables through impulse response analysis (section 3.4.4). Here, the accumulated responses of one variable to a one-time impulse of another variable are estimated for a period of up to eight years. Finally, the direction of causality between cointegrated variables is examined by applying Granger causality tests to the final VECM specifications (section 3.4.5). In this regard, a more accurate specification of the final VECM might also contribute to a more thorough understanding of the main causality patterns in a long-run cointegration relationship.

3.4.1 Stationarity of Time Series

In a seminal paper, Granger and Newbold (1974) demonstrated through Monte Carlo simulations that the inclusion of non-stationary variables in linear regressions frequently leads to apparently significant regression results between completely unrelated time series *(Spurious Regressions)*.[5] Most macroeconomic time series are non-stationary in their levels but stationary in first differences.[6] Estimation methods such as ordinary least squares (OLS) or generalised least squares (GLS) require the underlying time series to be stationary and, thus, cannot be applied for analysing the empirical link between the levels of macroeconomic time series. In contrast, cointegration analysis allows for an examination of the long-run relationships between non-stationary time series.

A variable y_t is integrated of order d, $y_t \sim I(d)$, if it is stationary after differencing d times. Thus, a stationary time series is $I(0)$. Stationarity of y_t is given if its mean and its variance are constant over time. In addition, the covariance between two values of the time series y_t must not depend on the actual period t at which they are observed but only on the number of periods, s, separating the two observations.

---

[5]Phillips (1986) shows that the incidence of spurious regressions does not decrease asymptotically but, instead, increases for higher sample sizes. The t-statistics of non-stationary variables do not follow a t-distribution but actually diverge from the latter as the sample size T approaches infinity, $T \to \infty$. Hence, the bias in a standard t-statistic significance test towards rejection of the null hypothesis (H_0: variable not significant) will increase for higher sample sizes and, as a result, so does the number of statistically significant variables in the linear regression model.

[6]Empirical analysis of the stationarity of macroeconomic time series goes back to Nelson and Plosser (1982). When running a ADF-test on 14 US macroeconomic time series, the authors found that 13 of these time series were non-stationary in levels. Since then, the Nelson-Plosser data set has become an important reference point for the application of new unit root tests. While the results of Nelson and Plosser have partly been challenged by the findings of other unit root tests (e.g. Perron 1989; Kwiatkowski et al. 1992; Zivot and Andrews 1992), the consensus view remains that most macroeconomic time series are non-stationary in levels.

$$E(y_t) = \mu \tag{3.1}$$

$$Var(y_t) = \sigma^2 \tag{3.2}$$

$$Cov(y_t, y_{t+s}) = Cov(y_t, y_{t-s}) = \gamma_s \tag{3.3}$$

Most macroeconomic time series (in levels) display trending behaviour and, as a result, do not meet conditions (3.1) - (3.3). If for example y_t exhibits a consistent upward trend, the mean and the variance of the sample are not constant but will increase with the size of the sample. Trends in time series can consist of a deterministic trend and/or a stochastic trend.

$$\textit{Deterministic trend:} \quad y_t = \alpha + \mu t + \epsilon_t, \quad \epsilon_t \sim (0, \sigma^2) \tag{3.4}$$

$$\textit{Stochastic trend:} \quad y_t = y_{t-1} + \epsilon_t, \quad \epsilon_t \sim (0, \sigma^2) \tag{3.5}$$

Both trends differ substantially with regard to the stability of their trending behaviour. In the case of a deterministic trend, y_t will grow by the constant rate μ in each period t. The error term ϵ_t is white noise with $E(\epsilon_t) = 0$ and $Var(\epsilon_t) = \sigma^2$. Hence, if the error term ϵ_t causes a deviation from the long-term trend in period t, y_t can be expected to revert to the trend in the following periods. Such a time series can be made stationary by detrending it *(Trend-Stationary)*. After detrending, y_t will always revert to a constant mean *(Mean Reversion)*. No differencing is necessary to make trend-stationary variables $I(0)$.

In contrast, a stochastic trend is a random walk. The trending behaviour of a stochastic trend cannot be predicted because it does not follow a clear pattern. This can be clarified by recursive substitution in equation (3.5):

$$y_t = y_{t-1} + \epsilon_t = y_{t-2} + \epsilon_{t-1} + \epsilon_t = \cdots = y_0 + \sum_{i=1}^{t} \epsilon_i \tag{3.6}$$

Thus, y_t comprises the sum of all error terms ϵ_t of previous periods. The trending behaviour of a stochastic trend is entirely driven by the stochastic error term ϵ_t. Each ϵ_t has a lasting impact on y_t *(Long Memory of Random Walks).* Whereas y_t has a constant mean, its variance tends to infinity:

$$E(y_t) = y_0 \tag{3.7}$$

$$Var(y_t) = tVar(\epsilon_t) = t\sigma^2 \tag{3.8}$$

The increasing variance implies that y_t may not revert to its mean. Stationarity of a random walk can only be achieved by differencing the respective variable *(Difference-Stationary).*

3.4.2 Unit Root Tests

Cointegration analysis is only applicable for variables which are integrated of the same order. Thus, prior to examining the existence of cointegrating relationships between different non-stationary variables, the order of integration of individual variables needs to be determined through unit root tests.[7]

The Augmented Dickey-Fuller test (ADF test) is still the most prevalent unit root test in empirical analyses of macroeconomic time series. However, Monte Carlo simulations have shown that the ADF test suffers from low power to discriminate between stationarity and non-stationarity if a time series contains a high degree of persistence (DeJong et al. 1992) or a structural break (Perron 1989).

As stated above, oil exporting countries have undergone prolonged periods of both low and high price levels on world oil markets during the last four decades. Therefore, GCC public expenditure time series might exhibit a slow process of mean reversion or structural breaks. In order to take into account these two cases, the variables are also examined by unit root tests which address a high degree of persistence in time series or a potential structural break (ADF-GLS test, unit root test with a structural break). In addition, the results of the ADF test are cross-checked by a stationarity test (KPSS test).

[7]In case a variable y_t is integrated of order one, the root of the lag polynomial equals unity which is why tests for the order of integration of a variable have been named unit root tests. Consider a first order autoregressive process $y_t = \rho_1 y_{t-1} + \epsilon_t$. As seen above, this process is a random walk and, thus, I(1) if $\rho_1 = 1$. The first order polynomial is given by $\rho(z) = 1 - \rho_1 z$, where z takes the place of a lag operator for the variable y_t. Solving for the root of the polynomial leads to $\rho(z) = 1 - \rho_1 z = 0$ and, in turn, $z = 1/\rho_1$, which is a unit root if $\rho_1 = 1$. See also Patterson (2010:46-48).

Augmented Dickey-Fuller Test (ADF Test)

The basic idea behind the approach of Dickey and Fuller (1979, 1981) is a testing procedure which gauges whether a time series y_t follows a random walk:

$$y_t = \rho y_{t-1} + \epsilon_t \tag{3.9}$$

If $\rho = 1$, y_t is a random walk and, thus, $I(1)$. As seen above, a random walk does not necessarily revert to its mean since the lasting impact of ϵ_t from previous periods leads to an ever increasing variance of y_t. In contrast, if $\rho < 1$, y_t is a stationary autoregressive process. Here, ϵ_t from previous periods might still impact y_t. Over time, however, this impact fades and y_t will eventually return to its mean.

Subtracting y_{t-1} on both sides of equation (3.9) leads to the test regression of the Dickey-Fuller (DF) unit root test:

$$y_t - y_{t-1} = \rho y_{t-1} - y_{t-1} + \epsilon_t \tag{3.10}$$

$$\Delta y_t = (\rho - 1) y_{t-1} + \epsilon_t \tag{3.11}$$

$$\Delta y_t = \gamma y_{t-1} + \epsilon_t \tag{3.12}$$

where $(\rho - 1) = \gamma$. The null hypothesis of non-stationarity for variable y_t is given by:

$$H_0 : \gamma = 0 \tag{3.13}$$

For a better representation of most time series, a deterministic part D_t (constant α, deterministic trend μt) can be added to the DF test regression in equation (3.12). In addition, Said and Dickey (1984) have augmented the DF unit root test by lags of Δy_t to account for autocorrelation. The test regression of the Augmented Dickey-Fuller (ADF) test can be written as:

$$\Delta y_t = \beta' D_t + \gamma y_{t-1} + \sum_{s=1}^{m} \lambda_s \Delta y_{t-s} + \epsilon_t \tag{3.14}$$

Hence, if the estimated coefficient γ in equation (3.14) is statistically not significant, y_t is non-stationary. In order to account for the small sample size of the variables, critical values are taken from Cheung and Lai (1995).[8]

[8] Again, the significance test for γ cannot be based on a t-distribution because the ADF test statistic includes the potentially non-stationary variable y_t. To reflect this, the

KPSS Test

As mentioned above, the ADF test suffers from low power for certain characteristics of some time series. Thus, the null hypothesis of non-stationarity may not be rejected for every stationary variable y_t *(Type II Error)*. In order to alleviate the risk of drawing wrong conclusions from type II errors in unit root tests, the order of integration might be cross-checked through a testing procedure which is based on a null hypothesis of stationarity *(Stationarity Test)*.

The most prominent stationarity test is the KPSS test which was developed by Kwiatkowski et al. (1992). For testing the null hypothesis of stationarity, the authors decompose variable y_t into a stationary deterministic part D_t (constant α, deterministic trend μt), a non-stationary random walk r_t and an error term ϵ_t:

$$y_t = \beta' D_t + r_t + \epsilon_t, \quad \epsilon_t \sim (0, \sigma^2) \tag{3.15}$$

$$\text{with } r_t = r_{t-1} + u_t, \quad u_t \sim (0, \sigma_u^2)$$

The null hypothesis of stationarity for y_t is given by:

$$H_0 : \sigma_u^2 = 0 \tag{3.16}$$

A zero variance of the random walk implies a constant value for r_t and, as a result, the absence of a stochastic trend. If so, y_t is either trend stationary (in case of a deterministic trend μt) or (level) stationary. The KPSS test statistic η for the null hypothesis of stationarity is based on a Lagrange Multiplier (LM) test:

$$\eta = (T^{-2} \sum_{t=1}^{T} \hat{S_t^2}) / \hat{\lambda^2} \tag{3.17}$$

test statistic of γ has been termed τ-statistic instead of t-statistic. One-tail significance tests are often based on MacKinnon (1991) who estimated critical values τ_c for each of the three ADF test set-ups (no constant or deterministic trend; constant only; constant and deterministic trend). If τ-statistic $\leq \tau_c$, the null hypothesis of non-stationarity for y_t is rejected. Cheung and Lai (1995) have refined the estimates of MacKinnon (1991) by adjusting the critical values τ_c for the effects of the chosen lag order and the particular sample size. These adjustments are particularly important for small sample sizes. Since the sample sizes of this empirical analysis are rather small due to the utilisation of annual data, I will draw on the critical values of Cheung and Lai (1995).

$$\text{with } \hat{S}_t = \sum_{j=1}^{t} \hat{\epsilon_j}$$

where $\hat{\epsilon_j}$ are the residuals of the regression of y_t on D_t and $\hat{\lambda^2}$ is an estimate of the long-run variance of ϵ_j using $\hat{\epsilon_j}$. Accordingly, low values of $\hat{\epsilon_j}$ and, as a result, low levels of the KPSS test statistic η indicate that variable y_t is sufficiently described by the stationary deterministic components D_t. Thus, the null hypothesis of stationarity is only rejected when $\eta > \eta_c$. Critical values η_c are taken from Kwiatkowski et al. (1992).

ADF-GLS Test

The ADF test has low power to differentiate between highly persistent $I(0)$ and $I(1)$ variables (DeJong et al. 1992). Going back to equation (3.9), a variable y_t can be characterised as highly persistent or near-integrated if it exhibits a value for ρ which is below, albeit close to 1. Hence, a highly persistent $I(0)$ variable is close to being $I(1)$ and its process of mean reversion is slow.

Elliott et al. (1996) show that the discriminatory power of the ADF test can be improved significantly with regard to highly persistent variables through *efficient detrending*. In this approach, y_t is detrended by generalised least squares (GLS) estimates of the trend parameters β before testing the null hypothesis of non-stationarity. Assume that variable y_t consists of a deterministic part D_t (constant α, deterministic trend μt) and an error term u_t:

$$y_t = \beta' D_t + u_t \tag{3.18}$$

$$\text{with } u_t = \rho u_{t-1} + \epsilon_t, \quad \epsilon_t \sim (0, \sigma^2)$$

where $D_t = (1, t)$ and $\beta = (\beta_0, \beta_1)$. The null hypothesis of non-stationarity is given for $\rho = 1$. The alternative hypothesis of stationarity requires a fading impact of the error term u_t over time and, hence, $\rho < 1$.

The *efficient detrending* approach of Elliott et al. (1996) encompasses choosing a near-integrated value for ρ under the alternative hypothesis and, subsequently, detrending y_t with the estimates of β in a way that is efficient given the fixed value of ρ. The specific value of ρ depends on the sample size T and is determined through the following formula:

$$H_A : \rho = 1 + c/T < 1 \tag{3.19}$$

in which c is set to -7 (in case of constant α) or to -13.5 (in case of a constant α and a deterministic trend μt). Since the error term u_t is near-integrated, the most efficient estimates of β will be obtained by generalised least squares (GLS) regressions (Phillips and Lee 1996).

The detrended y_t^d is given by:

$$y_t^d = y_t - (\hat{\beta}_0 + \hat{\beta}_1 t) \tag{3.20}$$

As a result, the test regression of the ADF-GLS test does not include a deterministic part D_t:

$$\Delta y_t^d = \gamma y_{t-1}^d + \sum_{s=1}^{m} \lambda_s \Delta y_{t-s}^d + \epsilon_t \tag{3.21}$$

Similar to the ADF test regression in equation (3.14), non-stationarity of the variable y_t is given if the γ coefficient in equation (3.21) is statistically not significant. Critical values are taken from Elliott et al. (1996).

Unit Root Test with a Structural Break

The development of unit root test set-ups which allow for structural breaks of time series goes back to Perron (1989) who has shown that standard unit root tests such as the ADF test have low power to reject the null hypothesis of non-stationarity in case of a stationary time series with a structural break. To overcome this bias towards non-stationarity of a time series, Perron (1989) modifies the ADF test set-up by including dummy variables to account for a structural break. Whereas the break point is assumed to be given exogenously in Perron's unit root test, subsequent contributions such as Zivot and Andrews (1992) developed unit root tests which determine the break point endogenously from the data.

In this empirical analysis, I draw on the minimum LM unit root test with one endogenously determined structural break from Lee and Strazicich (2004). In contrast to Zivot and Andrews (1992), the unit root test of Lee and Strazicich (2004) includes a structural break not only in the alternative hypothesis but also in the null hypothesis. Thus, a rejection of the null hypothesis in the Lee and Strazicich test cannot merely be caused by the existence of a structural break but can, instead, unambiguously be ascribed to the absence of a unit root.

The "break model" of Lee and Strazicich (2004) allows for a shift both in the constant and the deterministic trend:

$$y_t = \delta' Z_t + X_t \tag{3.22}$$

$$\text{with } X_t = \beta X_{t-1} + \epsilon_t, \quad \epsilon_t \sim (0, \sigma^2)$$

where y_t is the variable under consideration. Z_t comprises deterministic terms and dummy variables to account for a structural break at time period T_B and is described by $Z_t = (1, t, D_t, DT_t)$. D_t and DT_t are dummy variables for a shift in the constant and a change in the slope of the deterministic trend, respectively, and are defined as $D_t = 1$ for $t \geq T_B + 1$, and zero otherwise and $DT_t = t - T_B$ for $t \geq T_B + 1$, and zero otherwise. The variable y_t is non-stationary if $\beta = 1$.

The test regression of Lee and Strazicich (2004) is based on a Lagrange Multiplier:

$$\Delta y_t = \delta' \Delta Z_t + \phi \hat{S}_{t-1} + \sum_{s=1}^{m} \lambda_s \Delta \hat{S}_{t-s} + \epsilon_t \tag{3.23}$$

in which $\hat{S}_t$ is a detrended series of y_t and is obtained by:[9]

$$\hat{S}_t = y_t - y_1 - \hat{\delta}' Z_1 - \hat{\delta}' Z_t \tag{3.24}$$

Along the lines of the ADF and the ADF-GLS tests, the null hypothesis of non-stationarity is given by:

$$H_0 : \phi = 0 \tag{3.25}$$

The date of the break point T_B is chosen by searching all possible break points for the minimum (i.e. the most negative) τ-statistic. Hence, the unit root test will be performed with the least favourable τ-statistic towards the null hypothesis. Critical values τ_c are taken from Lee and Strazicich (2004).

[9] Lee and Strazicich (2004) utilise restricted maximum likelihood estimation in their detrending approach. The deterministic terms are estimated under the unit root hypothesis. It is assumed that the first and the last restricted residual are zero, hence, $\hat{X}_1 = 0$ and $\hat{X}_T = 0$. Since y_1 and $\hat{\delta}' Z_1$ are subtracted from y_t, the detrended series starts at zero ($\hat{S}_1 = 0$). The coefficients $\hat{\delta}$ are estimated from a differenced version of equation (3.22), that is a regression of Δy_t on ΔZ_t.(Schmidt and Phillips 1992; Vougas 2003)

3.4.3 Cointegration Analysis

Most macroeconomic time series are non-stationary in levels. The interaction between these time series can best be analysed through cointegration analysis since this econometric approach allows for an examination of long-run relationships between non-stationary variables. In contrast, linear regression analysis requires the utilisation of stationary time series in order to avoid the problem of spurious regressions. In case of time series which are non-stationary in levels, only the stationary first differences of these time series would be eligible for linear regression analysis. This approach, however, leads to a loss of information since the relationships between the levels of these time series are not taken into account.

The concept of cointegration goes back to Granger (1981) and describes a situation where different non-stationary time series move closely together in the long-run since they are driven by a *common stochastic trend.* Cointegration between different non-stationary variables was first formalised by Engle and Granger (1987). Consider a bivariate vector $y_t = (y_{1t}, y_{2t})'$ with the two variables y_{1t} and y_{2t} being integrated of the same order d, $y_{1t} \sim I(d)$ and $y_{2t} \sim I(d)$. A possible long-run equilibrium relationship between these variables is given by:

$$\beta' y_t = y_{1t} - \beta_2 y_{2t} = z_t \tag{3.26}$$

where $\beta = (1, -\beta_2)'$ is a cointegration vector and z_t represents deviations from the equilibrium.

Without cointegration, z_t will exhibit the same order of integration as the non-stationary variables y_{1t} and y_{2t}, $z_t \sim I(d)$. However, if there exists a cointegration vector $\beta \neq 0$ such that $z_t \sim I(d-b)$, with $d \geq b > 0$, the variables y_{1t} and y_{2t} are called cointegrated of order (d, b), denoted as $y_{1t}, y_{2t} \sim CI(d, b)$. In that case, the linear combination $y_{1t} - \beta_2 y_{2t}$ exhibits a lower order of integration than the non-stationary variables y_{1t} and y_{2t}. If y_{1t} and y_{2t} are both $I(1)$ and cointegrated, z_t is $I(0)$. Since z_t is stationary, it has the property of mean reversion. Thus, deviations from the equilibrium between y_{1t} and y_{2t} are only temporary departures from an economic steady-state. In the long run, movements of y_{1t} and y_{2t} will be bound together by the cointegration vector β. Accordingly, the existence of a non-zero cointegration vector β indicates a long-run equilibrium relationship between the variables y_{1t} and y_{2t}.

Since cointegration analysis focuses particularly on potential long-run relationships between different variables, I deem it the most appropriate econometric approach for analysing the long-run empirical link between different kinds of public spending and non-oil economic growth as well as labour productivity developments in the GCC countries. The starting point for cointegration analysis are cointegration tests which examine the existence of a cointegration vector β within a set of variables. As will be seen below, cointegration tests exhibit a small sample bias. Hence, when analysing annual data with a time span of around 35 years, this bias needs to be controlled for in order to obtain sensible results. In case the existence of a non-zero cointegration vector β is confirmed by cointegration tests, I will conduct zero restriction tests on β. These tests help to clarify whether the long-run cointegration relationship applies to all variables examined or only to some of them. Following, a vector error correction model (VECM) is estimated for the cointegrated variables. If a VECM estimate is found to be stable over time, Granger causality tests will be applied to the cointegrated variables. Examining the direction of causality is essential for addressing the question whether higher public spending causes economic growth or vice versa.

Cointegration Tests

In a multivariate set-up with $p \geq 2$ different variables, the number of cointegration relations between these variables can be determined by a test procedure developed by Johansen (1988, 1992, 1994). The Johansen cointegration test involves obtaining maximum likelihood estimates of potential cointegration relations which, subsequently, are examined in a statistical significance test. The starting point for the Johansen test is a VAR estimate for the potentially cointegrated variables:

$$\Delta y_t = \Pi y_{t-1} + \sum_{j=1}^{k} \Gamma_j \Delta y_{t-j} + \pi + \mu t + \epsilon_t \tag{3.27}$$

$$\text{with } \Pi = \alpha\beta'$$

where y_t is a vector of p different variables, $y_t = [y_{1,t}, ..., y_{p,t}]$. Potential cointegration dynamics between the different variables are reflected in the long-run matrix Π which is the matrix product of the cointegration matrix β and the adjustment matrix α, the latter describing the speed of adjustment towards the (cointegration) equilibrium. The short-run dynamics are accounted for by the k lags of Δy_{t-j}.

If needed, equation (3.27) also contains a constant π and a deterministic trend μt. Moreover, one has to distinguish whether these deterministic terms are restricted to the cointegration relations in the long-run matrix Π or apply also to the first differences Δy_{t-j}. For a better representation, both deterministic terms can be decomposed into

$$\pi = \alpha\nu + \gamma \quad \text{and} \quad \mu = \alpha\rho + \tau \tag{3.28}$$

where ν and ρ denote a constant and a linear trend, respectively, within the cointegration relations. The constant γ and the linear trend τ apply to the first differences Δy_{t-j}. In this empirical analysis, I deem a unrestricted constant ($\rho = \tau = 0$) and a restricted trend ($\tau = 0$) the most relevant set-ups.[10] The final deterministic set-up for equation (3.27) will be chosen by comparing the Hannan-Quinn information criterion (HQ) of these two set-ups for a given lag length k. Beforehand, the lag order k is determined by selecting the number of lags which minimise the HQ of the VAR estimates in equation (3.27). In case this procedure indicates different lag orders for both deterministic set-ups, I chose the deterministic set-up which is preferable which regard to autocorrelation, ARCH effects and normality of the residuals ϵ_t.

The general idea behind the Johansen cointegration test is to identify the number of cointegration relations or, alternatively, the cointegration rank r by determining the rank of matrix Π, $r(\Pi)$. For cointegration to occur, the matrix Π needs to have a reduced rank, $p > r(\Pi) > 0$, since there can be at most $p - 1$ linearly independent cointegration relations between p different variables. Instead, if the matrix has full rank, $r(\Pi) = p$, all variables are stationary. If $r(\Pi) = 0$, all variables are non-stationary and are driven by p different stochastic trends. This implies the absence of a common stochastic trend and, hence, no cointegration relationship between the non-stationary variables.

Johansen derives the maximum likelihood estimates of the cointegration matrix β and, following, of the adjustment matrix α by utilising the *reduced rank regression* methodology.[11] For obtaining a model which only comprises potential (long-run) cointegration dynamics between the vari-

---

[10]Note that an unrestricted trend implies a trend in the first differences Δy_{t-j} and, following, a quadratic trend for the variables in levels. I regard this deterministic set-up unrealistic for the time series in this analysis.

[11]The hypothesis that the long-run matrix Π has a reduced rank, $\Pi < p$, implies a reduced number of parameters in Π which, in turn, might lead to more efficient estimates. An overview of the reduced rank regression methodology is given by Velu et al. (1986).

ables, short-run dynamics and deterministic terms are concentrated out of equation (3.27). Let Z_t be a vector of the lagged differences and the deterministic terms, $Z_t = (\Delta y_{t-1}, ..., \Delta y_{t-k+1}, 1, t)$, which is regressed on Δy_t as well as on y_{t-1}. The residuals of both regressions lead to the concentrated model:

$$R_{0t} = \alpha\beta' R_{1t} + \epsilon_t \tag{3.29}$$

where R_{0t} and R_{1t} are the residuals from the regressions $\Delta y_t = \hat{b_1} Z_t + R_{0t}$ and $y_{t-1} = \hat{b_2} Z_t + R_{1t}$, respectively.[12]

Johansen shows that the maximum likelihood estimators for β can be derived by calculating a product moment matrix from the residuals and solving the following eigenvalue problem:

$$\mid \lambda S_{11} - S_{10} S_{00}^{-1} S_{01} \mid = 0 \tag{3.30}$$

$$\text{where } S_{ij} = T^{-1} \sum_{t=1}^{T} R_{it} R'_{jt} \ (i, j = 0, 1)$$

The solution of equation (3.30) leads to p eigenvalues λ_i, which are ordered such that $1 \geq \lambda_1 \geq ... \geq \lambda_p \geq 0$. Estimates of potential cointegration vectors β_i in the cointegration matrix β are given by the eigenvectors $v_1, ..., v_p$ corresponding to the eigenvalues $\lambda_1, ..., \lambda_p$. The eigenvalue λ_i is the squared canonical correlation between a linear combination of the levels, $\beta'_i R_{1t-1}$, and a linear combination of the stationary differences $w'_i R_{0t}$.[13] Since the correlation between a non-stationary random walk and a stationary process is zero asymptotically, the magnitude of each eigenvalues λ_i can be interpreted as a measure for the stationarity of the corresponding linear combination $v'_i y_t$ (Juselius 2006:131-132). If $\lambda_i = 0$, the linear combination $v'_i y_t$ is non-stationary and, hence, the eigenvector v_i is not a cointegration vector. Accordingly, the number of linearly independent cointegration vectors β_i or, equivalently, the cointegration rank r can be determined by

[12] This approach follows the Frisch-Waugh theorem which states that the OLS estimate of β_2 in the model, $y_t = \beta_1 x_{1t} + \beta_2 x_{2t} + \epsilon_t$, can be obtained in the following two step procedure. First, run the two regressions $y_t = \hat{b_1} x_{1t} + u_{1t}$ and $x_{2t} = \hat{b_2} x_{1t} + u_{2t}$ and save the residuals u_{1t} and u_{2t}. Second, estimate β_2 in a regression with both residuals: $u_{1t} = \beta_2 u_{2t} + \epsilon_t$. (Juselius 2006:115-117)

[13] Canonical correlations measure the strength of linear relationships between two sets of variables. Each canonical correlation denotes the correlation between distinct linear combinations of both sets. (Anderson 1958:288-306)

testing how many λ_i are statistically significantly different from zero.

Johansen's trace test is the main statistical significance test. The trace test is based on a likelihood ratio (LR) test procedure and assumes under the null hypothesis that the number of statistically significant eigenvalues λ_i is less or equal to r:[14]

$$H_0 : r(\Pi) = r \text{ against } H_A : r < r(\Pi) \leq r_p \tag{3.31}$$

Accordingly, the trace test checks for all eigenvalues $\lambda_i < \lambda_r$ whether they are statistically significant different from zero:

$$\lambda_{tr}(r) = -T \sum_{i=r+1}^{p} ln(1 - \lambda_i) \tag{3.32}$$

Because $\ln(1) = 0$ and $\ln(0) \uparrow -\infty$, the trace test statistic λ_{tr} will be small if the examined eigenvalues are close or equal to zero. Thus, the null hypothesis will be rejected if λ_{tr} is smaller than the respective critical value. The trace test does not follow any of the standard distributions. In addition, the critical values depend on the deterministic terms in equation (3.27). Therefore, I will apply critical values computed by Doornik (1998).

Cheung and Lai (1993) emphasise that the Johansen LR test is rather sensitive to the choice of the lag order k in equation (3.27). Moreover, Cheung and Lai (1993) demonstrate that both the trace test and the maximum eigenvalue test exhibit a finite-sample bias toward the over-rejection of the null hypothesis, i.e. cointegration relations are found more often in small samples than suggested by asymptotic theory. For reducing the risk of finding spurious cointegration relations, the test statistic λ_{tr} is adjusted by a Bartlett correction factor as suggested by Johansen (2002).

In addition, I apply a cointegration test developed by Saikkonen and Lütkepohl (2000a, 2000b) which, as shown by the authors, exhibits better small sample properties than the Johansen test. The Saikkonen and Lütkepohl cointegration test is a modified version of the Johansen test. In contrast

[14] In addition to the trace test, Johansen has developed an alternative likelihood ratio test, the maximum eigenvalue test, for examining the statistical significance of the eigenvalues λ_i. In contrast to the trace test, the maximum eigenvalue test considers a specific alternative $r + 1$ as alternative hypothesis: $H_0 : r(\Pi) = r$ against $H_A : r + 1$. With regard to the power of both tests, Lütkepohl et al. (2001) show in a Monte Carlo simulation that the trace test is superior to the maximum eigenvalue test which is why I will utilise the former test.

to the Johansen test, the deterministic term D_t (constant π, deterministic trend μt) are subtracted from y_t before applying the reduced rank regression methodology. Hence, the VAR estimate contains the detrended y_t^d:

$$\Delta y_t^d = \Pi y_{t-1}^d + \sum_{j=1}^{k} \Gamma_j \Delta y_{t-j}^d + \epsilon_t \tag{3.33}$$

$$\text{where} \quad y_t^d = y_t - \hat{D}_t$$

The estimates of the deterministic term are obtained through a generalised least squares (GLS) procedure. In the Saikkonen and Lütkepohl cointegration tests, I apply the same deterministic set-up and the same lag order k as in the respective Johansen cointegration tests. The statistical significance of the eigenvalues λ_i is tested along the lines of the Johansen trace test. However, as a result of the prior trend adjustment of y_t, the critical values applied in the likelihood ratio test differ. Thus, the null hypothesis of the Saikkonen and Lütkepohl cointegration test is checked through p-values computed by Trenkler (2008).

Estimation and Specification of a VECM

The short-run and long-run dynamics between cointegrated variables can best be estimated in a vector error correction model (VECM). A VECM is based on the methodology of a Johansen cointegration test. Building on equation (3.27), a VECM for three (endogenous) variables $y_{1,t}$, $y_{2,t}$ and $y_{3,t}$ can be written as:

$$\begin{bmatrix} \Delta y_{1,t} \\ \Delta y_{2,t} \\ \Delta y_{3,t} \end{bmatrix} = \alpha\beta' \begin{bmatrix} y_{1,t-1} \\ y_{2,t-1} \\ y_{3,t-1} \end{bmatrix} + \sum_{j=1}^{k} \Gamma_j \begin{bmatrix} \Delta y_{1,t-j} \\ \Delta y_{2,t-j} \\ \Delta y_{3,t-j} \end{bmatrix} \tag{3.34}$$

$$+ \begin{bmatrix} \pi_1 \\ \pi_2 \\ \pi_3 \end{bmatrix} + \begin{bmatrix} \mu_1 \\ \mu_2 \\ \mu_3 \end{bmatrix} t + \begin{bmatrix} \epsilon_{1,t} \\ \epsilon_{2,t} \\ \epsilon_{3,t} \end{bmatrix}$$

where the long-run cointegration relations between the three variables are described by the adjustment matrix α and the cointegration matrix β. The short-run dynamics are displayed in the (3×3) coefficient matrices Γ_j which quantify how the respective variables are impacted both by their own lags as well as by the lags of the two other variables. The lag order k and the deterministic set-up (unrestricted constant π or restricted trend μt) are the same as in the respective cointegration tests for the variables. In case the results from zero restriction tests or Chow breakpoint tests lead to the exclusion of an endogenous variable or to a shorter sample period, respectively, the lag order k and the deterministic set-up are determined anew according to the procedure outlined above for cointegration tests.

As a first step, however, the cointegration matrix β needs to be specified. The Johansen cointegration test procedure delivers maximum likelihood estimates of a $(p \times r)$ cointegration matrix β for a given cointegration rank r within a multivariate set-up with $p \geq 2$ variables. Yet, specification of the *unrestricted estimates* in the cointegration matrix β is necessary for clarifying the long-run dynamics between the cointegrated variables. This involves identification of the r cointegration vectors β_i in the matrix β as well as testing hypothesis on coefficients in the cointegration vectors.

Without further specification, the unrestricted cointegration vectors β_i are not uniquely identified. If cointegration rank $r = 1$, normalisation on one coefficient suffices to achieve identification of the cointegration vector. Instead, if cointegration rank $r > 1$, $(r-1)$ restrictions and one normalisation have to be imposed on each cointegration vector β_i for the matrix β to be just-identified.[15]

In addition, hypothesis on coefficients in the cointegration vectors can be tested for drawing conclusions on the underlying cointegration structure. For this, I employ the *zero restriction test* on β from Johansen and Juselius (1992, 1994). It tests whether a certain coefficient in a cointegration vector β_i is zero and, hence, can be excluded from the long-run relationship described in that vector. In particular for set-ups with $p > 2$ variables, this test yields very informative results as the existence of a cointegration relation does not necessarily imply that all variables are part of that long-term equilibrium relationship.[16]

With view to the potential impact of public spending on non-oil economic

[15]In contrast to over-identifying restrictions, just-identifying restrictions impose no more than $(r-1)$ restrictions on each vector. Just-identifying restrictions can be achieved by taking linear combinations of the unrestricted cointegration vectors β_i. As a result, these restrictions do not change the maximum likelihood function and are therefore not testable. (Johansen and Juselius 1994)

[16]In a bivariate set-up, zero restriction tests may be utilised as a cross check against the inclusion of $I(0)$ variables in cointegration analysis.

growth or labour productivity developments in the GCC countries, zero restriction tests help to differentiate the effects of different kinds of public expenditure. Moreover, these tests prevent from finding spurious cointegration relations between public spending on the one hand and non-oil economic growth or labour productivity on the other hand since a long-run cointegration relationship might even be confined to the spending patterns of different kinds of public expenditures without any long-term connection to non-oil economic growth or labour productivity.

The null hypothesis that a coefficient $\beta_{ij} = 0$ is tested through a likelihood ratio test procedure. For this purpose, the likelihood function is maximised both for a model where coefficient β_{ij} is set to zero as well as for the unrestricted model. The zero restriction test statistic is given by the ratio between the values of both likelihood functions:

$$\Lambda = \frac{L_{\max}(r)_{\text{restr.}}}{L_{\max}(r)_{\text{unrestr.}}} \tag{3.35}$$

The test statistic Λ follows asymptotically a $\chi^2(rm)$-distribution. The degrees of freedom are determined by the number of restrictions m imposed on each of the r cointegration vectors.

If the results of the zero restriction tests confirm the existence of a cointegration relationship with $p \geq 2$ variables, a VECM with the respective variables is estimated. Afterwards, the adequacy of the model set-up is tested through diagnostic tests. This comprises standard tests for checking the assumption of normality as well as the existence of autocorrelation or ARCH effects with regard to the residuals ϵ_t.

In addition, I apply a test for a structural change in the VECM. By testing for the stability of the VECM, it can be deduced whether cointegration relations have lasted for the full time span of the empirical analysis or have changed over time. Tests for a structural change in a sample period go back to the methodology of Chow (1960) and are therefore often referred to as *Chow tests*. The general idea behind a Chow test for structural change is to split a sample into two sub-samples and estimate separate regressions for both sub-samples and the full sample. If the estimated coefficients of the sub-samples are equivalent to the estimated coefficients of the full sample, it can be concluded that no structural change has occurred during the sample period.

For examining the stability of the VECM, I utilise the break point test from Lütkepohl (2004). In this test, separate estimates are obtained for a full sample with T observations and two sub-samples with T_1 and T_2 observations, respectively. The full sample is split at break date T_B. The null hypothesis of parameter constancy is tested by comparing the residual covariance matrices $\tilde{\Sigma}_{(...)}$ of the three estimates:

$$\lambda_{BP} = (T_1 + T_2) \log \det\tilde{\Sigma}_{(1,2)} - T_1 \log \det\tilde{\Sigma}_{(1)} - T_2 \log \det\tilde{\Sigma}_{(2)} \tag{3.36}$$

$$\text{with } \tilde{\Sigma}_{(1)} = T_1^{-1} \sum_{t=1}^{T_1} \hat{\epsilon}_t^{(1)} \hat{\epsilon}_t^{(1)\prime}, \quad \tilde{\Sigma}_{(2)} = T_2^{-1} \sum_{t=T-T_2+1}^{T} \hat{\epsilon}_t^{(2)} \hat{\epsilon}_t^{(2)\prime}$$

$$\text{and } \tilde{\Sigma}_{(1,2)} = T_1^{-1} \sum_{t=1}^{T_1} \hat{\epsilon}_t \hat{\epsilon}_t' + T_2^{-1} \sum_{t=T-T_2+1}^{T} \hat{\epsilon}_t \hat{\epsilon}_t'$$

The null hypothesis of parameter constancy is rejected for large values of the test statistic λ_{BP}. Since the potential break date T_B is not known a priori, the Chow test is repeated for a range of possible break dates. If the null hypothesis is rejected for a break date T_B, cointegration tests and VECM estimates are performed for the resulting sub-samples.

In contrast to a Chow test in a time series with one known potential break point T_B, the χ^2-distribution cannot be utilised for the above described sequential Chow tests since the results of these repeated tests are not independent. Asymptotically correct critical values for sequential Chow tests with an unknown break point are substantially larger than the comparable values provided by the χ^2-distribution (Andrews 1993). In addition, Candelon and Lütkepohl (2001) show that using a χ^2-distribution for Chow tests in small samples leads to a bias towards rejection of the null hypothesis and, as a result, to spurious break dates. As suggested by Candelon and Lütkepohl (2001), I utilise bootstrap p-values, which tend to be considerably larger than p-values based on an approximate χ^2-distribution.

3.4.4 Impulse Response Analysis

The long-term impact between cointegrated variables can best be simulated through impulse response analysis. While estimates of the long-run relationships between cointegrated variables are given by the cointegration matrix β and the adjustment matrix α in equation (3.34), the mutual impact between these variables cannot merely be inferred from relating the respective coefficients to each other. For example, a long-run relationship between the two variables $y_{1,t}$ and $y_{2,t}$ is not adequately described by the ratio β_1/β_2 since the latter does not capture the dynamic interactions and feedback effects between the variables in a VECM.

Instead, I employ impulse response analysis for simulating the extent to which the cointegrated variables impact one another. In this approach, the impact of a variable $y_{1,t}$ on the other variables in a VECM is gauged by measuring the responses of the other variables to a one-time impulse in $y_{1,t}$. Going back to a VECM representation as in equations (3.34) or (3.38), a one-time impulse for $y_{1,t}$ is given by one standard deviation of the residual $\epsilon_{1,t}$. The accumulated responses of the other variables are reported for a time period of up to eight years. A necessary condition for impulse response analysis to deliver interpretable results is that an impulse takes place only in one variable at a time. However, different variables in a VECM might be affected similarly by one shock during the same time period. As a result, the correlation of different residuals might not be zero. Therefore, the residuals need to be orthogonalised using a Cholesky decomposition of the residual covariance matrix Σ_ϵ.

The utilisation of orthogonalised residuals requires choosing a particular ordering of the variables. Within a orthogonalised residual covariance matrix, an impulse in the residual of the first variable impacts all other variables during the same time period. Instead, an impulse in the residual of the second variable has no instantaneous impact on the first variable but only the third variable and so forth. The impulse of the second variable starts to impact the first variable only from the second time period onwards. Here, a change in the variable order might lead to different impulse responses (Breitung et al. 2004:165-169).

With regard to the impulse responses of the GCC countries, public expenditure variables are ranked first and non-oil GDP is put on the second rank in the orthogonalised residual covariance matrix. This particular ordering of the variables is based on the notion that public expenditure in the GCC countries is more likely to exert an instantaneous impact on other variables than non-oil GDP. A substantial change in public expenditure levels might strongly influence aggregate demand in the economy and, hence, non-oil GDP levels in the same year. In contrast, non-oil GDP developments may reasonably be assumed not to exert a comparable impact on contemporaneous public expenditure levels given the negligible role of tax revenues for GCC public finances. As seen in table 3.2, GCC public revenues consist primarily of oil and gas export revenues. Hence, the leeway for public spending is largely determined by exogenous factors such as world market prices for oil and gas.

In order to check the robustness of the empirical results, impulse responses are also simulated for a modified order of variables. This robustness test draws on an orthogonalised residual covariance matrix where non-oil GDP is ranked before public expenditure variables (see figures C1-C3 in the appendix).

3.4.5 Granger Causality Tests

After a sufficiently specified VECM has been estimated, one can proceed with analysing cause and effect between the cointegrated variables through Granger causality tests. For evaluating the effectiveness of public spending in promoting non-oil economic growth, it is essential to examine the direction of causality between these variables. Here, Granger causality tests help to disentangle whether public spending patterns are a cause or an effect of economic growth.

The direction of causality between time series is examined by a methodology developed by Granger (1969). In this concept, causality is defined entirely in terms of predictability of time series. A variable x_t is said to cause the variable y_t if lags of x_t help to predict y_t. Hence, the direction of causality between two stationary variables can be examined by testing the statistical significance of lags in a simple causal model:

$$x_t = \sum_{j=1}^{m} a_j x_{t-j} + \sum_{j=1}^{m} b_j y_{t-j} + \epsilon_t \tag{3.37}$$

$$y_t = \sum_{j=1}^{m} c_j x_{t-j} + \sum_{j=1}^{m} d_j y_{t-j} + u_t$$

where y_t causes x_t if $b_j \neq 0$ for at least one j. Similarly, x_t causes y_t if $c_j \neq 0$ for at least one j. If both causality conditions are fulfilled, bi-directional causality is given.

For investigating the direction of causality in a VECM framework, both the long-term and the short-term relations between two cointegrated variables $y_{1,t}$ and $y_{2,t}$ have to be considered:[17]

$$\begin{bmatrix} \Delta y_{1,t} \\ \Delta y_{2,t} \end{bmatrix} = \alpha\beta' \begin{bmatrix} y_{1,t-1} \\ y_{2,t-1} \end{bmatrix} + \sum_{j=1}^{k} \Gamma_j \begin{bmatrix} \Delta y_{1,t-j} \\ \Delta y_{2,t-j} \end{bmatrix} + \begin{bmatrix} \epsilon_{1,t} \\ \epsilon_{2,t} \end{bmatrix} \tag{3.38}$$

$$\text{with } \alpha\beta' = \begin{bmatrix} \alpha_1\beta_1 & \alpha_1\beta_2 \\ \alpha_2\beta_1 & \alpha_2\beta_2 \end{bmatrix} \text{ and } \Gamma_j = \begin{bmatrix} \gamma_{11,j} & \gamma_{12,j} \\ \gamma_{21,j} & \gamma_{22,j} \end{bmatrix}$$

The null hypothesis that $y_{2,t}$ does not cause $y_{1,t}$ is given by $\alpha_1\beta_2 = \gamma_{12,j} = 0$ for all j. Testing whether these VECM coefficients equal zero is done through a Wald test. Despite the presence of non-stationary variables in the model, a χ^2-distribution may be utilised for a Wald test (Dolado and Lütkepohl 1996).[18]

In a higher dimensional VECM with $p > 2$ variables, the causal relation between two variables cannot be examined separatly. This can be shown in a trivariate VECM such as equation (3.34) where the two variables $y_{1,t}$ and $y_{2,t}$ might not only impact each other through direct causal links but also through indirect causal links via $y_{3,t}$. For instance, $y_{1,t}$ might affect $y_{3,t}$, which, in turn, might influence $y_{2,t}$. Therefore, it can only be tested whether one variable causes the set of remaining variables as a whole (*block exogeneity test*).

[17]For simplicity, no deterministic terms are modeled. The inclusion of deterministic terms does not change the results.

[18]Dolado and Lütkepohl (1996) show that the Wald test follows a χ^2-distribution if at least one coefficient matrix is not restricted under the null hypothesis. Therefore, the authors propose to increase the lag order k by one additional lag when estimating the VECM. Afterwards, the Wald test is performed on the coefficient matrices of the first k lags while the matrix of the redundant lag $k+1$ is ignored.

3.5 Empirical Results

The empirical results for unit root tests (section 3.5.1), cointegration and impulse response analysis (section 3.5.2), and Granger causality tests (section 3.5.3) are reported below. Thereupon, the robustness of the empirical results is analysed with regard to the omission of potentially relevant variables and to potential flaws in the underlying data sets (section 3.5.4). Finally, section 3.6 concludes.

3.5.1 Results of Unit Root Tests

The order of integration of the variables was examined by four different unit root tests (ADF test, KPSS test, ADF-GLS test, unit root test with a structural break). As can be seen from the empirical results in table 3.4, these four different unit root tests do not always indicate the same order of integration for the respective variables. In addition to the above mentioned difficulty to distinguish between stationarity and non-stationarity in cases of highly persistent time series or structural breaks, the power of the unit root tests might have also suffered from the rather small sample sizes of the variables which result from the utilisation of annual time series.

In case of ambiguity, the order of integration had to be gauged by evaluating the overall empirical evidence. Here, I have attached a higher importance to the empirical results of the ADF-GLS test by Elliott et al. (1996) and the break test by Lee and Strazicich (2004) since these tests have better power properties when determining the order of integration of time series which exhibit a high level of persistence or structural breaks.

With the exception of four variables, the overall empirical evidence suggests that all variables are I(1), i.e. integrated of order one. Instead, the variables education expenditure and health expenditure in Qatar were found to be I(2) and, hence, are not eligible for cointegration analysis. Furthermore, the variable non-oil GDP per worker is not I(1) both in case of Bahrain and Oman. Therefore, the impact of different public expenditure categories on the labour productivity indicator non-oil GDP per worker cannot be examined for Bahrain and Oman through cointegration analysis.

3.5.2 Cointegration and Impulse Response Analysis

The empirical analysis of potential long-run cointegration relationships between different categories of public expenditure on the one hand and non-oil

Table 3.4: Overview - Order of Integration

All variables in constant prices

Variable	Unit Root Test Results: ADF	KPSS	ADF-GLS	Break	Overall Evaluation
Bahrain (1979-2013):					
Total Expenditure	I(1)	I(1)	I(2)	I(1)	I(1)
Current Expenditure	I(2)	I(1)	I(2)	I(1)	I(1)
Capital Expenditure	I(2)	I(1)	I(1)	I(0)	I(1)
Education Expenditure	I(1)	I(1)	I(1)	I(1)	I(1)
Non-Education Expend.	I(1)	I(1)	I(2)	I(1)	I(1)
Health Expenditure	I(1)	I(1)	I(2)	I(0)	I(1)
Non-Health Expenditure	I(1)	I(1)	I(2)	I(1)	I(1)
Non-Oil GDP	I(1)	I(1)	I(1)	I(0)	I(1)
Non-Oil GDP per Worker	I(0)	I(0)	I(0)	I(0)	I(0)
Oman (1979-2013):					
Total Expenditure	I(1)	I(1)	I(2)	I(1)	I(1)
Current Expenditure	I(1)	I(1)	I(2)	I(1)	I(1)
Capital Expenditure	I(1)	I(1)	I(1)	I(1)	I(1)
Education Expenditure	I(0)	I(0)	I(1)	I(1)	I(1)
Non-Education Expend.	I(1)	I(1)	I(2)	I(1)	I(1)
Health Expenditure	I(0)	I(0)	I(1)	I(1)	I(1)
Non-Health Expenditure	I(1)	I(1)	I(2)	I(1)	I(1)
Non-Oil GDP	I(1)	I(0)	I(2)	I(1)	I(1)
Non-Oil GDP per Worker	I(1)	I(0)	I(2)	I(2)	I(2)
Qatar (1979-2013):					
Total Expenditure	I(1)	I(2)	I(2)	I(1)	I(1)
Current Expenditure	I(1)	I(2)	I(1)	I(1)	I(1)
Capital Expenditure	I(2)	I(2)	I(1)	I(1)	I(1)
Education Expenditure	I(2)	I(1)	I(2)	I(2)	I(2)
Non-Education Expend.	I(1)	I(2)	I(2)	I(1)	I(1)
Health Expenditure	I(1)	I(2)	I(2)	I(0)	I(2)
Non-Health Expenditure	I(1)	I(2)	I(2)	I(1)	I(1)
Non-Oil GDP	I(2)	I(2)	I(1)	I(1)	I(1)
Non-Oil GDP per Worker	I(1)	I(1)	I(1)	I(1)	I(1)

Note: For detailed unit root test results of the variables please refer to tables B1-B4 in the appendix.

GDP or non-oil GDP per worker on the other hand comprises two main parts. First, the different groups of variables were examined for the existence of a long-run cointegration relationship by two different cointegration tests (Johansen trace test, Saikkonen and Lütkepohl test). Second, the long-run dynamics of the variables which exhibit a cointegration relationship were estimated in a vector error correction model (VECM). The VECM was specified through zero restriction tests and Chow stability tests. The final VECM estimates serve as a basis for simulating the long-run mutual impact between the cointegrated variables through impulse response analysis.

As can be seen from table 3.5, the cointegration test results point to marked differences with regard to the long-term relationships between aggregate non-oil GDP and different public expenditure categories in the three GCC countries Bahrain, Oman and Qatar. The overall empirical evidence for cointegration relationships between public expenditure and non-oil GDP levels is stronger in Oman and Qatar than in Bahrain. In case of Bahrain, the Johansen trace test (JOH) and the Saikkonen and Lütkepohl test (SAI) detect one cointegration relationship between the variables non-oil GDP, public education expenditure and non-education expenditure. Instead, both cointegration tests do not support the existence of long-term links between non-oil GDP and other categories of public expenditure in Bahrain (total expenditure; current and capital expenditure; health and non-health expenditure).

The Johansen trace test points to a much higher number of cointegration relationships in Oman and in Qatar than in Bahrain. Empirical results of the Johansen trace test indicate that the development patterns of non-oil GDP in Oman and in Qatar are cointegrated with all four groups of public expenditure variables examined (total expenditure; current and capital expenditure; education and non-education expenditure; health and non-health expenditure). In this regard, it is important to note that the variables education expenditure and health expenditure, which are typically ascribed a potential growth-enhancing impact in the economic literature, have not been included in the respective cointegration tests in Qatar since they are integrated of order two (table 3.4).

While the Johansen trace test results indicate strong long-term links between public expenditure and non-oil GDP in Oman and Qatar, the Saikkonen and Lütkepohl test results offer very different conclusions about the

Table 3.5: Overview - Number of Cointegration Relations

All variables in constant prices

	Bahrain[1]		Oman[1]		Qatar[1]	
Variables	JOH	SAI	JOH	SAI	JOH	SAI
Total Expenditure & Non-Oil GDP	0	0	1*	0	1**	0
Total Expenditure & Non-Oil GDP p. Worker	na	na	na	na	0	0
Current Expenditure & Capital Expenditure & Non-Oil GDP	0	0	1**	0	1**	1***
Current Expenditure & Capital Expenditure & Non-Oil GDP p. Worker	na	na	na	na	1*	1**
Education Expenditure & Non-Education Expend. & Non-Oil GDP	1*	1**	1***	0	1**	0
Education Expenditure & Non-Education Expend. & Non-Oil GDP p. Worker	na	na	na	na	0	0
Health Expenditure & Non-Health Expenditure & Non-Oil GDP	0	0	1**	0	1**	0
Health Expenditure & Non-Health Expenditure & Non-Oil GDP p. Worker	na	na	na	na	0	0

Notes: Statistical significance levels of cointegration relationships are indicated by ***(1%), **(5%), and *(10%), respectively. For detailed cointegration test results of the Johansen trace test (JOH) and the Saikkonen and Lütkepohl test (SAI) please refer to tables B5-B7 in the appendix.

[1] The following variables have been excluded from the respective cointegration tests since they are not integrated of order one (table 3.4): non-oil GDP per worker (Bahrain), non-oil GDP per worker (Oman), education expenditure (Qatar) and health expenditure (Qatar).

existence of cointegration relationships between public expenditure and non-oil GDP in both countries. With the exception of a cointegration relationship between current expenditure, capital expenditure and non-oil GDP in Qatar, the Saikkonen and Lütkepohl test does not detect cointegration relations between public expenditure and non-oil GDP in Oman and in Qatar. These differing cointegration test results, in turn, highlight the need to cross-check the strength of the cointegration relations indicated by the Johansen trace test through a zero restriction test procedure.

In contrast to the variable non-oil GDP, the Johansen trace test offers much less support for the existence of long-term links between public expenditure and the labour productivity indicator non-oil GDP per worker in Qatar. Here, the Johansen trace test results report one cointegration relation between non-oil GDP per worker and one group of public expenditure variables (current expenditure, capital expenditure). Instead, all other groups of public expenditure variable are found not to be cointegrated with the variable non-oil GDP per worker in Qatar (table 3.5). Hence, the above mentioned empirical support of the Johansen trace test for strong links between public expenditure and non-oil GDP levels in Qatar does not seem to be primarily related to labour productivity developments. Unfortunately, the cointegration links between labour productivity and public expenditure could not be examined for Bahrain and Oman because the variable non-oil GDP per worker was found not to be integrated of order one in both countries.

Since cointegration tests pointed to the existence of long-run relationships between non-oil GDP and different categories of public expenditure in all three countries, the long-run dynamics between these cointegrated variables were estimated in a vector error correction model (VECM). For a better representation of long-run cointegration relationships, the VECM were specified through zero restriction tests and Chow stability tests. Zero restriction tests are conducive for elaborating the key elements of a cointegration relationship since they examine whether certain variables can be excluded from the cointegration vector. In addition, zero restriction tests serve as a cross-check for the strength of a cointegration relationship because they test the null hypothesis of variable exclusion for every variable in a cointegration vector. Chow breakpoint tests help to detect structural breaks in the cointegration relationship.

The empirical results of the zero restriction tests are given in table B8 in the appendix. These empirical results support the notion that the long-run cointegration relationship between public expenditure and aggregate non-oil GDP is somewhat weaker in Oman than in Qatar. Here, the null hypothesis of variable exclusion was not rejected four times in case of Oman (non-oil GDP (two times), current expenditure and education expenditure) but only one time in case of Qatar (current expenditure). In particular, the two long-run cointegration relationships in Oman between the variables non-oil GDP, education expenditure and non-education expenditure as well as non-oil GDP, health expenditure and non-health-expenditure appear to be weak since zero restriction tests point to the exclusion of non-oil GDP in both cases. As a result, no final VECM was estimated for these two cointegration relationships.

In addition, the variables current expenditure (Oman) and current expenditure (Qatar) were not included in the final VECM specifications in table 3.6 because zero restriction tests pointed to the exclusion of both variables from the respective cointegration vectors. Instead, the cointegration relationships seem to be confined to capital expenditure and non-oil GDP both in case of Oman and Qatar. In terms of Bahrain, zero restriction test results did not support the exclusion of a variable from the cointegration relation between non-oil GDP, education expenditure and non-education expenditure.

Chow stability tests do not indicate a structural change for most of the remaining cointegration relationships in Bahrain, Oman and Qatar as can be seen from table B9 in the appendix. Instead, only one cointegration relationship in Qatar was found to exhibit a structural break (current expenditure, capital expenditure and non-oil GDP per worker). A re-examination of the resulting sub-samples of the latter cointegration relationship reveals that the link between the labour productivity indicator non-oil GDP per worker, current expenditure and capital expenditure in Qatar is confined to the period 1979-1998. Therefore, the VECM for this cointegration relationship was only estimated for the period 1979-1998. The VECM of all other cointegration relationships were estimated for the full sample period (1979-2013).

The final VECM specifications for Bahrain, Oman and Qatar are displayed in table 3.6. In line with the procedure adopted for the two cointegration tests above, the deterministic terms and the lag order of the final VECM specifications were determined by the Hannan-Quinn information criterion.

Table 3.6: VECM - Final Specification

All variables in constant prices

Variables (& Trend)	Det. Terms	Lags	r	β-Vector
Bahrain (1979-2013):				
Education Expenditure	Restr. Trend	1	1	1.551
& Non-Education Expenditure				-1.474
& Non-Oil GDP				1.000
& Trend				-0.056
Oman (1979-2013):				
Total Expenditure	Restr. Trend	3	1	-0.400
& Non-Oil GDP				1.000
& Trend				-0.051
Capital Expenditure	Restr. Trend	1	1	-0.199
& Non-Oil GDP				1.000
& Trend				-0.048
Qatar (1979-2013):				
Total Expenditure	Restr. Trend	1	1	-0.846
& Non-Oil GDP				1.000
& Trend				-0.039
Capital Expenditure	Restr. Trend	2	1	-0.460
& Non-Oil GDP				1.000
& Trend				-0.050
Non-Education Expenditure	Restr. Trend	1	1	-0.817
& Non-Oil GDP				1.000
& Trend				-0.038
Non-Health Expenditure	Restr. Trend	1	1	-0.844
& Non-Oil GDP				1.000
& Trend				-0.039
Qatar (1979-1998):				
Current Expenditure	Restr. Trend	2	1	-1.146
& Capital Expenditure				-0.100
& Non-Oil GDP per Worker				1.000
& Trend				0.022

Notes: For detailed test results of the zero restriction and stability tests please refer to tables B8-B9 in the appendix. Coefficients in the β vector of the VECM have been normalised on the GDP coefficient. Lag order and deterministic terms have been determined by the Hannan-Quinn information criterion.

The cointegration rank, r, was set to one for all VECM specifications. Here, the interrelation between public expenditure and non-oil GDP or non-oil GDP per worker was deemed to be the only plausible long-run relationship in this set-up.

The long-run relationships between cointegrated variables are given by the β-vectors in table 3.6. For a unique identification of the β-vectors, the coefficients of the GDP variables were normalised to one. The coefficients of the GDP variables and almost all public expenditure categories in the β-vectors are estimated to have an opposite sign. The opposite signs of coefficient estimates might be interpreted as an indication for a positive long-run relationship between public expenditure and non-oil GDP[19]. Yet, assessing the long-run relationship between cointegrated variables merely by the coefficients in a β-vector can be misleading since this approach ignores dynamic interactions of the variables in a VECM. This applies particularly to β-vectors which include more than two variables such as the two trivariate cointegration relationships displayed in table 3.6.

Instead, a more comprehensive simulation of the long-run mutual impact between cointegrated variables is obtained in the following through impulse response analysis as laid out in section 3.4.4. The impulse responses for the cointegration relationships in Bahrain, Oman and Qatar are shown in figures 3.1-3.3. These figures illustrate the accumulated changes in the (natural log) level of a responding variable over a period of eight years after a positive one-time impulse in another variable.

The impulse responses in figures 3.1-3.3 point to a positive impact of public expenditure on non-oil GDP levels in Oman and, most notably, Qatar. All public expenditure categories in these two countries are estimated to exert a positive long-run impact on non-oil GDP (left columns of figures 3.1 and 3.2). This finding can be ascribed a high statistical significance because the 95% confidence intervals of all non-oil GDP responses both in Oman and in Qatar comprise only positive values.

[19]This may be exemplified by going back to equation (3.26) in section 3.4.3 where a long-run relationship between two variables y_{1t} and y_{2t} which are bound together by a normalised cointegration vector $\beta = (1, -\beta_2)'$ is given by $\beta' y_t = y_{1t} - \beta_2 y_{2t} = z_t$ with z_t denoting deviations from the long-run equilibrium. As discussed earlier, z_t is stationary in case of a cointegration relationship between two I(1) variables. In this case, deviations from the long-run equilibrium are only temporary since z_t can be expected to revert to its mean over time. Here, the opposite signs of the coefficients in the β-vector indicate that both variables move in the same directions when reinstating the long-run equilibrium after a temporary deviation.

Furthermore, the positive responses of non-oil GDP to public expenditure impulses are robust to changes in the variable order of the orthogonalised residual covariance matrix. As can be seen from the left columns of figures C1 and C2 in the appendix, public expenditure also exerts a positive long-run impact on non-oil GDP in Oman and Qatar in case non-oil GDP is ranked first in the orthogonalised residual covariance matrix. The statistical significance of the latter results, however, is higher for Qatar than for Oman. The confidence intervals of all non-oil GDP responses in Qatar contain only positive values (figure C2). Instead, the confidence interval of the positive non-oil GDP response in Oman to an impulse of total expenditure includes also negative values (figure C1).

The overall empirical evidence for a positive impact of public expenditure on non-oil GDP is weakest in Bahrain. This is particularly apparent from the ambiguous response of non-oil GDP to an increase in non-education expenditure. Here, the 95% confidence interval of the non-oil GDP response to an impulse in non-education expenditure indicates that positive and negative responses of non-oil GDP are equally probable. Instead, a one-time increase in public education expenditure exerts a statistically significant positive impact on non-oil GDP levels in Bahrain (left column figure 3.1).

While impulse response analysis confirms a clear positive impact of public expenditure on non-oil GDP, most notably, in Qatar, the responses of public expenditure to a positive one-time impulse in non-oil GDP are more ambiguous. As shown in the right columns of figures 3.1-3.2, the long-run responses of public expenditure in all three countries are mostly negative. Yet, these results cannot be considered robust since the responses of most public expenditure categories turn positive in case of a modified variable order in the orthogonalised residual covariance matrix (right columns of figures C1 and C2 in the appendix).

Furthermore, the 95% confidence intervals of many public expenditure responses contain positive as well as negative values. This, in turn, limits the statistical significance of these response estimates. In view of the small sample size, the magnitude of the impulse response estimates should be interpreted cautiously. Nevertheless, these estimates clearly highlight that the empirical evidence for a positive impact of public expenditure on non-oil GDP is much higher than for a long-run impact of non-oil GDP on public expenditure levels.

Figure 3.1: Impulse Response Analysis Bahrain & Oman

Bahrain: Public Expenditure and Non-Oil GDP

(a) Response Non-Oil GDP to Impulse Education Expend.

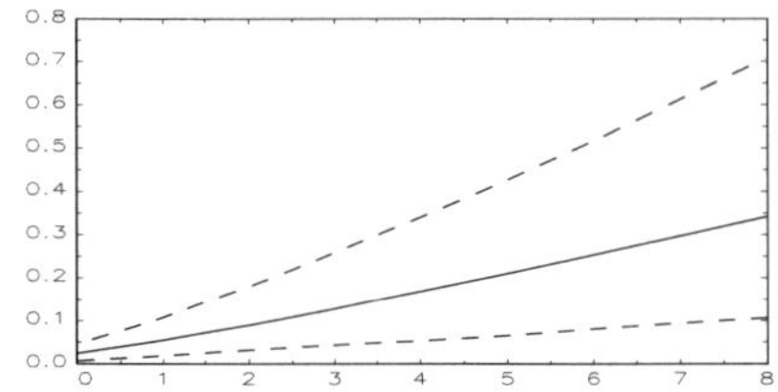

(b) Response Education Expend. to Impulse Non-Oil GDP

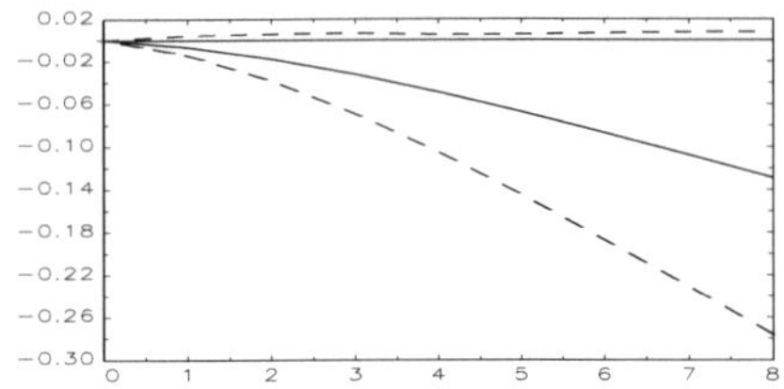

(c) Response Non-Oil GDP to Impulse Non-Education Exp.

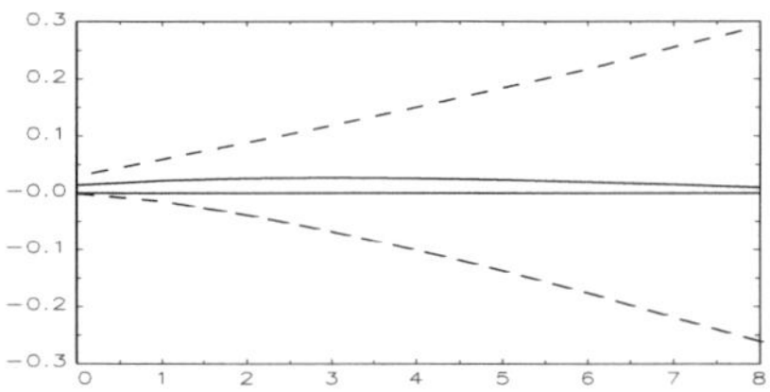

(d) Response Non-Educat. Exp. to Impulse Non-Oil GDP

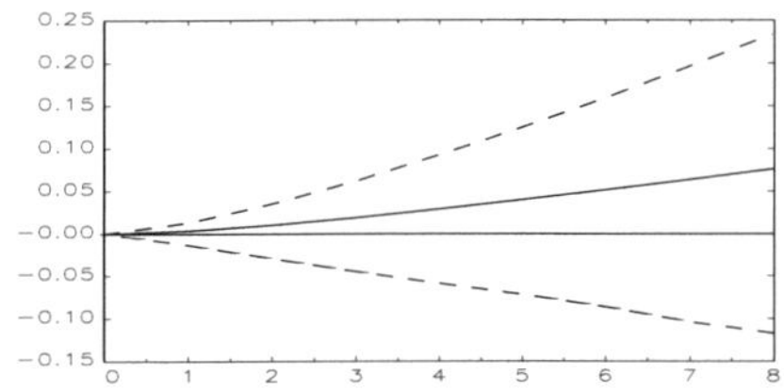

Oman: Public Expenditure and Non-Oil GDP

(e) Response Non-Oil GDP to Impulse Total Exp.

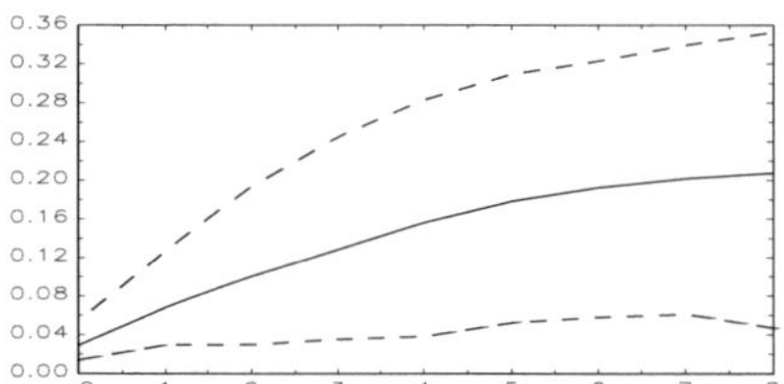

(f) Response Total Exp. to Impulse Non-Oil GDP

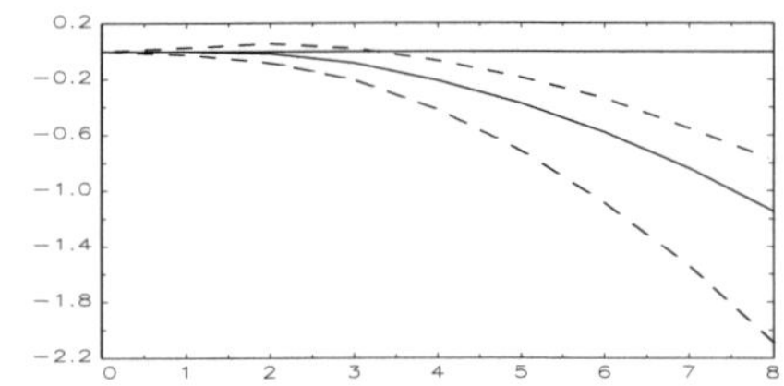

(g) Response Non-Oil GDP to Impulse Capital Exp.

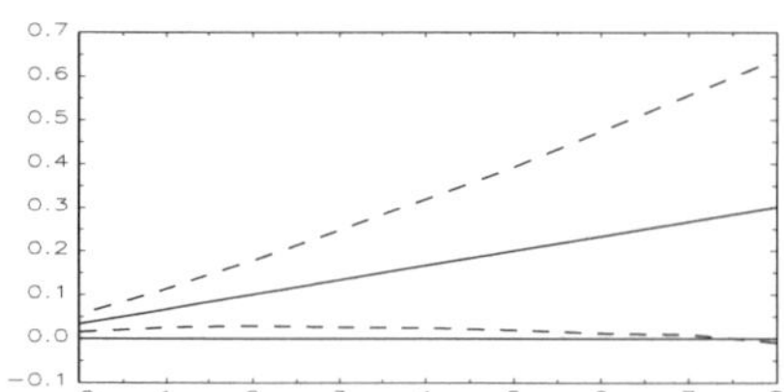

(h) Response Capital Exp. to Impulse Non-Oil GDP

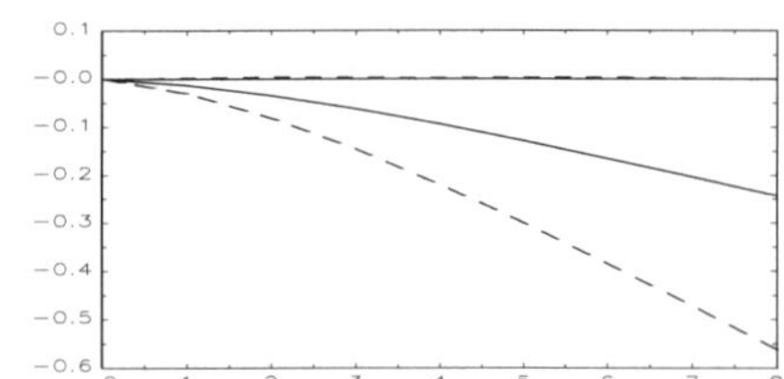

Notes: See figure 3.3

Figure 3.2: Impulse Response Analysis Qatar I

Qatar: Public Expenditure and Non-Oil GDP

(a) Response Non-Oil GDP to Impulse Total Exp.

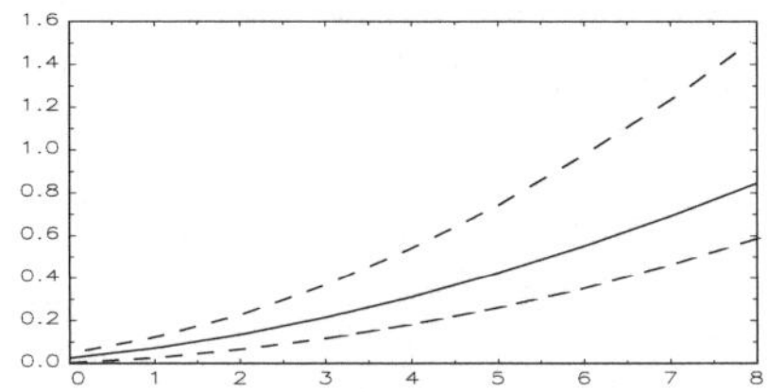

(b) Response Total Expend. to Impulse Non-Oil GDP

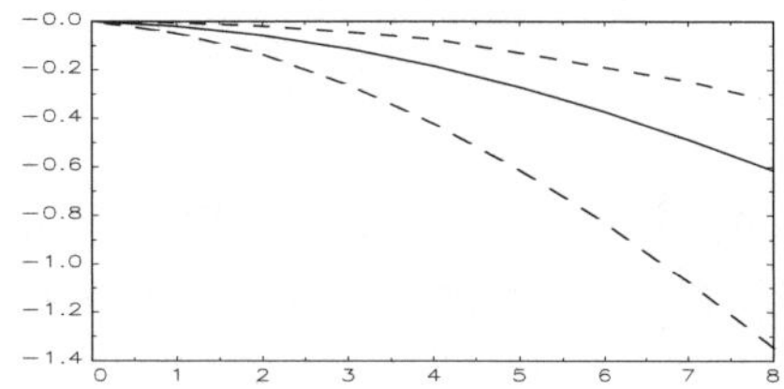

(c) Response Non-Oil GDP to Impulse Capital Exp.

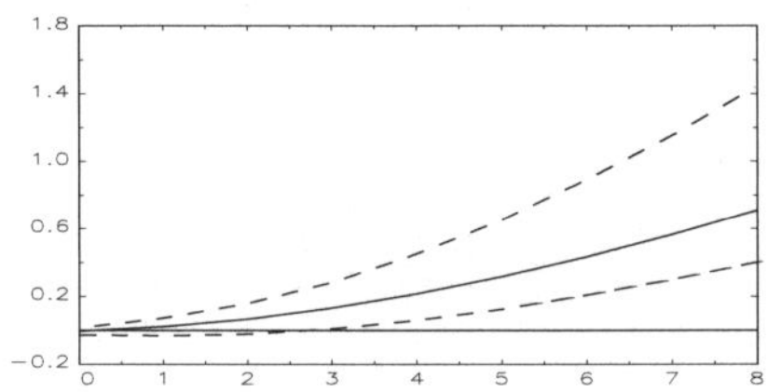

(d) Response Capital Exp. to Impulse Non-Oil GDP

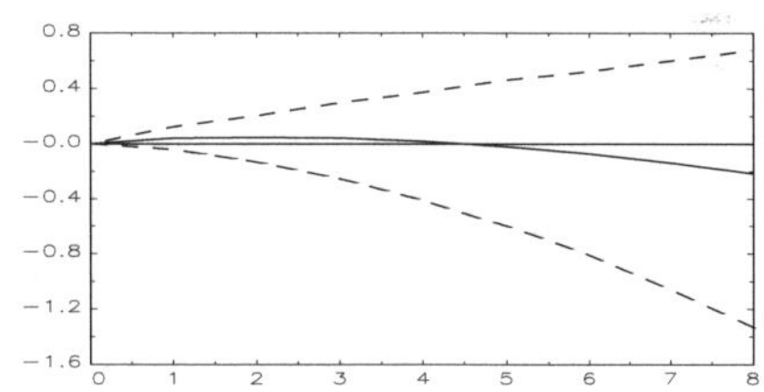

(e) Response Non-Oil GDP to Impulse Non-Education Exp.

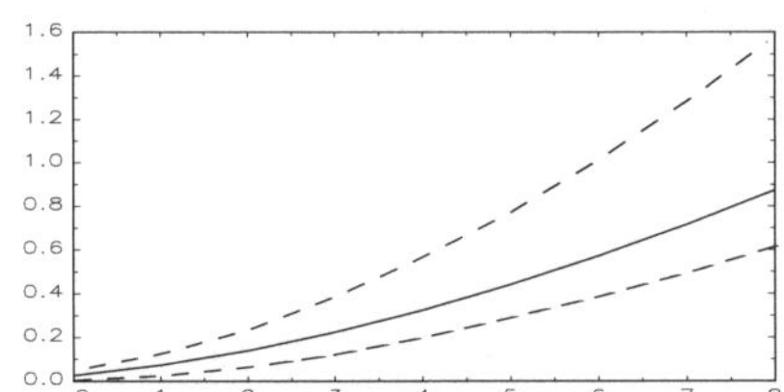

(f) Response Non-Educat. Exp. to Impulse Non-Oil GDP

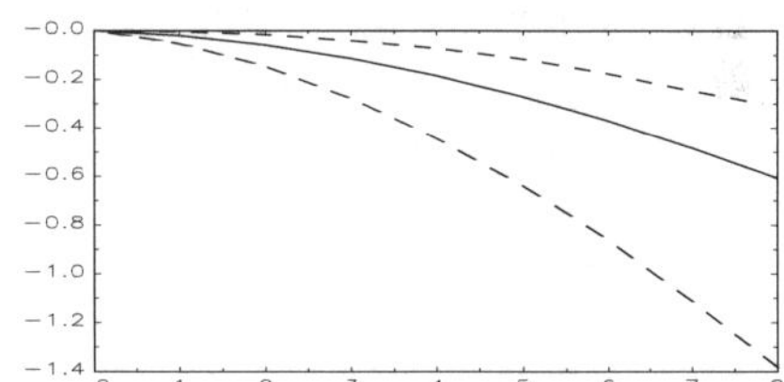

(g) Response Non-Oil GDP to Impulse Non-Health Exp.

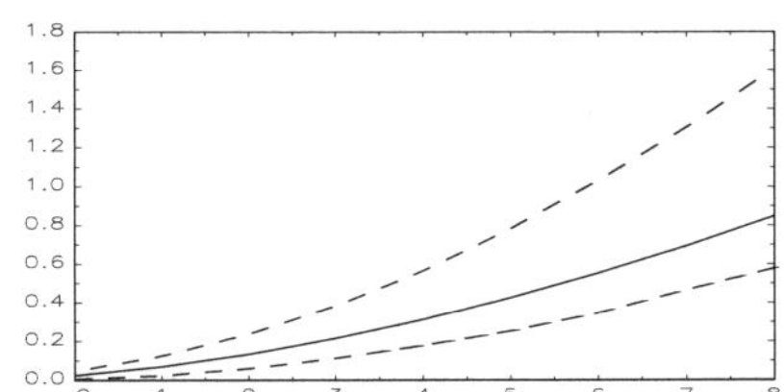

(h) Response Non-Health Exp. to Impulse Non-Oil GDP

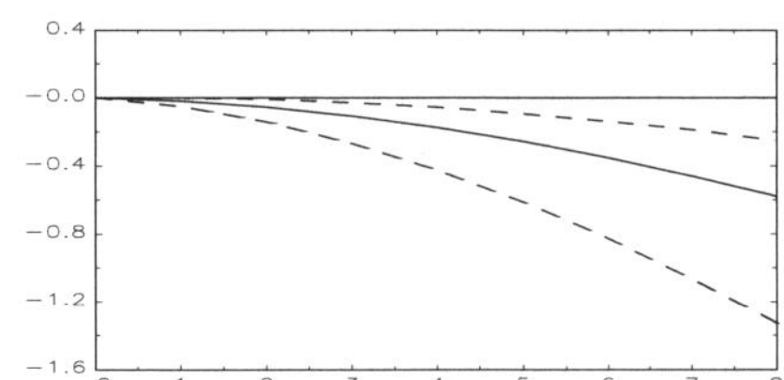

Notes: See figure 3.3

Figure 3.3: Impulse Response Analysis Qatar II

Qatar: Public Expenditure and Non-Oil GDP per Worker

(a) Response GDP per Worker to Impulse Current Exp.

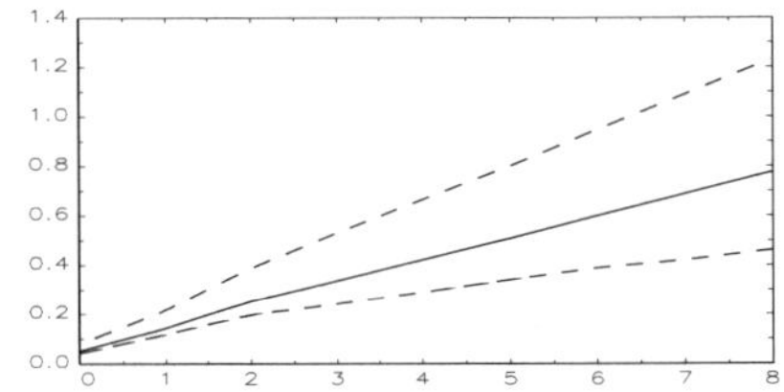

(b) Response Current Expend. to Impulse GDP per Worker

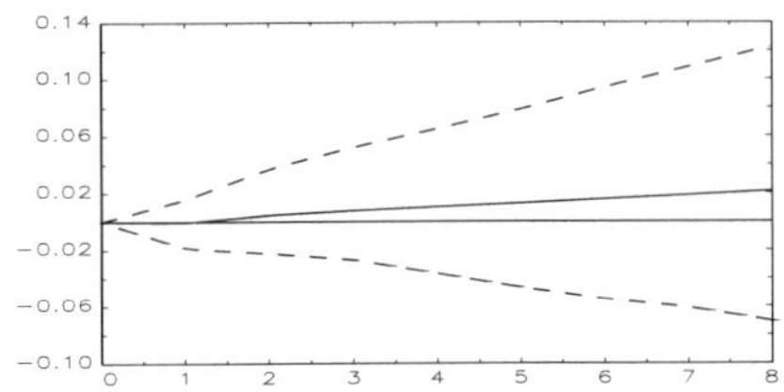

(c) Response GDP per Worker to Impulse Capital Exp.

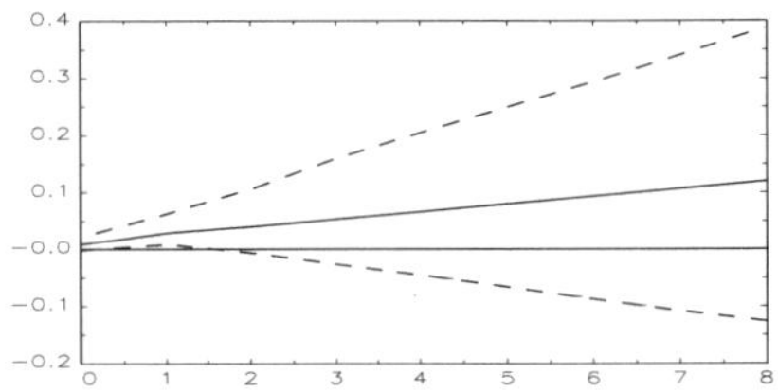

(d) Response Capital Expend. to Impulse GDP per Worker

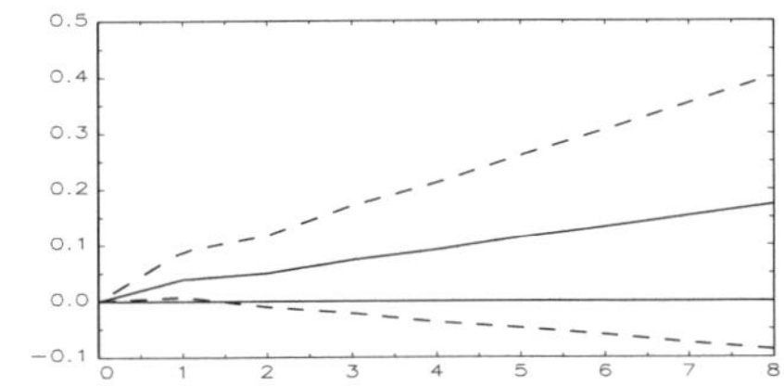

Notes: 95% Hall percentile confidence intervals (1000 bootstrap replications). VECM has been specified as shown in table 3.6. X-axis denotes number of years after initial impulse. Y-axis shows accumulated changes in the (natural log) level of responding variable. Impulse is given by one standard deviation of the orthogonalised residual of the impulse variable. Public expenditure variables have been ranked before non-oil GDP (per worker) in the orthogonalised residual covariance matrix.

In terms of the link between public expenditure and labour productivity in Qatar, the impulse response simulations in figure 3.3 show that capital and current expenditure tend to exert a positive impact on labour productivity developments, albeit in a less distinct manner than on non-oil GDP developments. A less clear-cut impact of public expenditure on labour productivity developments is particularly observable with regard to the variable capital expenditure. While an impulse in capital expenditure leads to a statistically significant positive response of non-oil GDP, the response of the labour productivity indicator non-oil GDP per worker to an impulse in capital expenditure is more ambiguous since the confidence interval of the labour productivity response comprises both positive as well as negative values (figures 3.2 and 3.3).

The finding that public expenditure in Qatar exerts a less distinct impact on labour productivity than on non-oil GDP developments is in line with other results of the cointegration analysis above. For example, the Johansen trace test results reported four cointegration relations between non-oil GDP and different public expenditure categories but only one cointegration relationship between labour productivity and public expenditure variables. Furthermore, all cointegration relationships between public expenditure and non-oil GDP were shown to be stable over the entire sample period (1979-2013) whereas the cointegration link between the labour productivity indicator non-oil GDP per worker, current expenditure and capital expenditure is confined to the period 1979-1998.

3.5.3 Empirical Results Granger Causality Tests

The direction of causality between the cointegrated variables was analysed through Granger causality tests. As discussed earlier, Granger causality tests infer causality patterns by examining whether changes in one variable precede changes of other variables and, hence, help to predict movements of the latter. Since cointegrated variables are driven by a common stochastic trend, at least one variable must "Granger cause" other variables.

The empirical evidence for a causal effect of public expenditure on non-oil GDP and on labour productivity levels is particularly strong for Qatar. As can be seen from table 3.7, Granger causality test results for Qatar uniformly point to public expenditure causing movements of aggregate non-oil GDP or non-oil GDP per worker levels. With regard to the cointegration relationships between different categories of public expenditure and aggregate non-oil GDP, the null hypothesis that public expenditure does not Granger cause the variable non-oil GDP is clearly rejected for all four public expenditure variables with the significance levels of the test statistics standing either at 1% (total expenditure, non-education expenditure, non-health expenditure) or at 5% (capital expenditure).

Furthermore, Granger causality in Qatar is found to be running solely from public expenditure to non-oil GDP in three out of four cases. In terms of the cointegration relationship between current expenditure, capital expenditure and the labour productivity indicator non-oil GDP per worker in Qatar during the period 1979-1998, the two public expenditure variables are found to Granger cause the other variables of this cointegration relationship either at a 1% (capital expenditure) or at a 5% statistical significance level (current expenditure).

Table 3.7: Granger Causality Tests

All variables in constant prices

Variables	Null Hypothesis	Test Statistic
Bahrain (1979-2013):		
Education Expend.	H_0: Ed. Exp. $\nRightarrow$ Non-Ed. Exp. & GDP	2.32[1]
& Non-Educat. Exp.	H_0: Non-Ed. Exp. $\nRightarrow$ Ed. Exp. & GDP	3.64**
& Non-Oil GDP	H_0: GDP $\nRightarrow$ Ed. Exp. & Non-Ed. Exp.	0.12
Oman (1979-2013):		
Total Expenditure	H_0: Total Exp. $\nRightarrow$ GDP	0.99
& Non-Oil GDP	H_0: GDP $\nRightarrow$ Total Exp.	4.07**
Capital Expenditure	H_0: Capital Exp. $\nRightarrow$ GDP	0.32
& Non-Oil GDP	H_0: GDP $\nRightarrow$ Capital Exp.	0.37
Qatar (1979-2013):		
Total Expenditure	H_0: Total Exp. $\nRightarrow$ GDP	9.18***
& Non-Oil GDP	H_0: GDP $\nRightarrow$ Total Exp.	0.26
Capital Expenditure	H_0: Capital Exp. $\nRightarrow$ GDP	4.92**
& Non-Oil GDP	H_0: GDP $\nRightarrow$ Capital Exp.	3.57**
Non-Education Exp.	H_0: Non-Education Exp. $\nRightarrow$ GDP	9.80***
& Non-Oil GDP	H_0: GDP $\nRightarrow$ Non-Education Exp.	0.36
Non-Health Expend.	H_0: Non-Health Exp. $\nRightarrow$ GDP	10.00***
& Non-Oil GDP	H_0: GDP $\nRightarrow$ Non-Health Exp.	0.49
Qatar (1979-1998):		
Current Expenditure	H_0: Cur. E. $\nRightarrow$ Cap. E. & GDP p. W.	3.33**
& Capital Expend.	H_0: Cap. E. $\nRightarrow$ Cur. E. & GDP p. W.	8.07***
& Non-Oil GDP per Worker	H_0: GDP p. W. $\nRightarrow$ Cur. E. & Cap. E.	1.14

Notes: The direction of causality between cointegrated variables has been analysed by Wald tests which examine whether the respective VECM coefficients in equation (3.38) are zero (section 3.4.5). Statistical significance levels of the test statistic for rejecting the null hypothesis, H_0, of no Granger causality are indicated by *** (1%), ** (5%), and * (10%), respectively. Here, the symbol $\nRightarrow$ denotes "does not Granger cause". The VECM have been specified as shown in table 3.6.
[1] Null hypothesis rejected at 15% significance level.

Granger causality tests also detect a causal impact of public expenditure on non-oil GDP in Bahrain, albeit at lower statistical significance levels than in Qatar. When applying Granger causality tests to the only cointegration relationship in Bahrain (education expenditure, non-education expenditure, non-oil GDP), the null hypothesis of no Granger causality is rejected for non-education expenditure (5% statistical significance level) and, less distinctly, for education expenditure (15%) but not for non-oil GDP. In case of education expenditure, the rather low statistical significance level for rejecting the null hypothesis of no Granger causality indicates that the empirical evidence for a causal impact of public expenditure in Bahrain is less distinct than in Qatar.

In contrast, Granger causality test results for Oman do not support the notion of a causal impact of public expenditure on non-oil GDP. With regard to the cointegration relationship between total expenditure and non-oil GDP, Granger causality tests show that non-oil GDP causes total expenditure at a 5% statistical significance level. Granger causality test results for the cointegration relationship between capital expenditure and non-oil GDP in Oman are inconclusive since they do not indicate any uni-directional or bi-directional causality patterns between both variables. Here, the null hypothesis of no Granger causality is not rejected in a single Wald test. The absence of any statistically significant causal effects calls into question the strength of the cointegration relationship between capital expenditure and non-oil GDP in Oman.

3.5.4 Robustness Analysis

The empirical results from cointegration and causality analysis can only be considered valid if the results are not biased by the omission of relevant variables in the empirical analysis or by potential flaws in the underlying data sets. In the following, the potential relevance of omitted variables is analysed with regard to cointegration relationships between non-oil GDP and public expenditure in the GCC countries. Thereupon, the robustness of the empirical results above is examined by looking into the results of two additional cointegration and causality analyses which utilise different data sets than the baseline empirical analysis. The first robustness check is a cointegration and causality analysis which draws on time series in current prices. This serves as a cross check against potential measurement errors resulting from the deflating procedure employed for time series in constant prices.

The second robustness check examines whether the finding of cointegration links between different categories of public expenditure and non-oil GDP in the baseline empirical analysis is related to problems of circularity in the underlying data sets. Problems of circularity between public expenditure and non-oil GDP variables might arise from the fact that certain components of public expenditure such as public sector wages are typically utilised as valuation parameters for the computation of gross value added by public sector activities (e.g. public administration) within national account statistics. Therefore, the second additional cointegration and causality analysis checks the robustness of the empirical results by drawing on a non-oil GDP measure which only includes gross value added generated outside the public sector (private sector non-oil GDP).

When examining the long-run developments of non-oil GDP and public expenditure patterns in the GCC countries separately, one can safely assume that each time series is impacted by a wide range of factors. However, if these time series are found to be cointegrated it might well be argued that the long-run interaction between these variables cannot be ascribed to the effects of an omitted factor. This assertion can be substantiated by looking into the structure of GCC fiscal accounts. As seen in table 3.2, public revenues of the GCC countries rely to a large extent on oil export revenues. Instead, tax revenues are only of minor importance for the public budget. Hence, public revenues and, following, the GCC countries' leeway for public spending are largely determined by exogenous factors (e.g. OPEC quotas, world demand for oil) and only to a small extent by business cycles of the domestic economy. As a result of the insignificant role of tax revenues, any omitted factor which might strongly impact economic growth in the non-oil sectors cannot be expected to have a similar effect on public finances in the GCC countries.

Conversely, the exogenous factors which affect GCC public finances are unlikely to exert a comparable separate influence on non-oil GDP developments. Exports of the GCC countries consist mainly of oil exports (see table 3.1). In view of the rather small size of non-oil exports, any exogenous factor such as the business cycle of the world economy which has a high relevance for oil export earnings, is unlikely to impact the non-oil sectors in the GCC countries in a similar vein. Given the difficulty to identify factors which have a profound long-run impact both on non-oil GDP developments and on public spending in the GCC countries, no additional endogenous or exogenous variables were included in the VECM estimates of the long-run cointegration relationship between these variables.

Examining the robustness of the empirical results against measurement errors is necessitated by potential flaws in the underlying data sets. Due to the limited availability of consistent time series, data quality is an important aspect for evaluating the validity of results from any empirical work on the GCC countries. As already discussed in section 3.3, available data for the GCC countries is particularly sparse with regard to price variables. Here, the total GDP deflator as well as the CPI index are the only variables which can be utilised for deflating time series in current prices into time series in constant prices. Given such reliance on rather imperfect price variables in the deflating procedure, time series in constant prices might exhibit measurement errors.[20]

While time series of non-oil GDP or public expenditure in current prices suffer from other substantial drawbacks such as a distortion through changes in the price level, they can be utilised for cross-checking the robustness of the empirical results above. Since the sources of potential measurement errors in time series in constant prices differ considerably from those of time series in current prices, the respective empirical analyses are unlikely to be biased in a uniform manner.

Apart from the deflating procedure for time series in constant prices, the results of the baseline empirical analysis might also be affected by problems of circularity in the underlying data sets because certain components of public expenditure might both be included in public expenditure and non-oil GDP time series. Due to the absence of market values for most public sector services, international standards for compiling national accounts data such as the System of National Accounts 1993 (1993 SNA) or the 2008 SNA recommend valuing public services by the costs which have been incurred for producing them (*cost of production approach*). Here, different components of public expenditure such public sector wages or consumption of fixed capital can be singled out as very important valuation parameters for gross value added in the public sector (European Commission et al.

[20]In contrast to OLS regressions, the empirical results of cointegration analysis are not affected by an asymptotic measurement error as long as the measurement error is stationary (Fischer 1990; Hassler and Kuzin 2009). However, this asymptotic property does not necessarily hold in this empirical work as a result of the rather small sample sizes utilised. Furthermore, imperfect price variables in the deflating procedure may lead to a systematic measurement error for some variables. In case of such high persistence of the errors, the stationarity assumption might not hold for all measurement errors.

1993:164-165, 2009:110-111).

The inclusion of these public expenditure components in both public expenditure as well as non-oil GDP time series might, in turn, give rise to the finding of spurious cointegration links. In order to examine the robustness of the cointegration links between different categories of public expenditure and non-oil GDP in the baseline empirical analysis, the second additional cointegration and causality analysis draws on a non-oil GDP measure which does not include gross value added within the public sector ("private sector non-oil GDP"). The latter measure is computed by subtracting gross value added in the public administration sector (ISIC, Rev. 3 Code: L) from the non-oil GDP figure utilised in the baseline empirical analysis.

Unfortunately, the latter robustness check cannot be applied in a reliable manner to the links between public expenditure and the labour productivity indicator non-oil GDP per worker due to data constraints. Annual time series of the labour force in Bahrain, Oman and Qatar are only available in an aggregated form for the total economy but not for single economic sectors. Instead, comprehensive information on the labour force in single economic sectors is only published for census years.[21]

In contrast to the oil and gas sector, a substantial share of employment in Bahrain, Oman and Qatar during census years falls upon the public administration sector (tables 4.9, 5.10 and 6.9). Therefore, relating the above mentioned private sector non-oil GDP (excl. gross value added by public administration) to the total number of persons in the labour force appears as a highly distorted measure for labour productivity developments in the private sector non-oil economy. As a result, the second additional cointegration and causality analysis examines only the links between public expenditure and total private sector non-oil GDP but not the links between public expenditure and labour productivity. Detailed empirical results of both robustness checks (unit root tests, cointegration tests, zero restriction tests, stability tests, final VECM specifications and Granger causality tests) can be found in tables C1-C21 in the appendix.

The two robustness tests confirm the empirical results of the baseline em-

[21]Bahrain, Oman and Qatar publish sectoral breakdowns of employment in annual statistical yearbooks. Yet, these employment figures exhibit strong discrepancies with the respective census year figures, most notably, with regard to public sector employment since the employment figures in annual statistical yearbooks typically do not include employment in security and defence.

pirical analysis only partially. Unfortunately, the explanatory power of the two additional cointegration and causality analyses is limited by the findings of the respective unit root tests which show that several variables are not integrated of order one and, hence, are not eligible for cointegration analysis (tables C1 and C11). As a result, a robustness check for several empirical results of the baseline empirical analysis was not feasible. This applies particularly to Oman since the variables non-oil GDP (current prices), non-oil GDP per worker (current prices) and private sector non-oil GDP (constant prices) were all found to be integrated of order two. Therefore, the impact of public expenditure on non-oil GDP or on labour productivity developments in Oman could not be examined by the two additional cointegration and causality analyses.

In contrast to Oman, unit root test results for Bahrain allowed for an extensive robustness analysis of the baseline empirical results. Except for the variable health expenditure (current prices), all variables of the two robustness tests for Bahrain were found to be eligible for cointegration analysis. With regard to the link between public expenditure and non-oil GDP in Bahrain, the two robustness tests do not provide uniform results. The first robustness test does not find empirical evidence for any cointegration links between public expenditure and non-oil GDP in Bahrain. Instead, the second robustness test fully confirms the findings of the baseline empirical analysis since it points to a cointegration relationship between the variables non-oil GDP, education expenditure and non-education expenditure but does not find evidence for any additional cointegration links between non-oil GDP and other categories of public expenditure.

In line with the results of the baseline empirical analysis for Bahrain, the cointegration link between the variables non-oil GDP, education expenditure and non-education expenditure is indicated both by the Johansen trace test and the Saikkonen and Lütkepohl test within the second robustness analysis (tables 3.5 and C16). Furthermore, Granger causality test results in the baseline empirical analysis and in the second robustness analysis reveal similar causality patterns as non-education expenditure and, less clearly, education expenditure are shown to Granger cause movements of the other cointegrated variables in both analyses (tables 3.7 and C21).

Figure 3.4 displays the impulse response simulations of the second robustness analysis for the variables private sector non-oil GDP, education expenditure and non-education expenditure. The impulse responses in figure

3.4 almost exactly resemble the impulse responses of these three variables within the baseline empirical analysis in figure 3.1. Here, public education expenditure is shown to exert a statistically significant positive impact on non-oil GDP while the impact of non-education expenditure on non-oil GDP is less distinct in both impulse response simulations. In view of the high congruence between the empirical results in the baseline empirical analysis and in the second robustness analysis, one can ascertain that the positive impact of public education expenditure on non-oil GDP in Bahrain is not caused by the above described problems of circularity.

The cointegration link between education expenditure, non-education expenditure and non-oil GDP in Bahrain, however, is not confirmed by the first robustness test as the cointegration analysis of time series in current prices does not find evidence for any stable cointegration links of public expenditure with non-oil GDP or with the labour productivity indicator non-oil GDP per worker. With regard to the link between public expenditure and labour productivity within the first robustness analyis, the Johansen trace test and the Saikkonen and Lütkepohl test indicate cointegration relations of the variable non-oil GDP per worker with all groups of public expenditure variables in Bahrain. The existence of the latter cointegration relations, however, is questioned by the results of the zero restriction and Chow stability tests. Here, the cointegration relation between education expenditure, non-education expenditure and non-oil GDP per worker does not appear to be robust since zero restriction tests point to the exclusion of both public expenditure variables from the cointegration vector. The other cointegration relationships of public expenditure variables with non-oil GDP per worker are shown to exhibit different structural breaks in the first half of the 1990s. Since the cointegration analysis of the resulting subsamples does not indicate the existence of cointegration links, no VECM were estimated for the respective variables (tables C7, C9 and C10).

In a similar vein, the cointegration analysis of time series in current prices does not find evidence for cointegration links of public expenditure with non-oil GDP or non-oil GDP per worker in Qatar. The scope of this cointegration analysis on Qatar, however, is limited by the results of the unit root tests since four out of seven public expenditure variables were found to be integrated of order two. Here, the only public expenditure variables which were found to be eligible for cointegration analysis are non-education expenditure, health expenditure and non-health expenditure (table C1). Whereas the baseline empirical analysis showed that non-oil GDP is coin-

Figure 3.4: Impulse Response Analysis Bahrain (Private Sector)

Bahrain: Public Expenditure and Private Sector Non-Oil GDP

(a) Response Non-Oil GDP to Impulse Education Expend.

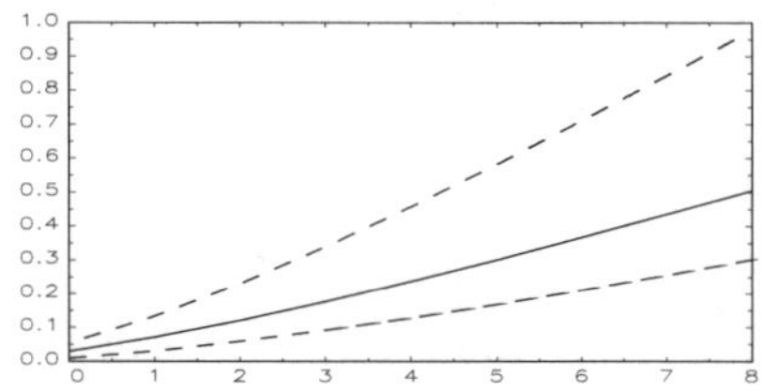

(b) Response Education Expend. to Impulse Non-Oil GDP

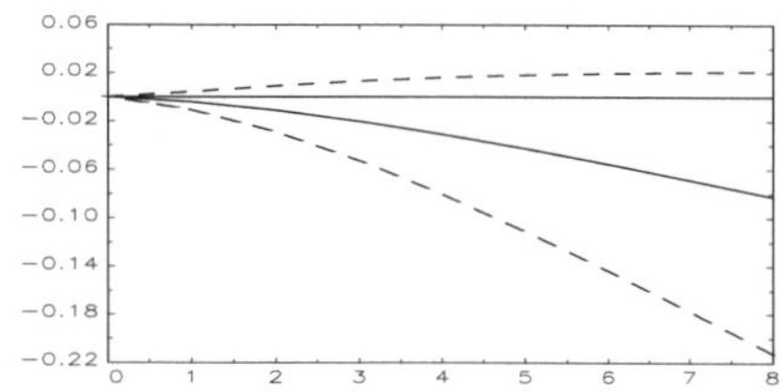

(c) Response Non-Oil GDP to Impulse Non-Education Exp.

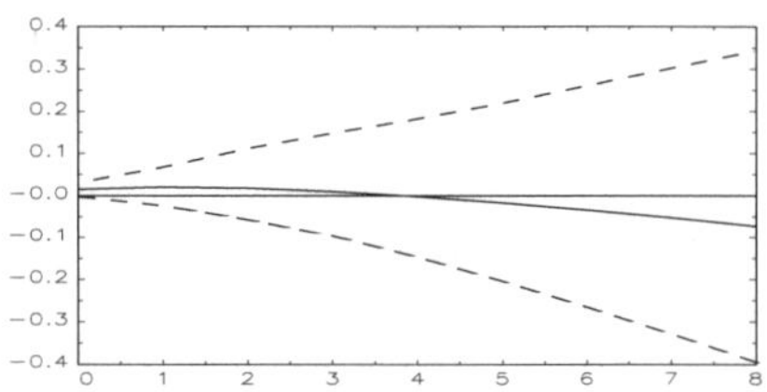

(d) Response Non-Educat. Exp. to Impulse Non-Oil GDP

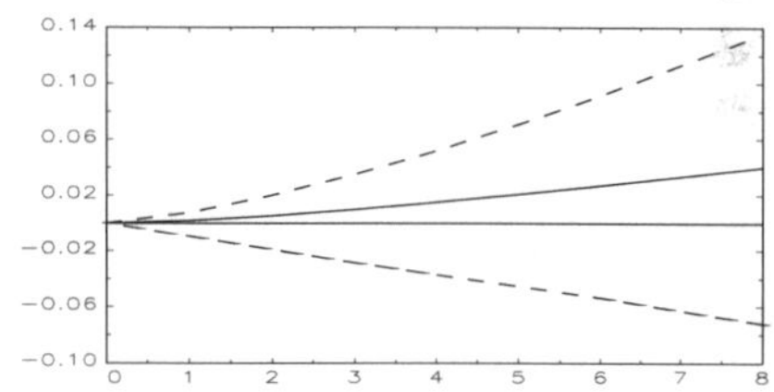

Notes: 95% Hall percentile confidence intervals (1000 bootstrap replications). VECM has been specified as shown in table C20 in the appendix. X-axis denotes number of years after initial impulse. Y-axis shows accumulated changes in the (natural log) level of responding variable. Impulse is given by one standard deviation of the orthogonalised residual of the impulse variable. Public expenditure variables have been ranked before non-oil GDP (per worker) in the orthogonalised residual covariance matrix.

tegrated with non-education expenditure and non-health expenditure, the latter two cointegration links are not confirmed by the cointegration analysis of time series in current prices (table C8). Unfortunately, a cross-check of these potential cointegration links through the second additional robustness analysis is not feasible since the variable private sector non-oil GDP is integrated of order two (table C11).

Overall, the explanatory power of the robustness analysis suffers from the fact that several variables in Oman and Qatar were found not to be eligible for the two additional cointegration and causality analyses. Despite these shortcomings, however, the robustness analysis underscored the empirical validity of the results of the baseline econometric analysis in two important aspects. First, the positive impact of different public expenditure categories on non-oil GDP developments in all three coutries does not appear to be driven by the effects of an omitted factor. As outlined above, public expenditure and non-oil GDP development patterns in the GCC countries are influenced by very differing sets of domestic and external factors. Therefore, the long-run interaction between public expenditure and non-oil GDP is unlikely to be shaped lastingly by another (omitted) variable.

Second, the finding of cointegration links between different categories of public expenditure and non-oil GDP does not appear to be related to problems of circularity within the underlying data sets. With regard to Bahrain, the empirical results of the second robustness analysis almost exactly match the empirical results of the baseline econometric analysis as both analyses detect a cointegration relationship between education expenditure, non-education expenditure and non-oil GDP. Furthermore, the impulse response simulations in both analyses show that public education expenditure exerts a positive impact on non-oil GDP in Bahrain.

Unfortunately, this robustness analysis against problems of circularity was not feasible for Oman and Qatar since the variables private sector non-oil GDP (Oman) and private sector non-oil GDP (Qatar) were not integrated of order one. Given the very high congruence between the empirical results of the baseline and the second robustness analyses in Bahrain, however, one might argue that the empirical results for Oman and Qatar in the baseline empirical analysis are also unlikely to be biased markedly by problems of circularity.

3.6 Conclusion

Empirical results from cointegration and causality analysis allow for two main conclusions about the long-run relationships between public expenditure and non-oil economic growth in the three GCC countries Bahrain, Oman, and Qatar. First, the long-term link between different categories of public expenditure and aggregate non-oil GDP exhibits considerable cross-country heterogeneity. While the baseline empirical analysis clearly points to a positive impact of different public expenditure categories on non-oil GDP developments in Qatar, the empirical evidence for such a growth stimulating role of public expenditure is less distinct for Bahrain and Oman.

Second, the impact of public expenditure on economic growth differs from the impact typically envisaged by economic growth theory. As seen earlier, economic growth theory ascribes a potential growth-enhancing impact to different categories of public expenditure (capital, education and health) since the latter public expenditure categories are deemed to have a positive influence on the long-run productivity levels of an economy. However, empirical results highlight that public expenditure in the GCC countries has predominantly impacted aggregate non-oil GDP levels. Instead, the empirical evidence for a long-run link between public expenditure and the labour productivity measure non-oil GDP per worker is much more limited.

A strong disparity between the impact of public expenditure on labour productivity developments and on aggregate non-oil GDP levels is evident in Qatar. One the one hand, only one group of public expenditure variables (capital and current expenditure) was found to exhibit a cointegration relationship with the labour productivity indicator non-oil GDP per worker. Moreover, this cointegration relationship does not extend to the full sample period (1979-2013) but only to the sub-period 1979-1998. On the other hand, the empirical evidence for a positive impact of public expenditure on aggregate non-oil GDP levels in Qatar is comparatively strong. The Johansen trace test points to cointegration relations of non-oil GDP with all four groups of public expenditure variables examined. Furthermore, the continuance of these cointegration relationships over the full sample period is confirmed by the results of zero restriction and Chow stability tests.

The impulse response simulations for the latter cointegration relationships in Qatar clearly highlight that different public expenditure variables exert a statistically significant positive impact on non-oil GDP levels while the impact of non-oil GDP on public expenditure levels is much more ambiguous. In addition, the notion of a positive causal impact of public expenditure on non-oil GDP in Qatar is also supported by the Granger causality test results which show that different public expenditure variables Granger cause non-oil GDP developments either at a 1% statistical significance level (total expenditure, non-education expenditure, non-health expenditure) or at a 5% statistical significance level (capital expenditure). The clarity of these findings might appear somewhat surprising in view of the fact that the two potentially growth-enhancing public spending categories education expenditure and health expenditure could not be utilised in the cointegration analysis for Qatar since the variables are not integrated of order one. In contrast to the results of the baseline empirical analysis, the cointegration analysis of time series in current prices does not confirm two of the above mentioned cointegration relationships (non-education expenditure & non-oil GDP; non-health expenditure & non-oil GDP).

The baseline empirical analysis also points to a positive impact of public expenditure on non-oil GDP in Oman, albeit in a less distinct manner than for Qatar. While the Johansen trace test indicates that non-oil GDP in Oman is cointegrated with all four groups of public expenditure variables examined, zero restriction tests confirm only the existence of two cointegration relationships (total expenditure & non-oil GDP; capital expenditure & non-oil GDP). Impulse response simulations for the latter two cointegration relationships clearly show that positive impulses of the two public expenditure variables lead to positive responses of non-oil GDP. Instead, Granger causality test results do not point to a causal impact of public expenditure on non-oil GDP.

Unfortunately, the robustness of the cointegration links in Oman could not be examined by the two robustness analyses since the respective variables are not integrated of order one. Similarly, a cointegration analysis on the link between labour productivity and public expenditure in Oman was not feasible since the labour productivity indicator non-oil GDP per worker was found to be integrated of order two both when examined in constant and in current prices.

The empirical evidence for a positive impact of public expenditure on non-oil GDP is weakest for Bahrain. The baseline empirical analysis points to one cointegration relationship between non-oil GDP, education expenditure and non-education expenditure but does not indicate the existence of any additional cointegration links between non-oil GDP and other categories of public expenditure. Furthermore, the impulse response simulations for the cointegration relationship in Bahrain are less clear-cut than those for the cointegration relationships in Oman and Qatar.

While a positive impulse in education expenditure leads to a statistically significant positive response of non-oil GDP, the impact of non-education expenditure on non-oil GDP is much less distinct. The existence of a cointegration relationship between non-oil GDP, education expenditure and non-education expenditure is confirmed by the second robustness analysis but not by the first robustness test. Due to unit root test results, the link between public expenditure and labour productivity could only be scrutinised for time series in current prices. The cointegration analysis of time series in current prices did not find evidence for stable cointegration links between public expenditure and labour productivity in Bahrain.

Chapter 4

Bahrain: Non-Oil Development Efforts in a Semi-Rich Oil Rentier Economy

4.1 Overview

Public expenditure plays an important role in the Bahraini non-oil economy. Substantial external rents from oil exports have allowed the Bahrani government to pursue a rapid modernisation of the economy as exemplified by a strong improvement of the country's socio-economic development level over the last decades. In comparison to other GCC countries, however, the overall impact of public expenditure on non-oil economic development patterns in Bahrain is less pronounced. While being a resource-rich country on a global scale, Bahrain is endowed with much smaller oil and gas reserves than neighbouring GCC states. As a result, the Bahraini government has commanded over less abundant financial means than the latter countries for fostering the development of non-oil sectors.

A lower prominence of public spending within Bahrain's non-oil economy is indicated by a comparatively small relative size of total public expenditure when compared to other GCC countries. For example, total public expenditure in Bahrain amounted to 33.2% of non-oil GDP in the years 1976-2013 while the share of total public expenditure at non-oil GDP stood at 86.1% in Oman and at 81.5% in Qatar during the same period (tables 4.3, 5.3, and 6.3).

Table 4.1: Bahrain - Average Annual Growth Rates Public Expenditure, Non-Oil GDP and Labour Productivity 1979-2013

(in per cent)

	1979–1985	1986–2001	2002–2013	1979–2013
Total Public Expenditure	4.8	2.9	10.0	5.7
Aggregate Non-Oil GDP	4.4	4.4	7.9	5.6
Non-Oil GDP per Worker	-2.3	0.4	0.6	-0.1
Memo: Labour Force	6.8	3.9	7.2	5.6

Sources: Appendix A.
Notes: Calculations by the author. Average annual growth rates refer to compound annual growth rates for the respective time periods. Labour productivity is proxied by non-oil GDP per worker. Non-oil GDP and public expenditure time series in constant Bahraini dinar prices.

In addition to being the least wealthy GCC state, Bahrain stands out among the GCC countries since its has pioneered the development both of oil-related and of non-oil-related economic activities. For one, Bahrain was the first GCC country where international oil companies commenced the production of crude oil back in the year 1934. Three years later, this was followed by the launch of operations at Bahrain Refinery, the oldest oil refinery on the Arabian peninsula.

Not least as a result of comparatively low oil reserves, Bahrain has also led the way in promoting the development of non-oil sectors particularly during the 1960s and the 1970s. Even before the declaration of independence in 1971, the by then semi-autonomous government of Bahrain has actively fostered the diversification of the economy. In this regard, particularly the incorporation of Aluminium Bahrain in 1968 as the first aluminium producing company of the GCC countries stands out. Moreover, Bahrain has become an important regional financial center following the government's decision to start licensing offshore banks in 1975.

Yet, in more recent decades the structural transformation towards a more diversified economy has lost steam. Here, the financial sector has been the only non-oil sector which has seen a substantial rise in importance within the sectoral structure of the economy since the 1970s. Until now, the production of crude oil and natural gas continues to be the most important economic activity in Bahrain. A strong reliance on public oil export proceeds becomes particularly evident with regard to the labour market where the public sector remains the largest employer for Bahraini nationals, albeit at lower levels than in Oman and in Qatar.

The expansion of employment both in the public administration and, to a lesser extent, in the public education and health sectors can be singled out as a major cause for the strong rise in public expenditure (section 4.2). As can be seen from table 4.1 total public expenditure (in constant prices) grew at an average annual rate of 5.7% between the years 1979 and 2013. In addition to the public wage bill, overall public spending was also increased by rising levels of capital expenditure in particular during periods of high oil price levels (1974-1985, 2002-2013). The strong expansion of public expenditure during the 2000s, however, has increasingly constrained the fiscal leeway of the Bahraini government.

Similar to public expenditure, the overall size of the non-oil economy in Bahrain grew substantially over the last decades (section 4.3). While economic growth has been particularly strong in the financial sector, several other non-oil sectors have also witnessed a marked increase in economic activity levels. Despite similar long-term trends, clear links between public expenditure and non-oil economic growth are discernible only for some non-oil sectors. Here, public spending has facilitated rising levels of gross value added in these sectors either through public outlays for wages and salaries (government services) or through capital expenditure (electricity production, wholesale trade).

Instead, a growth-enhancing impact of public expenditure is much less apparent for the financial sector, the biggest non-oil sector in Bahrain. This applies particularly for the offshore banking industry whose strong growth was primarily induced by non-fiscal economic policy measures such as the adoption of a laissez-faire regulatory framework. The latter finding as well as the comparatively small size of public expenditure within the Bahraini non-oil economy might also explain why the econometric evidence for a long-term link between public expenditure and aggregate non-oil GDP levels was found to be weaker in Bahrain than in Oman or Qatar (chapter 3).

In stark contrast to the high growth rates of public expenditure and aggregate non-oil GDP, labour productivity levels in Bahrain decreased by an annual average of -0.1% between the years 1979 and 2013 (section 4.4).

This slight overall decrease of the labour productivity measure non-oil GDP per worker is attributable to the fact that the strong growth of aggregate non-oil GDP was accompanied by an even higher increase of the country's labour force. The diverging development patterns of the two time series total public expenditure and non-oil GDP per worker, in turn, might also explain why the econometric analysis in chapter 3 did not find evidence for a stable link between public expenditure and labour productivity in Bahrain.

Two important developments in the Bahraini labour market help to explain why average output levels per worker have not seen sustained increases over the last four decades. First, a substantial fraction of employment growth took place in low value added sectors (construction, wholesale and retail trade, household services). This applies particularly to periods of strong employment growth. Second, the employment patterns of Bahraini nationals have not undergone a structural shift towards sectors with higher levels of value added per worker.

4.2 Public Expenditure

Public expenditure in Bahrain has risen to markedly higher levels over the last decades. Yet, the pace of expansion has not been uniform over time as can be seen from figure 4.1. Here, public spending patterns have been closely linked to oil price movements which, in turn, can be ascribed to the important role of oil export revenues for Bahrain's fiscal account (table 3.2).
The sample period of the econometric analysis (1979-2013) in chapter 3 comprises two periods of strongly rising oil price levels (1974-1985, 2002-2013) which both have been characterised by a massive expansion of current and capital expenditure. This applies particular to the first period (1974-1985) which is not fully captured in the sample period due to missing data. Rising numbers of public sector employees as well as a modernisation of the public infrastructure can be singled out as the two main effects of the increases in public expenditure during these two periods.

Instead, public expenditure growth has been more muted in years of low oil price levels (1986-2001). Fiscal restraint during these years has primarily been achieved by scaling back public capital spending. This change in relative importance is reflected in a strongly decreasing share of capital expenditure in total expenditure. While the cyclicality of public capital spending in Bahrain resembles capital expenditure patterns of other GCC countries, the relative size of capital expenditure in Bahrain is typically lower than in more affluent GCC countries. For example, capital expenditure in Bahrain averaged 9.3% of non-oil GDP during the years 1976 and 2013 compared to 24.2% in Oman and 16.1% in Qatar (tables 4.3, 5.3, and 6.3).

Bahrain is endowed with much less proven oil reserves than other GCC countries. Yet, public finances in Bahrain were impacted by oil revenues at an early stage since Bahrain was the first oil producing country on the Arabian peninsula. In 1934 Bahrain Petroleum Company (BAPCO) which at that time was fully owned by the American oil company Standard of California started oil production in Bahrain (Longrigg 1968:102). Over the following decades oil concession payments by BAPCO quickly became a major income stream for local rulers. According to figures provided in Rumaihi (1976:75) the average contribution of oil revenues to the state budget was 53% between the years 1934 and 1971.

For the decades prior to the 1970s available public expenditure data is very patchy. This applies particularly to public education and health expenditures. However, existing time series clearly show that the size of public expenditure was on a substantially lower level than after the oil price hikes of the 1970s. For example, total public expenditure (in current prices) increased from a mere 5.3 million Bahraini dinar in 1960 to 308.1 million Bahraini dinar in 1980 (BH/MFNE 1991:99).

While smaller in size, public expenditure in the decades prior to the 1970s seems to have led to considerable socio-economic changes in Bahrain. As can be seen from table 4.2 the levels both of adult literacy as well as of life expectancy improved substantially during the period 1960-1970. Despite the difficulty to account for the impact of other factors at least part of this improvement may reasonably be ascribed to a strong expansion of public education and health services. Here, the strong increase in the number of public schools was accompanied by much higher enrollment rates in primary education (table 4.2). Between 1950 and 1970 the number of students in public schools rose from 5,555 to 50,071 (Rumaihi 1976:128). Furthermore, the first public hospital in Bahrain was opened in the year 1957 (BH/EDB 2013). This, in turn, yielded a much higher health care provisioning level for the Bahraini population a can be seen from the strong increase in the number of hospital beds in table 4.2.

Figure 4.1: Bahrain - Oil Prices and Total Expenditure 1960-2013 (Index, 1960=100)

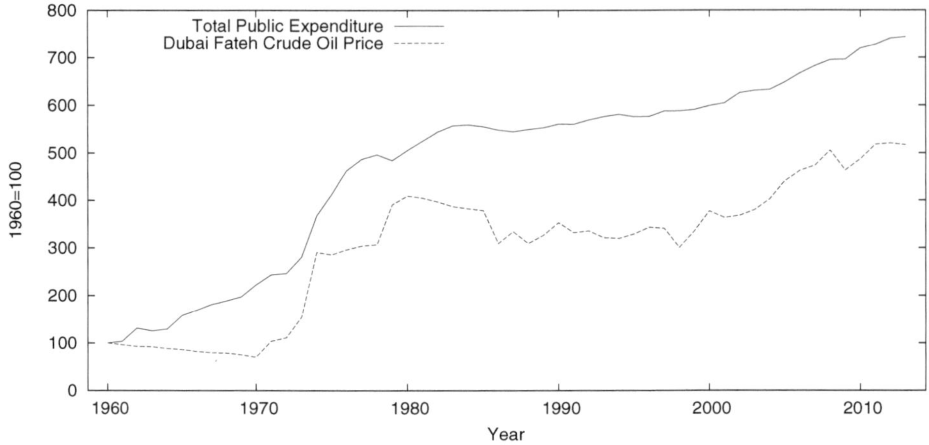

Notes: Time series in logarithms and in current prices. Due to a lack of data prior to 1970, public expenditure time series has not been deflated by CPI of Bahrain.
Sources: World Bank, *GEM Commodities*; national sources (see table A1)

The oil price hike during the first oil crisis in 1973/74 marks a turning point for government spending in Bahrain. Here, public revenues were primarily boosted by the high oil prices levels which resulted from the oil crisis in 1973/74 and 1979. In addition, the important role of oil export revenues for the public budget was further strengthened by the acquisition of a 60% stake in BAPCO through the State of Bahrain in September 1974 (Lawson 1989:80). Facilitated by spiraling oil export earnings, the size of total public expenditure rose to markedly higher levels during the years 1974-1985 (figure 4.1). This comprised an expansion both of current and capital expenditure. Here, the share of capital expenditure at total expenditure during the years 1979-1985 stood at a much higher level than in later periods (table 4.3).

The strong increase of public expenditures altered the economy in different aspects. In particular, a rapid modernisation of the public infrastructure as well as a growing size of the public sector in Bahrain stand out as the two main effects of high spending levels during the years 1974-1985. Rising capital expenditures led to a substantial modernisation of the public infrastructure. For example, the combined production capacity of public electricity providers in Bahrain increased by 1,010% between 1974 and 1985 (BH/MFNE 1991:146). Furthermore, this period saw an enlargement of the country's main transportation facilities such as the port Mina Salman or the international airport in the capital city Manama (World Bank 1978:26-27). In the year 1986, University of Bahrain was established (BH/UB 2009). The modernisation of public infrastructure also entailed a considerable improvement of the living conditions of the Bahraini population. This latter point is exemplified by the rapidly rising number of houses exhibiting a connection to the public sewage and electricity system between the census years 1971 and 1991 (table 4.2).

The main reason for the rapidly growing size of current expenditure since the year 1974 is a rising wage bill for employees in the public sector. Here, the public wage bill comprises primarily salaries for employees in the public administration (e.g. ministries, public agencies). The second largest component of the public wage bill are salaries for public employees in the education and health sectors. As a result of a free provision of education and health services to Bahraini citizens the cost for the provision of these services is fully reflected in the Bahraini government accounts.

As will be discussed at greater length in section 4.4 the number of Bahraini employees in the public administration has risen constantly since the 1970s. In part, the rising number of employees in public administration during the 1970s can be ascribed to the need for building up of government capacity after Bahrain achieved full independence in 1971. Yet, the strong expansion of the public sector during this period has also been criticised as being excessive (e.g. Franklin 1985:10; Abdel-Latif 1985:98-102). In this view, distributing newly gained oil wealth among the citizens of Bahrain was the main motive for enlarging the size of public sector employment. As an example for the latter, Abdel-Latif (1985:99) points to an increase in the number of ministries in Bahrain from 13 in the year 1973 to 29 in 1978.

In addition, the high oil revenue windfalls of the 1970s enabled the government of Bahrain to establish a generous social security system for Bahraini citizens as well as price subsidies on various consumer goods. With regard to the latter, in particular the introduction of food subsidies in 1973 led to rising levels of current expenditure (World Bank 1978:36).[1] As can be seen

[1]Since food prices have been lowered through direct subsidies, the cost of these subsidies is fully reflected in government accounts. In contrast, most other subsidised prices in Bahrain (e.g. electricity, water, gasoline) stem from indirect subsidies which makes the cost of the latter subsidies less transparent.

Table 4.2: Bahrain - Education, Health, and Infrastructure Indicators 1950-2013

Indicator	1950	1960	1970	1980	1990	2000	2013
Gross Enrollment Primary Education (% of age cohort)	24.0	72.0	98.4	104.2	110.0	103.4	na
Gross Enrollment Secondary Education (% of age cohort)	na	na	51.3	59.0	87.0	100.1	95.5[3]
Gross Enrollment Tertiary Education (% of age cohort)	na	na	1.4	5.1	16.7	21.0	33.5[3]
Adult Literacy Rate (% of adults aged 15 and above)	na	25.3	50.9	71.2	82.1	87.5	94.6[4]
Public Schools (Number)	21	55	111	125	158	193	206
Beds in Public Hospitals (Number)	0	729	907	1,012	1,320[2]	1,642	2,093
Life Expectancy at Birth (Years)	na	52.1	63.7	69.8	72.5	74.6	76.7
Telephone Lines (Number in 1,000)	na	na	6.3	41.2	94.0	171.0	251.0
House Connections Sewerage (Number in 1,000)	na	na	9.0[1]	23.6[1]	83.3[1]	104.9[1]	140.4[1]
House Connections Electricity (Number in 1,000)	na	na	29.2[1]	52.0[1]	83.1[1]	105.7[1]	191.6[1]
Length of Paved Road Network (km)	na	na	na	na	1,996	2,537	3,544
Memo: Population (Persons in 1,000)	116	163	213	360	496	667	1,349

Sources: World Bank (2008); World Bank, *World Development Indicators*; Rumaihi (1976); BH/MFNE (1991); BH/CSO (1991); BH/CIO (2001-2014); BH/CIO (2011b); United Nations, *World Population Prospects - The 2015 Revision.*

Notes: Gross enrollment rates divide the total number of students enrolled (regardless of age) by the population in the official age cohort of the respective educational level. Due to grade repetitions and the enrollment of over-aged or under-aged students, gross enrollment rates may exceed 100%.

[1] Figures for the years 1970, 1980, 1990, 2000 and 2013 refer to the census years 1971, 1981, 1991, 2001 and 2010 respectively.

[2] Figure refers to year 1989.

[3] Figure refers to year 2012.

[4] Figure refers to year 2010.

from table 4.3 wages and salaries of public sector employees, direct price subsidies and social security transfer payments continue to form the bulk of current expenditures in Bahrain.

Following the strong decline of the oil price in early 1986 the rapid expansion of public expenditure came to an end in the second half of the 1980s. Faced with much lower oil export revenues and, as a result, soaring budget deficits the Bahraini government was compelled to rein in public spending. Here, the government budget balance deteriorated from annual average of 1.8% of GDP during the years 1980-1985 to -7.2% of GDP in 1986-1990 (World Bank 1993:9). The necessary fiscal adjustments primarily took the form of cut backs in capital expenditure. As a result, the share of capital expenditure in total expenditure decreased rapidly. Until the start of the second oil price boom in 2002 public investment activity remained modest. The decrease in public investment levels during the years 1986-2001 is particularly evident with regard to public utilities (electricity & water) and public housing schemes (table 4.3).

Contrary to capital expenditure, current expenditure continued to grow during the second half of the 1980s and the 1990s, albeit at a slower pace. In this regard, it is important to note that the public wage bill (in current prices) saw continuous increases during the years 1980-2001. Rising government outlays for salaries and wages are also the main cause for the increase in current expenditure during the second oil price boom (2002-2013). Here, the public wage bill (in current prices) rose by an annual average of 10.0% between 2002 and 2013 (compared to an annual average of 4.4% between 1986 and 2001). Furthermore, the cost of public subsidies increased particularly during the second half of the 2000s which can in large part be attributed to strongly rising world market prices of subsidised food products.

The Bahraini government also expanded capital expenditure levels markedly during the period 2002-2013 (annual average growth rate nominal capital expenditure levels 2002-2013: 9.4%). This upswing in public investment activity during 2002-2013 is primarily due to higher public investments in the country's road and drainage networks as well as in the production facilities of public utilities. Furthermore, the Bahraini government resumed large-scale public housing programmes during this period (table 4.3). Public investment needs in these fields can be attributed to continuously high rates of population growth during the 1980s and the 1990s. Similarly to the

Table 4.3: Bahrain - Composition & Size of Public Expenditure 1976-2013

	1976 -1985	1986 -2001	2002 -2013	1976 -2013
	(% of total public expenditure)			
Composition of Public Expenditure				
Expenditure by Economic Type:				
Current Expenditure	56.2	79.8	77.0	72.7
Of which: Salaries & Wages[1]	35.6	51.2	40.9	44.8
Of which: Subsidies & Transfers[1]	5.8	10.7	21.7	13.7
Capital Expenditure	43.8	20.2	23.0	27.3
Of which: Electricity & Water[2]	15.3	6.9	7.2	7.9
Of which: Roads, Drainage & Public Buildings[3]	5.6	4.9	4.7	4.9
Of which: Housing[3]	6.7	2.3	4.6	3.6
Expenditure by Economic Function:				
Education Expenditure	10.5	13.8	12.5	12.5
Non-Education Expenditure	89.5	86.2	87.5	87.5
Health Expenditure	7.2	8.0	7.8	7.7
Non-Health Expenditure	92.8	92.0	92.2	92.3
	(% of non-oil GDP)			
Size of Public Expenditure				
Total Expenditure	35.6	32.5	32.2	33.2
Current Expenditure	19.9	25.8	24.9	23.9
Capital Expenditure	15.7	6.6	7.4	9.3
Education Expenditure	3.7	4.5	4.0	4.1
Health Expenditure	2.6	2.6	2.5	2.5

Sources time series: BH/CIO (2003-2010); BH/CSO (1984-1996); BH/MoF (2005, 2007-2014); BH/MFNE (1991, 1996, 2000); UN Data, *National Accounts Official Country Data*; World Bank (1993:178).

Notes: Time series in current prices. Calculations by the author.

[1] Time series only available from 1980 until 2013.

[2] Time series only available from 1983 until 2008.

[3] Time series only available from 1983 until 2013.

first oil price boom, the considerable enlargement of public infrastructure during the second oil price boom is exemplified by the rapid increase of the number of house connections to the public sewage and electricity systems between the census years 2001 and 2010 (table 4.2).

In addition, the strong expansion of capital expenditure was also driven by a renewed focus of the government on the development of non-oil sectors. Here, the government aimed at facilitating economic growth in several non-oil sectors through publicly financed infrastructure projects such as the construction of different economic zones (e.g. Bahrain Logistics Zone, Bahrain Investment Wharf) and of the new Khalifa Bin Salman port (Thomas 2009; BH/MoW 2009:19). These infrastructure projects coincided with several government initiatives which aimed to enhance the long-term development prospects of the non-oil economy in Bahrain. In May 2005, the Economic Development Board (EDB), a government body established along the lines of the Economic Development Board in Singapore, was entrusted with the official mandate for long-term economic planning in Bahrain (BH/BNA 2005).[2] This was followed by the launch of Economic Vision 2030, a long-term economic development strategy, in October 2008 (BH/BNA 2008).

The substantial upswing of public expenditure levels during the 2000s, however, has put considerable strain on public finances in Bahrain. According to estimates by the IMF (2015:110), the world market price for crude oil necessary to balance the national budget of the Bahraini government stood at a very high 107 US-Dollar in the year 2015. Instead, the corresponding estimates for fiscal break-even oil prices in Oman and Qatar during the year 2015 amount to 95 US-Dollar and 56 US-Dollar, respectively and, hence, point to a much higher fiscal leeway particularly in case of Qatar.

4.3 Non-Oil GDP

The size of the non-oil economy in Bahrain expanded significantly over the last four decades. As can be seen in table 4.4, aggregate non-oil GDP increased almost sixfold between the years 1979 and 2013. In contrast, the labour productivity measure non-oil GDP per worker witnessed a slight decline during the same period. This strong divergence between both time

[2] The establishment of the Economic Development Board (EDB) dates back to the year 2000. However, the EDB has assumed an important role in designing economic policy only after being handed the *national economy* mandate for strategic economic planning from the Ministry of Finance and National Economy (*now:* Ministry of Finance) in May 2005. BH/EDB (2010:4)

series indicates that the high rates of aggregate non-oil GDP growth cannot be ascribed to improvements in labour productivity. The development pattern of the labour productivity measure non-oil GDP per worker needs to be analysed in the context of labour market developments in Bahrain and, hence, will be examined in section 4.4. Beforehand, the sectoral sources of the strong increase in aggregate non-oil GDP are analysed in this section.

The increase in aggregate non-oil GDP between 1979 and 2013 has been driven by a broad based expansion of economic activity in the non-oil economy in Bahrain. As can be seen from the indicators displayed in table 4.5 different non-oil sectors such as wholesale trade, air transport, financial services, electricity production or several manufacturing industries have all exhibited rising levels of economic activity between the years 1979 and 2013. With regard to the oil and gas sector, the production of natural gas has been expanded heavily since the 1970s. Rising production levels of natural gas, however, were not utilised for exports but have instead primarily been allocated to domestic power companies or energy intensive manufacturing industries such as the production of aluminium or petrochemicals (BH/CIO 2011: table 13.08).

The total gross value added in the Bahraini economy increased considerably, yet, the pace of expansion has been uneven across sectors. Therefore, the structure of economic activity has changed over the last four decades. This becomes evident when looking at the sectoral contributions to gross value added (GVA) in table 4.6. In particular, the financial sector has gained importance since its contribution to the nominal GVA in Bahrain rose from 6.6% in 1976 to 15.3% in 2013. As a result, the financial sector became the biggest non-oil sector in the economy. Furthermore, manufacturing and government services stand out as important non-oil sectors. Overall, the production of crude oil and natural gas remains the most important economic activity in Bahrain, even though the relative size of this sector has fluctuated strongly due to changes in the world market prices for crude oil and natural gas.

The rising economic importance of the financial sector between the years 1976-2013 is attributable to the emergence of Bahrain as a regional financial center during this period. In the earlier decades of the sample period, this development was primarily driven by an increasing size of offshore banking activities in Bahrain. During the 1990s and the 2000s the status as a regional financial center has been reinforced by the strong growth of the

Islamic finance industry in Bahrain.

Offshore banking in Bahrain dates back to October 1975 when the government of Bahrain started to offer offshore banking licenses to foreign banks. These banking licenses allowed foreign banks to conduct their international business activities from an offshore banking branch in Bahrain.[3] Instead, the offshore banking licenses permitted only a very limited access to the domestic market in Bahrain such as the provision of banking services to public agencies or domestic (onshore) banks. The government of Bahrain utilised several regulatory and tax incentives in order to convince foreign banks to base their offshore banking activities in Bahrain.

As to regulatory incentives, these included the absence of capital account restrictions on the banks' international transactions. Furthermore, offshore banking branches were not obliged to fulfill any minimum reserve or liquidity requirements. In addition, offshore branches enjoyed a favourable tax treatment since their income as well as the interest income of the banks' depositors were both exempted from domestic taxes. Offshore banks operating in Bahrain were only levied with an annual license fee amounting to 25,000 US Dollar (Pfeiffer 1991:52-54; Gerakis and Roncesvalles 1983:272-274).

The size of the offshore financial sector grew particularly strong during the second half of the 1970s and the 1980s. By year-end 1976, the Bahraini authorities had already granted 26 offshore banking licenses (Pfeiffer 1991:16). During the period 1975-1979, the proportion of total offshore banking assets to Bahrain's GDP jumped from 142% to 951%. As can be seen from table 4.5, total assets of the offshore financial sector continued to expand faster than nominal GDP during the 1980s.

As a result of the strong growth of offshore banking, Bahrain quickly became the most important money market center in the Middle East. Here, the business activities of offshore banks primarily comprised intermediation of short-term funds between regional banks, dealings of foreign exchange transactions on the currencies of the neighbouring Gulf countries as well

[3] The government of Bahrain aimed at the establishment of branches and not of subsidiaries of international banks. In contrast to subsidiaries, branches are no separate legal entities from the parent bank which potentially ensures a stronger commitment of the latter. Furthermore, the offshore banking licenses required the branches of international banks to be fully operational and equipped with staff (Gerakis and Roncesvalles 1983:274-275).

Table 4.4: Bahrain - Levels Public Expenditure, Non-Oil GDP and Labour Productivity 1979-2013
(in constant 2010 US-Dollar prices)

	1979	1990	2000	2013
Total Public Expenditure (Billion US-Dollar)	1.0	1.8	2.5	8.4
Aggregate Non-Oil GDP (Billion US-Dollar)	3.8	5.7	8.6	22.5
Non-Oil GDP per Worker (1,000 US-Dollar)	31.7	26.3	28.5	30.4

Sources: National sources (see Appendix A)
Note: US $ exchange rates from IMF (International Financial Statistics).

as the provision of trade finance facilities such as letters of credit (Pfeiffer 1991:69-78; Wilson 1983:110-119).

The financial sector continues to be the most important non-oil sector in Bahrain. However, the dominant role of offshore banking within the financial sector has diminished between the years 2000 and 2013 as can be seen in table 4.6. Since the 1990s, growth in the financial sector has increasingly been driven by the Islamic banking and insurance industries. Between 1990 and 2015 the number of Islamic banks and Islamic insurance companies operating in Bahrain increased from 5 to 25 and from 2 to 11, respectively (BH/CBB 2016).

In terms of economic policy, several government initiatives can be singled out which aided the development of the Islamic finance industry in Bahrain during this period. These initiatives typically aimed at strengthening the Islamic finance market infrastructure. In 2001 the Bahrain Monetary Agency issued the first sovereign Islamic bond *(Sukuk)* on the Arabian peninsula which helped to establish a capital market for Islamic finance securities (Obaidullah 2007:197-198). In addition, Bahrain's reputation as a global Islamic finance center was also strengthened by setting up international Islamic finance bodies in Bahrain. Among others, this included the establishment of standard setting organisations such as the Accounting and Auditing Organization for Islamic Financial Institutions, the main accounting body in Islamic finance, in 1991 and the International Islamic Financial Market, a standard setting body for Islamic finance products on money and capital markets, in 2002 (Baba 2007:388-391).

As seen above, the Bahraini government has played an active role in promoting the growth both of offshore banking and Islamic finance. In doing so, it adopted a rather diverse set of economic policies which ranged from offering a laissez-faire regulatory framework to offshore banks to promoting the development of Islamic finance capital markets through the issuance of Sukuk. With regard to the economic policies pursued, the role of public expenditure does not figure prominently. While a positive impact of public expenditure categories such as education expenditure cannot be precluded, public expenditure does not stand out as a main economic policy tool fostering economic growth in the financial sector.

The Bahraini government has not only fostered economic growth in the financial sector but also in other services sectors. For example, the international operations of Gulf Air, a Bahrain based airline, were strongly expanded after the government of Bahrain and three other GCC countries (Oman, Qatar, Emirate Abu Dhabi) became sole shareholders of the company in 1973 (BH/GA 2013). The year 1981 saw the incorporation of Bahrain Telecommunications Company (Batelco) as a joint venture between the government of Bahrain and the British company Cable & Wireless (MEED 1981). Yet, diversification efforts in the transport and telecommunications sectors have been less successful than in the financial sector. Here, the combined share of both sectors at total gross value added even exhibited a slight decline between 1976 and 2013 (table 4.6).

In comparison to the financial sector, the manufacturing sector underwent much less structural change since the 1970s. Important manufacturing industries such as aluminium production and oil refining had been established in Bahrain prior to the start of the first oil price boom in 1974. The production of petrochemicals and a shipyard have been the only new major manufacturing activities which commenced operations since the mid-1970s.

Oil refining is the oldest modern day manufacturing activity in Bahrain since the first refinery in Bahrain ("Bahrain Refinery") was set up as early as 1937 by BAPCO (Longrigg 1968:103). The beginning of the aluminium industry dates back to the incorporation of Aluminium Bahrain (ALBA) in the year 1968. Established as a joint venture between the by then semi-autonomous government of Bahrain and four international companies ALBA has been the first aluminium producing company on the Arabian peninsula (Lawson 1989:99-101). Not least as a result of a comparatively early start of oil refining and aluminium production contemporaneous economic research evaluated the industrial structure in Bahrain as being the

Table 4.5: Bahrain - Indicators of Economic Activity 1979-2013

Economic Activity	1979	1990	2000	2013
Oil and Natural Gas Production:				
Crude Oil (Million metric tons/year)	9.5	9.4	9.3	9.9
Natural Gas (Billion cubic meters/year)	2.9	4.3	6.1	14.2
Manufacturing Production:				
Aluminium (1,000 metric tons/year)	139	213	509	913
Refined Oil (1,000 barrels/day)	254	254	262	265
Ammonia (1,000 metric tons/year)	0	325	350	378
Electricity Production:				
Gross Domestic Production (TWh)	1.5	3.5	6.3	25.9
Wholesale Trade Seaports:				
Containers Handled (1,000 TEU/year)	43	69[1]	122[2]	356
Air Transport:				
Airport Arrivals (1,000 Passengers/year)	450	995	1,682	3,627
Financial Sector:				
Total Assets Financial Sector (% of GDP)	1,019	1,321	1,174	584
Of which: Offshore Banks	951	1,219	1,027	355[3]

Sources: International Energy Agency (IEA), *Oil Information*, various issues; IEA, *Natural Gas Information*, various issues; IEA, *Energy Statistics of Non-OECD Countries*, various issues; IEA, *Electricity Information*, various issues; US Geological Survey, *Minerals Yearbook*, various issues; Containerisation International, *Containerisation International Yearbook*, various issues; BH/CSO (1991); BH/CIO (2001, 2014); BH/MFNE (1991); BH/CBB (2001, 2005, 2006, 2014); UN Data, *National Accounts Main Aggregates Database*

[1] Refers to year 1989.

[2] Refers to year 1999.

[3] Includes offshore banks and investment banks.

most diversified among the six GCC member countries during the late 1970s and the early 1980s (e.g. Looney 1989).

While oil refining levels did not witness a strong upswing, aluminium production increased more than sixfold during the period 1979-2013 following several capacity expansions at ALBA's production plants (see table 4.5). In addition, this period saw the start of production of the petrochemical products ammonia and methanol after the Gulf Petrochemical Industries Company (GPIC), a joint venture involving the government of Bahrain and two petrochemical companies from Kuwait and Saudi Arabia, commenced operations in the year 1985 (Looney 1989:17-18). The Arab Shipbuilding and Repair Yard (ASRY), a Bahraini shipyard jointly owned by the government of Bahrain and six other petroleum exporting countries, started operations in November 1977 (Al-Yousef 1985:126-128).

The indicators of economic activity displayed in table 4.5 point to the aluminium and the petrochemicals industries as important growth drivers in the manufacturing sector between the years 1979-2013. In this regard, one may reasonably assume that the increase in production at ALBA and GPIC during the sample period necessitated substantial capital investment. Yet, the impact of public expenditure on economic growth in the manufacturing sector is difficult to trace since the expenditures of partly state-owned companies such as ALBA or GPIC are not included in the government accounts.[4] Given the energy-intensive nature of these manufacturing industries, however, one may well suppose an indirect impact of capital expenditure in public electricity production on the output capacities of manufacturing companies like ALBA and GPIC.

In addition to the financial sector and manufacturing, government services play an important role in the non-oil economy of Bahrain. Yet, compared to the former two sectors, the impact of government expenditure on the growth rates of government services is much more obvious. This follows from the valuation method which is typically adopted for estimating the gross value added by government services in national accounts. Since government services (e.g. education, health, maintenance of public infrastructure, law enforcement) are usually provided free of charge or at highly subsidised prices, the monetary value of these services cannot be estimated by drawing on observable market prices. Instead, internationally agreed standards for compiling national accounts data such as the System of National Accounts 1993 (1993 SNA) or the 2008 SNA recommend valuing government services by the costs which have been incurred when producing them *(cost of production approach)* (European Commission et al. 1993:164-165, 2009:110-111).

In this regard, public expenditure on wages and salaries can be singled out as the most important production input for the valuation of government services' gross value added. On average, 80.0% of the gross value added levels for government services in Bahraini national accounts between 1984

[4]For an overview about the ministries and the public agencies included in Bahraini government accounts, please refer to the national sources mentioned in tables A3 and A4.

Table 4.6: Bahrain - Gross Value Added by Economic Activity 1976-2013 (in % of total gross value added)

	1976	1980	1990	2000	2013
Agriculture & Fishing	1.5	0.9	0.9	0.7	0.3
Mining & Quarrying	27.8	31.7	18.9	25.2	26.9
Of which: Production Oil & Gas	27.7	31.6	18.9	25.0	26.4
Manufacturing	12.8	14.8	15.2	10.3	14.8
Of which: Refining & Petrochem.	na	na	na	3.0	4.7
Of which: Aluminium	na	na	na	3.9	4.1
Electricity & Water	0.2	0.9	1.7	1.3	1.2
Construction	8.0	6.4	5.7	3.2	5.9
Wholesale & Retail Trade	14.5	9.4	7.0	7.2	4.0
Hotels & Restaurants	1.9	1.3	1.9	1.8	2.1
Transport & Telecommunications	6.8	7.9	8.5	6.3	6.2
Of which: Air Transportation	na	na	na	1.4	na
Of which: Communications	na	na	na	2.9	na
Financial Sector	6.6	8.3	11.7	19.2	15.3
Of which: Offshore Banking	3.6	4.8	7.1	10.3	6.2
Real Estate	6.0	4.7	4.7	7.4	3.7
Other Business Services	na	na	na	0.8	1.3
Social & Personal Private Services	3.4	3.1	4.8	3.0	5.9
Of which: Private Education Serv.	na	na	na	0.5	1.8
Of which: Private Health Services	na	na	na	0.3	1.2
Government Services	10.6	10.7	19.0	13.6	12.3
Of which: Public Education Serv.	na	na	na	2.7	2.7
Of which: Public Health Services	na	na	na	1.5	1.8
Total Gross Value Added	100.0	100.0	100.0	100.0	100.0

Sources: UN Data; BH/CSO (1985, 1991, 1996); BH/CIO (2005, 2014b, 2014c)
Notes: Calculations by the author. Gross value added in current producers' prices. In the official national accounts time series for the years 1976-2000, financial intermediation services indirectly measured (FISIM) have not been allocated as intermediate consumption to the sectors which used these services. Instead, the total amount of FISIM was deducted from the sum of gross value added of the different sectors within official time series. In contrast, national account figures for the year 2013 do not include FISIM figures as these services have been allocated to the respective sectors. To ensure consistency of sectoral shares at gross value added during 1976-2013, gross value added figures for the years 1976-2000 include FISIM.

and 1990 accrue from compensation of public employees. A further 20.0% of gross value added in this period relates to consumption of fixed capital (BH/CSO 1991:486, 1991:501, 1996:612).[5] Hence, the strong increase of government services' contribution to total gross value added between 1976 and 1990 in table 4.6 can primarily be ascribed to the rapid rise of the public wage bill during the first oil boom 1974-1985 (see section 4.2). Concurrent with public spending patterns the expansion of government services has slowed down as a result of much lower oil price levels between 1986 and 2001. Here, the average annual growth rate of gross value added by government services (in current prices) dropped from 16.7% during the period 1977-1985 to 4.0% between 1986 and 2001. Even though this growth rate accelerated to 10.2% during the second oil boom (2002-2013), this expansion was outweighed the higher growth rates of gross value added in other sectors.[6] As a result, the relative size of government services in the Bahraini economy declined from 13.6% in 2000 to 12.3% in 2013 (table 4.6).

Similar to government services, it may well be argued that public expenditure has also facilitated economic growth in the electricity production and the wholesale trade sectors. Rising levels of economic activity in these sectors are indicated by the increases in gross domestic electricity production and by rising volumes of containers handled at Bahraini seaports, respectively (table 4.5). As seen in section 4.2, public financing for the expansion both of the port infrastructure as well as of the production capabilities of public utilities constituted a considerable share of capital expenditure in Bahrain. Here, a rising demand for electricity as well as for higher levels of imports can in part be attributed to high population growth rates in Bahrain over the sample period (see table 4.2). Yet, despite rising levels of economic activity, the relative size of these two sectors within the Bahraini economy has either declined as in the case of the trade sector or remained on a low level as in the case of water and electricity production (table 4.6).

Overall, a discernible impact of government expenditure on aggregate non-oil GDP growth can be observed for some non-oil sectors such as govern-

[5] All other operating costs of government such as purchases of goods and services are treated as intermediate consumption and, hence, do not affect the level of gross value added. For the period 1984-1990, the levels of gross value added by governments services are given in BH/CSO (1991:486, 1996:612). A breakdown of the production inputs for government services can be found in BH/CSO (1991:501). Unfortunately, the latter time series are not publicly available for the entire sample period.

[6] Average annual growth rates relate to compound annual growth rates between the respective years. Data for the levels of gross value added by government services has been taken from BH/CSO (1985, 1991, 1996) and BH/CIO (2001, 2005, 2009, 2014b).

ment services, electricity production and wholesale trade. Furthermore, energy-intensive manufacturing industries seem to have benefitted from substantial public investments in electricity production. Instead, there exists much less evidence for a positive impact of public spending on economic growth in the financial sector which has become the biggest non-oil sector in Bahrain since the 1970s. This latter point as well as the comparatively small size of public expenditure in Bahrain might also explain why the econometric evidence for a positive impact of public expenditure on aggregate non-oil GDP is weaker in case of Bahrain than in case of Oman and Qatar (section 3.5).

4.4 Labour Productivity

The evolution of labour productivity levels in Bahrain stands in stark contrast to the long-term trends in the levels of aggregate non-oil GDP and of total public expenditure. While the latter two time series increased substantially, labour productivity levels in Bahrain have not witnessed a sustained upswing since the late 1970s. Instead, the labour productivity measure non-oil GDP per worker declined by an annual average of -0.1% between the years 1979 and 2013 (table 4.1).

The rather stagnant development pattern of the labour productivity measure non-oil GDP per worker is due to the fact that the country's labour force expanded at a similar rate as total value added within the non-oil economy of Bahrain. Here, the strong gap between the growth rates of labour productivity and of aggregate non-oil GDP needs to be examined with a view to labour market developments in Bahrain. In this regard, particularly two factors help to explain why the strong increase in total employment was not accompanied by an upswing of output levels per worker. First, a large fraction of additional jobs has been created in low value added sectors, particularly during periods of strong employment growth. Second, the labour market for Bahraini nationals has not undergone a structural change during the sample period. Here, labour productivity developments have not benefitted from a substantial shift in employment of Bahraini nationals towards sectors with higher levels of gross value added per worker.

Figure 4.2 compares the evolution of labour productivity, aggregate non-oil GDP and the total labour force during the period 1979-2013. Unlike the levels of aggregate non-oil GDP and the labour force which both feature a clear upward trend, the productivity measure non-oil GDP per worker does not exhibit a consistent long-term trend over the course of the sample period. Instead, labour productivity developments in Bahrain have been characterised by prolonged periods both of rising as well as falling productivity levels. In addition, periods of falling labour productivity levels (1979-1986, 2005-2009) appear to be associated with particular high rates of growth in the country's labour force.[7] This suggests that a substantial part of the employment growth during such boom periods took place in low value added sectors of the non-oil economy.

The analysis of labour market developments in Bahrain is complicated by the limited availability of detailed labour force data. Breakdowns of the labour force by sectoral employment or nationality are not available on an annual basis for Bahrain. Therefore, employment patterns in Bahrain are analysed by drawing on employment figures from the five most recent censuses in Bahrain (1971, 1981, 1991, 2001 and 2010). This includes census year data about overall employment levels (table 4.7) and the distribution of employment by sector and nationality (tables 4.8 and 4.9).

Official census year figures in table 4.7 show a substantial increase of overall employment levels over the last four decades. The total number of employees increased by a factor of almost 12 between the census years 1971 and 2010. However, the expansion of employment has been highly uneven both with regard to time and to the nationality of employees. Timewise, a large fraction of employment growth took place during periods of strongly rising oil price levels (1974-1985; 2002-2013). For example, overall employment during the periods 1971-1981 and 2001-2010 increased by 128.7% and 141.3%, respectively. In contrast, employment growth between the years 1991 and 2001 stands at a much lower 37.4% (table 4.7).

The fluctuations of employment growth rates between census years are particularly distinct for non-Bahraini nationals. Yet, overall, the number of non-Bahraini employees has risen at much higher rates than the number of Bahraini employees during the period 1971-2010. As will be discussed at greater length below, this divergence in employment growth can be ascribed to much higher employment shares of non-Bahraini nationals in most private sector activities. Therefore, the share of Bahraini nationals at total employment decreased from 62.9% in 1971 to 25.2% in 2010 (table 4.7).

[7] Given the logarithmic representation of the time series in figure 4.2, increasing rates of growth for a particular variable are indicated by a rise in the steepness of the variable's slope.

Figure 4.2: Bahrain - Labour Productivity, Aggregate Non-Oil GDP and Labour Force 1979-2013
(Index, 1979=100)

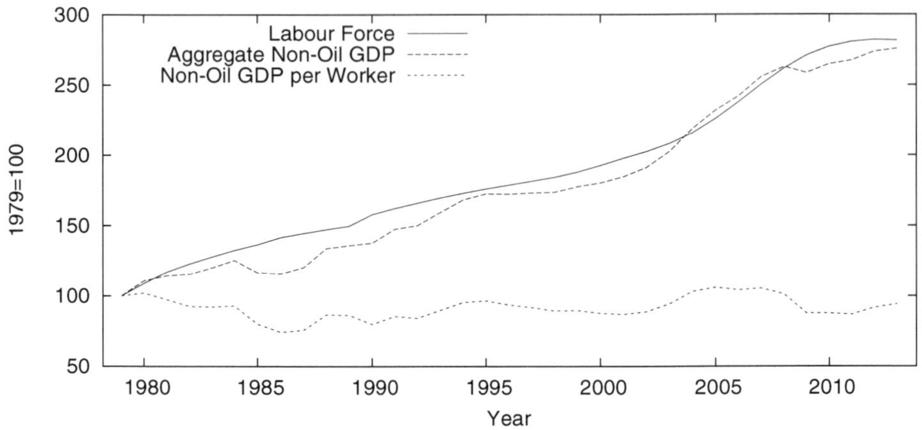

Notes: Time series in logarithms. Non-Oil GDP in constant prices.
Sources: Appendix A.

In terms of the sectoral sources of employment growth, the overall increase in the number of employees between the census years 1971 and 2010 has been particularly strong in the construction as well as in the wholesale and retail trade sectors (table 4.8). Here, the construction sector has witnessed a much more volatile pattern of employment growth than the trade sector with periods of strong growth (1971-1981, 2001-2010) typically coinciding with high levels of capital expenditure (table 4.3).

Despite the strong employment growth in the construction and the trade sectors, the shares of both sectors at total gross value added declined substantially over the last four decades (table 4.6). In a similar vein, the gross value added of household services, which exhibited the third largest sectoral increase in employment over the period 1971-2010 (table 4.8), has remained on a very modest level since the 1970s.[8] This, in turn, indicates that the average levels of value added per worker in the construction, the trade and the household services sectors are much below the comparative values of most other non-oil sectors. The latter comparison holds particular for the

[8]The gross value added shares of household services are included in the category social & personal private services in table 4.6.

financial sector. Despite a comparatively low increase in employment, the contribution of the financial sector to total gross value added rose substantially between the years 1976 and 2013 (table 4.6).

The census year employment figures also highlight a segmentation of the Bahraini labour market. As can be seen from table 4.9, non-Bahraini nationals continue to be employed primarily in private sector activities of the economy such as construction, wholesale and retail trade, household services and manufacturing. Here, the strong expansion of employment in the latter sectors has been the main cause for the substantial increase in the overall number of non-Bahraini employees between 1971 and 2010.

Instead, a substantial part of employment for Bahraini nationals falls upon public sector activities such as public administration and, to a lesser extent, public health and education services.[9] While employment of Bahraini nationals in certain private sector activities (e.g. construction, wholesale and retail trade, manufacturing) has also risen to markedly higher levels during the 1990s and the 2000s, non-Bahraini nationals still account for a large fraction of total employment growth in these sectors. Overall, public administration has been by far the biggest provider of new jobs for Bahraini nationals during the the periods 1971-1981, 1981-1991, and 2001-2010. Here, employment increases in the public sector are particularly pronounced during periods of rising oil prices (1974-1985; 2002-2013) in line with the above discussed public expenditure patterns.

The low employment levels of Bahraini nationals in the private sector are typically ascribed to two main factors. First, a substantial wage gap between salaries in the public sector and comparatively low wages for most private sector activities in Bahrain (Hertog 2012b:87-88). This applies in particular with regard to the private sector activities which exhibited the highest rates of employment growth (e.g. construction, manufacturing, trade, household services). Second, a general preference for government jobs among Bahraini nationals given the low prestige of most of the above mentioned private sector activities (World Bank 1993:29-30).

[9] Unfortunately, official census year employment data does not distinguish between employees in the private and in the public sectors with regard to education and health services. Yet, in view of the fact that the gross value added by public education and health services exceeds the gross value added by private providers of education and health services (table 4.6), it seems reasonable to assume that a major fraction of the census year employment figures for education and health services relates to the public sector.

Table 4.7: Bahrain - Total Employment Census Years 1971-2010

	1971	1981	1991	2001	2010
Number of Employees (in 1,000):					
Total Employees	60.3	137.9	212.1	291.4	703.2
Bahraini Employees	38.0	57.2	77.3	111.0	177.0
Non-Bahraini Employees	22.4	80.7	134.8	180.4	526.2
Share at Total Employment (%):					
Bahraini Employees	62.9	41.5	36.4	38.1	25.2
Non-Bahraini Employees	37.1	58.5	63.6	61.9	74.8
Rate of Change to Previous Census Year (%):					
Total Employees	na	128.7	53.8	37.4	141.3
Bahraini Employees	na	50.7	35.1	43.6	59.5
Non-Bahraini Employees	na	261.1	67.0	33.8	191.7

Sources: BH/MFNE (1972); BH/MCA (1982); BH/CIO (2001, 2004, 2011b).
Notes: Calculations by the author. Due to rounding errors numbers of Bahraini and non-Bahraini employees may not add up to the number of total employees. In contrast to the labour force data sources mentioned in table A5, employment data in this table does not include unemployed persons.

Faced with a growing public wage bill, the government of Bahrain has attempted to foster employment of Bahraini nationals in the private sector since the early 1980s. Over the course of the following three decades the government has aimed at a *Bahrainisation* of the workforce through different approaches. The first government initiative for increasing the employment shares of Bahraini nationals in the private sector goes back to 1981 when "Project 10,000", a training scheme for young Bahrainis citizens, was launched.

A quite different approach was taken in 1995 with the imposition of quota rules for employment in the private sector. Here, the employment share of Bahraini nationals in a single company had to be increased by an annual 5% until the employment share reached 50%. However, in most companies these quotas were not reached (Dito 2007; Hertog 2012b:99). Furthermore, mandatory employment quotas for Bahraini nationals were increasingly seen as detrimental to private sector growth by the government of Bahrain. In this regard, particularly the newly established Economic Development Board, a government body for strategic economic planning, has criticised the mandatory employment approach for raising business costs as well as for failing to incentivise Bahraini nationals for work performance (BH/EDB 2004:12).

Therefore, employment quotas were reduced, albeit not abolished, by the labour market reforms in the year 2007. Instead, the Bahraini government sought to enhance employment opportunities of Bahraini nationals by starting to charge companies annual and monthly levies on foreign workers and, by doing so, narrowing the wage gap between local and foreign workers particularly in labour intensive low-wage industries. In addition, 80% of the funds collected were deemed to be utilised for training programmes of Bahraini nationals.

Yet, this fee-based approach of the Bahraini government for lowering the wage gap between local and foreign workers was short-lived. Private sector businesses which rely heavily on non-national workers strongly opposed the imposition of levies on foreign labour as these fees increased their business costs. Following the outbreak of mass protests during the course of the Arab Spring, the Bahraini government eliminated the fees on foreign labour during the year 2011 in order to secure the political support of private sector businesses (AlHasan 2012; Hertog 2012b:99-102, 2013:44-45).

So far, the impact of different Bahrainisation policies on the employment patterns of Bahraini nationals has been limited. During the census year 2010, the public administration sector continued to be, by far, the most important employment sector for Bahraini nationals (table 4.9). A lack of structural change is particularly evident with regard to the financial sector. Despite a substantial rise in gross value added, the relative importance of the financial sector on the Bahraini labour market barely rose over the last three decades. While the employment shares of the trade, the manufacturing and the construction sectors increased between the census years 1991 and 2010, employment growth for Bahraini nationals in these sectors has been far from sufficient to provide enough jobs for new entrants on the labour market. As a result, employment levels of Bahraini nationals in public sector activities (public administration, public education and health sector) continued to expand strongly during the 1990s and the 2000s (table 4.8).

Table 4.8: Bahrain - Employment by Sector and Nationality Census Years 1971-2010

(Number of Employees in 1,000)

	1971	1981	1991	2001	2010
Construction	10.4	29.2	26.7	26.4	160.7
Of which: Bahraini	5.6	3.9	2.1	4.4	14.1
Of which: Non-Bahraini	4.8	25.4	24.6	22.0	146.6
Wholesale and Retail Trade	6.7	14.7	23.0	34.5	109.5
Of which: Bahraini	4.5	5.5	6.1	10.5	23.5
Of which: Non-Bahraini	2.1	9.2	16.9	24.0	86.0
Household Services	3.6	14.2	17.8	29.6	84.4
Of which: Bahraini	1.1	2.1	0.1	0.1	0.0
Of which: Non-Bahraini	2.5	12.0	17.7	29.5	84.4
Manufacturing	4.1	11.4	26.6	50.0	84.4
Of which: Bahraini	1.7	3.8	6.4	13.5	19.1
Of which: Non-Bahraini	2.3	7.5	20.2	36.4	65.3
Public Administration	5.2	18.1	41.0	52.4	83.1
Of which: Bahraini	3.7	11.0	26.8	33.2	55.0
Of which: Non-Bahraini	1.5	7.1	14.1	19.2	28.1
Real Estate & Other Bus. Serv.	0.3	0.3	12.0	16.2	41.4
Of which: Bahraini	0.2	0.2	2.2	5.2	10.0
Of which: Non-Bahraini	0.1	0.1	9.8	11.0	31.4
Restaurants & Hotels	1.0	3.8	6.9	13.1	35.5
Of which: Bahraini	0.3	0.3	0.8	2.4	4.0
Of which: Non-Bahraini	0.7	3.5	6.2	10.6	31.6
Education & Health Services[1]	7.5	13.6	15.6	21.1	27.7
Of which: Bahraini	5.3	8.6	10.6	16.1	19.0
Of which: Non-Bahraini	2.2	5.0	5.0	5.0	8.7
Financial Sector	0.8	4.3	5.3	6.5	17.4
Of which: Bahraini	0.5	2.6	3.7	4.6	10.1
Of which: Non-Bahraini	0.3	1.7	1.6	1.9	7.3
Other Sectors	20.7	28.4	37.2	41.6	59.3
Of which: Bahraini	14.8	19.2	18.6	20.9	22.4
Of which: Non-Bahraini	5.9	9.2	18.7	20.7	36.8

Sources: BH/MFNE (1972); BH/MCA (1982); BH/CIO (2001, 2004, 2011b).

Note: Due to rounding errors numbers of Bahraini and non-Bahraini employees may not add up to the number of total employees.

[1] Includes employment in public and private sectors.

Table 4.9: Bahrain - Sectoral Employment Shares Bahraini and Non-Bahraini Nationals 1971-2010

	1971	1981	1991	2001	2010
	(in % of Bahraini Employees)				
Bahraini Nationals:					
Main Sectors:					
Public Administration	9.8	19.2	34.7	29.9	31.1
Wholesale and Retail Trade	11.9	9.6	7.9	9.4	13.3
Manufacturing	4.6	6.7	8.3	12.2	10.8
Education & Health Services[1]	14.1	15.0	13.7	14.5	10.7
Construction	14.9	6.7	2.8	4.0	7.9
Memo:					
Financial Sector	1.4	4.6	4.8	4.1	5.7
Oil and Gas & Quarrying	10.2	6.3	3.6	1.9	0.2
	(in % of Non-Bahraini Employees)				
Non-Bahraini Nationals:					
Main Sectors:					
Construction	21.3	31.4	18.2	12.2	27.9
Wholesale and Retail Trade	9.6	11.4	12.6	13.3	16.4
Household Services	11.2	14.9	13.1	16.3	16.0
Manufacturing	10.4	9.3	15.0	20.2	12.4
Restaurant & Hotels	3.2	4.3	4.6	5.9	6.0
Memo:					
Financial Sector	1.1	2.1	1.2	1.0	1.4
Oil and Gas & Quarrying	2.3	1.4	0.6	0.4	0.3

Sources: BH/MFNE (1972); BH/MCA (1982); BH/CIO (2001, 2004, 2011b).

Note: Calculations by the author.

[1] Includes employment in public and private sectors.

Chapter 5

Oman: A Late Non-Oil Economic Blooming Caused by Rising Public Oil Rents

5.1 Overview

Oman's economy was transformed by the inflow of oil export proceeds at a much later time than other GCC countries. For a large part of the twentieth century, size and structure of the Omani economy barely changed. Oman was the last GCC country to commence the production of crude oil in the year 1967. Until the late 1960s, Oman remained a closed-off subsistence economy without almost any modern day infrastructure, public schools or medical facilities.

The development pattern of the Omani economy changed rapidly after the start of oil production and, even more so, following spiralling public oil export revenues during the years of the first oil price boom (1974-1985). An unprecedented increase of public expenditure levels contributed to a tremendous improvement of Oman's infrastructure as exemplified by the first build-up of countrywide transportation, electricity and communication networks.

Likewise, strongly rising government outlays on the provision of education and health services led to a substantial upswing of the educational level and the health status of Oman's population. The growing inflow of oil export proceeds has also set off a lasting structural change in the Omani economy. Here, the relative importance of subsistence agriculture and fishing within

Table 5.1: Oman - Average Annual Growth Rates Public Expenditure, Non-Oil GDP and Labour Productivity 1979-2013

(in per cent)

	1979–1985	1986–2001	2002–2013	1979–2013
Total Public Expenditure	17.2	0.8	10.6	7.2
Aggregate Non-Oil GDP	20.4	4.5	6.6	8.3
Non-Oil GDP per Worker	7.1	2.3	-0.7	2.2
Memo: Labour Force	12.4	2.2	7.4	5.9

Sources: Appendix A.

Notes: Calculations by the author. Average annual growth rates refer to compound annual growth rates for the respective time periods. Labour productivity is proxied by non-oil GDP per worker. Non-oil GDP and public expenditure time series in constant Omani Rial prices.

the economy was dwarfed by high rates of growth in several modern industry and service sectors.

Over the following decades, the size of the non-oil economy grew substantially with the largest rates of non-oil economic growth taking place during the years of the two oil price booms (1974-1985, 2002-2013). Endowed with smaller oil and gas reserves than most other GCC countries, the government of Oman fostered the development of non-oil sectors through various economic policy measures particularly since the mid-1990s.

Yet, the strong expansion of the non-oil economy since the 1970s did not diminish the economic importance of the oil sector lastingly. Instead, the Omani economy increasingly resembled features of an oil-rentier economy along the lines of other GCC countries. In terms of gross value added, the production of crude oil remains, by far, the most important economic activity in Oman. Furthermore, public expenditure patterns continue to be shaped heavily by the size of oil export proceeds since the latter constitute the main source of public revenues.

Public expenditure contributed to a substantial upswing of the country's socio-economic development level over the last decades. Oman's non-oil economy, however, still relies heavily on a steady inflow of oil export proceeds since public expenditure is an important catalyst of economic activity in most non-oil sectors. In addition, a high importance of public oil revenues is evident on the Omani labour market where the public sector (public administration & defence, public education services, public health services) has emerged as the main employer of the national workforce similar to the employment patterns in other GCC countries.

Continued increases in the public wage bill are also a major cause for the substantial rise of public expenditure levels since the 1970s (section 5.2). As can be seen from table 5.1, total public expenditure (in constant prices) grew by an annual average of 7.2% between the years 1979-2013. In addition to the public wage bill, overall spending levels were elevated by large-scale public investments in the country's infrastructure over the last decades. During the years of the second oil price boom (2002-2013), public infrastructure expenditure increasingly comprised investments which aimed at facilitating economic growth of different non-oil sectors (e.g. build-up of special economic zones, wholesale ports and gas supply networks for energy-intensive industries).

The strong increase of non-oil GDP levels over the last decades was driven by an upswing of economic activity in various industry and service sectors (section 5.3). Here, the largest growth contributions fall upon government services (public administration & defence, public education services, public health services), wholesale & retail trade and manufacturing. While private sector companies figure prominently in the trade and manufacturing sectors, a positive impact of public expenditure on economic growth is observable for all three sectors as the increases of gross value added were either fostered by a rising public wage bill (government services) or by large-scale public infrastructure investments (wholesale trade, manufacturing).

Furthermore, the public sector bore a substantial share of the initial investments for the build-up of production capacities in several capital-intensive manufacturing industries. These observations confirm the results of the baseline econometric analysis in chapter 3 which found a positive impact of two public expenditure categories (total expenditure, capital expenditure) on aggregate non-oil GDP growth.

Beyond high rates of aggregate non-oil GDP growth, Oman is the only country examined in this analysis which witnessed a considerable increase of the labour productivity measure non-oil GDP per worker since the late 1970s (section 5.4). Starting out on a much lower level than in Bahrain or Qatar, labour productivity in Oman converged towards the productivity levels of the two latter countries over the last decades.

The impact of public expenditure on the long-term evolution of labour productivity, however, is much more ambiguous than is the case for aggregate non-oil GDP. On the one hand, public spending can be assigned an important role in facilitating the above mentioned catch-up process of labour productivity because rising levels of government expenditure contributed to a tremendous improvement of the human and physical capital endowment levels within the Omani economy.

On the other hand, the publicly financed large expansion of public sector employment seems to have impeded sustained increases of labour productivity particularly with regard to the private sector. Adversely affected by high public sector wages for Omani nationals, private sector employment patterns have so far not undergone a structural transformation towards more skill-intensive sectors. Despite rising levels of potentially productivity enhancing spending categories such as education or health expenditures, economic growth in most private sector activities continues to rely heavily on the availability of cheap foreign labour and on high capital investments.

5.2 Public Expenditure

Public expenditure in Oman started to exert a substantial impact on economic development patterns at a much later time than in other GCC countries since Oman became an oil-exporting country only in 1967. The start of oil production in 1967 led to a strong upswing of public revenues which allowed for a massive expansion of public expenditure levels over the following decades. This, in turn, transformed the economy of Oman lastingly in several aspects.

Not least as a result of a very low economic development level back in the late 1960s, the impact of public expenditure was particularly pronounced during the 1970s and the 1980s. Here, an unprecedented increase of government expenditures on education, health and infrastructure projects until the end of the first oil boom in early 1986 contributed to a substantial improvement of the socio-economic development level as well as to the build-up of a modern day public infrastructure.

Over the course of the last decades, continued increases of public sector employment for the national workforce stand out as a main cause for rising levels of current expenditure. Furthermore, a renewed upswing of capital expenditure during the years of the second oil price boom (2002-2013) led to a substantial enlargement of the non-oil economic infrastructure (e.g. build-up of special economic zones, wholesale ports and gas supply networks for energy-intensive industries). In view of the growing importance of the public wage bill within Oman's fiscal accounts, public expenditure patterns can be seen to have increasingly resembled features of other GCC countries.

Public expenditure patterns in Oman were impacted by oil export revenues at a much later time than in other GCC countries since Oman was the last GCC country to commence the production of crude oil. While Bahrain and Qatar had already started to produce oil in the years 1934 and 1949, respectively, crude oil in commercial quantities was not discovered in Oman before the period 1962-1964. The first barrels of Omani crude oil were exported as late as July 1967 following the granting of oil concessions to Petroleum Development Oman (PDO), by then a wholly foreign-owned joint venture, and the completion of a pipeline from the newly discovered oilfield Fahud to the Mina al Fahal oil terminal near Muscat (Wells 1967; Longrigg 1968:478-479).

The inflow of oil concession payments by PDO strongly altered public finances in Oman. Government revenues, which prior to the start of oil exports depended primarily on custom duties and grants by the British government, were multiplied by 24 between the years 1967-1973 (IBRD 1972:8; IBRD 1974:35). Public revenues continued to spiral during the years of the first oil price boom (1974-1985) as a result both of strongly rising oil prices and increasing crude oil production levels. Moreover, the government's share in PDO's profits went up following the acquisition of a 60% stake in the company during the year 1974 (World Bank 1976:12).

The strong upswing of public revenues allowed for a massive expansion of public expenditure until the end of the first oil price boom in early 1986 (figure 5.1). Total public expenditure (in current prices) rose from just under OMR 2 million to OMR 1,928 million between the years 1967 and 1985. During the latter period, various categories of public spending witnessed an unprecedented increase. With regard to functional categories of public expenditure, a substantial part of increased spending levels falls upon rising government outlays for defence and security (table 5.3). The build-up of defence and security forces was particularly advanced by Sultan Qaboos after assuming power from his father, Sultan Saʿid, in a coup in

Figure 5.1: Oman - Oil Prices and Total Expenditure 1967-2013 (Index, 1967=100)

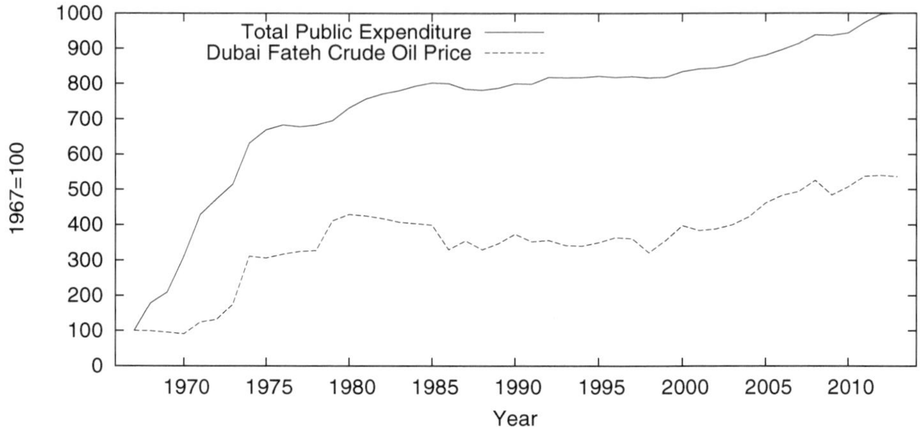

Notes: Time series in logarithms and in current prices. Due to a lack of data prior to 1970, public expenditure time series has not been deflated by CPI of Oman. *Sources:* World Bank, *GEM Commodities*; Sources table A1

July 1970. Here, Sultan Qaboos sought to strengthen the Omani armed forces considerably both in terms of manpower and of military equipment in order to defeat the popular uprising in the south-western province of Dhofar (1965-1975).

Defence and security expenditures continued to figure prominently in the public budget after the end of the Dhofar uprising in 1975. This can be related to security concerns of the Omani government resulting from its hostile relationship with neighbouring South Yemen as well as from border and maritime disputes with Saudi Arabia, the United Arab Emirates and Iran during the late 1970s and the early 1980s (Allen and Rigsbee 2000:65-78).

Facilitated by rising oil revenues, the period 1967-1985 also saw a strong increase of public education and health expenditures. In addition, a substantial part of public funds was allotted to infrastructure projects. As can be seen from table 5.3, capital expenditure accounted for 35.4% of total expenditure during the years 1976-1985 and, hence, for a much higher portion of total public expenditure than in later periods.

The continued rise of government outlays on education, health and infrastructure projects during the 1970s and the first half of the 1980s led to a strong expansion of public education and health services as well as to a rapid modernisation of the public infrastructure. This, in turn, contributed to a tremendous improvement of Oman's socio-economic development level. Adult literacy rates in Oman increased substantially between the years 1970 and 1990 from 18.5% to 54.7%. In a similar vein, life expectancy of the Omani people rose by around 17 years during the same period (table 5.2).

Oman's socio-economic development level back in the year 1970 was very low as can be seen from the different education, health and infrastructure indicators displayed in table 5.2. Here, school enrollment rates as well as the levels of adult literacy and life expectancy were far below the comparative values of Bahrain and Qatar in the same year (tables 4.2 and 6.2).

Prior to the start of oil exports in 1967, public education and health services were virtually non-existent in Oman. In the year 1967, the number of public primary schools in the entire country amounted to a mere 3 with the bulk of primary schooling provided by 5 private primary schools and 45 Koranic schools. In addition, public medical services were confined to 9 small medical centers with very limited facilities until the first public hospital in Oman opened in February 1972 (IBRD 1972:33-36). Likewise, very large parts of the country at that time lacked basic infrastructure such as paved roads as well as access to electricity and communication networks (table 5.2).

After taking power in July 1970, the new government under Sultan Qaboos launched ambitious building programmes which resulted in a much higher provisioning level of public education and health services.[1] By the year 1985, the number of public hospitals and public schools had increased to 40 and 588 (including 49 secondary schools), respectively. This was com-

[1]There is no consensus in the academic literature about the importance of the change in power for the tremendous economic and social progress experienced by Oman since the early 1970s. Most scholars ascribe the new ruler, Sultan Qaboos, a much stronger focus on socio-economic development goals than his deposed father, Sultan Saʿid as exemplified by the establishment of the first ministries for education and health in Oman (e.g. Birks and Sinclair 1987:145-156; Allen 1987:89-94; Valeri 2009:64-69, 84-87). Instead, Allen and Rigsbee (2000) downplay the importance of development policies adopted under the new government and ascribe the social progress in the 1970s and the 1980s primarily to the growing inflow of oil export proceeds. In a departure from earlier work by Allen (1987), the authors emphasise a high degree of continuity in economic and political patterns between the reigns of Sultan Saʿid and Sultan Qaboos (e.g. organisation of the armed forces, dominant economic role of traditional merchant elites).

Table 5.2: Oman - Education, Health, and Infrastructure Indicators 1950-2013

Indicator	1950	1960	1970	1980	1990	2000	2013
Gross Enrollment Primary Education (% of age cohort)	na	na	3.0	48.7	81.9	94.7	112.9
Gross Enrollment Secondary Education (% of age cohort)	na	na	0.0	8.8	42.1	79.6	93.5[2]
Gross Enrollment Tertiary Education (% of age cohort)	na	na	na	0.0	4.2	7.8	28.1[3]
Adult Literacy Rate (% of adults aged 15 and above)	na	na	18.5	36.2	54.7	71.7	86.9[4]
Public Schools (Number)	na	na	16	363	779	993	1,042
Beds in Public Hospitals[1](Number)	na	na	12	1,784	3,431	4,534	4,821
Life Expectancy at Birth (Years)	na	42.7	50.3	59.7	67.3	72.4	76.9
Telephone Lines (Number in 1,000)	na	na	1	15	107	225	351
House Connections Water (Number in 1,000)	na	na	na	20	61	116	392
House Connections Electricity (Number in 1,000)	na	na	1	53	241	438	859
Length of Paved Road Network (km)	na	na	10	2,173	4,976	8,477	32,605
Memo: Population (Persons in 1,000)	456	552	724	1,154	1,812	2,239	3,907

Sources: World Bank (2008); World Bank, *World Development Indicators*; OM/DC (1981, 1986, 1992); OM/MoNE (2001, 2012); OM/NCSI (2015); United Nations, *World Population Prospects - The 2015 Revision.*

Notes: Gross enrollment rates divide the total number of students enrolled (regardless of age) by the population in the official age cohort of the respective educational level. Due to grade repetitions and the enrollment of over-aged or under-aged students, gross enrollment rates may exceed 100%.

[1] Includes beds in public hospitals and in public medical centers.

[2] Refers to year 2012.

[3] Refers to year 2011.

[4] Refers to year 2010.

plemented by the opening of Sultan Qaboos University as the first public university in Oman during the year 1986 (OM/DC 1987:15-20, 62).

In addition, large-scale infrastructure investments led to a rapid build-up of transportation and public utility networks. Civil aviation services in Oman were strongly expanded following the opening of Seeb International Airport in 1972. Two years later, Mina Qaboos (now: Port Sultan Qaboos), Oman's first deep-water port, was inaugurated. Furthermore, total installed production capacity at government power stations increased from a mere 4 megawatts in the year 1970 to 938 megawatts in 1985. In a similar vein, the rapid build-up of a road network provided large parts of Oman for the first time with a modern day public infrastructure (Allen and Rigsbee 2000:155-158; World Bank 1988b:170).

The increase in the provisioning level of government services since the early 1970s was accompanied by a strongly growing size of the public sector. Between the years 1970 and 1985, the number of government employees in Oman's civil service went up from 1,750 to 66,648. Here, the largest shares of government manpower in 1985 were falling upon the Ministry of Education (15,050 employees) and the Ministry of Health (8,441). In contrast to later years, this increase was driven by rising employment levels not only of Omani nationals but also of non-Omani nationals. In the year 1985, non-Omani nationals accounted for 41.2% of the civil service workforce (OM/DC 1986:99-102). As will be discussed in more detail in section 5.4, the employment level of Omani nationals in the public sector has continued to rise constantly since then.

In part, the build-up of a government apparatus during the early years of Sultan Qaboos' reign was necessitated by an almost complete lack of administrative capacity prior to the coup in 1970 (Townsend 1977:64-76). However, expansion of public sector employment during recent decades has also been utilised as a means for enhancing the government's political legitimacy. By acting as an employer of last resort for a growing national labour force, the Omani government sought to alleviate pressures on the labour market and, hence, to ensure political stability (Valeri 2009:87-91). Not least as a result of these employment policies a contemporary report of the World Bank (1994:70) ascribed the public sector in Oman high levels of overstaffing as evidenced by "many unnecessary departments" as well as a "low level of efficiency" in the provision of government services.

Table 5.3: Oman - Composition & Size of Public Expenditure 1976-2013

	1976 -1985	1986 -2001	2002 -2013	1976 -2013
	(% of total public expenditure)			
Composition of Public Expenditure				
Expenditure by Economic Type:				
Current Expenditure	64.6	78.7	73.1	73.2
Capital Expenditure	35.4	21.3	26.9	26.8
Memo: Salaries & Wages (in % of total civilian expenditure)	16.8	31.8	29.7	27.2
Expenditure by Economic Function:				
Education Expenditure	5.1	10.3	11.2	9.2
Non-Education Expenditure	94.9	89.7	88.8	90.8
Health Expenditure	2.9	5.0	4.6	4.3
Non-Health Expenditure	97.1	95.0	95.4	95.7
Defence & Security Expenditure	42.5	34.0	29.1	34.7
Civilian Expenditure	57.5	66.0	70.9	65.3
	(% of non-oil GDP)			
Size of Public Expenditure				
Total Expenditure	119.4	75.0	72.9	86.1
Current Expenditure	76.5	58.9	53.6	61.8
Capital Expenditure	43.0	16.2	19.4	24.2
Education Expenditure	5.9	7.6	8.1	7.3
Health Expenditure	3.4	3.7	3.3	3.5

Sources time series: OM/DC (1981-1993); OM/MoD (1994-1996); OM/MoNE (1998-2012); OM/NCSI (2013-2015); UN Data, *National Accounts Official Country Data.*

Notes: Time series in current prices. Calculations by the author. No public information available for share of salaries & wages in public defence & security expenditure. Capital expenditure comprises defence & security expenditure on construction projects with civilian nature. All other defence & security related public spending is included in current expenditure.

While public expenditure on salaries and wages constituted only a small portion of overall civilian expenditure during the years of the first oil price boom (1974-1985), the importance of the public wage bill within Omani fiscal accounts has risen markedly since then. Following the strong decline of oil prices in early 1986, the Omani government compensated for lower public revenues primarily by scaling back capital expenditure. Instead, the wage bill of civil ministries and government agencies continued to grow, albeit at a slower pace than prior to 1986. As a result, the share of salaries and wages at overall civilian expenditures has increased to much higher levels since the mid-1980s (table 5.3).

Similarly, the rising importance of public expenditure on education and health since the end of the first oil price boom can to a large part be attributed to the high portion of salary costs within these functional categories of public expenditure. Another factor for the rise in public expenditure on education was a continued expansion of public education services as evidenced by strongly increasing numbers of students in public schools, Sultan Qaboos University and miscellaneous colleges since the mid-1980s (OM/MoNE 2001:502-505).

No public information is available on the size of the public wage bill for security and defence personnel. Yet, in view of a presumably high demand for manpower in public security and defence services it seems reasonable to assume that a substantial fraction of public expenditure on security and defence relates to salaries and wages.[2]

The strong expansion of public expenditure came to an end as a result of the oil price drop in early 1986. Here, the fall in public oil revenues put substantial pressure on the government's fiscal accounts. Even when including off-budget transfers to sovereign wealth funds such as the State General Reserve Fund or the Oman Oil Fund, the average fiscal balance of the Omani government stood at -1.2% of GDP between the years 1986 and 2001 (Treichel 1999:23; IMF 2002). As mentioned above, the government responded to lower public revenues after 1986 primarily by cutting back capital expenditure which remained on a low level until the start of the

[2] Manpower estimates for Oman's security and defence services differ considerably. Valeri (2009:87-88) puts the total size of armed forces, police and security services at 150,000 persons for the year 2007. According to CSIS (2010:15), the total active military manpower stood at 42,600 persons in the year 2010. This compares with a total of 163,982 employees in Oman's civil service and public corporations by 2010 (OM/MoNE 2012).

second oil price boom in the year 2002 (table 5.3).

Given the limited availability of public funds during the 1990s, the Omani government increasingly started to rely on private investors for financing the expansion of the country's infrastructure. Since the mid-1990s, the involvement of the private sector was particularly advanced with regard to the production of electricity. Financed by national and international private investors, the Al Manah power station commenced operations in May 1996 as the first privately owned power plant in the Middle East. This was followed by the opening of six additional private power plants until the year 2010. By year end 2010, privately owned power stations accounted for 79% of the total electricity production capacity in Oman (Ambinder et al. 2000:1042-1045; OM/UPC 2011:13; OM/OPWP 2011:18-19).

The increased reliance on the private sector in the expansion of the electricity infrastructure reflects a general realignment of economic policy in Oman since the mid-1990s. Faced with comparatively low oil export earnings during these years, the Omani government started to envisage a more important role of the private sector for spurring the long-term economic development of non-oil sectors.

A stronger focus of the government on the private sector became particularly evident in the year 1995 with the adoption of Vision 2020, a 25-year economic development strategy. Within this long-term strategy, the private sector was planned to provide 600,000 new employment opportunities for Omani nationals until the year 2020. This compares with only 100,000 planned new jobs for Omani nationals in the public sector over the same time period.

In terms of sectoral sources of economic growth, the Omani government attached a particular importance to the trade and manufacturing sectors which were both planned to account for 15% of GDP in 2020. Furthermore, the production of natural gas was singled out as an important economic sector with a targeted share of 10% at GDP by the year 2020. In contrast, the sectoral contribution of the oil sector was envisaged to decline to about 9% of GDP by 2020 (OM/MoNE 2007b:88, 115-120).

Since the mid-1990s, the Omani government adopted different economic policies for fostering the development of the private sector. In part, it pursued a policy of economic liberalisation as shown by Oman's accession to the World Trade Organisation in 2000 or by the passage of a foreign investment law in 1994 which allowed foreign investors majority ownerships at Omani companies (subject to an approval of the Ministry of Industry and Commerce). In addition, the government partially privatised some state-owned enterprises such as Oman Cement Company as well as National Bank of Oman in the year 1994 and Omantel, a telecommunications company, in 2005 (Ernst & Young 2011:12; Al-Maawali 2000:181-220; OM/Otel 2013:32).

Yet, the stronger emphasis on the private sector did not reduce the importance of public expenditure in the economic policy framework of the Omani government. This became particularly evident during the second oil price boom (2002-2013). Facilitated by rising oil revenues, this period witnessed a substantial upswing of capital expenditure levels.

A major reason for the renewed increase in capital expenditure levels were rising public investments in the production of natural gas. Furthermore, the government of Oman embarked on large infrastructure projects such as the construction of a seaport in Sohar and the building of several large-scale economic zones which were deemed to attract national and international investors from the private sector by tax exemptions and relaxed regulations (e.g. Sohar Industrial Port, Salalah Free Zone, Duqm Special Economic Zone, Al-Mazunah Free Zone, Knowledge Oasis Muscat).

In addition to public infrastructure outlays, the government actively fostered the development of the non-oil economy by forming several joint ventures with multinational companies particularly in the wholesale trade sector and in energy-intensive manufacturing industries such as the production of aluminium, petrochemicals and liquified natural gas (LNG). In this regard, substantial public sector investments in the build-up of production capacities at some of these companies (e.g. Oman LNG Company, Oman India Fertilizer Company, Sohar Refinery, Sohar Aluminium) contributed to the strong rise in capital expenditure levels (OM/MoNE 2002b:147-150; Salisbury 2012).

Despite the economic policy goal of raising the employment share of Omani nationals in the private sector, the Omani government continues to use public sector employment as an important means for enhancing its political legitimacy. This became particularly apparent with the start of the Arab Spring in the year 2011. Following mass demonstrations in other

Arab countries against domestic governments, the Omani government expanded public sector employment by around 100,000 employees during the years 2011-2013 (IMF 2013a). Over the course of the second oil price boom (2002-2013), public expenditure on salaries and wages (in current prices) grew by an annual average of 11.8% (compared to 6.8% between 1986 and 2001).

As a result of the continued increases in the public wage bill and the renewed upswing of capital expenditure, the reliance of public finances on oil export revenues has increased markedly since the early 2000s. According to estimates of the IMF (2015:110), the fiscal break-even oil price for Oman stood at 95 US-Dollar in the year 2015 and, hence, strongly above the oil price levels prevailing prior to the start of the second oil price boom (2002-2013).

5.3 Non-Oil GDP

The start of oil production in the year 1967 altered the economy of Oman lastingly. Prior to the inflow of oil export proceeds, Oman was largely a subsistence economy. Modern industry and service sectors were virtually absent. Instead, large parts of the population were engaged in small-scale agriculture and fishing. Size and structure of Oman's non-oil economy changed rapidly following the start of oil exports in 1967 as well as spiralling oil export revenues during the early years of the first oil price boom (1974-1985).

While nominal non-oil GDP had amounted to only USD 64 million in the year 1967, it rose by an annual average of 24.4% between 1967 and 1978 (World Bank 1979:34). Not least as a result of rising government outlays on infrastructure projects and public sector employment, economic growth during these years was particularly strong in construction, the trade sector and government services (public administration & defence, public education services, public health services). In contrast, the importance of agriculture and fishing within Oman's economy diminished rapidly during the 1970s due to much higher growth rates in other sectors (table 5.6).

The scale of non-oil economic activity continued to increase strongly over the following decades. Between the years 1979 and 2013, the size of Oman's non-oil economy witnessed a twelvefold increase when measured in constant 2010 US-Dollar prices (table 5.4). As will be discussed at greater length in section 5.4, Oman is the only country of this empirical analysis which saw a substantial upswing of labour productivity since the late 1970s. Here, labour productivity levels in Oman have converged towards labour productivity levels in Bahrain (tables 4.4 and 5.4).

In terms of sectoral sources, non-oil economic growth since the 1970s was broad based. As can be seen from the indicators displayed in table 5.5, the levels of economic activity within various sectors increased strongly between the years 1979 and 2013 (e.g. electricity production, air transport, financial sector). Overall, the biggest contributions to non-oil GDP growth fall upon manufacturing, government services (public administration & defence, public education services, public health services) and the trade sector.

The substantial upswing of public expenditure levels after the start of oil production fostered economic growth in various non-oil sectors. This applies particularly to government services since continued increases in the public wage bill have been the main driver of rising levels of gross value added from government services. With regard to other important non-oil sectors such as trade and manufacturing, a substantial share of economic activity falls upon private sector companies. Yet, economic activity in these two sectors benefitted substantially from large-scale public investments in seaports, industrial zones and natural gas supplies.

While the overall size of the non-oil economy rose strongly, Oman's economic structure continues to be dominated by the production of crude oil. Despite a declining sectoral share at total gross value added, the production of crude oil remained, by far, the most important economic activity in Oman in the year 2013. Here, manufacturing is the only non-oil sector which has seen a substantial rise in importance within the economic structure over the last decades (table 5.6).

The importance of the manufacturing sector within the economy of Oman increased substantially since the 1970s. Following the establishments of several new manufacturing industries in Oman, the sectoral share of manufacturing at total gross value added rose from a mere 0.8% to 9.9% between the years 1980 and 2013 (table 5.6). Public expenditure fostered economic growth in the manufacturing sector primarily in two ways. First, the public sector bore a substantial share of the initial investments for building up production capacities in several manufacturing industries. Second, manufacturing activity was facilitated by large public infrastructure investments

Table 5.4: Oman - Levels Public Expenditure, Non-Oil GDP and Labour Productivity 1979-2013
(in constant 2010 US-Dollar prices)

	1979	1990	2000	2013
Total Public Expenditure (Billion US-Dollar)	2.5	4.9	6.6	23.9
Aggregate Non-Oil GDP (Billion US-Dollar)	2.2	6.5	10.3	26.6
Non-Oil GDP per Worker (1,000 US-Dollar)	7.8	11.8	13.6	14.7

Sources: National sources (see Appendix A)
Note: US $ exchange rates from IMF (International Financial Statistics).

in the construction of economic zones or in the gas supply for energy-intensive manufacturing industries.

At the start of the 1970s, modern manufacturing industries were non-existent in Oman. Instead, manufacturing activities at that time were largely confined to local handicrafts (e.g. metal works, pottery) and to shipbuilding (dhows). The size of the manufacturing sector remained on a very low level during the first years of Sultan Qaboos' reign.

Only by the late 1970s, manufacturing witnessed an upswing of economic activity. In the following decade, rising numbers of both private and public manufacturing companies led to a substantial improvement of Oman's industrial development level. According to figures provided by World Bank (1994:79), the number of registered industrial establishments increased from a mere 10 to 3,643 between the years 1975 and 1991. Growth in the manufacturing sector during the latter period was particularly pronounced in the production of food and beverages, construction materials, furniture, fabricated metals and plastic products.

A large share of the new industrial establishments falls upon small manufacturing companies from the private sector. Here, the government of Oman sought to facilitate growth of the private manufacturing sector by various measures such as custom exemptions for imports of raw materials and factory equipment, low-interest loans by the Oman Development Bank (founded in 1977) and the building of industrial sites like the Rusayl Industrial Estate (opened in 1984).[3]

[3]World Bank (1994:81) estimates the cost of industrial subsidies in the year 1991 at 11.0% of industrial value added.

While considerably smaller in number than private companies, public manufacturing companies advanced several large-scale industrial projects since the investment needs for these projects typically exceeded the capacity of private Omani investors at that time. The first large-scale industrial venture in this regard was the (partly) state-owned Oman Flour Mills which came on stream in the year 1977. This was followed by the start of operations at Oman's first refinery in November 1982 (Oman Refinery Corporation) and at the country's first two cement plants in early 1984 (Oman Cement Company, Raysut Cement Company) (World Bank 1988b:58-61, 137-138, 1994:75-82, 97-99; Allen and Rigsbee 2000:148-152).

The importance of the manufacturing sector within Oman's economy continued to increase in the 1990s and, particularly, in the 2000s (table 5.6). Strongly rising levels of manufacturing activity during the 2000s can primarily be ascribed to the launch of several large-scale industrial plants in energy-intensive industries such as the production of liquified natural gas (LNG), petrochemicals and aluminium.

Here, gross value added of the manufacturing sector rose substantially following the start of operations at Oman LNG in the year 2000 as well as the launch of several petrochemical companies since the mid-2000s (e.g. Oman India Fertiliser Company, Octal Petrochemicals, Oman Methanol Company, Oman Polypropylene). Furthermore, the year 2008 saw the startup of Oman's first Aluminium producing plant at Sohar Aluminium Company (OM/OLNG 2010:21; OM/OOC 2012; OM/OMZEST 2013; Mirza 2009).

Compared to earlier decades, the private sector played a bigger role in establishing these new capital-intensive manufacturing industries in Oman. As discussed above, many large-scale industrial ventures of the late 1970s and the early 1980s were conducted by fully state-owned companies (e.g. Oman Refinery Corporation, Oman Cement Company).

In contrast, most manufacturing companies which commenced operations during the 2000s were incorporated either as joint ventures between public sector entities and national or international investors from the private sector (e.g. Oman LNG, Oman India Fertiliser Company, Oman Polypropylene, Sohar Aluminium Company) or, in some cases, even as joint ventures entirely owned by different investors from the private sector (e.g. Octal Petrochemicals, Oman Methanol).

Table 5.5: Oman - Indicators of Economic Activity 1979-2013

Economic Activity	1979	1990	2000	2013
Oil and Natural Gas Production:				
Crude Oil (Million metric tons/year)	15.0	34.8	50.2	46.2
Natural Gas (Billion cubic meters/year)	0.3	3.0	11.7	34.8
Manufacturing Production:				
Aluminium (1,000 metric tons/year)	0	0	0	354
Refined Oil (1,000 barrels/day)	0	65	81	184
Ammonia (1,000 metric tons/year)	0	0	0	1,100
Electricity Production:				
Gross Domestic Production (TWh)	0.6	4.5	9.1	26.2
Wholesale Trade Seaports:				
Containers Handled (1,000 TEU/year)	12	169	1,162	3,930
Air Transport:				
Airport Arrivals (1,000 Passengers/year)	214	567	1,322	4,180
Financial Sector:				
Total Assets Financial Sector (% of GDP)	30.3	36.3	53.0	73.0

Sources: International Energy Agency (IEA), *Oil Information*, various issues; IEA, *Natural Gas Information*, various issues; IEA, *Energy Statistics of Non-OECD Countries*, various issues; IEA, *Electricity Information*, various issues; US Geological Survey, *Minerals Yearbook*, various issues; Containerisation International, *Containerisation International Yearbook*, various issues; OM/DC (1981); OM/MoNE (2002); OM/NCSI (2015); Central Bank of Oman, *Quarterly Statistical Bulletin*, various issues; UN Data, *National Accounts Main Aggregates Database*

Yet, despite higher shareholdings of the private sector, public outlays continued to play an important role in fostering the build-up of new manufacturing industries in terms both of project-related investments and public infrastructure expenditure. With regard to the former, OM/MoNE (2001b:19) puts the total public investment of the years 1996-2000 for the build-up of LNG production and storage capacities at OMR 856 million (USD 2.2 billion).

Furthermore, the Omani government fostered the development of the petrochemicals industry by investing in ancillary industries. This is exemplified by the publicly financed construction of Sohar Refinery, Oman's second refinery. Apart from increasing the country's refining capacity, Sohar Refinery also served as a polypropylene supplier for the newly incorporated

Oman Polypropylene company. In addition to such project-related investments, economic growth in the manufacturing sector was facilitated by large public infrastructure expenditures on the construction of several industrial zones which provided production sites for many of the newly established manufacturing companies (e.g. Rusayl Industrial Estate, Sohar Industrial Port, Salalah Free Zone).

Beyond, manufacturing growth during the 2000s was strongly aided by public investment in the production of natural gas since energy-intensive manufacturing industries such as the production of LNG, petrochemicals and aluminium utilised natural gas heavily as a cheap energy source or as a raw material. Here, total (on budget) government expenditure on gas production amounted to OMR 4.3 billion (USD 11.1 billion) during the years 2004-2013 (OM/MoNE 2007, 2009, 2012; OM/ NCSI 2014, 2015). As a result of high investment levels, natural gas production in Oman almost tripled between the years 2000 and 2013 (table 5.5).

Furthermore, the publicly financed construction of gas pipelines to the economic zones in Sohar and Salalah helped to secure rising gas supplies to expanding manufacturing industries. During the year 2013, industrial projects accounted for 59% of domestic natural gas consumption (OM/MoNE 2002b: 147-149; OM/NCSI 2016:200).

In addition to the establishment of several new manufacturing industries, aggregate non-oil GDP growth since the 1970s was also driven by strongly rising levels of gross value added in government services (public administration & defence, public education services, public health services) and in the trade sector. The importance of government services and trade within Oman's economic structure had started to rise at a much earlier time than manufacturing. Following the build-up of manpower in government services throughout the 1970s and the completion of infrastructure projects such as Mina Qaboos (now: Port Sultan Qaboos) in 1974, both sectors had already attained a high economic importance by the year 1980 (table 5.6). Yet, concurrent with a rapidly growing size of the overall non-oil economy, the scale of economic activities in both sectors continued to expand substantially over the following decades.

This applies particularly to government services (public administration & defence, public education services, public health services) which constituted the biggest non-oil sector in 2013 as a result of a rapidly growing size of

Table 5.6: Oman - Gross Value Added by Economic Activity 1967-2013 (in % of total gross value added)

	1967	1980	1990	2000	2013
Agriculture & Fishing	34.0	2.6	3.3	2.0	1.2
Mining & Quarrying	37.1	62.3	49.8	49.2	48.2
Of which: Production Crude Oil	37.1	61.7	48.4	47.6	44.2
Of which: Product. Natural Gas	0.0	0.6	1.2	1.3	3.6
Manufacturing	0.2	0.8	3.8	5.5	9.9
Of which: Refining	0.0	na	0.4	0.5	0.2
Of which: LNG & Petrochemicals	0.0	na	na	1.7	5.8
Electricity & Water	0.0	0.8	1.5	1.0	1.1
Construction	19.7	5.7	3.1	1.9	6.0
Wholesale & Retail Trade	1.9	8.9	11.0	10.7	6.4
Hotels & Restaurants	0.0	0.3	0.6	0.7	0.7
Transport, Storage, Communication	0.7	1.9	3.2	5.9	4.6
Of which: Transport	na	1.6	2.0	4.4	3.3
Financial Sector	0.2	1.7	3.4	3.4	4.4
Real Estate	2.9	5.2	4.7	4.3	2.0
Other Business Services	0.0	1.0	0.7	1.3	1.6
Education Services	na	1.1	3.2	4.2	4.1
Of which: Public Education Serv.	na	1.1	2.9	na	3.6
Health Services	na	0.5	1.3	1.6	1.7
Of which: Public Health Services	na	0.5	1.2	na	1.5
Other Social & Personal Services	1.9	0.6	1.1	1.6	1.3
Public Administration & Defence	1.4	7.9	12.3	9.4	8.7
Memo: Government Services	na	9.5	16.4	na	13.8
Less: FISIM	na	-1.2	-3.0	-2.7	-1.9
Total Gross Value Added	100.0	100.0	100.0	100.0	100.0

Sources: IBRD (1972); OM/DC (1986, 1992); OM/MoNE (2002); OM/NCSI (2015b)

Notes: Calculations by the author. Gross value added in current producers' prices. Government services comprise public administration & defence, public education services and public health services. In the national accounts time series of the above stated sources, financial intermediation services indirectly measured (FISIM) have not been allocated as intermediate consumption to the sectors which have used these services. Instead, the total amount of FISIM has been deducted from the sum of gross value added of all sectors. Due to rounding errors sum of sectoral shares may not add up to 100%.

the public sector (table 5.6). Between the years 1980 and 2014, the number of employees in public corporations and Oman's public administration (excluding security and defence) increased from 40,340 to 232,980 (OM/DC 1992; OM/NCSI 2016).

As already discussed at greater length in section 4.3, the gross value added of government services in national accounts is typically measured by a cost of production approach due to a lack of market prices for these services. Here, public expenditure on salaries and wages can be singled out as the most important valuation parameter for gross value added by government services. For example, compensation of employees accounted on average for 85.5% of gross value added by public administration and defence services in Oman during the years 2000-2010 (OM/MoNE 2012: Table 14.8). Hence, the strong increase of the public wage bill during the sample period can be seen as the major cause for rising levels of gross value added by government services.

Similar to government services, the importance of the trade sector within Oman's economy rose strongly after the start of oil production in 1967. By the end of the 1970s, the trade sector had already attained a comparatively high sectoral share at gross value added (table 5.6). Over the following decades the trade sector continued to witness a substantial expansion of economic activity. For example, a strong upswing of wholesale trade activity between the years 1979-2013 is exemplified by a more than three-hundred-fold increase in the container throughput volume handled at Omani seaports (table 5.5).

High rates of economic growth in the retail and wholesale trade sector during the 1970s and the 1980s can to a large extent be attributed to the rising prominence of import trade within the Omani economy. While non-oil exports remained on a rather modest level, imports both of consumer and capital goods surged particularly during the years of the first oil price boom (1974-1985). Here, the strong growth of merchandise imports was propelled primarily by a rising affluence of Omani citizens, large public infrastructure development programmes, low foreign trade barriers as well as a small domestic industrial base at that time.

The increasing importance of the import trade sector during the 1970s and the 1980s is depicted by domestic private sector credit data from World Bank (1994:91) according to which 24.3% of total commercial bank credit by year end 1991 related to import trade companies. Similar to the years of the first oil price boom (1974-1985), merchandise imports increased considerably during the second oil price boom (2002-2013). The latter period also witnessed rising exports of the above mentioned energy-intensive manufacturing industries (LNG, petrochemicals, aluminium), which, however, remained on a much lower level than imported goods (World Bank 1977:40-41, 1988b:112-116; OM/NCSI 2013).

The distribution and warehousing of import products in Oman continues to be dominated since the 1970s by a few traditional merchant families which have evolved over time into large conglomerates with a wide range of business activities (e.g. Khimji Ramdas, Suhail Bahwan Group, Omar Zawawi Establishment). These private sector trading companies benefitted strongly from the legal framework in Oman such as the Agency Law of 1977 which granted exclusive distribution rights for imports to local merchants. From a political economy perspective, the granting of import monopolies can be considered an important tool of the government of Sultan Qaboos for ensuring political support among traditional merchant families over the last decades (Allen and Rigsbee 2000:113-120; Valeri 2009:103-107).

In line with growing trade volumes, the scale of seaport operations in Oman increased strongly over the last decades. Container handling capacities at Port Sultan Qaboos, Oman's main import hub, were expanded considerably during the 1980s and the 1990s. In addition, large-scale seaports in Salalah and in Sohar commenced operations in the years 1997 and 2004, respectively. Here, particularly the port of Salalah saw strongly rising levels of container throughput in the 2000s as a result of the port's important role in transshipment trade.

Operations at Omani seaports have typically been managed by public-private ventures. Port Services Corporation, operator of Port Sultan Qaboos, was founded 1976 as a joint venture between the government of Oman (shareholding: 35%) and three local private sector businesses (Bahwan, Zawawi, Zubair). During later years, the government of Oman increasingly relied on multinational companies for founding port operators. For example, the biggest shareholders of the publicly listed Salalah Port Services Company are the Ministry of Finance in Oman (20%) and APM Terminals (30%), a global port operator. Likewise, Sohar Industrial Port Company is a joint venture between the government of Oman (50%) and the Port of Rotterdam Authority (50%) (Fossey 2010; Allen and Rigsbee 2000:156;

Salisbury 2012).

Despite the important role of the private sector, it seems reasonable to ascribe public expenditure a positive impact on economic growth in the trade sector. For one, public expenditure in Oman appears as an important determinant of the gross value added by import trade businesses. In view of the high import propensity of the Omani economy, rising government outlays on infrastructure projects and public sector wages particularly during the years of the two oil price booms can be seen as a major cause for increasing levels of imports both of capital and consumer goods. Furthermore, rising trading activities were facilitated by a publicly funded expansion of the seaport infrastructure.

Similar to import trade volumes, construction activity in Oman resembled public expenditure patterns over the last decades. Here, the importance of the construction sector within Oman's economy typically increased during periods of high capital expenditure levels (tables 5.3 and 5.6). While construction activity in Oman was also fostered by several large-scale private sector projects particularly in the tourism sector during the 2000s, one can reasonably ascribe rising public infrastructure outlays during the years of the two oil price booms a positive impact on economic growth in the construction sector.

5.4 Labour Productivity

Labour productivity in Oman improved considerably over the last decades. Between the years 1979 and 2013, the labour productivity measure non-oil GDP per worker grew by an annual average of 2.2% (table 5.1). While labour productivity levels in Oman increased at a much lower rate than aggregate non-oil GDP (8.3%) and total public expenditure (7.2%), Oman stands out as the only country of this empirical analysis which has seen a substantial improvement of labour productivity since the late 1970s.

The differing evolution of labour productivity in Oman can to a large extent be understood as a catch-up process to the development levels and the economic structures of other oil-producing countries on the Arabian peninsula. Labour productivity in Oman started out on a significantly lower level than in Bahrain, but converged to the latter over the course of the last decades (tables 4.4 and 5.4). Since Oman became an oil exporter only in the year 1967, the impact of new gained oil wealth on several factors of

Figure 5.2: Oman - Labour Productivity, Aggregate Non-Oil GDP and Labour Force 1979-2013
(Index, 1979=100)

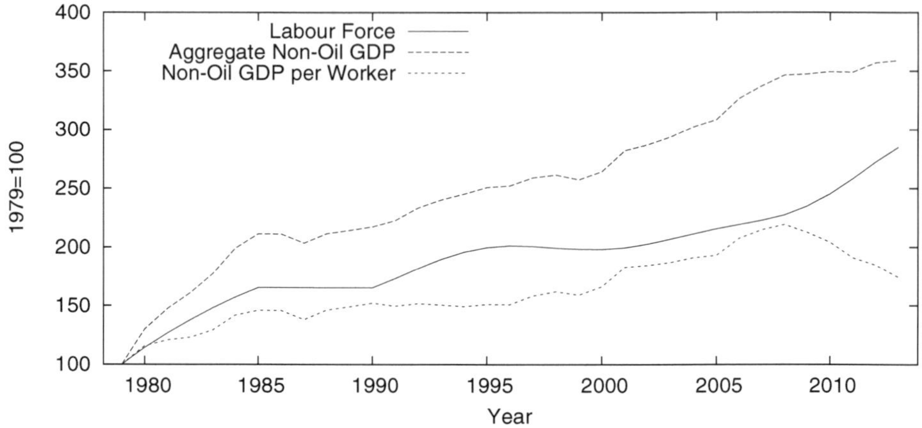

Notes: Time series in logarithms. Non-Oil GDP in constant prices.
Sources: Appendix A.

labour productivity (e.g. educational level and health status population, capital intensity economy, sectoral structure labour market) started to unfold at a much later time than in other GCC countries.

Not least as a result of Oman's comparatively low development stage at the end of the 1970s, labour productivity levels stood out to gain from strongly rising endowments of human and physical capital over the following decades. Furthermore, labour productivity levels in Oman benefitted from a strongly declining share of employees engaged in low productivity sectors such as small-scale agriculture. Instead, the public sector has emerged as the main employer for the national labour force along the lines of other GCC countries. Not least because gross value added by public sector activities in national accounts is measured by a cost of production approach, this sectoral shift in employment patterns led to an upswing of the labour productivity measure non-oil GDP per worker.

The impact of public expenditure on the evolution of labour productivity in Oman is ambiguous. On the one hand, a strong increase in public education and health services, high public investments in the economy's capital stock as well as the publicly financed shift in employment from small-scale agriculture to the public sector contributed to rising labour productivity levels particularly during the 1970s and the 1980s.

On the other hand, the strong expansion of the public sector wage bill seems to have impeded a structural transformation of private sector employment patterns towards more skill-intensive industries and services. Instead, most private sector non-oil economic activities continue to rely either on the availability of cheap foreign labour (construction, wholesale trade, household services) or on high capital investments (LNG and petrochemicals production).

Labour productivity in Oman developed in an uneven way between the years 1979 and 2013. As shown in figure 5.2, the labour productivity measure non-oil GDP per worker increased considerably during the later years of the first oil price boom (1979-1985) while remaining stagnant over the following decade (1986-1996). In the year 1997, labour productivity resumed an upward trend which lasted until the year 2007. This was followed by a marked decline of labour productivity levels during the period 2008-2013.

In the following, this analysis seeks to identify factors which contributed to the overall improvement of labour productivity levels in Oman since the late 1970s. In general, rising endowments of physical and human capital appear as important determinants of labour productivity developments in Oman even though quantifying the impact of both factors is impeded by a lack of detailed data.

As discussed in section 3.3, public available data in the GCC countries does not allow for a (reliable) calculation of multi factor productivity measures (e.g. growth accounting analysis) but only of single factor productivity measures such as labour productivity. While being less susceptible to measurement errors in the time series of factor inputs than multi factor productivity measures, single factor productivity measures such as non-oil GDP per worker do not provide insights into the relative importance of different potential sources of labour productivity growth. For example, rising levels of non-oil GDP output per worker might both be related to a higher human capital endowment and, as a result, a higher productivity of the factor input labour or to increases in other factor inputs such as the country's capital stock.

Despite the lack of multi factor productivity measures, a positive impact of both the physical capital stock and the human capital endowment on

Table 5.7: Oman - Average Annual Growth Rates Capital Intensity and Labour Productivity 1979-2013

(in per cent)

	1979–1985	1986–1996	1997–2007	2008–2013
Change Capital Stock per Worker	4.7	1.3	6.3	0.1
Change Non-Oil GDP per Worker	7.1	0.4	6.0	-6.5
Memo: Level GFCF (% of GDP)	23.8	16.0	22.1	28.5

Sources: Appendix A; UN Data, *National Accounts Official Country Data.*
Notes: Capital intensity is defined as capital stock per worker. The aggregate capital stock has been estimated by drawing on the perpetual inventory method as laid out by Nehru and Dhareshwar (1993:41). In this approach, the capital stock in period t, K_t, depends on the initial stock of capital, K_0, and the sum of subsequent investments in the capital stock, $\sum_{i=0}^{t-1} I_{t-i}$, which both depreciate by an annual rate of δ: $K_t = (1-\delta)^t K_0 + \sum_{i=0}^{t-1} I_{t-i}(1-\delta)^i$. In line with Nehru and Dhareshwar (1993) the annual rate of depreciation, δ, was set to 4%. Annual investments in the capital stock are proxied by gross fixed capital formation (at constant prices). Given Oman's very low economic development level in the early 1970s, the gross fixed capital formation (GFCF) figure for the year 1970 was deemed a reasonable estimate for the initial stock of capital.

labour productivity levels in Oman is suggested by the development patterns of these factors over the last decades. Here, the important role of physical capital for the evolution of labour productivity is indicated by an apparent link between the growth rates of labour productivity and capital intensity (stock of physical capital per worker).

As shown in table 5.7, the largest increases of the labour productivity measure non-oil GDP per worker typically fall upon periods of strongly rising capital intensity levels (1979-1985, 1997-2007). Instead, the much slower increases of capital intensity levels during the periods 1986-1996 and 2008-2013 were accompanied by a stagnation or even declines of labour productivity levels.[4]

In addition to high public infrastructure investments during the two oil

[4]The period 2008-2013 witnessed comparatively high rates of investment as can be seen from table 5.7. These years, however, also saw a strong increase in employment levels (figure 5.2). A large fraction of this employment growth falls upon non-oil sectors with low levels of labour productivity (e.g. construction) which, in turn, lowered average labour productivity levels across the non-oil economy of Oman.

price booms, a positive impact of an increasing capital stock on non-oil GDP output levels per worker appears particularly likely for capital-intensive industries. In this regard, the above discussed strong increase of gross value added in Oman's manufacturing sector since the 1970s stands out (section 5.3). Here, high (public and private) investments in the build-up of production capacity in new manufacturing industries during the first half of the 1980s (e.g. cement production) and during the 2000s (e.g. LNG, petrochemicals, aluminium) appear as major causes for rising manufacturing output levels per worker during these periods.

Beyond physical capital, labour productivity development patterns are likely to have benefitted from a tremendous increase of Oman's human capital endowment. Here, both the educational level and the health status of Oman's population improved considerably over the last decades. Various socio-economic indicators in Oman such as school enrollment rates, adult literacy rates or life expectancy levels started out on much lower levels than in Bahrain or Qatar, but converged to the latter between the years 1980 and 2013 (tables 4.2, 5.2 and 6.2). In view of the comparatively large improvement of Oman's socio-economic development level, it seems very plausible to assume a rising productivity of Oman's (national) labour force since the 1970s.

Concurrent with a considerable improvement of socio-economic conditions, Oman witnessed a structural transformation of employment patterns since the 1970s. While traditional economic activities such as agriculture and fishing still accounted for a substantial share of employment by the late 1970s, their relative importance on the Omani labour market was dwarfed over the following decades by strongly rising employment levels in various industry and service sectors.

Between the years 1978 and 2010, the overall level of employment increased from 0.2 to 1.1 million employees (table 5.8). This strong growth was accompanied by an increased reliance on foreign workers particularly in sectors like construction and household services. Instead, the public sector in Oman has emerged as the main employer for the national workforce during this time period. In view of an increasing segmentation between the national and the non-national workforce, the labour market in Oman has started to resemble characteristics of labour markets in other GCC countries.

Table 5.8: Oman - Overview Employment 1975-2010

	1975	1978	1993	2003	2010
Number of Employees (in 1,000):					
Total Employees	209.0	241.0	682.6	736.6	1,099.2
Omani Employees	137.0	141.0	251.4	312.4	447.0
Non-Omani Employees	72.0	100.0	431.3	424.2	652.2
Share at Total Employment (%):					
Omani Employees	65.6	58.5	36.8	42.4	40.7
Non-Omani Employees	34.4	41.5	63.2	57.6	59.3

Sources: World Bank (1979:4); OM/MoD (1994b); OM/MoNE (2004); OM/NCSI (2013c).
Notes: Due to rounding errors numbers of Omani and non-Omani employees may not add up to the number of total employees. In contrast to the labour force data sources mentioned in table A5, employment data in this table does not include unemployed persons.

The analysis of labour market developments in Oman is complicated by a scarcity of comprehensive employment data. Annual figures on Omani and non-Omani employment levels are publicly available from official publications such as the Statistical Year Book (SYB). However, SYB overall employment figures exclude employment in public security and defence services. Furthermore, the SYB publications do not contain detailed breakdowns of Omani employment in the private sector.

Sectoral employment breakdowns in official census year publications are more comprehensive but cover the time period of this analysis only partially since Oman's first ever census was conducted as late as 1993. Since SYB employment estimates exhibit substantial discrepancies to the respective figures in census year publications, they have not been utilised for the years prior to 1993. Instead, census year results (1993, 2003, 2010) in tables 5.8 - 5.10 are complemented with employment estimates by World Bank (1979:4) for the years 1975 and 1978.

Despite a rather limited scope, available employment data clearly highlight the structural changes on the labour market in Oman since the 1970s. This applies particularly to the marked sectoral shift in the employment of Omani nationals from agriculture and fishing towards the public sector. While 56.7% of Omani employment in the year 1978 fell upon agriculture and fishing, the latter sector's employment share dropped to 9.3% in the year 1993 and to a mere 2.5% by 2010 (table 5.10). Instead, government services (public administration & defence, public education services, public health services) quickly became the main provider of employment for Omani nationals. Here, the combined sectoral share of government public administration & defence and education & health services increased from 19.5% to around 65% between the years 1978 and 1993.[5]

Over the following decades, the employment level of Omani nationals continued to expand in public administration & defence and to a lesser extent, in the education and health sectors. The expansion of employment in public administration & defence was particularly pronounced during the years of the two oil price booms (1974-1985, 2002-2013) as can be seen from the large increases of Omani employees between the years 1978-1993 and 2003-2010. Overall, government services (public administration & defence, public education services, public health services) account for around 70% of the total increase in Omani employment levels between the years 1978 and 2010 (tables 5.8-5.10).

In addition to strongly rising numbers of Omani employees in the public sector, the labour market in Oman has also been transformed by the rapid growth of non-Omani employment levels since the 1970s. Between the years 1978 and 2010, the number of non-Omani employees rose from an estimated 100,000 to 652,222.

The expansion of non-Omani employment followed a markedly different pattern than the employment growth of Omani nationals. First, growth of non-Omani employment levels was much less steady and typically took place during periods of high oil price levels such as 1974-1985 and 2002-2013 (table 5.8). Second, employment growth of non-Omani nationals was not driven by the public sector but, instead, by private sector activities.

With the exception of the financial sector as well as the transport, storage and communications sectors, non-Omani employees outnumbered Omani employees in every private sector economic activity in the census year 2010. The reliance on non-national employees is particularly distinct in labour-

[5]Breakdowns of employment levels in the education and health sectors into public sector and private sector employees are not publicly available for the census years 1993, 2003 and 2010. However, since a large share of gross value added by education and health services accrues to the public sector (table 5.6), it seems reasonable to assume that a large fraction of employment in education and health services relates to the public sector.

Table 5.9: Oman - Employment by Sector and Nationality 1975-2010 (Number of Employees in 1,000)

	1975	1978	1993	2003	2010
Construction	na	na	108.2	118.3	280.5
Of which: Omani	na	na	4.8	10.1	19.6
Of which: Non-Omani	na	na	103.3	108.1	260.9
Public Administration & Defence[1]	30.0	43.0	165.6	162.7	207.8
Of which: Omani	24.0	27.5	139.9	144.7	190.4
Of which: Non-Omani	6.0	15.5	25.7	18.0	17.4
Wholesale and Retail Trade	na	na	89.6	86.8	120.0
Of which: Omani	na	na	11.9	21.7	44.0
Of which: Non-Omani	na	na	77.7	65.2	76.0
Household Services	na	na	33.5	51.8	82.1
Of which: Omani	na	na	0.2	0.5	1.7
Of which: Non-Omani	na	na	33.3	51.3	80.4
Education & Health Services[2]	na	na	53.3	75.9	78.3
Of which: Omani	na	na	25.0	52.2	57.4
Of which: Non-Omani	na	na	28.2	23.7	20.8
Manufacturing[3]	na	na	60.4	59.5	61.7
Of which: Omani	na	na	4.6	13.8	16.8
Of which: Non-Omani	na	na	55.9	45.7	44.9
Agriculture & Fishing	86.0	82.0	64.2	58.1	55.3
Of which: Omani	85.0	80.0	23.3	14.2	11.1
Of which: Non-Omani	1.0	2.0	40.8	43.9	44.2
Transport, Storage, Communication	na	na	24.8	27.7	46.5
Of which: Omani	na	na	11.8	17.2	32.3
Of which: Non-Omani	na	na	13.0	10.5	14.2
Other Sectors[4]	93.0	116.0	83.1	95.8	167.1
Of which: Omani	28.0	33.5	29.9	38.0	73.6
Of which: Non-Omani	65.0	82.5	53.2	57.8	93.4

Sources: World Bank (1979:4); OM/MoD (1994b); OM/MoNE (2004); OM/NCSI (2013c).

Note: Due to rounding errors numbers of Omani and non-Omani employees may not add up to the number of total employees.

[1] Figures for the years 1975 and 1978 refer to all public sector activities (e.g. public education services). [2] Includes employment in public and private sectors.

[3] Manufacturing census figures are likely to exclude employees in gas-based manufacturing industries such as LNG and petrochemicals. Instead, these employees seem to be included in the oil and gas & quarrying sectors. Employment in the latter sectors rose by around 25,000 employees between the census years 2003 and 2010. [4] Due to the lack of more detailed data employment figures of "Other Sectors" in the years 1975 and 1978 comprise all economic activities outside agriculture & fishing and outside the public sector.

intensive economic activities such as construction or household services. In a similar vein, the agriculture & fishing sector saw a partial substitution of Omani employees by non-Omani employees between 1978 and 2010 (table 5.9).

Since the mid-1990s, the Omani government has tried to reverse the increasing segmentation of the Omani labour market by fostering the participation of Omani nationals in the private sector. A much stronger emphasis on the *Omanisation* of labour in the private sector became particularly apparent in the year 1995 with the publication of Vision 2020, a 25 year economic development strategy. Here, the private sector was singled out as the main source of employment growth and was planned to employ an additional 600,000 Omani nationals by the year 2020. In contrast, Vision 2020 envisaged an increase of only 100,000 Omani employees in the public sector over the same time period (OM/MoNE 2007b:88).

The Omani government adopted various measures for increasing the participation of Omani nationals in the private sector. In October 1994, the government announced target quotas for the employment of Omani nationals in several private sector economic activities which, however, were not fulfilled in most economic sectors. Furthermore, a levy on foreign employees was enacted in the year 1995 in order to increase the competitiveness of Omani employees in the private sector labour market.[6] The proceeds of this levy, in turn, were utilised for funding different vocational training schemes for Omani nationals such as the Sanad self-employment programme. Launched in the year 2003 by the Ministry of Manpower, the Sanad programme aims to increase the number of Omani small businesses by providing state-funded training and subsidised loans (Valeri 2009:201-213).

So far, the results of these Omanisation policies have been mixed. While participation levels of Omani nationals increased notably in some private sector economic activities since the mid-1990s, overall Omani employment growth in the private sector has been far from sufficient to accommodate the needs of a growing national labour force.

The largest increases of Omani private sector employment during the period

[6] In the year 2010, employers were obliged to contribute 200 Omani Rials for every non-Omani employee once every two years. In proportion to the minimum wage for unskilled Omani employees at that time, this corresponds to a levy of 6.0% on foreign labour (Ernst & Young 2011:19).

Table 5.10: Oman - Sectoral Employment Shares Omani and Non-Omani Nationals 1975-2010

	1975	1978	1993	2003	2010
	(in % of Omani Employees)				
Omani Nationals:					
Main Sectors:					
Public Administration & Defence[1]	17.5	19.5	55.7	46.3	42.6
Education & Health[2]	na	na	10.0	16.7	12.9
Retail and Wholesale Trade	na	na	4.7	6.9	9.8
Transport, Storage, Communications	na	na	4.7	5.5	7.2
Oil and Gas & Quarrying	na	na	3.3	3.8	5.5
Memo:					
Agriculture & Fishing	62.0	56.7	9.3	4.5	2.5
Manufacturing	na	na	1.8	4.4	3.8
	(in % of Non-Omani Employees)				
Non-Omani Nationals:					
Main Sectors:					
Construction	na	na	24.0	25.5	40.0
Household Services	na	na	7.7	12.1	12.3
Retail and Wholesale Trade	na	na	18.0	15.4	11.7
Manufacturing	na	na	13.0	10.8	6.9
Agriculture & Fishing	1.4	2.0	9.5	10.4	6.8
Memo:					
Public Administration & Defence[1]	8.3	15.5	6.0	4.3	2.7
Education & Health[2]	na	na	6.5	5.6	3.2

Sources: World Bank (1979:4); OM/MoD (1994b); OM/MoNE (2004); OM/NCSI (2013c).

Note: Calculations by the author.

[1] Figures for the years 1975 and 1978 refer to all public sector activities (e.g. public education services). [2] Includes employment in public and private sectors.

1993-2010 fall upon the wholesale and retail trade as well as the transport, storage and communication sectors. Here, the Sanad programme can be ascribed an important role in raising the Omani (self-)employment level in small-scale retail trade. By year-end 2009, 12,750 beneficiaries of the Sanad programme (46.6% of total beneficiaries) had set up a small business in grocery or vegetables trade (OM/MoNE 2011b:92).

In addition, Omani employees figure prominently in the financial sector. According to figures in OM/NCSI (2013c), the share of Omani nationals at total financial sector employment stood at a high 81.2% in 2010. However, since the financial sector accounts only for 1.3% of total employment, this high degree of Omanisation did not lead to a substantial relief of pressure on the national labour market.

Instead, public administration & defence continued to be the main source of new jobs for Omani nationals between the census years 1993 and 2010. Even though public administration & defence witnessed a slightly decreasing employment share since 1993, it remained by far the most important employment sector for Omani nationals in the year 2010 (tables 5.9-5.10).

The obstacles for a greater participation of Oman's national workforce in the private sector are similar to the ones discussed for Bahrain in section 4.4. A poll conducted by Al-Lamki (1998) reveals a high preference among Omani students for public sector employment. Here, compensation and benefits in the public sector were perceived to be much higher than in the private sector.

Furthermore, the competitiveness of Omani employees on the private sector labour market is impaired by a substantial wage gap between national and foreign employees particularly with regard to labour-intensive economic activities (e.g. construction, household services). This wage gap, in turn, is caused by dual labour market structures such as a minimum wage which applies only to Omani employees.

At times, Omanisation policies were also thwarted by other political objectives of the Omani government. In order to enhance the attractiveness of newly built special economic zones for national and international investors during the 2000s, employment quotas for Omani nationals in these economic zones were typically set to comparatively low levels. For example, the minimum employment quota in the Sohar Industrial Port, Oman's main economic zone, stands at only 15% whereas the applicable quota for industrial ventures outside of economic zones is 35% (OM/SPF 2013; OM/MoM 2014).

In addition, public sector employment also serves as an important tool for enhancing the government's political legitimacy. This became particularly apparent with the start of the Arab Spring in the year 2011. Following mass demonstrations in other Arab countries against domestic governments the Omani government expanded public sector employment by around 100,000 employees during the years 2011-2013. Beyond, the minimum wage for Omani employees in the private sector was raised in two steps from 140 to 325 Omani Rials (IMF 2013a). Both measures have strongly reinforced the segmentation of the Omani labour market.

Overall, the above analysis suggests that public expenditure has exerted a considerable impact on several factors of labour productivity (e.g. educational level and health status population, capital intensity economy, sectoral structure labour market), albeit in opposing directions. On the positive side, labour productivity in Oman benefitted from a tremendous increase of human and physical capital endowment levels. This, in turn, was facilitated by a strong expansion of public expenditure particularly during the 1970s and the 1980s. In this regard, one can point to strongly rising levels of public education and health services as well as to substantial public investments in the economy's infrastructure or in the build-up of production capacities in capital-intensive industries like manufacturing.

Beyond, the level of the labour productivity measure non-oil GDP per worker was elevated by a publicly financed sectoral shift in employment from small-scale agriculture to the public sector. Here, the average gross value added per worker in government services is typically at a much higher level than in traditional economic activities such as small-scale agriculture because international standards for the compilation of national accounts data such as the 1993 SNA or the 2008 SNA recommend a cost of production approach for measuring the gross value added by government services (European Commission et al. 1993:164-165, 2009:110-111).

However, the strong expansion of the public sector wage bill can also be singled out as a major impediment for sustained increases of labour productivity. This applies particularly to the private sector since high public sector wages diminished the attractiveness of private sector employment for the national labour force. So far, rising levels of potentially productivity enhancing public spending categories such as education, health or infrastructure expenditures have not led to a structural transformation of private sector employment patterns towards more skill-intensive industries or services.

Instead, the largest increases of private sector employment over the course of the last decades fall upon low value added sectors such as construction, wholesale trade or household services. In addition, economic growth in sectors like manufacturing was not primarily driven by a rising productivity of the factor input labour but, instead, by large-scale investments in the build-up of production capacities in capital-intensive industries such as LNG or petrochemicals production.

Unfortunately, the impact of public expenditure on labour productivity could not be examined for Oman through the cointegration and causality analysis in chapter 3 because the labour productivity indicator non-oil GDP per worker was found to be integrated of order two both when examined in constant and in current prices and, hence, not to be eligible for cointegration analysis. In view of the above described conflicting impact of public expenditure on labour productivity patterns in Oman, however, one might argue that public expenditure fostered increases of labour productivity in a much less distinct way than is the case for aggregate non-oil GDP.

Chapter 6

Qatar: Big Push Non-Oil Investment by Qatar Inc.

6.1 Overview

Public expenditure has been an important source of non-oil economic growth in Qatar over the last decades. High levels of public investment in the country's infrastructure and in the business expansions of several state-owned companies contributed to a strongly growing size of Qatar's non-oil economy. The large increases of total public expenditure and aggregate non-oil GDP levels, however, were not accompanied by sustained increases of labour productivity within Qatar's non-oil economy (table 6.1). Instead, public expenditure facilitated non-oil economic growth primarily by fostering an accumulation of the factor inputs physical capital and labour.

Similar to other GCC countries, public expenditure patterns in Qatar are largely determined by the size of oil and gas export proceeds since the latter constitute the main source of public revenues. As a result, a growth-enhancing impact of public expenditure typically emerged during periods of rising oil and gas revenues.

Public expenditure only started to play an important role in the Qatari economy after the launch of oil production in the year 1949. The ensuing rise in public oil revenues provided the Qatari government with sizeable funds for fostering the first time build-up of public education and health services and of a modern public infrastructure over the 1950s and 1960s.

A positive impact of public expenditure on non-oil GDP levels is par-

Table 6.1: Qatar - Average Annual Growth Rates Public Expenditure, Non-Oil GDP and Labour Productivity 1980-2013

(in per cent)

	1980–1985	1986–2001	2002–2013	1980–2013
Total Public Expenditure	-0.7	0.8	16.9	5.9
Aggregate Non-Oil GDP	5.3	2.6	17.0	8.0
Non-Oil GDP per Worker	-4.9	-1.4	2.7	-0.6
Memo: Labour Force	10.7	4.1	13.9	8.6

Sources: Appendix A.
Notes: Calculations by the author. Average annual growth rates refer to compound annual growth rates for the respective time periods. Labour productivity is proxied by non-oil GDP per worker. Non-oil GDP and public expenditure time series in constant 2005 Qatari Rial prices. Due to a lack of CPI data prior to 1979, growth rates for time series in constant prices are only available since the year 1980.

ticularly apparent for the years of the two oil price booms (1974-1985, 2002-2013) as both the Qatari government and several state-owned companies embarked on various large-scale investment projects. Here, economic growth in several non-oil sectors during these years was strongly aided by large public infrastructure investments such as the enlargement of domestic electricity production capacity, the construction of industrial cities as well as the expansion of wholesale seaports and airports.

In addition, several (partly) state-owned companies in various non-oil sectors invested heavily in a rapid business expansion (e.g. Qatar Steel Company, Qatar Fertilizer Company, Qatari Diar, Qatar Airways). These large-scale investments, in turn, were partially funded by substantial off-budget transfers from the Qatari government, most notably, in the 2000s.

In addition to rising world market prices for oil and gas, Qatar's fiscal stance during the 2000s was bolstered by a strong expansion of liquified natural gas (LNG) export volumes since the mid-1990s. This enabled the Qatari government to increase capital expenditure levels during the 2000s by much higher rates than Bahrain or Oman. The comparatively high level of publicly financed investment projects during the 2000s appears as an important factor why the empirical evidence for a positive impact of different public expenditure categories on non-oil GDP levels in Qatar was found to be very strong within the baseline econometric analysis in chapter 3.

As will be discussed at greater length in section 6.2, overall public expenditure levels have risen substantially since the late 1940s with the largest increases falling upon the 1970s and the 2000s. The strong upswing of public expenditure altered the Qatari economy lastingly in several aspects. Rising government outlays on public infrastructure and on public education and health services led to a substantial improvement of Qatar's socio-economic development level. Furthermore, Qatar's labour market was strongly impacted by continued increases in the public wage bill. Following a rapid expansion of employment since the mid-1970s, the public sector has emerged as the country's main employer for Qatari nationals.

In a similar vein as public expenditure, non-oil GDP growth accelerated during periods of high oil price levels (section 6.3). Public expenditure fostered non-oil economic activity in these years primarily through an accumulation of the factor inputs physical capital and labour. A multitude of investment projects by the Qatari government and state-owned companies raised gross value added levels of several important non-oil sectors markedly (e.g. manufacturing, trade, construction, real estate).

In addition to raising the economy's stock of physical capital, these investment booms gave rise to large increases of foreign labour. Qatar's total labour force grew by an annual average of 13.9% during the years 2002-2013 (table 6.1). Yet, while public expenditure increased the size of various non-oil sectors, high levels of public investment on human and physical capital did not raise productivity levels of Qatar's labour force lastingly.

Despite an improving socio-economic development level, Qatar has witnessed an overall decline of the labour productivity measure non-oil GDP per worker since the late 1970s (section 6.4). The lack of sustained improvements in labour productivity can be attributed to two main reasons. First, high levels of investment exerted a growth-enhancing impact particularly on those sectors which exhibit either a high capital intensity (e.g. production of petrochemicals or steel) or a high reliance on low-skilled labour (e.g. construction, trade). As a result, investment booms in Qatar typically did not lead to a rising importance of skill-intensive economic activities but were, instead, accompanied by a strong increase of low-skilled, mostly foreign, labour.

Second, a structural change of employment patterns for Qatari nationals towards more skill-intensive economic activities is inhibited by high public sector wages for Qatari nationals. The incentives for Qatari nationals to seek employment outside the public sector are strongly diminished by a substantial wage gap between the public sector and economic activities in the private sector. With regard to the employment patterns of the national workforce, the Qatari labour market continues to resemble strong features of a rentier economy.

6.2 Public Expenditure

Public expenditure patterns in Qatar over the last decades were strongly shaped by the size of public oil and gas export proceeds. The start of oil production in the year 1949 gave rise to a much more prominent role of public expenditure within the Qatari economy as growing oil export revenues financed the first time build-up of public education and health services during the 1950s and the 1960s.

Over the following decades, public expenditure levels were closely linked to oil price developments. During the years of the two oil price booms (1974-1985, 2002-2013), rising public export revenues facilitated an upswing of the public wage bill and the launch of several large-scale public investment projects. High levels of investment particularly during the 2000s fostered not only a modernisation of the public infrastructure but also business expansions of several state-owned companies. The strong increase of public expenditure during the 2000s, in turn, can partly be ascribed to the fact that public finances at that time were bolstered by an upswing in liquified natural gas (LNG) export volumes.

In general, the analysis of public expenditure patterns in Qatar is complicated by a lack of detailed data. Breakdowns of public expenditure by civilian ministries and government agencies are published in the official "Annual Statistical Abstract". Yet, total expenditures of these ministries and departments account only for around 47% of overall public spending during the sample period of the econometric analysis (1979-2013) in chapter 3. With regard to the remainder of public expenditure, very limited information is publicly available about the scope and the deployment of public spending on defence and security.[1]

[1] According to figures published in Al-Kuwari (1978:132), the allocation for the ruling family in Qatar accounted for 36% of overall public expenditure during the fiscal year

Furthermore, overall expenditure figures in Qatar contain transfers to around 40 extrabudgetary accounts of different government institutions. While budgetary transfers to these accounts are classified as current expenditure within overall public spending figures, the operations of these autonomous accounts (e.g. lending, investment) are not covered in the official public expenditure data (IMF 2011:26, 2014c).

As will be discussed below, these off-budget funds were partially utilised for financing large-scale investments by state-owned companies such as Qatar Petroleum during the 2000s. In view of the latter, capital expenditure figures in officially published breakdowns of public expenditure can be seen to understate the total investment activity of Qatar's public sector.

The economic importance of public expenditure in Qatar increased substantially after the start of oil production in late 1949. Over the following decades, crude oil extraction from the Dukhan oilfield by Petroleum Development (Qatar) Limited, an international oil company, provided the by then semi-autonomous government of Qatar with a growing inflow of oil concession payments.

This new gained oil wealth, in turn, facilitated the first time build-up of public education and health services as well as of a modern public infrastructure in Qatar. Similar to Bahrain which had become an oil producing country in the year 1934, public outlays in Qatar on education and health had already increased considerably by the start of the first oil price boom (1974-1985).

Data on public expenditure in Qatar prior to the 1970s is very fragmentary. Yet, available figures from Al-Kuwari (1978:132) show large increases of public spending following the inflow of oil concession payments since the year 1949. For example, overall public expenditure on social services (e.g. education, health) increased from a mere QAR 0.8 million in the fiscal year 1953/1954 to QAR 95.9 million in 1970/1971. This, in turn, led to a massive expansion of public education and health services in Qatar over the 1950s and the 1960s.

Prior to the start of oil exports in the year 1949, public education and health facilities were non-existent in Qatar. The first public schools for boys and girls were only established in the years 1952 and 1955, respec-

1970. No such information is available for later fiscal years.

Figure 6.1: Qatar - Oil Prices and Total Expenditure 1967-2013 (Index, 1967=100)

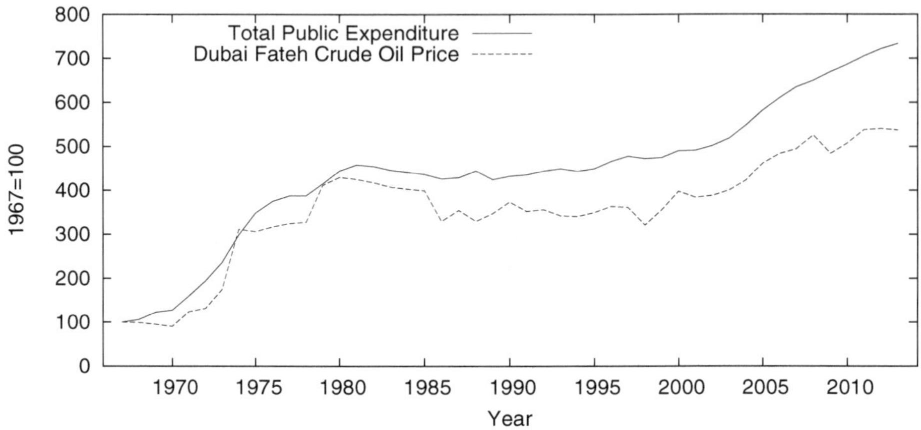

Notes: Time series in logarithms and in current prices. Due to a lack of data prior to 1979, public expenditure time series has not been deflated by CPI of Qatar.
Sources: World Bank, *GEM Commodities*; Sources table A1

tively. Yet, by the early 1970s the total number of public schools in Qatar had risen to 88 (table 6.2). Similarly, the first public hospital in Qatar opened only in 1959. In the year 1970, already three pubic hospitals were operating in Qatar (El Mallakh 1979:109-114; Crystal 1995:156).[2]

As a result of the much higher provisioning level of public health and education services, life expectancy and literacy levels of the Qatari population improved considerably. As can be seen in table 6.2, life expectancy of the Qatari population increased by around 11 years between 1960 and 1980. Furthermore, literacy levels of the Qatari population rose strongly as a result of rising school enrollment levels. While adult literacy rates are not available for Qatar prior to the year 1970, estimates cited in Crystal (1995:141) put the number of indigenous literates in Qatar at only 630 persons by the mid-1950s which corresponds to less than 2% of the total population at that time. In contrast, Qatar's adult literacy rate stood at almost 70% in 1980.

[2]Similar to other GCC countries the private sector played only a very minor role in the provision of education and health services during Qatar's early development stages. According to figures in Sadik and Snavely (1972:100-101) the number of hospital beds in non-public health facilities amounted only to 37 in the year 1970 compared to 621 beds in public hospitals.

Public expenditure levels in Qatar were strongly elevated during the years of the first oil boom (1974-1985) as can be seen from figure 6.1. This upswing in public spending was facilitated by a surge in public oil export proceeds which followed from a strong increase of world market prices for crude oil. Furthermore, Qatar's gradual takeover of oil producing companies during the years 1973-1976 led to a rising public share at oil export revenues. Between the fiscal years 1973/74 and 1984/85, public revenues (in current prices) witnessed an almost eightfold increase from QAR 1,720 million to QAR 13,610 million (El Mallakh 1979:34-35,60; QA/CSO 1988:321).

Similar to other GCC countries during this period, the upswing of public oil export proceeds led to large-scale public investments both in the infrastructure and in the industrial capacity of Qatar as well as to a strongly rising public wage bill. High capital expenditure outlays during the first oil price boom (1974-1985) contributed to a substantial expansion of the country's social and physical infrastructure.

The number of public schools and medical facilities continued to rise strongly throughout the 1970s and the 1980s (table 6.2). In addition, the year 1977 saw the foundation of Qatar University as the country's first university (QA/QU 2013). In terms of the physical infrastructure, the Qatari government invested heavily in the expansion of road and telecommunication networks as well as in the enlargement of cargo handling facilities at the country's two main wholesale ports (Doha port, Umm Said industrial port). Furthermore, production capacities of public utilities were expanded strongly. For example, domestic electricity production levels in Qatar went up by a factor of 13 during the period 1971-1986 (El Mallakh:1979:96-108; QA/CSO 1981:68, 1988:290).

Beyond modernising the public infrastructure, the Qatari government played an active role in fostering the country's industrial development during the first oil price boom. This comprised large-scale public infrastructure investments in the development of the Umm Said industrial area (now: Mesaieed Industrial City).

Furthermore, the public sector bore a substantial share of the investments for building up industrial production capacities. Here, the Qatari government set up several industrial ventures together with multinational companies such as the Qatar Iron and Steel Company (Government shareholding: 70%) or the Qatar Petrochemical Company (Government shareholding:

Table 6.2: Qatar - Education, Health, and Infrastructure Indicators 1950-2013

Indicator	1950	1960	1970	1980	1990	2000	2013
Gross Enrollment Primary Education (% of age cohort)	na	67.0	96.2	104.6	100.5	104.0	102.9[6]
Gross Enrollment Secondary Education (% of age cohort)	na	na	36.3	70.1	79.9	86.4	111.6[7]
Gross Enrollment Tertiary Education (% of age cohort)	na	na	na	10.4	21.6	21.1	14.3
Adult Literacy Rate (% of adults aged 15 and above)	na	na	58.3	69.8	77.0	na	96.7[8]
Public Schools (Number)	0	60	88[1]	141	192	220[4]	280[4]
Beds in Public Hospitals (Number)	0	na	621	713	1,075	1,346	2,223[8]
Life Expectancy at Birth (Years)	na	61.2	68.5	72.9	75.3	76.8	78.6
Telephone Lines (Number in 1,000)	na	0.6	8.1	30.6	92.1	160.2	337.8
House Connections Water (Number in 1,000)	na	na	12.7[2]	27.2	37.3[3]	53.4[5]	119.4[6]
House Connections Electricity (Number in 1,000)	na	na	na	na	46.2[3]	62.2[5]	124.7[6]
Memo: Population (Persons in 1,000)	25	47	109	224	476	593	2,101

Sources: World Bank (2008); World Bank, *World Development Indicators*; El Mallakh (1979:109-110); Crystal (1995:156); Sadik and Snavely (1972:100); QA/CSO (1981, 1982, 1987b, 1992); QA/PC (1999b, 2002); QA/MDPS (2013-2015); QA/SA (2010b); United Nations, *World Population Prospects - The 2015 Revision.*

Notes: Gross enrollment rates divide the total number of students enrolled (regardless of age) by the population in the official age cohort of the respective educational level. Due to grade repetitions and the enrollment of over-aged or under-aged students, gross enrollment rates may exceed 100%.

[1] Figure refers to year 1971.

[2] Figure refers to year 1974.

[3] Figure refers to census year 1986.

[4] Figure does not include schools set up by Qatar Foundation.

[5] Figure refers to census year 1997.

[6] Figure refers to year 2010.

[7] Figure refers to year 2011.

[8] Figure refers to year 2012.

80%) which commenced operations in the years 1978 and 1981, respectively. In addition, the production capacities of several already existing partly state-owned manufacturing companies (e.g. Qatar National Cement Company, Umm Said Refinery, Qatar Fertilizer Company) were strongly expanded during the years of the first oil price boom (UN-IDO 1980:9-11, 55-68; QA/QAPCO 2014).

Current expenditure levels during the years of the first oil price boom (1974-1985) were elevated by a rapid expansion of the public wage bill. The build-up of manpower in the public sector was accelerated considerably by the Qatari government after the year 1974 following the inflow of spiraling public oil export revenues. Between the census years 1970 and 1986, the number of employees within the public administration surged from 6,194 to 42,141 (UN-ECWA 1980; QA/CSO 1987b).

This strong increase in public sector employment can partly be ascribed to the need for enlarging the administrative capacity of a still evolving civil service. Similar to other GCC countries, an institutionalised system of government administration was only established in Qatar after the start of oil production. For example, a formal civil court was set up as late as 1949 (Al-Kuwari 1978:115).

While increasing the scope of public services, the rapid growth of Qatar's government administration over the following decades has been criticised as taking place without sufficient control. According to Sadik and Snavely (1972:158) "the rapid multiplication of new administrative units occurred without adequate efforts to coordinate them with each other or with already existing departments. This proliferation and fragmentation of governmental activities resulted in poor coordination and not infrequent duplication."

In addition, government employment policies particularly during the years of the first oil price boom (1974-1985) were often dominated by social welfare objectives and not by efficiency considerations. The latter point is exemplified by the fact that 45% of the Qataris which were employed in the country's civil service during the year 1986 had not even completed primary school (Crystal 1995:158-161; QA/CSO 1988:71).

The strong expansion of public expenditure came to an end in the early 1980s due to declining oil revenues. Here, public finances in Qatar were strained both by a downward slide in world oil prices during the first half

Table 6.3: Qatar - Composition & Size of Public Expenditure 1976-2013

	1976 -1985	1986 -2001	2002 -2013	1976 -2013
	(% of total public expenditure)			
Composition of Public Expenditure				
Expenditure by Economic Type:				
Current Expenditure	78.7	87.4	71.5	80.1
Of which: Salaries & Wages	25.1[1]	35.0	18.8	27.4[2]
Capital Expenditure	21.3	12.6	28.5	19.9
Expenditure by Economic Function:				
Education Expenditure	8.9[1]	9.8	6.2	8.4[2]
Non-Education Expenditure	91.1[1]	90.2	93.8	91.6[2]
Health Expenditure	4.7[1]	5.4	5.7	5.3[2]
Non-Health Expenditure	95.3[1]	94.6	94.3	94.7[2]
	(% of non-oil GDP)			
Size of Public Expenditure				
Total Expenditure	116.5	72.2	64.9	81.5
Current Expenditure	91.7	63.1	46.6	65.4
Capital Expenditure	24.8	9.1	18.3	16.1
Education Expenditure	9.8[1]	7.1	4.1	6.7[2]
Health Expenditure	5.2[1]	3.9	3.7	4.1[2]

Sources time series: QA/CSO (1983-1998); QA/MDPS (2012-2015); QA/QCB (1982a-2015d); QA/PC (2003, 2006, 2008); QA/SA (2010a); UN Data, *National Accounts Official Country Data.*

Notes: Time series in current prices. Calculations by the author.

[1] Figure refers to period 1978-1985.

[2] Figure refers to period 1978-2013.

of the 1980s as well as by declining levels of domestic oil production. As a result, public expenditure was scaled back during the 1980s, albeit, it continued to be on a much higher level than prior to the start of the first oil price boom in 1974 (figure 6.1).

Fiscal pressures in Qatar were further aggravated by a sharp drop in world oil prices in February 1986. Due to dwindling oil export revenues the fiscal deficit averaged 26.4% of GDP between the fiscal years 1986/87 and 1988/89 (QA/CSO 1992:366). The ensuing cutbacks in public spending were particularly pronounced with regard to capital expenditure. Between the years 1986-2001, the average share of capital expenditure at total expenditure stood only at 12.6% (table 6.3). As a result of these austerity measures, several development projects were shelved during the second half of 1980s.

Qatar's economic policy became more active again in the early 1990s as the Qatari government embarked on different industrial projects, most notably, the development of a liquified natural gas (LNG) export industry. In line with overall expenditure patterns, capital expenditure increased gradually over the 1990s before surging to much higher levels during the 2000s.

This shift in economic policy was triggered by the presence of continued public deficits in the early 1990s. As a result of the latter, the Qatari government sought to increase future public export revenues by advancing the exploitation of the North Dome gas field, the largest offshore gas field in the world. While the decision to start exploiting the North Dome gas field had already been taken by the government in the 1980s, most projects related to the extraction and liquefaction of natural gas were only implemented in the 1990s.

A stronger emphasis by the government on the development of a LNG industry during the first of half of the 1990s is exemplified by substantial public infrastructure investments which led to the opening of the Ras Laffan industrial city in 1996, the country's main LNG production hub (Hindley 1996). In addition, the state-owned Qatar Petroleum (QP) company formed several joint ventures for the production of LNG with multinational companies such as Qatargas 1 (QP shareholding: 65%) or RasGas 1 (QP shareholding: 63%).

Given still strained public finances during the 1990s, a substantial part of these large-scale investments was financed by borrowing on the international capital markets. Here, the combined external debt of the Qatari government and state-owned companies rose from USD 1.9 billion (25.8% of GDP) in 1990 to USD 14.4 billion (81.1% of GDP) in 2000 (IMF 2013b:41).[3]

During the years 2001-2005, Qatar Petroleum invested heavily in a further expansion of domestic LNG production capacities as it founded several additional joint ventures for the production of LNG with multinational companies (Qatargas 2, Qatargas 3, Qatargas 4, RasGas 2, RasGas 3). While Qatar's first LNG cargo had only been shipped in December 1996, the country became the world's largest LNG exporter by the year 2006 (EIA 2014; Gray 2013:93-102).

The growing size of LNG exports as well as strongly rising oil and gas export prices since the year 2002 led to spiralling public export proceeds during the 2000s. Between the years 2002 and 2013, public revenues (in current prices) witnessed a more than thirteen-fold increase (IMF 2014d). This surge in public revenues allowed for a much stronger upswing of public expenditure levels than in other GCC countries. Between the years 2002 and 2013, total public expenditure (in constant prices) grew by an annual average of 16.9% in Qatar compared to 10.0% in Bahrain and 10.6% in Oman (tables 4.1, 5.1 and 6.1).

In a similar vein as during the second half of the 1970s, the Qatari government undertook large investments in the public infrastructure as well as in the production capacities of (partly) state-owned companies across different sectors. Following the surge in public investment activity the relative importance of capital expenditure within overall public expenditure patterns increased strongly during 2002-2013 as can be seen from table 6.3.

The upswing of capital expenditure was particularly pronounced during the second half of the 2000s. Here, the Qatari government invested heavily in the expansion of public utilities, road and telecommunication networks. Furthermore, several ambitious public infrastructure projects such as the

---

[3]The share of capital expenditure at total expenditure during the years 1986-2001 in table 6.3 most likely understates the share of public funds allotted to investment projects. As will be discussed below, operations of Qatar Petroleum during the 2000s were partially funded by large loans from Qatar's Ministry of Finance. While no such figures are available for the 1990s, one may reasonably assume that some portion of the large LNG-related investments by Qatar Petroleum during the 1990s were funded by loans and transfers by extrabudgetay accounts of the Qatari government.

construction of a new international airport or the development of a new major port near the Mesaieed industrial city were launched during the 2000s (IMF 2010:11; Gray 2013:130-132).

In addition to (budgetary) capital expenditure, the Qatari government also fostered the build-up of infrastructure and production capacities by providing large amounts of public funds to public entities whose operations are not covered in official government accounts such as state-owned companies (e.g. Qatar Petroleum, Qatar Airways, Qatari Diar) or other off-budget entities (e.g. Qatar Foundation). This applies particularly to the state-owned industrial conglomerate Qatar Petroleum (QP) whose large-scale investments in oil and gas operations as well as in energy-intensive manufacturing activities during the 2000s were partially funded by loans from the Qatari government. According to Qatar Petroleum's financial statements, the amounts due to Qatar's Ministry of Finance increased from QAR 11.6 billion (USD 3.2 billion) at year-end 2003 to QAR 76.6 billion (USD 21.0 billion) by December 2009 (QA/QP 2005, 2010).

Apart from the above mentioned expansion of LNG production capacity, investments of QP comprised the establishments of Qatar Chemical Company (QP share: 51%) in the year 1999 and of the Aluminium producing company Qatalum (QP share: 50%) in 2007. Furthermore, the production capacities of several petrochemical companies of the QB group were strongly expanded since the late 1990s (e.g. Qatar Fertilizer Company, Qatar Petrochemical Company, Qatar Fuel Additives Company). (Gray 2013:102-104; QA/QALU 2013)

Except for Qatar Petroleum, off-budget public entities in Qatar typically do not publish data on government loans or budgetary transfers from the government. While state-owned companies increasingly borrowed on international capital markets during the 1990s and even more so during the 2000s as shown in IMF (2013b:41), it seems unlikely that the substantial investments by some state-owned companies or other public entities during these years were fully financed by debt and retained earnings.

Instead, one may reasonably assume that these substantial investments were partially funded by the Qatari government. In this regard, particularly the large-scale investments of the national carrier Qatar Airways, the real estate company Qatari Diar and Qatar Foundation stand out. For example, the fleet size of the national carrier Qatar Airways (Government shareholding: 50%) increased from 4 to 100 aircrafts during the period 1997-2011 (IMF 2013b:40; QA/QAir 2014).[4]

Furthermore, Qatari Diar, a real estate company wholly owned by Qatar's sovereign wealth fund Qatar Investment Authority, and its subsidiary Barwa (Share Qatari Diar: 45%) launched several ambitious real estate projects in Qatar since the mid-2000s such as Barwa City or the ongoing Lusail City project which is planned to provide new housing units for up to 200,000 residents (QA/QD 2012).

Apart from advancing the business expansion of state-owned companies, the Qatari government also pursued other economic policy objectives through off-budget public entities. This applies in particular to the publicly funded Qatar Foundation which has embarked on several education projects since its inception in 1995. Qatar Foundation's most prominent project has been the development of Education City, a 14 square kilometer education zone which hosts campus branches of several international universities (e.g. Weill Cornell Medical College, Carnegie Mellon University, Northwestern University) (Brandenburg 2012:227-244).

The strong focus of Qatar Foundation on advancing tertiary education in Qatar is consistent with the long-term economic development goals by the Qatari government. Within the long-term economic strategy "Qatar National Vision 2030" published in July 2008, the government postulated the long-term economic development goal of transforming Qatar into "a knowledge-based economy characterised by innovation" (QA/GSDP 2008:29).

In addition, several government initiatives which aimed at raising Qatar's international profile were funded by off-budget entities over the past decade. A prominent example in this regard is the Aspire Zone Foundation which fostered the construction of large sport venues (e.g. Aspire Dome) for hosting major sport events such as the 2006 Asian Games (QA/AZF 2013).

6.3 Non-Oil GDP

The size of Qatar's non-oil economy increased considerably over the last decades. Between the years 1979 and 2013, Qatar's non-oil GDP witnessed

[4]Qatar Airways became a fully state-owned company in 2014 after the sovereign wealth fund Qatar Investment Authority bought the stakes held by private investors (e.g. Qatar's former prime minister Scheikh Hamad bin Jassim Al-Thani) (Reuters 2014).

a fourteen-fold increase when measured in constant 2010 US-Dollar prices (table 6.4). This upswing of aggregate non-oil GDP levels was facilitated by rising stocks of the factor inputs physical capital and labour. Large-scale investments both in the country's infrastructure as well as in the production capacities of different industry and service companies fostered substantial output growth across various non-oil sectors.

Furthermore, a large increase in Qatar's labour force contributed to a strongly rising scale of the non-oil economy. Between the census years 1970 and 2010, Qatar's labour force went up from a mere 48,390 to 1,270,183 workers (UN-ECWA 1980; QA/SA 2010b). In contrast, economy-wide gains in productivity do not stand out as an important driver of non-oil GDP growth. As will be discussed at greater length in section 6.4, the labour productivity measure non-oil GDP per worker witnessed an overall decrease between the years 1979 and 2013 (table 6.4).

The sectoral sources of aggregate non-oil GDP growth over the last four decades were broad-based. Since the end of the 1970s, several non-oil economic activities such as manufacturing, electricity production, wholesale trade, air transportation and finance exhibited strongly rising levels of economic activity. For example, the volume of container throughput at domestic seaports and the number of air passengers arriving in Qatar rose by factors of 85 and 41, respectively between the years 1979 and 2013 (table 6.5). In terms of gross value added, the most important non-oil sectors are government services, manufacturing, trade, construction, real estate and financial services (table 6.6).

Despite a large expansion of different non-oil economic activities, the overall importance of the oil and gas sector has not diminished lastingly. Instead, most non-oil sectors have grown along with the oil and gas sector which has remained, by far, the most important economic activity in Qatar. In the year 2013, around 55% of nominal gross value added within the Qatari economy fell upon the production of crude oil and natural gas (table 6.6). Here, nominal gross value added levels of the oil and gas sector were further elevated during the 2000s by the upswing of oil and gas prices since the year 2002 as well as by the strong expansion of natural gas production since the mid-1990s (table 6.5). Moreover, strongly rising public oil and gas export proceeds during the 2000s allowed the Qatari government to advance the development of the non-oil economy through large investment projects.

Table 6.4: Qatar - Levels Public Expenditure, Non-Oil GDP and Labour Productivity 1979-2013
(in constant 2010 US-Dollar prices)

	1979	1990	2000	2013
Total Public Expenditure (Billion US-Dollar)	8.1	6.7	9.2	59.4
Aggregate Non-Oil GDP (Billion US-Dollar)	6.2	10.2	12.4	87.1
Non-Oil GDP per Worker (1,000 US-Dollar)	63.8	37.3	37.5	53.7

Sources: National sources (see Appendix A)
Note: US $ exchange rates from IMF (International Financial Statistics).

Public expenditure appears as a very important catalyst of non-oil economic activity in Qatar. Most notably, rising government outlays on public infrastructure and on business expansions of (partly) state-owned companies during times of high oil prices (1974-1985, 2002-2013) elevated output levels of various non-oil sectors markedly. Furthermore, continued increases in the public sector wage bill raised gross value added from government services since the 1970s.

A growth-enhancing impact of public infrastructure expenditure is particularly apparent for energy-intensive manufacturing industries, trade and transport services. Here, the strong increase of economic activity in these sectors since the 1970s was heavily aided by several large-scale public investments such as the enlargement of domestic electricity production capacities, the construction of a new international airport, the expansion of seaports as well as the development of the industrial cities Mesaieed and Ras Laffan (section 6.2).

Furthermore, the scale of economic activities in sectors like manufacturing, real estate and air transport was strongly increased by rapid business expansions of either fully state-owned companies or public-private joint ventures in these sectors (e.g. Qatar Fertilizer Company, Qatalum, Qatar Diar, Qatar Airways). While detailed figures about the size of public funds directed to the business expansion of these companies are publicly not available in most cases, it seems very unlikely that investment projects of this scale were fully financed by borrowings on financial markets or retained earnings of the respective companies. Beyond the build-up of production capacities in certain sectors, implementation of these large investment projects also spurred economic activity in other parts of the non-oil economy as exemplified by strongly rising levels of gross value added in the construction and finance sectors during these periods.

Overall, these findings confirm the results of the baseline econometric analysis in chapter 3 which found a positive impact of different public expenditure categories (total expenditure, capital expenditure, non-education expenditure, non-health expenditure) on aggregate non-oil GDP levels in Qatar.

Similar to public expenditure patterns, economic growth in most non-oil sectors accelerated during times of high oil prices (1974-1985, 2002-2013). This applies in particular to important non-oil sectors such as manufacturing, finance, real estate and construction since gross value added levels in these sectors were elevated by an upswing of public and private investment activity during these years.

As shown in table 6.3, the Qatari government devoted a much higher share of public funds to investment projects during periods of oil price booms. The much stronger focus of the government on economic development, in turn, also fuelled investment spending by the private sector.

A strong impact of investment on the scale of economic activity is visible for the manufacturing sector. Here, high levels of investment by the Qatari government and multinational companies stand out as the main cause for rising levels of gross vale added in the manufacturing sector over the last decades. Economic growth in the manufacturing sector was particularly strong during the 1980s and the 2000s. As can be seen from table 6.6 the sectoral share of manufacturing at total gross value added in the Qatari economy rose markedly during the years 1975-1990 and 2000-2013.

The upswing of manufacturing gross value added during these two periods was primarily driven by large-scale production expansions at partly state-owned companies in capital-intensive manufacturing industries such as oil refining or the production of petrochemicals, steel and aluminium. In addition to the strong build-up of production capacities in heavy industries, the manufacturing sector witnessed a considerable increase of the number of small-scale private sector establishments in different light manufacturing industries since the early 1980s.

Qatar's manufacturing sector exhibits characteristics of a dual economy. On the one hand, capital-intensive heavy manufacturing industries are domi-

Table 6.5: Qatar - Indicators of Economic Activity 1979-2013

Economic Activity	1979	1990	2000	2013
Oil and Natural Gas Production:				
Crude Oil (Million metric tons/year)	24.5	19.6	30.8	40.3
Natural Gas (Billion cubic meters/year)	2.7	6.2	24.5	163.3
Manufacturing Production:				
Aluminium (1,000 metric tons/year)	0	0	0	634
Refined Oil (1,000 barrels/day)	7	60	66	250
Ammonia (1,000 metric tons/year)	334	584	1,097	2,985
Electricity Production:				
Gross Domestic Production (TWh)	2.0	4.8	9.1	34.7
Wholesale Trade Seaports:				
Containers Handled (1,000 TEU/year)	5	22	80[2]	424
Air Transport:				
Airport Arrivals (1,000 Passengers/year)[1]	287	548	1,327	11,802
Financial Sector:				
Total Assets Financial Sector (% of GDP)	30.5	75.5	77.7	123.5

Sources: International Energy Agency (IEA), *Oil Information*, various issues; IEA, *Natural Gas Information*, various issues; IEA, *Energy Statistics of Non-OECD Countries*, various issues; IEA, *Electricity Information*, various issues; US Geological Survey, *Minerals Yearbook*, various issues; Containerisation International, *Containerisation International Yearbook*, various issues; QA/CSO (1981, 1991, 1992); QA/PC (2002); QA/MDPS (2012-2015); UN Data, *National Accounts Main Aggregates Database*

[1] Airport arrivals in Qatar include transit passengers.

[2] Figure refers to year 1999.

nated by large joint ventures between the Qatari government and multinational companies (e.g. Qatar Fertilizer Company, Qatar Steel Company, Qatar Petrochemical Company, Qatalum, Laffan Refinery Company). On the other hand, economic activity in light manufacturing industries typically falls upon small-scale companies from the local private sector (e.g. food and beverages, textiles, wood products, printing).

While a large part of gross value added in the manufacturing sector is generated by public-private joint ventures in capital-intensive heavy industries, the bulk of Qatar's manufacturing workforce is employed by small-scale companies in light industries. For example, the three manufacturing industries oil refining, production of chemicals and production of metals accounted for around 86% of gross value added but only for 18% of employment within the manufacturing sector during the year 2013 (QA/MDPS 2014c).

The government of Qatar fostered the development of different manufacturing industries since the 1960s by setting up several joint ventures with mostly foreign private sector investors. The first large-scale industrial project was the formation of Qatar Cement Company in the year 1965 (government share: 40%). This was followed by the establishment of Qatar Fertilizer Company in 1969 (government share: 70%).

Bolstered by rising oil export proceeds, the government intensified the promotion of industrial development since the start of the first oil price boom (1974-1985). During the latter period, Qatar's industrial capacity increased considerably due to the launch of several new companies (e.g. Qatar Steel Company, Umm Said Refinery, Qatar Petrochemical Company).

Furthermore, several state-owned companies invested heavily in the expansion of production capacities, a large part of which came on stream during the 1980s. For example, Qatar Steel Company, a joint venture established in June 1974 between the Qatari government (shareholding: 70%) and two Japanese companies, increased steel production by 56% during the years 1979 and 1990 (UN-IDO 1980:55-68; QA/CSO 1982:149, 1992:223).

In a similar vein, gross value added levels in the manufacturing sector during the second oil price boom (2002-2013) were elevated by large-scale investments in the production capacities of several heavy industries. This is exemplified by Qatar Fertilizer Company which became the world's largest on-site producer of ammonia and urea by the year 2010 as a result of considerable production increases since 2004.

In addition, the fully state-owned Qatar Petroleum Company and its subsidiary Qatar Industries (Share Qatar Petroleum: 70%) spearheaded the manufacturing sector's development push since the late 1990s by forming several joint ventures with multinational companies in different manufacturing industries (e.g. Qatar Chemical Company, Laffan Refinery Company, Qatalum). Here, the establishment of the Laffan Refinery Company (Share Qatar Petroleum: 51%) in the year 2006 contributed to a substantial upswing of the country's refining capacity (table 6.5). Furthermore, Qatar turned into the third largest aluminium producing country in the Middle East by the year 2011 following the commissioning of the country's first

Table 6.6: Qatar - Gross Value Added by Economic Activity 1975-2013 (in % of total gross value added)

	1975	1980	1990	2000	2013
Agriculture & Fishing	0.7	0.5	0.8	0.4	0.1
Mining & Quarrying	68.3	66.8	38.2	60.7	55.1
Of which: Production Crude Oil	na	na	na	na	16.3
Of which: Product. Natural Gas	na	na	na	na	37.3
Manufacturing	2.6	3.3	13.0	5.5	10.1
Of which: Refining	na	na	na	1.3	1.8
Of which: Petrochemicals	na	na	na	1.2	6.1
Of which: Metals	na	na	na	1.3	0.8
Electricity & Water	0.3	0.2	1.5	1.2	0.5
Construction	7.8	6.0	4.2	3.6	5.2
Trade, Restaurants & Hotels	5.1	4.5	5.6	5.8	6.2
Of which: Trade	na	4.0	4.9	5.2	5.6
Transport, Storage, Communication	1.7	1.7	2.6	3.1	3.1
Of which: Air Transportation	na	0.4	0.3	0.3	0.8
Of which: Communication	na	0.2	1.4	1.7	0.8
Finance, Real Estate & other Business Services	7.5	5.9	9.6	7.3	11.9
Of which: Finance	na	1.9	3.2	2.8	5.6
Of which: Real Estate	na	3.9	5.9	3.5	4.1
Social & Personal Private Services	1.1	0.8	1.9	1.8	1.3
Of which: Private Education Serv.	na	na	na	0.3	0.4
Of which: Private Health Services	na	na	na	0.1	0.2
Government Services	6.3	11.7	25.0	12.7	9.2
Less: FISIM	-1.6	-1.4	-2.4	-2.2	-2.6
Total Gross Value Added	100.0	100.0	100.0	100.0	100.0

Sources: QA/CSO (1982, 1983, 1992); QA/PC (2002); QA/MDPS (2014c, 2014d, 2015b)

Notes: Calculations by the author. Gross value added in current producers' prices. In the national accounts time series of the above stated sources, financial intermediation services indirectly measured (FISIM) have not been allocated as intermediate consumption to the sectors which have used these services. Instead, the total amount of FISIM has been deducted from the sum of gross value added of the different sectors.

aluminium plant at Qatalum (Share Qatar Petroleum: 50%) in December 2009 (Gray 2013:102-104; QA/QG 2014; QA/QP 2011; USGS 2013).

As can be seen from table 6.6, the bulk of gross value added in the manufacturing sector is generated by the refining, the petrochemicals and the metals industries. Nevertheless, manufacturing activity outside these heavy industries also increased considerably over the last decades. An industrial survey conducted in the year 1982 puts the number of manufacturing establishments outside the refining, chemical and metal industries at 1,036 (10,341 employees). By the year 2013, the number of manufacturing establishments had risen to 2,404 (87,945 employees) a large part of which falls upon private sector companies in light industries such as food and beverages, wearing apparels, printing and furniture and fabricated metal products (QA/CSO 1984b, QA/MDPS 2014c).

Overall, economic growth patterns in the manufacturing sector seem to have been strongly impacted by public expenditure. The Qatari government embarked on large-scale investment projects in the refining, chemicals and metals industries in particular during periods of high oil price levels. These industrial projects were typically spearheaded by state-owned companies such as Qatar Petroleum which received substantial off-budgetary funds by the Qatari government as discussed in section 6.2.

Similar to the manufacturing sector, economic activity in the financial sector is linked to oil price developments. Financial intermediation services of Qatari banks increased considerably during periods of high oil price levels. Between the years 1975-1985 and 2002-2013 the share of the banking sector's total assets at GDP rose from 26.7% to 66.2% and from 88.9% to 123.5%, respectively (QA/CSO 1981, 1988; QA/PC 2004; QA/MDPS 2015).

Rising levels of gross value added in the financial sector during these periods were facilitated by the inflow of high oil and gas export proceeds since the latter provided Qatar's commercial banks with a strong increase of customer deposits. A large part of these funds was lent to domestic borrowers due to a multitude of investment projects at that time. Here, domestic credit growth was particularly strong with regard to public sector entities, retail customers, trade, construction and the real estate sector.

In contrast to Bahrain, rising levels of gross value added in the Qatari financial sector over the last decades were primarily driven by a substantial increase of lending by existing commercial banks rather than by a structural transformation of the financial sector. As discussed in section 4.3, the strong upswing of gross value added in Bahrain's financial sector was largely caused by the development of an offshore banking industry since the mid-1970s.

The most important change in the Qatari financial sector since the 1970s has been the rise of Islamic finance banks such Qatar Islamic Bank or, more recently, Masraf Al Rayan. Furthermore, the government sought to promote the development of Qatar towards a regional financial center along the lines of Dubai and Bahrain by attracting foreign financial institutions through several initiatives such as the opening of the Qatar Financial Centre in May 2005 (Hancock 2008).

Overall, financial intermediation services in Qatar, however, continue to be dominated by the established market leader Qatar National Bank (government shareholding: 50%), the country's oldest domestic commercial bank which was founded in the year 1965. As of September 2013, Qatar National Bank accounted for almost 45% of total banking sector assets in Qatar (Gray 2013:68; QA/QCB 2013).

Credit growth rates in Qatar's financial sector can also be seen as an important determinant of economic growth in the real estate and the construction sectors. The credit boom of the 2000s was accompanied by the launch of several unprecedented mega-projects in Qatar's real estate sector such as the ongoing Lusail City or The Pearl projects. The gigantic Lusail City development was commenced by the fully state-owned real estate company Qatari Diar in 2005 and is planned to accommodate 200,000 residents eventually. In a similar vein, private sector company United Development Company embarked on The Pearl project in 2004, a 400-hectare artificial island (QA/QD 2012).

Beyond credit supply, building activity in times of oil price booms (1974-1985, 2002-2013) was also fueled by high levels of public infrastructure spending as well as by strong population growth rates. The important role of public spending for the construction sector is exemplified by data from QA/SA (2011b:40) which shows that around 40% of the total value of Qatari construction projects in the year 2010 related to projects which had been commissioned by the Qatari government.

Furthermore, the broad-based economic expansions during the oil price booms were accompanied by a strong influx of foreign workers which, in turn, increased the demand for housing in Qatar. Here, the number of completed buildings in Qatar rose by 38,239 between census years 2004 and 2010 compared to an increase of only 15,324 during the period 1997-2004 (QA/PC 1999b:209, 2004b:297; QA/SA 2010b:281).

While economic activity in the above discussed non-oil sectors was primarily impacted by capital expenditure, the public wage bill can be singled out as the most important determinant of gross value added in government services (public administration & defence, public education services, public health services). According to the recommendations of international standards for compiling national accounts data (e.g. 1993 SNA, 2008 SNA), gross value added by government services is best measured by a cost of production approach because market prices for these services are typically not available and, hence, cannot be utilised for the valuation of gross value added (European Commission et al. 1993:164-165, 2009:110-111). The most important valuation parameter in such a cost of production approach is the public wage bill. During the period 1980-2004, salaries and wages in Qatar's public sector accounted for 83.5% of gross value added by government services (QA/PC 2006b:23).

As discussed in section 6.2, public sector employment increased particularly strong during the years of the first oil price boom (1975-1985). As a result of the ensuing upswing of the public wage bill, the sectoral share of government services at total gross value added rose rapidly from 6.3% to 25.0% between the years 1975 and 1990 (table 6.6). Over the following decades, this sectoral share declined even though the build-up of public sector manpower started to accelerate again during the years of the second oil price boom (2002-2013). Yet, the marked increases of gross value added by government services in the latter period were surpassed by the strong growth of other economic activities during these years.

6.4 Labour Productivity

The substantial increase in the overall size of Qatar's non-oil economy over the last decades was not accompanied by sustained improvements of labour productivity levels. Instead, the labour productivity measure non-oil GDP per worker declined by around 19% between the years 1979 and 2013 when measured in constant 2010 Qatari Rial prices.

Figure 6.2: Qatar - Labour Productivity, Aggregate Non-Oil GDP and Labour Force 1979-2013
(Index, 1979=100)

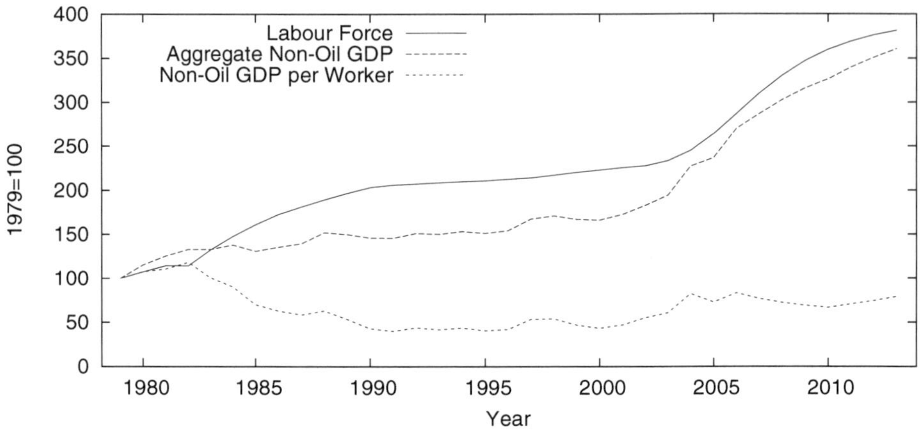

Notes: Time series in logarithms. Non-Oil GDP in constant prices.
Sources: Appendix A.

The lack of sustained increases in labour productivity can primarily be ascribed to developments on the Qatari labour market over the last decades. Even though a strong expansion of non-oil economic activity led to a considerable upswing of employment levels particularly for non-Qatari nationals, a large fraction of this employment growth took place in sectors with low labour productivity levels such as construction, trade and household services.

Furthermore, employment of Qatari nationals has not undergone a structural change towards sectors with higher productivity levels but, instead, continues to be concentrated in government services (public administration & defence, public education services, public health services). Here, the segmentation of the Qatari labour market between nationals and non-nationals is more distinct than in Bahrain and Oman. Not least as a result of comparatively high oil and gas endowments, the Qatari government adopted less comprehensive measures than the latter two countries for increasing the employment level of the national workforce outside the public sector.

The evolution of labour productivity in Qatar since the late 1970s has not been uniform. As can be seen from figure 6.2, the labour productivity measure non-oil GDP per worker does not exhibit a clear long-term trend.

Instead, labour productivity developments in Qatar have been characterised by periods both of prolonged declines and modest increases. Labour productivity levels in Qatar typically declined in periods of strong employment growth such as the 1980s and the second half of the 2000s.[5] These declines in non-oil GDP output per worker can largely be ascribed to the substantial increases in employment for low-skilled labour during these years, most notably, in the construction sector.

In contrast to labour productivity, the development patterns of aggregate non-oil GDP and employment levels were closely aligned over the last decades. A close association between non-oil economic activity and employment is particularly apparent for the years of the second oil price boom (2002-2013) which saw large increases both in non-oil GDP output and in employment levels. In terms of the growth contribution of the factor input labour, non-oil economic growth in Qatar seems to have been driven by increases rather in the scale than in the productivity level of the labour force.

The analysis of labour market developments in Qatar is complicated by a limited availability of detailed employment figures particularly prior to the 2000s. Yet, available data from official census year publications highlight strong employment growth in Qatar over the last decades. Between the census years 1970 and 2010, the number of employees surged from 48,390 to 1,270,183 persons (UN-IDO 1980; QA/SA 2010b). The rates of employment growth accelerated during periods of high oil price levels (1974-1985, 2002-2013). Furthermore, a very large share of the overall employment increases falls upon non-Qatari nationals. As a result of the latter, the share of Qatari employees at total employment stood at only 5.6% in the census year 2010 (table 6.7).

The sectoral sources of employment growth since the 1970s differ considerably for Qatari and non-Qatari nationals. Following the inflow of spiralling

[5] The decline of the labour productivity measure non-oil GDP per worker was less pronounced during the second half of the 2000s than during the 1980s despite a very large increase of employment in sectors with low labour productivity levels (e.g. construction) between the census years 2004 and 2010 (table 6.8). In part, this can be related to much higher (public and private) investment levels during the 2000s. Here, total investment in the Qatari economy stood at an annual average of 39.6% of GDP between the years 2005 and 2010 compared to only 16.1% of GDP during 1980-1990 (IMF 2014d). These comparatively high investment levels during the 2000s positively impacted non-oil GDP output levels per worker particularly in capital-intensive manufacturing industries (e.g. petrochemicals).

Table 6.7: Qatar - Total Employment Census Years 1970-2010

	1970	1986	1997	2004	2010
Number of Employees (in 1,000):					
Total Employees	48.4	200.2	280.1	437.6	1,270.2
Qatari Employees	8.2	20.8	36.3	50.3	71.1
Non-Qatari Employees	40.2	179.4	243.8	387.3	1,199.1
Share at Total Employment (%):					
Qatari Employees	16.9	10.4	12.9	11.5	5.6
Non-Qatari Employees	83.1	89.6	87.1	88.5	94.4
Rate of Change to Previous Census Year (%):					
Total Employees	na	313.8	39.9	56.2	190.3
Qatari Employees	na	154.7	74.3	38.6	41.4
Non-Qatari Employees	na	346.1	35.9	58.8	209.6

Sources: UN-IDO (1980); QA/CSO (1987b, 1992); QA/PC (1999b, 2004b); QA/SA (2010b).

Notes: Calculations by the author. Due to rounding errors numbers of Qatari and non-Qatari employees may not add up to the number of total employees. In contrast to the labour force data sources mentioned in table A5, employment data in this table does not include unemployed persons.

oil export proceeds during the years of the first oil price boom (1974-1985) the Qatari government expanded the employment of Qatari nationals in government services such the country's public adminstration strongly.[6]

Over the following decades, the public sector continued to absorb a large share of a growing national workforce in particular during years of high oil price levels. By the census year 2010, public administration as well as public education and health services provided employment to 74.5% of all employed Qatari nationals. Furthermore, an additional 7.1% of Qatari employment in this year fell upon the mining & quarrying sector which is dominated by state-owned companies such as Qatar Petroleum.

Overall, the importance of public sector activities for the employment of the national workforce is much higher in Qatar than in Bahrain or in Oman.

[6]Unfortunately, publicly available data sources for the census year 1986 provide only figures about the overall employment level in Qatar's public administration but no breakdown of employment in this sector into Qatari and non-Qatari nationals (table 6.8). However, given the strong increase of the overall employment level in Qatar's pubic administration between the census years 1970 and 1986, it seems reasonable to assume that a substantial share of this employment growth falls upon Qatari nationals.

This becomes evident when comparing the sectoral employment shares of public administration which constitutes the main source of public sector employment for GCC nationals. Qatar's public adminstration employed 58.9% of all Qatari employees in the year 2010. Instead, the corresponding employment shares of public administration stood at 31.1% in Bahrain and at 42.6% in Oman (tables 4.9, 5.10, 6.9).

In stark contrast to Qatari nationals, non-Qatari nationals are largely employed in the private sector. The main sectoral sources of employment growth for non-Qatari nationals over the last decades were construction, trade, household services and manufacturing. Between the census years 1970 and 2010, the number of non-Qatari employees within these four sectors increased by around 860,000 persons. This compares with an increase of approximately 500 Qatari employees in these sectors over the same time span (table 6.8). Here, the very low employment levels of Qatari nationals in various private sector activities exemplify a strong segmentation of the Qatari labour market.

In a similar vein as in other GCC countries, higher employment shares of Qatari nationals in the private sector are impeded by a substantial wage gap between jobs in the public sector and the private sector particularly with regard to low-skilled labour. According to the results of an employment survey from June 2005, the average monthly salary in the public sector at that time was 2.6 times higher than in the private sector even though average working hours in the former sector accounted only for 88% of the private sector's average working time (QA/PC 2006c:27). This relative attractiveness of public sector jobs can be seen as a major obstacle for a structural change in the employment patterns of Qatari nationals towards private sector activities.

So far, the Qatari government has not adopted comprehensive measures for increasing the employment share of Qatari nationals in the private sector *(Qatarisation)*. In this regard, Qatar pursued a much more lenient labour market policy than less affluent GCC countries like Bahrain or Oman. As discussed in sections 4.4 and 5.4, the governments of Bahrain and Oman sought to increase participation levels of the national workforce in the private sector over the last decades through various policy measures such as employment quotas, vocational training programmes (e.g. "Sanad", "Project 10,000") and the imposition of levies on wages by foreign workers.

Table 6.8: Qatar - Employment by Sector and Nationality Census Years 1970-2010

(Number of Employees in 1,000)

	1970	1986	1997	2004	2010
Construction	7.8	40.5	56.1	117.0	506.3
Of which: Qatari	0.2	0.3	0.3	0.3	0.6
Of which: Non-Qatari	7.6	40.3	55.8	116.7	505.7
Wholesale and Retail Trade	7.9	18.0	30.6	54.4	142.8
Of which: Qatari	0.9	na	0.8	0.7	1.9
Of which: Non-Qatari	7.0	na	29.8	53.7	140.9
Household Services	na	34.3	45.1	53.4	132.5
Of which: Qatari	na	na	0.1	0.1	0.1
Of which: Non-Qatari	na	na	45.0	53.2	132.4
Manufacturing	5.2[1]	13.9	24.1	40.0	100.6
Of which: Qatari	1.8[1]	0.4	0.6	0.7	0.8
Of which: Non-Qatari	3.4[1]	13.5	23.5	39.3	99.9
Mining & Quarrying	2.2	4.8	9.4	18.0	85.7
Of which: Qatari	1.3	1.4	2.1	3.8	5.1
Of which: Non-Qatari	1.0	3.4	7.3	14.2	80.7
Public Administration	6.2	42.1	49.9	53.4	72.0
Of which: Qatari	1.4	na	20.7	27.5	41.8
Of which: Non-Qatari	4.8	na	29.2	25.9	30.1
Real Estate & Other Business Serv.	na	1.4	4.6	11.9	68.2
Of which: Qatari	na	na	0.2	0.3	1.2
Of which: Non-Qatari	na	na	4.5	11.5	67.0
Education & Health Services[2]	na	na	19.4	31.4	45.3
Of which: Qatari	na	na	8.2	11.9	11.5
Of which: Non-Qatari	na	na	11.2	19.6	33.7
Transport, Storage, Communication	3.2	7.4	9.6	15.2	43.1
Of which: Qatari	0.7	na	0.9	1.1	2.9
Of which: Non-Qatari	2.6	na	8.7	14.1	40.1
Other Sectors	15.9	37.7	31.3	42.7	73.7
Of which: Qatari	2.0	na	2.4	3.7	5.2
Of which: Non-Qatari	13.9	na	28.9	39.0	68.5

Sources: UN-IDO (1980); QA/CSO (1987b, 1992); QA/PC (1999b, 2004b); QA/SA (2010b).

Note: Due to rounding errors numbers of Qatari and non-Qatari employees may not add up to the number of total employees.

[1] Includes employment in public utilities.

[2] Includes employment in public and private sectors.

Instead, the most important *Qatarisation* measure was the imposition of employment quotas for Qatari nationals on 24, mostly state-owned, companies in the oil and gas sector as well as in the manufacturing sector. In the year 2000, these companies were obliged by the Qatari government to attain a 50% employment quota for Qatari nationals until the year 2005 (QA/QSC 2014). However, a large share of these companies were either subsidiaries or joint ventures of the fully state-owned Qatar Petroleum company. Therefore, the subsequent increase of Qatari employees in these companies cannot be considered a structural change of employment patterns towards a reduced reliance on the Qatari government as the main employer for the national workforce.

More recently, the national development strategy of the Qatari government for the years 2011-2016 set out the target to increase the proportion of Qataris working in the entire private sector to 15% by 2016 (QA/GSDP 2011:151-152). However, this goal was thwarted by other measures of the Qatari government. For example, wages in the public sector were increased by 60%-120% in September 2011, thus further aggravating the wage gap between the public and private sectors in Qatar (Gray 2013:225).

Comparatively high public sector wages for the national workforce can also be seen as a major reason why strongly rising levels of potentially productivity enhancing public expenditure categories have not translated into sustained improvements of labour productivity over the last decades. Here, large increases of public investment, education and health expenditures contributed to an improvement of several factors of labour productivity such as the economy's endowment of human and physical capital (e.g. educational level and health status of population, quality of public infrastructure, capital intensity of industrial production). Yet, these higher endowments of human and physical capital did not lead to an increase in non-oil GDP output levels per worker since a structural change in employment patterns of Qatari nationals towards more skill-intensive economic activities was impeded by high public sector wages.

These findings confirm the results of the baseline econometric analysis in chapter 3 which found a much stronger evidence for a positive impact of public expenditure on non-oil GDP levels than on labour productivity. Here, only one group of public expenditure variables (capital and current expenditure) was found to exhibit a long-term link with the labour productivity indicator non-oil GDP per worker.

Table 6.9: Qatar - Sectoral Employment Shares Qatari and Non-Qatari Nationals 1970-2010

	1970	1986	1997	2004	2010
	(in % of Qatari Employees)				
Qatari Nationals:					
Main Sectors:					
Public Administration	17.0	na	57.1	54.7	58.9
Education & Health Services[1]	na	na	22.6	23.6	16.2
Of which: Public Sector	na	na	na	23.3	15.6
Mining & Quarrying	15.4	6.9	5.7	7.7	7.1
Transport, Storage, Communication	8.0	na	2.4	2.1	4.1
Memo:					
Wholesale and Retail Trade	10.8	na	2.2	1.5	2.6
Manufacturing	22.3[2]	2.0	1.8	1.4	1.1
	(in % of Non-Qatari Employees)				
Non-Qatari Nationals:					
Main Sectors:					
Construction	18.8	22.4	22.9	30.1	42.2
Wholesale and Retail Trade	17.4	na	12.2	13.9	11.8
Household Services	na	na	18.5	13.7	11.0
Manufacturing	8.5[2]	7.5	9.6	10.2	8.3
Mining & Quarrying	2.4	1.9	3.0	3.7	6.7
Memo:					
Real Estate & Other Business Serv.	na	na	1.8	3.0	5.6
Public Administration	11.9	na	12.0	6.7	2.5

Sources: UN-IDO (1980); QA/CSO (1987b, 1992); QA/PC (1999b, 2004b); QA/SA (2010b).
Note: Calculations by the author.
[1] Includes employment in public and private sectors.
[2] Includes employment in public utilities.

Furthermore, this cointegration link did not extend to the full sample period (1979-2013) but, instead, only to the sub-period 1979-1998. As can be seen from figures 6.1 and 6.2, the period 1979-1998 largely witnessed stagnant or even declining levels of both public expenditure and labour productivity. Therefore, the cointegration link between public expenditure and labour productivity in Qatar within this period does not appear as a strong evidence for a productivity enhancing impact of increases in public expenditure.

Part III

The Impact of Public Expenditure on Potential Sources of Non-Oil Economic Growth

Chapter 7

Public Expenditure and Private Sector Investment

7.1 Introduction

Investment patterns of the private sector are an important aspect when analysing the overall impact of public expenditure on non-oil economic growth in Bahrain, Oman and Qatar. Large increases of public expenditure during years of high oil price levels exerted not only a direct impact on non-oil economic growth patterns but shaped the latter also by influencing private sector investment activity.

The link between public expenditure and private investment in Bahrain, Oman and Qatar differs from that in most other countries. Most importantly, public expenditure in the GCC countries is largely funded by external oil and gas export proceeds and not by taxes on domestic households or private businesses.

Therefore, strong increases of public expenditure like those seen during the years of the two oil price booms (1974-1985, 2002-2013) typically do not necessitate increases in taxes or higher levels of borrowing at domestic banks and, hence, do not limit the financial resources for private sector investments. Instead, the increases in public expenditure particularly during the 2000s were accompanied by a surge in private investment activity. This, in turn, can be ascribed to the finding that public expenditure in all three countries exhibits a much stronger tendency to crowd-in than to crowd-out private investment.

A crowding-in effect is particularly observable for large-scale public investments in the economic infrastructure which aimed to improve the production conditions for the private sector markedly (build-up economic cities and wholesale ports, expansion electricity production capacities). Furthermore, public and private investment levels were both elevated as the governments in all three countries formed several joint ventures with private sector investors, most notably, in capital-intensive manufacturing industries (e.g. chemicals, fertilisers, aluminium). With regard to the build-up of production capacities in these industries, private investment can be seen to have amplified the impact of public expenditure on non-oil economic growth in Bahrain, Oman and Qatar markedly.

Apart from raising economic activity levels in different non-oil sectors, the interplay between public expenditure and private investment also shaped the characteristics of non-oil economic growth dynamics lastingly. The country studies in chapters 4-6 highlighted that non-oil economic growth in Bahrain, Oman and Qatar over the last decades was primarily driven by an accumulation of the factor inputs physical capital and labour and not by sustained improvements of labour productivity.

Public and private investment patterns strongly contributed to this input-driven growth dynamic. A growth-enhancing impact of public and private investments is particularly observable for non-oil sectors which rely on high investments in the stock of physical capital (capital-intensive manufacturing) or on a high availability of low-skilled, typically foreign, labour (e.g. construction, trade). Hence, while fostering a growing size of the non-oil economy, the concurrent increases of public expenditure and private investment during the years of the two oil price booms did not ignite a structural change of non-oil economic production patterns towards more skill-intensive economic activities.

The following chapter elaborates the country-specific characteristics of the link between public expenditure and private investment in Bahrain, Oman and Qatar in more detail. Section 7.2 puts the interplay between public expenditure and private investment into context by examining the economic roles of the public and private sectors in Bahrain, Oman and Qatar.

Building on that, section 7.3 explores the impact of total public expenditure on private investment through an econometric analysis. By drawing on cointegration and causality analysis, this section examines whether increases in total public expenditure crowd-in or crowd-out private sector investment in a statistically significant manner. The respective strength of these two opposing effects, in turn, is an important factor for shaping the overall impact of public expenditure on non-oil economic growth.

Section 7.4 turns to the characteristics of non-oil economic growth dynamics and analyses how public and private investment activity strengthened the input-driven growth pattern within the non-oil economies of Bahrain, Oman and Qatar.

7.2 The Economic Roles of the Public and Private Sectors

The economic roles of the public and private sectors in Bahrain, Oman and Qatar changed over the last decades. While public sectors continue to shape economic development patterns, their dominant economic role nowadays manifests itself in a less distinct manner than during earlier decades.

This becomes particularly evident when comparing the relative importance of public capital expenditures for economy-wide investment levels during the periods of the two oil price booms (1974-1985, 2002-2013). Budgetary capital expenditures in the latter period financed a lower share of large-scale investment projects than during the years of the first oil price boom (1974-1985). Instead, the public sector relied to a greater extent on private sector capital during the 2000s as the economic policy of GCC countries increasingly aimed at stimulating private sector investment activity. The rising prominence of private sector capital, in turn, resulted from a substantial accumulation of financial funds both by households and private business over previous decades.

Despite being a more important source of capital, however, GCC private sectors do not appear as an increasingly independent economic force. Instead, investment spending of the GCC private sectors is closely aligned to investment patterns of GCC governments. For example, rising levels of private investment in energy-intensive manufacturing industries during the years of the second oil price boom (2002-2013) were strongly facilitated by high public investments in the economic infrastructure (e.g. build-up of economic cities, gas supplies for energy-intensive manufacturing industries). Furthermore, GCC public sectors increased private investment activity by forming several joint ventures with private sector investors.

A strong, albeit indirect, impact of GCC governments on private sector activity is also exemplified by large government shareholdings at several publicly listed companies. In addition, different senior political figures in the GCC countries stand out as important private sector investors.

The origins of the public sectors' dominant economic role in Bahrain, Oman and Qatar can be traced back to the discovery of oil on the Arabian peninsula. The start of oil production and, even more so, spiralling world market prices for crude oil during the years of the first oil price boom (1974-1985) gave rise to huge inflows of public oil export proceeds. This, in turn, allowed GCC governments to exert considerable influence on economic developments.

Employment patterns in the GCC economies have been shaped lastingly by a strong build-up of manpower in the countries' public sectors. As a result, the GCC governments evolved into an employer of last resort for the local workforce. Furthermore, the substantial increase in the public wage bill served as an important source of economic demand by providing large parts of the local population with rising incomes. In addition, large public investments in the infrastructure and in the industrial capacities of local economies spurred economic growth across various non-oil sectors (e.g. trade, transport, manufacturing, construction).

The strong decline of world market prices for crude oil after the years of the first oil price boom (1974-1985) exposed the limits of this oil rent driven growth strategy. Substantial budgetary pressures during the second half of the 1980s and the 1990s prompted GCC governments to search for alternative ways of generating both economic growth as well as employment for an increasing national workforce. In this context, the private sector was increasingly ascribed an important economic role.

A stronger emphasis on the private sector is exemplified by the economic policy goals set out in *Vision 2020*, a long-term development growth strategy adopted by the Omani government in the year 1995. Here, *Vision 2020* strived for "the creation of a leading and highly competitive private sector characterised by being efficient, self-reliant and integrated into the global economy". Furthermore, the private sector was planned to become "the main source of provision of fair employment opportunities for people" (OM/MoNE 2007b:131).

In a similar vein, the long-term development strategies published by the governments of Bahrain and Qatar during the 2000s envisaged the private sector as the main source of sustained economic growth in future. For example, the long-term development strategy *Economic Vision 2030 for Bahrain* postulates that "the private sector should be able to drive economic growth in Bahrain independently [by the year 2030]" (BH/BNA 2008). Likewise, the long-term development strategy *Qatar National Vision 2030* aims at the creation of "a diversified economy that gradually reduces its dependence on hydrocarbon industries [and] enhances the role of the private sector" (QA/GSDP 2008:29).

Since the mid-1990s, most GCC governments implemented different economic policy reforms which aimed at increasing private sector investment. These reforms included a partial privatisation of state-owned companies (e.g. Qatar Telecom, Industries Qatar, Omantel), the launch of privately owned power plants (e.g. Al Manah, Al Ezzel), the opening of certain sectors to foreign investment (e.g. real estate, financial sector) and the end of monopolies in sectors such as telecommunication (Gray 2013:122-130; Valeri 2009:220-224; Fasano and Iqbal 2003).

Furthermore, governments sought to attract private sector investors by improving the economic infrastructure. Facilitated by an upswing of public export proceeds during the years of the second oil price boom (2002-2013), GCC governments embarked on several large-scale investment projects such as the build-up of economic cities, new wholesale ports or gas supplies for energy-intensive manufacturing activities.

Over the last decades, the economic balance between the public and the private sectors has shifted. GCC governments still exert a strong influence on economic developments, albeit in a more indirect manner than during earlier decades. Government expenditure, most notably, on public sector wages continues to be the main source of income for large parts of the local population. Yet, decades of large government outlays on public wages and infrastructure projects allowed for a substantial accumulation of financial funds both by households and private businesses (Hertog 2011). This accumulation of private capital as well as a growing availability of domestic credit from the financial sector gave room to a rising prominence of private investment within GCC economies particularly during the years of the second oil price boom (2002-2013).

Table 7.1: Indicators Private Sector Investment Bahrain, Oman and Qatar 1979-2013

	1979 -1985	1986 -2001	2002 -2013
	(in % of non-oil GDP)		
Domestic Credit Private Sector (household & business)			
Bahrain[1]	43.5	43.3	74.2
Oman	34.8	49.9	72.8
Qatar	40.7	51.9	74.9
	(in % of non-oil GDP)		
Domestic Credit Private Business			
Bahrain[1]	35.3	29.0	49.0
Oman	28.9	33.4	41.3
Qatar	31.5	31.1	46.6
	(in % of total GFCF)		
Private Sector Gross Fixed Capital Formation			
Bahrain[2]	61.6	64.5	70.1
Oman[3]	22.9	32.2	59.8
Oman (excluding housing)[3]	11.9	16.7[4]	na
Qatar[2]	na	na	75.8[5]
	(in % of total GFCF)		
Foreign Direct Investment			
Bahrain	-0.5	24.6	19.9
Oman	6.0	3.6	10.4
Qatar	0.2	4.5	10.1
	(in % of non-oil GDP)		
Memo: Public Capital Expenditure			
Bahrain	13.3	6.6	7.4
Oman	36.8	16.2	19.4
Qatar	21.9	9.1	18.3

Sources time series: Appendix A; UN Data, *National Accounts Official Country Data*; UNCTAD.

Notes: Time series in current prices. Calculations by the author.

[1] Time series domestic credit to private sector and private business in Bahrain do (most likely) include loans to public corporations (see Appendix A).

[2] Figures refer to oil and non-oil sectors and include both public and private companies. [3] Private sector and total gross fixed capital formation (GFCF) figures in Oman comprise only non-oil sectors.

[4] Figure refers to period 1986-1994. [5] Figure refers to period 2002-2008.

The analysis of investment spending by the public and private sectors is complicated by a scarcity of detailed data, most notably, on gross fixed capital formation. Time series on (budgetary) capital expenditure point to a declining relative importance of investment spending by the central governments in Bahrain, Oman and Qatar.

Yet, while the levels of non-government investment increased markedly, publicly available data on gross fixed capital formation provides only limited insights into the main drivers of this increase. Except for Oman, figures on gross fixed capital formation do not allow for a differentiation between investments by households, private businesses or (partly) state-owned companies. Furthermore, Oman is the only country which publishes disaggregated data on gross fixed capital formation in the non-oil economy. Instead, figures in Bahrain and Qatar refer to gross fixed capital formation in both the oil and the non-oil sectors (appendix A).

A growing economic importance of private sector investment in Bahrain, Oman and Qatar is indicated by strongly rising levels of credit by domestic commercial banks to borrowers from the private sector (households & businesses). When measured in relation to non-oil GDP, the share of domestic credit to the private sector increased by around 30-40 percentage points in all three countries between the periods 1979-1985 and 2002-2013 (table 7.1).

In contrast to private sector investment levels, the relative size of public capital expenditure has decreased over the last decades. Even though GCC governments embarked on several large public infrastructure projects during the years of the second oil price boom (20002-2013), the share of capital expenditure at non-oil GDP during this period stood at much lower levels than during the first oil price boom (1974-1985).

The decrease in the relative size of public capital expenditure is particularly pronounced in Bahrain and in Oman. Whereas capital expenditure in Bahrain and in Oman had accounted for 13.3% and 36.8%, respectively of non-oil GDP during the period 1979-1985, the corresponding shares stood only at 7.4% and 19.4% between the years 2002 and 2013 (table 7.1).

Yet, while the prominence of public sector investment has decreased, it is important to point out that capital expenditure figures might understate the extent of public sector investment activity. As will be discussed below, figures on capital expenditure by central governments typically do not entail investment by (partly) state-owned companies.

In view of both the rising prominence of private sector investment vis-a-vis public capital expenditure and the implementation of different economic policy reforms since the mid-1990s (e.g. privatisation, establishment of stock markets), Hodson (2013) ascertains a general (albeit slowly evolving) trend towards a declining dependence of private sectors on GCC governments. Yet, this notion of GCC private sectors' as an increasingly independent source of future economic growth is put into question by two important factors.

First, a large fraction of the increase in private sector credit falls upon households and not on private sector businesses. Here, a substantial part of rising private sector investment levels appears to have been directed to the construction of (household) dwellings. These investments, in turn, cannot be regarded as a generator of sustainable long-term economic growth.

Second, even though the prominence of private business capital has increased, GCC governments continue to exert a large impact on overall investment patterns. In comparison to the years of the first oil price boom (1974-1985), this impact is less distinct since a lower share of overall gross fixed capital formation was financed through budgetary outlays.

However, GCC governments played a very important, albeit more indirect, role during the 2000s in facilitating the build-up of production capacities in different industry and service sectors. This is exemplified by large-scale public investments in the economic infrastructure (e.g. build-up of economic cities and new wholesale ports) and by the formation of several joint ventures with private sector investors. Furthermore, the GCC economies exhibit a very close proximity between political and economic elites.

Breakdowns of private sector credit data into households and private businesses indicate that a substantial fraction of rising credit levels was utilised for residential investment and not for the build-up of production capacities by different industry or service companies. If loans to households are excluded from private credit data, the overall increase in credit levels is much less pronounced. When measured as a share of non-oil GDP, domestic credit to private businesses increased by around 15 percentage points since the early 1980s and, hence, by much smaller rates than domestic credit to the overall private sector (households and business) as can be seen from table 7.1.

In terms of the financing purposes of household loans, one may presume that the rising stock of household loans was primarily utilised for the purchase of consumer goods or the construction of household dwellings. Here, a high importance of housing within private sector investment patterns is indicated by disaggregated gross fixed capital formation data in Oman. The share of the private sector at total gross fixed capital formation in Oman is substantially lower, albeit still rising over time, if public and private sector investment in housing is excluded (table 7.1).

Unfortunately, no such breakdowns of gross fixed capital formation are publicly available for Bahrain and Qatar. Yet, in view of the high stock of household loans in both countries, it may reasonably be assumed that investment in housing played an important role for private sector gross fixed capital formation in Bahrain and Qatar as well.

With regard to private sector businesses, the indicator domestic credit to private businesses in table 7.1 points to an acceleration of credit growth during the years of the second oil price boom (2002-2013). The main sectoral sources of private business credit growth during these years were manufacturing, trade, construction and real estate.

Rising levels of private business activity over the last decades are exemplified by the business expansions of various family conglomerates in the GCC countries (e.g. Nass Group, Omar Zawawi Establishment, WJ Towell, Jaidah Group, Almana Group). During the years of the first oil price boom (1974-1985), these companies operated primarily in the construction sector, light manufacturing or as (sole) distributors of certain import goods. The accumulation of substantial earnings from the former business activities as well as the liberalisation measures of the 1990s and the 2000s allowed these companies to launch operations in various additional sectors (e.g. real estate, energy-intensive manufacturing industries, private education and health services). (Gray 2013:70-74; Valeri 2013)

In view of the rising shares of private business credit at non-oil GDP, the importance of private sector business investment appears to have increased within all three countries during the 2000s. Yet, despite being a more important source of gross fixed capital formation, a large part of private business investment seems to be closely aligned to the investment patterns of GCC public sectors. For example, the increase of private business investment in energy-intensive manufacturing industries was strongly facilitated by large public infrastructure investments (e.g. build-up of economic cities, wholesale ports or gas supplies for energy-intensive manufacturing activities).

In addition, GCC governments spurred business investment in different non-oil sectors by setting up several joint ventures between public sector entities and private sector investors particularly during the 2000s. As seen in sections 5.3 and 6.3, the establishment of these joint ventures is particularly observable for Oman (e.g. Oman LNG, Oman India Fertiliser Company, Sohar Industrial Port) and for Qatar (e.g. Qatalum, Qatar Chemical Company, Barwa Real Estate Company).

The publicly financed shares of investment by these joint ventures are typically not captured by budgetary capital expenditure figures. General government accounts do not comprise the operations of (semi-)public corporations but only budgetary transfers to these entities (IMF 2001:10-15, 70-71). Furthermore, as discussed with regard to Qatar, operations of public corporations have partially been funded by off-budgetary accounts (section 6.2). Hence, data on capital expenditure by general governments might strongly understate the total investment activity of the public sector in some GCC countries.[1]

A continued strong clout of GCC governments on private sector business activities is also indicated by large government shareholdings at domestic companies as well as by substantial business activities of different senior political figures in the GCC countries. Table 7.2 displays the shareholdings of domestic governments entities in the five largest publicly listed compa-

[1]The distinction between investments by general governments and public corporations is also a very important aspect when analysing private sector gross fixed capital formation figures in Bahrain and Qatar. As discussed in appendix A, officially published time series on private sector gross fixed capital formation in Bahrain and Qatar entail the investments both of private and public companies. The latter point might lead to misleading conclusions about potential shifts in the economic roles of the private and public sectors. This applies particularly to Qatar since the share of private sector investment stood at a very high 75.8% of total gross fixed capital formation during the years 2002-2008 (table 7.1). As discussed in chapter 6.2, various fully or partly state-owned companies in Qatar embarked on large-scale investment projects during the 2000s (e.g. Qatar Airways, Qatari Diar, Qatar Fertilizer Company). Hence, one may reasonably assume that a substantial fraction of the high private sector investment levels during the years 2002-2008 falls upon (partly) state-owned companies.

nies in Bahrain, Oman and Qatar.

In particular, the governments of Bahrain and Qatar stand out as dominant investors on local stock exchanges since both governments hold a combined share of at least 50% in three of the five largest publicly listed companies. Here, the government of Bahrain is the majority shareholder of National Bank of Bahrain, Aluminium Bahrain (Alba) and Bahrain Telecommunication. Likewise, the Qatari government exerts control over Qatar National Bank, Industries Qatar and Ooredoo (previously: Qatar Telecom). Furthermore, the Qatari government's sway over the business developments of Industries Qatar and Qatar National Bank is strengthened by regulations which limit the maximum shareholding of other investors to 2% (QA/IQ 2003:6; QA/QNB 2014:23).

Apart from shareholdings by government entities, various senior politicians in Bahrain, Oman and Qatar figure prominently as private sector investors. The analysis of private business activities from senior politicians is complicated by a limited availability of information, most notably, on the shareholder structure of private companies. Yet, qualitative case studies such as Valeri (2013) or Gray (2013) point to a very close proximity between economic and political elites in all three countries.

Large economic activities of different members of the ruling families are particularly observable for Bahrain and Qatar. For example, Hamad bin Jassim bin Jabr Al-Thani, the former foreign minister (1992-2013) and former prime minister (2007-2013) of Qatar, has been one of the most important private sector investors in Qatar over the last two decades. Among other investments, he has been an important investor in the large-scale real estate development The Pearl as well as in the trading firm Al-Fardan. Furthermore, he held a 50% stake at the national carrier Qatar Airways until the year 2014 (Gray 2013:62-63; Reuters 2014).

Likewise, different members of the ruling family in Bahrain were reported to be major investors in large-scale real estate projects during the 2000s. The most prominent investments in this regard are a 50% stake in the Bahrain Financial Harbour Project owned by Bahrain's prime minister Khalifa bin Salman Al-Khalifa as well as a 40% stake of the King of Bahrain, Hamad bin Isa Al-Khalifa in Bahrain Bay, a USD 2.5 billion real estate project (Reuters 2011; Financial Times 2014).

Table 7.2: Government Shareholdings in the Five Largest Publicly Listed Companies

Company	Market Cap. (USD Bln)	Shareholdings by Domestic Government Entities	Other Major Shareholders
<u>Bahrain:</u>			
Al-Ahli United Bank	4.9	9.7%: Social Insurance Organ.	17.9%: Gov. of Kuwait
Arab Banking Corporation	2.2	na	59.4%: Central Bank Libya 29.7%: Kuwait Invest. Auth.
National Bank of Bahrain	2.1	49.0%: Mumtalakat, 7.1%: Social Insurance Organ.	na
Aluminium Bahrain	2.0	69.4%: Mumtalakat	20.6%: SABIC
Bahrain Telecommunication	1.5	36.7%: Mumtalakat, 20.6%: Social Insurance Organ., 20.0%: Amber Holding	na
<u>Oman:</u>			
Bank Muscat	3.5	23.6%: Royal Court Affairs, 6.5%: Ministry of Defence Pension Fund	12.3%: Dubai Financial Group
Oman Telecommunication	3.2	70.0%: Government of Oman	na
Bank Dhofar	1.2	10.1%: Civil Service Employees' Pension Fund	27.8%: Dhofar International Development & Invest.

continued on next page

continued from previous page

Company	Market Cap. (USD Bln)	Shareholdings by Domestic Government Entities	Other Major Shareholders
Oman (continued):			
Nawras	1.1	na	55.0%: Oooredoo (*previously:* Qatar Telecom)
National Bank of Oman	1.1	23.8%: combined share of three different entities (e.g. Civil Service Employees' Pension Fund)	34.9%: Commercial Bank of Qatar 14.7%: Suhail Bahwan Group
Qatar:			
Qatar National Bank	40.3	50.0%: Qatar Investment Auth.	na
Industries Qatar	30.6	51.0%: Qatar Petroleum (100% state-owned)	na
Ezdan Holding	12.5	na	54.2%: Khalid Thani A. Al Thani
Ooredoo (*previously:* Qatar Telecom)	10.3	51.7%: Qatar Holding 12.5%: General Retirement and Social Insurance Auth.	10.0%: Abu Dhabi Investment Council
Masraf al Rayan	9.5	27.7%: combined share of five different entities (e.g. Qatar Holding)	13.1%: Hamad Abdulla Al Thani

Sources: Bahrain Bourse, Muscat Securities Market, Qatar Stock Exchange, company sources (annual reports, homepages, corporate governance reports).
Note: Market capitalisation as of 4 December 2014.

In comparison to Bahrain and Qatar, the ruling family in Oman appears to be less involved in private sector business activities which might partly be ascribed to the ruling family's small size. Instead, close links between economic and political elites in Oman are rather exemplified by a strong political clout of important business families. As pointed out by Valeri (2013:20-21), several ministries of the Omani government were headed by different members of leading business families over the last decades (e.g. Qays al Zawawi, Salim bin Hilal, Abd al-Malik bin Abd Allah).

7.3 Crowding-In or Crowding-Out - An Econometric Analysis

The public sectors in Bahrain, Oman and Qatar impacted the economic activities of private sectors in different ways over the last decades. A positive impact of public sectors on private sector business activities is observable for large-scale public infrastructure investments (e.g. build-up of wholesale ports and economic cities, expansion of electricity production) since the latter improved the production conditions for private sector companies markedly. In addition, public sectors facilitated private sector economic activity by forming several public-private joint ventures.

Instead, public sectors played a detrimental role in fostering the employment of national employees within the private sectors. As a result of a strong expansion of public sector employment since the 1970s and comparatively high public sector wages for national employees, private sector business activities in all three countries largely continue to rely on the availability of cheap foreign labour.

The following section seeks to examine the economic links between public and private sectors in more detail by analysing the impact of public expenditure on private sector investment. The economic literature highlights that increases in public expenditure might exert both a positive (*crowding-in*) as well as a negative (*crowding-out*) impact on private sector investment activity. Therefore, the country-specific characteristics of the long-term link between public expenditure and private sector investment in Bahrain, Oman and Qatar are examined below through a cointegration and causality analysis.

Section 7.3.1 shortly discusses the underlying causes for the occurrence of crowding-in and crowding-out effects as well as their applicability to the

GCC countries. The data and methodology of the econometric analysis are described in section 7.3.2. Section 7.3.3 presents the econometric results and concludes.

7.3.1 Causes of Crowding-In and Crowding-Out Effects

The overall impact of increases in public expenditure on private sector investment activity varies considerably across countries. This cross-country heterogeneity can be ascribed to the observation that rising levels of public expenditure potentially influence private sector gross fixed capital formation in different ways. An increase in public expenditure levels might both stimulate (*crowding-in effect*) as well as reduce (*crowding-out effect*) private sector investment activity. The respective strength of these two opposing effects depends on a range of country-specific factors.

Economic theory ascribes a potential crowding-in effect to public spending categories which exert a positive impact on the production conditions within an economy and, as a result, raise the profitability of private sector investment (section 2.1). In this regard, the economic literature typically points to public spending on infrastructure (e.g. electricity production, road networks, wholesale ports) and on human capital (e.g. public provision of health and education services).

An increase in these public spending categories might stimulate private sector investment activity by removing infrastructure bottlenecks or by improving the educational level and the health status of the population. Hausmann and Rodrik (2003) extend this line of thought and advocate that governments in developing countries should foster private sector investment in the build-up of new industries through different incentives (e.g. public sector credit, investment subsidies).

In this view, the rationale for government interventions is based on the assumption that private sector investment levels in certain production factors such as infrastructure or education services are below the social optimum of an economy. This under-investment of private sector agents in the provisioning level of these production factors, in turn, is ascribed to the existence of positive externalities (e.g. education services) or to high initial investment needs (e.g. infrastructure, build-up production capacity in new industries). Accordingly, the strength of a crowding-in effect within a particular country is seen to depend on whether rising levels of public expenditure help to alleviate any potential shortfalls of human or physical capital in the economy.

In contrast, the crowding-out effect applies a very different perspective on the link between public expenditure and private investment than the crowding-in effect. As seen above, the crowding-in effect analyses the impact of public expenditure on private investment primarily with regard to the productive capacity of an economy. Instead, the crowding-out effect highlights potential consequences of increases in public expenditure on the availability of financing for private sector investments.

The crowding-out effect refers to a situation where a strong expansion of public expenditure limits the financial resources for private sector gross fixed capital formation. This applies particularly if rising levels of public expenditure are funded by increases in taxes or by higher levels of borrowing at domestic banks. In the latter two cases, the crowding-out hypothesis states that increases in public expenditure do not complement but, instead, substitute private investment.

The links between public expenditure and private investment in the GCC countries differ considerably from those in most other countries. Most importantly, public expenditures of the GCC governments are largely funded by inflows of oil and gas export proceeds and not by taxes. Moreover, as GCC governments command over sizeable resource endowments, taxation is virtually absent in the GCC economies.

Public spending levels of GCC governments increased strongly during the years of the two oil price booms (1974-1985, 2002-2013). A large fraction of these increases in public expenditure falls upon spending categories which are typically not considered to be conducive to the production conditions within an economy. This applies particularly to the strong expansion of public sector employment for local populations during the periods of the two oil price booms. Since external rents from oil and gas exports constitute the main source of public revenues, however, strong increases in the public wage bill do not necessarily limit the financial resources for private sector investment activity.

Instead, the existence of crowding-out effects appears more likely for periods of low oil price levels. During the latter years, GCC governments exhibited, at times, substantial fiscal deficits as a result of comparatively low oil and gas export revenues. Here, government borrowing at domestic

Figure 7.1: Public Expenditure and Private Gross Fixed Capital Formation
(Index, 1979=100)

(a) Bahrain

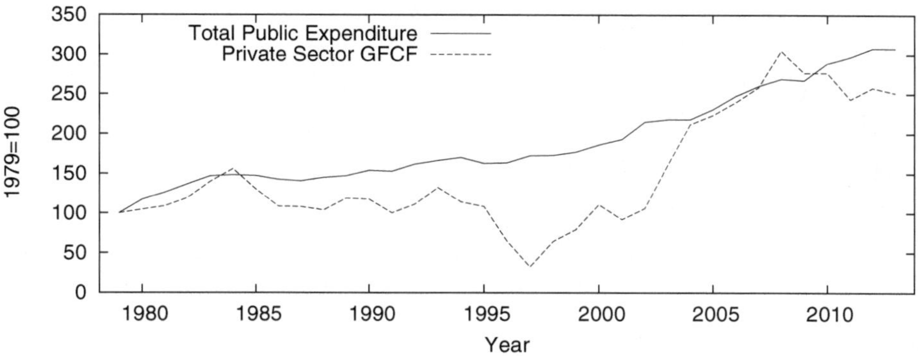

(b) Oman

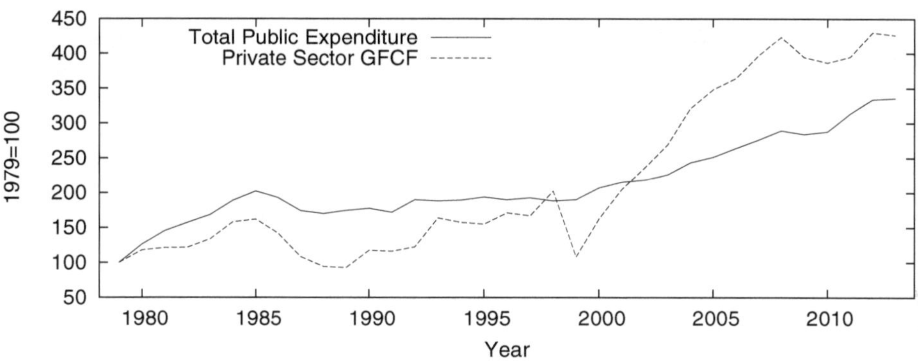

Notes: Times series in logarithms and in constant prices. Breakdowns of total gross fixed capital formation (GFCF) in Qatar into public and private sector GFCF are publicly not available for the years prior to 2002.
Sources: Appendix A.

Figure 7.2: Public Expenditure and Domestic Credit to Private Sector (Index, 1979=100)

(a) Bahrain

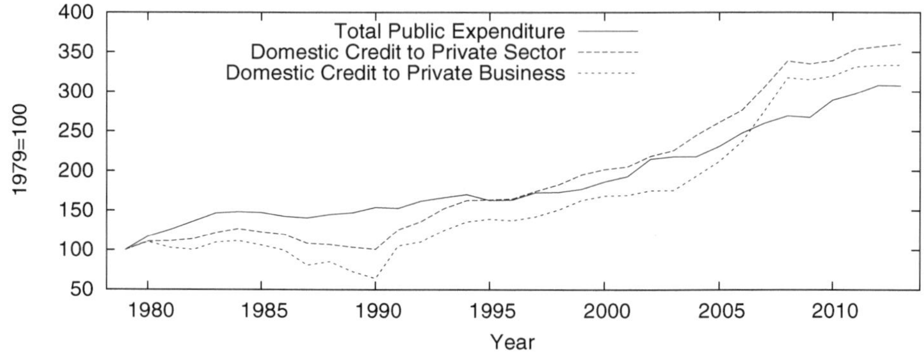

(b) Oman

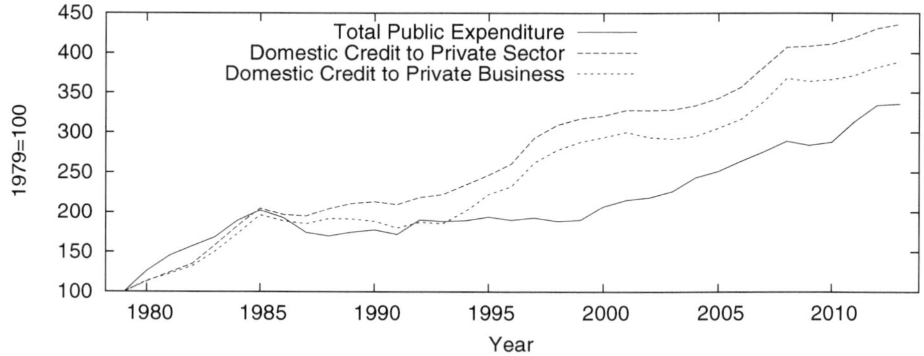

(c) Qatar

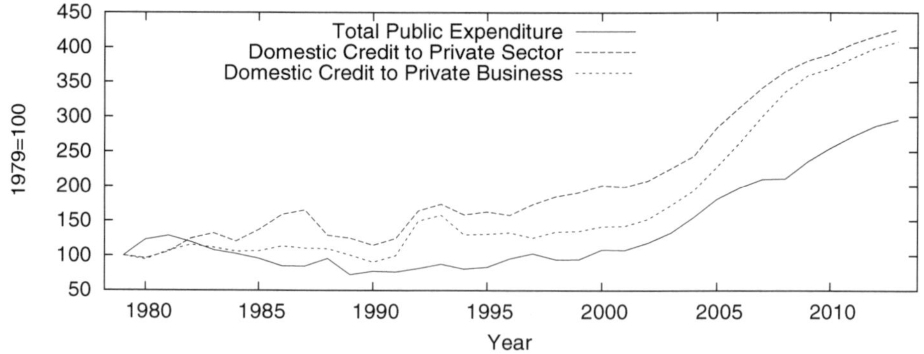

Notes: Times series in logarithms and in constant prices.
Sources: Appendix A.

banks during years of fiscal deficits might have reduced the availability of funding for private sector investments.

Figures 7.2 and 7.1 compare the developments of total public expenditure and private sector investment. Due to a scarcity of detailed data on private gross fixed capital formation (GFCF), time series of domestic credit to the private sector (households and private businesses) and to private businesses serve as additional proxies for private sector investment activity within the GCC countries.

At first sight, a crowding-in effect appears more likely for the GCC countries than a crowding-out effect since large increases of public expenditure were typically accompanied by an upswing of private sector investment activity. This is particularly evident for the years of the second oil price boom (2002-2013).

In this regard, one may hypothesise that certain public spending categories such as public investments in the economic infrastructure and in the production capacities of various non-oil sectors stimulated private investment. Bolstered by rising oil revenues, GCC governments aimed to improve private sector production conditions by large public investments in the (non-oil) economic infrastructure during the 2000s (e.g. economic cities, wholesale ports, gas-supply for energy-intensive manufacturing industries). Furthermore, GCC governments sought to increase the production capacities in non-oil sectors such as manufacturing or trade by forming different joint ventures with private sector investors.

For gaining a more accurate understanding of the overall impact of public expenditure on private sector capital formation in Bahrain, Oman and Qatar, I will examine the long-term interaction between these time series through a cointegration and causality analysis.

7.3.2 Data and Econometric Methodology

The econometric analysis below elaborates the country-specific characteristics of the long-term link between public expenditure and private sector investment in Bahrain, Oman and Qatar. The main question of this analysis is whether increases in public expenditure tend to crowd-in or to crowd-out private sector investment. Building on cointegration and causality analysis, the following econometric approach indicates the existence of a crowding-in (crowding-out) effect if increases in public expenditure are found to cause increases (decreases) of private sector investment in a statistically significant manner.

In terms of public expenditure, the econometric analysis draws on time series of total public expenditure. As discussed above, the impact of different categories of public expenditure (e.g. public wage bill, infrastructure investments) on private investment activity is likely to vary considerably. Hence, time series of total public expenditure are suitable for gauging the overall impact of public expenditure.

With regard to private sector investment, the analysis is complicated by a limited availability of time series on private sector gross fixed capital formation (GFCF). Oman is the only country which publishes disaggregated data on private sector GFCF in the non-oil economy. Instead, GFCF data in Bahrain refers to both the oil and the non-oil sectors. Furthermore, figures on private sector GFCF in Qatar are publicly not available for the years prior to 2002.

Given the scarcity of private sector GFCF data, I utilise two additional proxy variables for private sector investment (domestic credit to private sector, domestic credit to private business). Since the availability of funding appears as an important determinant of private sector investments, time series on domestic credit to the private sector can be assumed to approximate private investment activity reasonably well.

As discussed above, a substantial share of credit to the private sector in the GCC countries falls upon households. One may suppose that the intended uses of loans to households and private businesses differ considerably. Therefore, the econometric analysis examines the impact of total public expenditure not only with regard to domestic credit to the private sector (households and private business) but also with regard to time series of domestic credit to private business.

The sample period of the econometric analysis is 1979-2013 and, hence, the same as in the econometric analysis in chapter 3. Due to a lack of more accurate deflators, time series are deflated by the consumer price index (CPI) of the respective country. In order to control for potential measurement errors which might result from this deflating procedure, the robustness of the empirical results is examined by conducting a separate econometric analysis for time series in current prices.

The econometric methodology applied in this chapter resembles the econometric approach which was explained extensively in section 3.4. Therefore, I sketch out the econometric approach utilised in this chapter only briefly below.

The econometric analysis starts by examining whether total public expenditure exhibits a long-term link with one of the private investment time series (private GFCF, domestic credit to private sector, domestic credit to private business). The existence of such long-term links can be scrutinised by cointegration analysis as the latter econometric method identifies potential co-movements of different variables over the long-run.

In order to be eligible for cointegration analysis, however, variables need to be integrated of order one. Therefore, the order of integration of the different time series is first determined by four different unit root tests (ADF test, KPSS test, ADF-GLS test, Lee and Strazicich test with a structural break).

Provided that the respective variables are integrated of order one, the existence of cointegration relationships between public expenditure and private investment time series are examined by two cointegration tests (Johansen trace test, Saikkonen and Lütkepohl test). In addition, the strength of any potential cointegration relationship is checked by a zero restriction test. Furthermore, Chow breakpoint tests examine the stability of a potential cointegration relationship.

In case public expenditure and private investment are found to exhibit a stable long-term link, the interaction between these (cointegrated) variables is estimated in a vector error correction model (VECM). These VECM estimates, in turn, allow for an analysis of the mutual impact between the cointegrated variables through Granger causality tests and impulse response analysis.

Granger causality tests identify the direction of causality between cointegrated variables. Impulse response analysis is an appropriate tool for simulating the overall impact of an increase in public expenditure on private sector investment. If public expenditure is shown to exert a positive (negative) causal impact on private sector investment, the existence of a crowding-in (crowding-out) effect is confirmed.

7.3.3 Empirical Results and Conclusion

The empirical results allow for two main conclusions about the long-term impact of total public expenditure on private sector investment activity in Bahrain, Oman and Qatar. First, increases in total public expenditure tend to crowd-in private sector investment. Instead, the existence of crowding-out effects is not indicated by the results of the econometric analysis. Granger causality tests and impulse response analysis of time series which were found to exhibit a stable cointegration relationship clearly show that increases in public expenditure cause increases and not decreases of private sector investment levels.

This finding is consistent with the development patterns of public expenditure and private investment variables in figures 7.2 and 7.1 which showed that increases in total public expenditure were typically accompanied by increases in private sector gross fixed capital formation (GFCF) and by rising levels of domestic credit to the private sector.

The lack of empirical support for the existence of crowding-out effects might be ascribed to the fact that public expenditure in the GCC countries is largely funded by external oil and gas rents. Therefore, increases of public expenditure particularly during periods of rising oil price levels do not necessarily limit the financial resources for private sector investment activity.

Second, the strength of this potential crowding-in effect, however, seems to vary across the GCC countries. A strong tendency for public expenditure to crowd-in private investment is observable for Qatar. Instead, the econometric results do not confirm a long-term link between total public expenditure and private investment times series in Oman.

Unfortunately, the scope of the cointegration analysis is limited by the results of the unit root tests and data limitations. The two time series domestic credit to private sector (Oman) and domestic credit to private business (Qatar) are not eligible for cointegration analysis because both time series were not found to be integrated of order one. Furthermore, time series on private sector GFCF are publicly not available for Qatar prior to the years 2002. As a result, the long-term interactions between public expenditure and private sector investment activity in Qatar can only be examined through the variable domestic credit to private sector.

Table 7.3 summarises the results of the baseline cointegration and causality analysis. In addition, table 7.4 displays the main results of the cointegration and causality analysis of time series in current prices which serves as a robustness test for the results in the baseline cointegration and causality analysis.

The empirical results for Bahrain can be seen to be very robust since the findings on Bahrain in table 7.3 are confirmed by the results in table 7.4. Unfortunately, no such robustness test could be applied to the empirical results for Oman and Qatar in table 7.3 since the variable total public expenditure is not integrated of order one when measured in current prices both in case of Oman and Qatar.

The results of the baseline econometric analysis in table 7.3 show that increases in total public expenditure exert a crowding-in effect on the two variables domestic credit to private business (Bahrain) and domestic credit to private sector (Qatar). Total public expenditure is shown not only to exhibit a long-run cointegration relationship with these two variables but also to cause the development patterns of the latter variables at a 1% statistical significance level.

Furthermore, impulse response simulations for these cointegration relationships clearly point to a positive long-term impact of increases in total public expenditure on private sector investment activity. As can be seen in the left-hand panel of figure 7.3, a positive impulse of total public expenditure leads to positive responses of the variables domestic credit to private business (Bahrain) and domestic credit to private sector (Qatar), respectively. These impulse response dynamics can be ascribed a high statistical significance since the 95% confidence intervals of both responses in the left-hand panel contain only positive values.

In addition, the impulse response dynamics of the variables total public expenditure (Bahrain) and domestic credit to private business (Bahrain) are confirmed by the impulse response analysis of time series in current prices in figure 7.4. Here, the impulse responses of the variables total public expenditure (Bahrain) and domestic credit to private business (Bahrain) in figure 7.4 almost exactly resemble the impulse responses of both variables within the baseline econometric analysis in figure 7.3.

The overall empirical evidence, however, for a crowding-in effect in Bahrain is less distinct than in case of Qatar. This is apparent when comparing the

Table 7.3: Overview - Cointegration and Causality Analysis

All variables in constant prices

Variables	CI Tests[1] JOH	SAI	β-Vector VECM	Direction of Causality
Bahrain (1979-2013):				
Total Expenditure & Private GFCF	0	0	na	na
Total Expenditure & Credit Private Sector	0	0	na	na
Total Expenditure & Credit Private Business	2*	0	1.000 -0.645	Expenditure ⇒ Credit***
Oman (1979-2013):				
Total Expenditure & Private GFCF	0	0	na	na
Total Expenditure & Credit Private Sector	na	na	na	na
Total Expenditure & Credit Private Business	0	0	na	na
Qatar (1979-2013):				
Total Expenditure & Credit Private Sector	2*	1*	1.000 -1.071	Expenditure ⇒ Credit***
Total Expenditure & Credit Private Business	na	na	na	na

Notes: Cointegration (CI) test results refer to the number of cointegration relations between the respective variables in the Johansen trace test (JOH) and the Saikkonen and Lütkepohl test (SAI). The symbol ⇒ denotes the direction of Granger causality. Statistical significance levels of 1%, 5%, and 10% are indicated by ***, **, and *, respectively. For detailed test results please refer to tables D1-D10 in the appendix.

[1] The following variables have been excluded from the respective cointegration tests since they are not integrated of order one (table D1): credit to private sector (Oman), credit to private business (Qatar).

Table 7.4: Overview - Cointegration and Causality Analysis (Current Prices)

All variables in current prices

Variables	CI Tests JOH	CI Tests SAI	β-Vector VECM	Direction of Causality
Bahrain (1979-2013):				
Total Expenditure & Private GFCF	0	0	na	na
Total Expenditure & Credit Private Sector	0	0	na	na
Total Expenditure & Credit Private Business	1*	0	1.000 -0.705	Expenditure $\Rightarrow$ Credit***
Oman (1979-2013):				
Total Expenditure & Private GFCF	na	na	na	na
Total Expenditure & Credit Private Sector	na	na	na	na
Total Expenditure & Credit Private Business	na	na	na	na
Qatar (1979-2013):				
Total Expenditure & Credit Private Sector	na	na	na	na
Total Expenditure & Credit Private Business	na	na	na	na

Notes: Cointegration (CI) test results refer to the number of cointegration relations between the respective variables in the Johansen trace test (JOH) and the Saikkonen and Lütkepohl test (SAI). The symbol $\Rightarrow$ denotes the direction of Granger causality. Statistical significance levels of 1%, 5%, and 10% are indicated by ***, **, and *, respectively. Cointegration tests could not be conducted for Oman and Qatar since the variable total expenditure was found to be integrated of order two in both cases (table D11). For detailed test results please refer to tables D11-D20.

cointegration test results for both cointegration relationships within the baseline econometric analysis. While the existence of a long-term link between the variables total public expenditure (Qatar) and domestic credit to private business (Qatar) is confirmed both by the Johansen trace test (JOH) and the Saikkonen and Lütkepohl test (SAI), the cointegration link between the variables total public expenditure (Bahrain) and domestic credit to private business (Bahrain) is only indicated by the Johansen trace test (table 7.3).

In addition, the notion of a crowding-in effect in Bahrain is not supported by the empirical results of two other private investment time series. In contrast to the variable domestic credit to private business (Bahrain), the two variables private sector GFCF (Bahrain) and domestic credit to private sector (Bahrain) do not exhibit a long-term cointegration relationship with total public expenditure (Bahrain) both when examined in constant and in current prices. These differing cointegration test results suggest that the strength of a crowding-in effect in Bahrain is weaker than in Qatar.

With regard to Oman, the results of the baseline econometric analysis do not indicate the existence of a crowding-in effect. Neither the variable private sector GFCF (Oman) nor the variable domestic credit to private business (Oman) are found to exhibit a cointegration link with total public expenditure (Oman).

In terms of these cross-country differences, the existence of a comparatively strong crowding-in effect in Qatar might be ascribed to the observation that the non-oil development push in Qatar was more pronounced than in Bahrain and Oman, most notably, during the years of the second oil price boom (2002-2013). While the governments of Bahrain and Oman embarked on several large-scale public investments projects which aimed at improving non-oil economic production conditions, the Qatari government expanded public investment levels far more rapidly than the former two countries since the early 2000s.

Facilitated by rapidly rising liquified natural gas (LNG) exports proceeds, the Qatari government pursued a big push development strategy which aimed at advancing the development of several non-oil sectors through various large-scale investment projects. High levels of public investments contributed to the build-up of economic infrastructure (e.g. construction of new economic cities and whosesale ports) and to a rapid business expan-

Figure 7.3: Impulse Responses Cointegrated Variables

Bahrain: Total Public Expenditure & Credit Private Business

(a) Response Credit to Impulse Total Expenditure

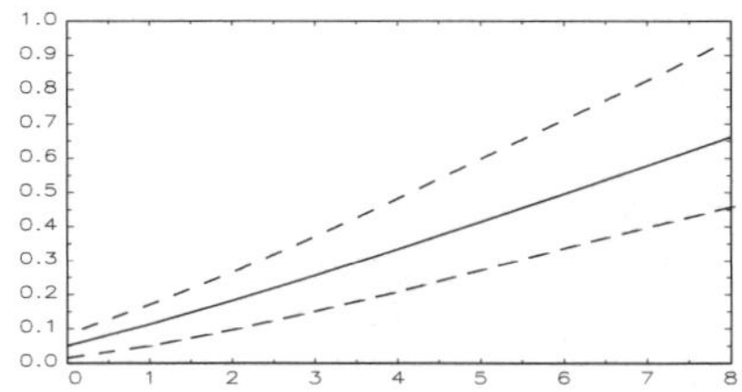

(b) Response Total Expenditure to Impulse Credit

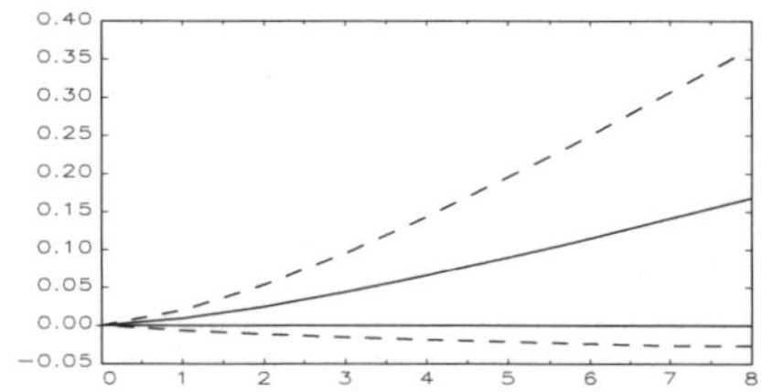

Qatar: Total Public Expenditure & Credit Private Sector

(c) Response Credit to Impulse Total Expenditure

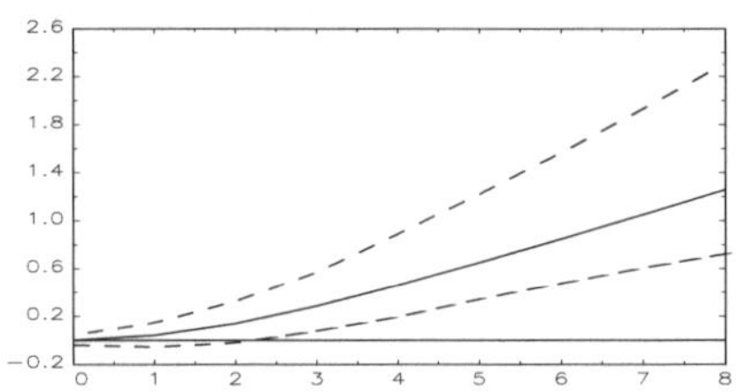

(d) Response Total Expenditure to Impulse Credit

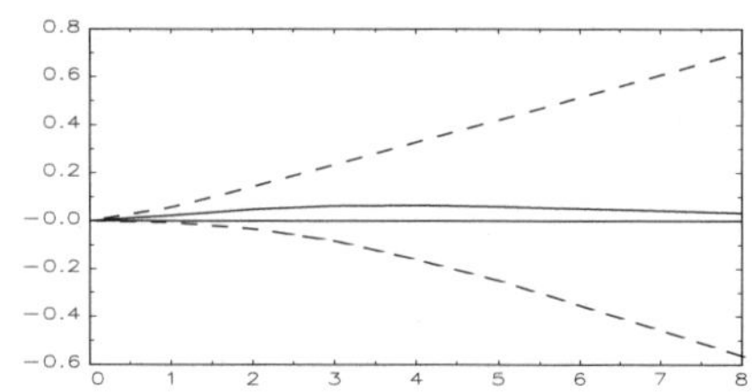

Notes: 95% Hall percentile confidence intervals (1000 bootstrap replications). VECM specifications refer to table D9 in the appendix. X-axis denotes number of years after initial impulse. Y-axis shows accumulated changes in the (natural log) level of responding variable. Impulse is given by one standard deviation of the orthogonalised residual of the impulse variable. In view of the results of the respective Granger causality tests in table D10, total public expenditure has been ranked first in the orthogonalised residual covariance matrix.

Figure 7.4: Impulse Responses Cointegrated Variables (Current Prices)

Bahrain: Total Public Expenditure & Credit Private Business

(a) Response Credit to Impulse Total Expenditure

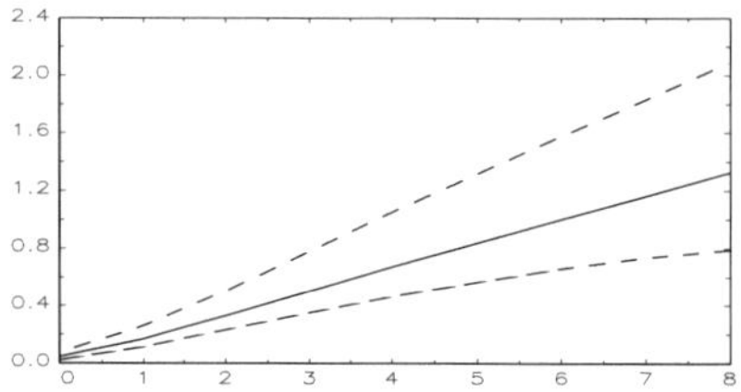

(b) Response Total Expenditure to Impulse Credit

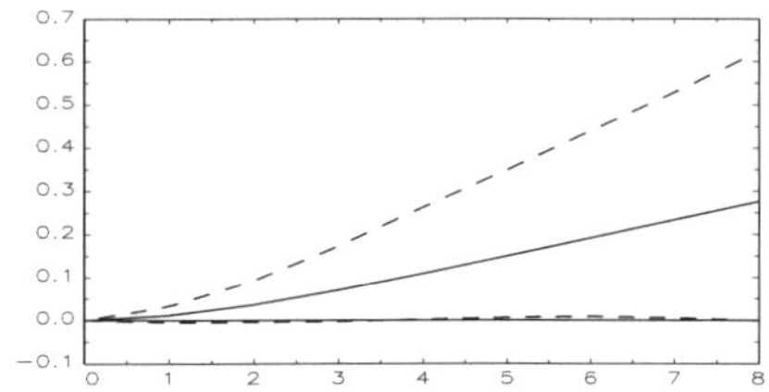

Notes: 95% Hall percentile confidence intervals (1000 bootstrap replications). VECM specifications refer to table D19 in the appendix. X-axis denotes number of years after initial impulse. Y-axis shows accumulated changes in the (natural log) level of responding variable. Impulse is given by one standard deviation of the orthogonalised residual of the impulse variable. In view of the results of the respective Granger causality tests in table D20, total public expenditure has been ranked first in the orthogonalised residual covariance matrix.

sion of several joint ventures of the Qatari government with private sector investors (e.g. Qatar Fertilizer Company, Qatalum, Qatar Airways). Not least with regard to the business expansions of public-private joint ventures, this big push investment strategy of the Qatari government appears to have broadened the investment opportunities for private sector investors markedly.

A positive impact of public expenditure on private sector investment activity in Qatar is not only observable for budgetary capital expenditure (e.g. build-up of economic infrastructure) but also for some current expenditure categories. As discussed in section 6.2, official current expenditure figures in Qatar contain transfers to extrabudgetary accounts which have partially been utilised for funding large-scale investments of (partly) state-owned companies during the 2000s. Between the years 2002 and 2013, the Qatari government increased total public expenditure (in constant prices) by an annual average of 16.9% compared to 10.0% in Bahrain and 10.6% in Oman (tables 4.1, 5.1 and 6.1).

Overall, the strength of a crowding-in effect in Bahrain, Oman and Qatar seems to be related to the scale of publicly financed investment projects. Since public expenditure in the GCC countries is largely financed by external oil and gas rents, a strong expansion of public investment expenditure typically does not limit the resources for private sector investment activity. In contrast, a high willingness of governments to foster a rapid economic expansion in various sectors through large-scale investments projects appears to stimulate private sector investment activity in the GCC countries.

7.4 The Impact of Investment on Non-Oil Economic Growth Dynamics

Investment patterns of the public and private sectors have shaped non-oil economic growth dynamics in Bahrain, Oman and Qatar lastingly over the last decades. A strong impact of investment on non-oil economies is particularly observable for periods of high oil and gas price levels (1974-1985, 2002-2013) during which GCC governments typically increased public investment considerably.

Large-scale public investment projects during the years of the two oil price booms altered the non-oil economies in all three countries markedly by expanding both the economic infrastructure (e.g. economic cities, wholesale ports, electricity production) and the production capacities of (partly) state-owned companies. The impact of these large-scale public investments on local economies was partly amplified by private investment. As shown by the econometric analysis in the previous section, public expenditure in all three countries exhibits a tendency to crowd-in private investment. Hence, public expenditure exerts not only a direct impact on local economies but shapes the latter also in an indirect manner through its impact on private investment activity.

The important role of oil and gas price levels for overall investment patterns is illustrated by table 7.5 which displays the average shares of total investment at GDP in Bahrain, Oman and Qatar during the years 1975 and 2013. The share of total investment at GDP typically stood at much higher levels during periods of high oil prices (1975-1985, 2002-2013) than during periods of low oil prices (1986-2001). Therefore, the size of public oil and gas export proceeds appears as an important determinant of total investment activity in all three economies.

The following section analyses the impact of public and private invest-

Table 7.5: Total Gross Fixed Capital Formation 1975-2013
(in % of GDP)

	1975 -1985	1986 -2001	2002 -2013
Bahrain	35.9	18.6	24.5
Oman	27.0	17.5	25.2
Qatar	20.8[1]	21.9	34.6
Memo: Average Crude Oil Price (US-Dollar/bbl)	23.8	17.1	68.1

Sources: UN Data, *National Accounts Official Country Data*; IMF, *International Financial Statistics*; World Bank, *Global Economic Monitor Commodities*
Notes: Gross fixed capital formation (GFCF) figures above comprise oil and non-oil sectors since sectoral breakdowns of GFCF are publicly not available for Bahrain and Qatar. Crude oil prices refer to the annual averages of Dubai Fateh crude oil prices during the respective time periods. Time series in current prices. Calculations by the author.
[1] Figure refers to period 1976-1985.

ment on non-oil economic growth dynamics in more detail. In particular, this section aims to examine to what extent public and private investment patterns shaped the characteristics of non-oil economic growth dynamics in Bahrain, Oman and Qatar.

The focus on the characteristics of non-oil economic growth dynamics arises from the findings of the country studies in chapters 4-6 which showed that the strong increases in aggregate non-oil GDP levels since the late 1970s were to a very large extent driven by an accumulation of the factor inputs labour and physical capital. Instead, measures of productivity such as labour productivity levels have either decreased (Bahrain, Qatar) or increased by much smaller rates than aggregate non-oil GDP levels (Oman) over the same time period.

A strong disparity between aggregate non-oil GDP and labour productivity is also observable with regard to a potential growth-enhancing impact of public expenditure. The econometric analysis in chapter 3 showed that public expenditure influences the long-run development patterns of aggregate non-oil GDP to a much greater extent than the long-term trajectory of labour productivity.

The central argument laid out in the following is that public and private investment patterns strongly contributed to this input-driven growth dynamics since a growth-enhancing impact of investment is particularly evident for non-oil sectors which rely on high initial investments (e.g. capital-intensive manufacturing industries) or on cheap, typically foreign, labour (e.g. construction, wholesale trade).

GCC governments fuelled this investment pattern in different ways such as large-scale investments in the economic infrastructure (build-up of wholesale ports and gas supply networks for energy-intensive industries), the foundation of fully or partly state-owned companies as well as the provision of different production inputs at comparatively low prices (e.g. oil and gas feedstocks, electricity).

The important role of investment for fostering non-oil economic growth is particularly evident when looking into the main drivers of export and employment growth over the last decades (tables 7.6 and 7.8). As can be seen from table 7.6, all three countries witnessed a substantial increase of non-hydrocarbon exports since the year 1980. These strong increases were mainly driven by rising export levels of capital-intensive manufacturing industries (e.g. production of aluminium, iron ore, chemicals, fertilisers, plastics).

In addition, an upswing of re-exports elevated non-hydrocarbon export volumes, most notably, in Oman since the 1990s. Here, a large share of re-exports in Oman falls upon the port of Salalah which became a regional hub for entrepot trade following a strong expansion of handling capacities in the mid-1990s.

In view of the large investments needs for the build-up of production capacities in capital-intensive manufacturing industries and for the expansion of handling capacities at wholesale ports, high levels of investments can be singled out as the main cause for the strong increase of exports in these non-oil sectors. These large-scale investments were carried out both by public sector entities and by private sector investors. A large share of rising exports levels outside the oil and gas sector originates from expansions of production capacities at joint ventures between the public and the private sectors (e.g. Aluminium Bahrain, Oman India Fertiliser Company, Oman Polypropylene, Salalah Port Services Company, Qatar Fertiliser Company, Qatar Chemical Company, Qatar Petrochemical Company).

Beyond the formation of joint ventures, GCC governments facilitated eco-

Table 7.6: Main Export Goods 1980-2010
(in US-Dollar million)

	1980	1990	2000	2010
Bahrain				
Hydrocarbon	3,209	2,939	4,478	11,515
Of which: Refined Oil	na	na	na	11,508
Non-Hydrocarbon (incl. Re-Exports)	233	822	1,717	4,545
Of which: Aluminium	105	410	779	1,573
Of which: Iron Ore	0	0	197	1,187
Of which: Manufacture of Metals	32	72	15	252
Of which: Road Vehicles	17	13	21	227
Memo: Total Re-Exports	11	36	82	560
Oman				
Hydrocarbon	3,608	5,039	9,365	25,203
Of which: Crude Oil	3,608	4,898	8,716	20,799
Of which: LNG	0	0	465	3,055
Non-Hydrocarbon (incl. Re-Exports)	145	458	1,939	11,350
Of which: Chemicals	0	0	10	955
Of which: Fertilisers	0	0	0	777
Of which: Food & Live Animals	13	88	228	733
Of which: Plastics	0	1	24	629
Memo: Total Re-Exports	131	279	1,295	4,991
Memo: Re-Export Transport Equipment	na	156	698	3,779
Qatar				
Hydrocarbon	5,345	2,967	10,663	72,634
Of which: Crude Oil	5,336	2,783	6,588	21,951
Of which: LNG	0	0	3,512	23,394
Non-Hydrocarbon (incl. Re-Exports)	295	674	931	6,436
Of which: Plastics	0	194	228	1,494
Of which: Chemicals	0	78	49	1,379
Of which: Fertilisers	163	89	189	861
Of which: Steel & Iron	133	180	127	746
Total Re-Exports	na	112	170	na

Sources: Comtrade; BH/CSO (1986, 1992); BH/CIO (2002); OM/DC (1992); OM/MoNE (2002, 2012); OM/CBO (1981d); Nafi (1983); QA/PC (2002); IMF (2012).

nomic growth in capital-intensive manufacturing industries through large-scale investments in the economic infrastructure (e.g. build-up of economic cities and gas supply networks) and by providing production inputs such as electricity or oil and gas feedstocks at comparatively low prices.

The build-up of economic cities is a widely adopted economic policy approach for stimulating economic activity across the GCC countries. This became particularly apparent during the second half of the 1990s and the 2000s as the governments of Bahrain, Oman and Qatar embarked on the establishment of several new economic cities (e.g. Bahrain Investment Wharf, Sohar Industrial Port, Salalah Free Zone, Ras Laffan Industrial City, Mesaieed Industrial City).

Public investments in the build-up of economic zones comprised not only the construction of modern production sites but also several related investments such as the building of logistics facilities in economic zones (e.g. ports) and a substantial expansion of production capacities at public utilities (e.g. electricity). In addition to rising electricity production levels, the strong expansion of oil-related manufacturing activities (chemicals, fertilisers, plastics) during the 2000s necessitated also large public investments in the supply of oil and gas feedstocks. For example, the government of Oman embarked on the construction of gas pipelines to the economic zones in Sohar and Salalah during the early 2000s in order to secure gas supplies for manufacturing companies in these economic zones (OM/MoNE 2002b:147-149).

Furthermore, the governments of Bahrain, Oman and Qatar aided the growth of manufacturing export industries by providing important production inputs such as electricity as well as oil and gas feedstocks at comparatively low prices. As can be seen from table 7.7, industrial electricity prices in Bahrain, Oman and Qatar are substantially lower than in OECD countries. These comparatively low electricity prices constitute an important comparative advantage for manufacturing exporters in all three countries given the high energy consumption levels in most GCC manufacturing industries (e.g. production of aluminium, iron ore, chemicals, fertilisers, plastics).

The important role of low electricity prices for stimulating manufacturing activity, in turn, exemplifies the extensive nature of non-oil economic growth patterns in Bahrain, Oman and Qatar. Not least as a result of rising

Table 7.7: Industrial Electricity Prices and Energy Use

	Industrial Electricity Price (US-Dollar/KWh)	Annual Energy Use per Capita (tonne of oil equiv.)
Bahrain	0.04	7.4
Oman	0.04[1]	8.4
Qatar	0.02	17.4
Memo: OECD Countries	0.12	4.2

Sources: Kingdom of Bahrain: Electricity & Water Authority; Muscat Electricity Distribution Company; Qatar Electricity & Water Company; International Energy Agency, *Electricity Information 2014*; World Bank, *World Development Indicators.*

Notes: Industrial electricity prices in Bahrain, Oman and Qatar refer to tariffs as of March 2015 whereas the average electricity price for OECD countries corresponds to the year 2012. World Bank data on energy use refers to year 2011.

[1] Corresponds to the annual average as the industrial electricity price amounts to 0.03 between September and April and 0.06 between May and August, respectively.

energy needs of manufacturing industries over the last decades, Bahrain, Oman and, most notably, Qatar exhibit much higher levels of per capita energy consumption than OECD countries (table 7.7). In view of this high energy dependency, continued increases in electricity production capacities appear as a crucial precondition for economic growth in the manufacturing sectors of all three economies.

Overall, while large-scale (public and private) investments spurred aggregate GDP growth across different non-oil sectors markedly, they did not reduce the dependence of non-oil economies on the oil and gas sector lastingly. In contrast, economic growth patterns in different non-oil sectors continue to depend largely on developments in the oil and gas sector.

This link applies not only to the demand of certain manufacturing activities (e.g. plastics, chemicals) for oil and gas feedstocks but also to the important role of public oil and gas export proceeds for stimulating non-oil economic activity. Here, large inflows of oil and gas export revenues can be singled out as a main cause for the upswing of non-oil economic activity particularly during periods of high oil price levels since these inflows allowed GCC governments for large-scale investments in the economic infrastructure and in the production capacities of different non-oil sectors.

In particular, a high importance of public oil and gas export proceeds is observable for manufacturing export industries since the strong increases of production in these industries necessitated large-scale public investments in the stock of physical capital over the last decades. In view of the capital-intensive nature of most manufacturing export industries, non-oil exports in Bahrain, Oman and Qatar can rather be characterised as complements than as substitutes to oil and gas exports.

In addition to increasing the stock of physical capital, investment by public and private sectors also spurred non-oil economic activity through an accumulation of the factor input labour. A positive impact of investment on employment growth is evident for different sectors of the three economies, most notably, during periods of high oil price levels.

Table 7.8 displays the main employment sectors in Bahrain, Oman and Qatar for different census years since the 1970s. These census year figures point to strong employment growth over the last decades within the construction sector, wholesale & retail trade, household services, manufacturing and public administration & defence.

The strong employment growth in the construction sector can be ascribed to the implementation of various large-scale investment projects during periods of high oil price levels which led to a strong upswing of construction activity and, as a result, rising numbers of, typically foreign, construction workers. Following the surge in (public and private) investment activity during the 2000s, the construction sector constituted the largest employment sector in all three economies during the census year 2010.

In a similar vein, rising levels of public and private investment stimulated employment growth in the wholesale & retail trade and manufacturing sectors. Here, large-scale investments in the expansion of container handling capacities at wholesale ports or in the build-up of production capacities in different manufacturing industries can be singled out as important factors for rising employment levels in both sectors.

Yet, while high levels of investment clearly increased the overall size of employment within non-oil economies, they did not set off a structural change in employment patterns towards a higher importance of skill-intensive eco-

Table 7.8: Main Employment Sectors Census Years
(Number of Employees in 1,000)

Bahrain

	1971	1981	1991	2001	2010
Construction	10.4	29.2	26.7	26.4	160.7
Wholesale and Retail Trade	6.7	14.7	23.0	34.5	109.5
Household Services	3.6	14.2	17.8	29.6	84.4
Manufacturing	4.1	11.4	26.6	50.0	84.4
Public Administration & Defence	5.2	18.1	41.0	52.4	83.1
Memo: Total Employment	60.3	137.9	212.1	291.4	703.2

Oman

	1975	1978	1993	2003	2010
Construction	na	na	108.2	118.3	280.5
Public Administration & Defence[1]	30.0	43.0	165.6	162.7	207.8
Wholesale and Retail Trade	na	na	89.6	86.8	120.0
Household Services	na	na	33.5	51.8	82.1
Education & Health Services[2]	na	na	53.3	75.9	78.3
Memo: Total Employment	209.0	241.0	682.6	736.6	1,099.2

Qatar

	1970	1986	1997	2004	2010
Construction	7.8	40.5	56.1	117.0	506.3
Wholesale and Retail Trade	7.9	18.0	30.6	54.4	142.8
Household Services	na	34.3	45.1	53.4	132.5
Manufacturing	5.2[3]	13.9	24.1	40.0	100.6
Mining and Quarrying	2.2	4.8	9.4	18.0	85.7
Memo: Total Employment	48.4	200.2	280.1	437.6	1,270.2

Sources: BH/MFNE (1972); BH/MCA (1982); BH/CIO (2001, 2004, 2011b); World Bank (1979); OM/MoD (1994b); OM/MoNE (2004); OM/NCSI (2013c); UN-IDO (1980); QA/CSO (1987b, 1992); QA/PC (1999b, 2004b); QA/SA (2010b).
[1] Figures for the years 1975 and 1978 refer to all public sector activities (e.g. public education services). [2] Includes employment in public and private sectors.
[3] Includes employment in public utilities.

nomic activities. Instead, a very large fraction of the overall increases in employment levels over the last decades falls upon sectors which rely heavily on low-skilled labour (e.g. construction, trade, household services).

The nature of employment growth exemplifies the non-oil economic growth dynamics in Bahrain, Oman and Qatar. On the one hand, large increases in total employment, most notably during periods of high oil price levels, contributed to an upswing of aggregate non-oil GDP levels by raising the economic demand for goods and services within local economies markedly.

On the other hand, the strong growth of low-skilled employment during these periods inhibited marked improvements of average labour productivity levels within the non-oil economies of Bahrain, Oman and Qatar. The economic demand for low-skilled labour, in turn, was fuelled by public and private sector investment activity. Here, employment growth in sectors such as construction and trade typically accelerated during periods of high investment levels.

As will be argued in the following chapter, a potential explanation for the lack of a structural change towards more skill-intensive employment is the continued segmentation of labour markets in Bahrain, Oman and Qatar. The strong increases of employment levels in most private sector activities (e.g. construction, trade, manufacturing, household services) fall to a very large extent on foreign employees as shown in the country studies in chapters 4-6 (tables 4.8, 5.9 and 6.8).

Instead, large parts of the national workforce in all three countries continue to be employed in public sector activities (e.g. public administration & defence, public education and health services). High inflows of oil and gas export proceeds allowed GCC governments to expand public sector employment for the national workforce strongly, most notably, during the years of the two oil price booms.

Furthermore, the incentives for national employees to seek employment outside the public sector are diminished by a substantial wage gap between the public and private sectors. As a result, high levels of potentially productivity enhancing investments in both human and physical capital have so far not succeeded in igniting a structural change of employment patterns for national employees towards more skill-intensive economic activities.

Chapter 8

Public Expenditure and Labour Productivity

8.1 Introduction

Public expenditure has shaped non-oil economic development patterns in Bahrain, Oman and Qatar lastingly. The impact of public expenditure on non-oil economic growth in these three countries, however, differs substantially from the effects envisaged by economic growth theory. Endogenous growth models typically relate a growth-enhancing impact of certain public expenditure categories (e.g. infrastructure, education, health) to increases in productivity. In this view, public spending might raise the productivity of economic activities and, hence, long-term economic growth prospects by removing infrastructure bottlenecks, promoting the development of skill-intensive industries or by improving the educational level and the health status of a country's workforce.

In contrast, public expenditure in the GCC countries fostered non-oil economic growth primarily through an accumulation of the factor inputs labour and physical capital and not by sustained improvements in economy-wide productivity levels. Large increases in public expenditure levels since the 1970s contributed to a strongly growing overall size of non-oil economies in the GCC countries. Instead, measures of productivity such as the labour productivity indicator non-oil GDP per worker witnessed either a decrease (Bahrain, Qatar) or much smaller increases than aggregate non-oil GDP levels (Oman) over the same time period.

The following chapter seeks to analyse why increases in labour productivity are only a minor source of non-oil economic growth in Bahrain, Oman and Qatar. The main question in this regard is whether public expenditure patterns in the GCC countries have impeded sustained increases in labour productivity. For answering this question, the following chapter examines the impact of public expenditure on two potential drivers of labour productivity (human capital, structural change).

The importance of human capital for long-term productivity developments is particularly emphasised by different endogenous growth models which point to the educational level and the health status of a country's workforce as crucial determinants of labour productivity. The link between structural change and labour productivity was highlighted early on by Kuznets (1966, 1973). Here, a structural change in employment or production patterns is seen to raise economy-wide labour productivity levels through a reallocation of the factor inputs labour and capital from low-productivity to high-productvity sectors.

Section 8.2 starts by putting labour productivity developments in Bahrain, Oman and Qatar in an international perspective. A cross-country comparison of non-oil economic growth patterns during the period 1980-2013 shows that increases in labour productivity constitute a much less important source of non-oil economic growth in Bahrain, Oman and Qatar than in most of the five comparator countries examined (Indonesia, Malaysia, Mexico, Singapore, United States). While the non-oil economies of the GCC countries witnessed comparatively large increases in aggregate gross value added levels, these large increases in non-oil economic activity were primarily driven by a strongly rising size of the countries' labour force and not by increasing labour productivity levels.

Section 8.3 points out that the lack of sustained increases in labour productivity levels stands in stark contrast to a substantial improvement of human capital stocks within the GCC countries since the 1970s. GCC governments expanded public education and health services strongly over the last decades which, in turn, contributed to a large improvement of the educational level and the health status of GCC populations. Not least as a result of the GCC countries' resource wealth, the relative size of public education and health expenditures in the GCC countries is on a much higher level than in most of the comparator countries examined in section 8.2. Hence, the scale of public education and health expenditures does not appear to be the binding constraint for increases in labour productivity within GCC non-oil economies.

Instead, as will be argued in section 8.4, different institutional characteristics of GCC labour markets appear as an important factor why high public outlays on human capital formation have not translated into sustained increases of labour productivity within GCC non-oil economies. In particular, a high segmentation of labour markets inhibited structural changes in employment patterns towards a rising importance of skill-intensive economic activities and, as a result, sustained improvements of labour productivity.

Public expenditure strengthened the segmentation of labour markets in different ways. This applies particularly to the high public wage bill of GCC governments since a strong expansion of public sector employment and the payment of comparatively high public sector wages diminished the incentives of national employees for working outside the public sector. In view of the high public sector wages for national employees, the resource wealth of GCC countries can be singled out as an important impediment for structural changes in employment patterns.

In addition, various large-scale investment projects of GCC governments did not foster the development of skill-intensive economic activities but, instead, reinforced the importance of low-skilled labour and capital as the main factors of production within non-oil economies. While high public investments in the economic infrastructure and in the production capacities of (partly) state-owned companies contributed to a strong increase in non-oil GDP levels, this upswing of economic activity was primarily driven by capital-intensive manufacturing industries and non-oil sectors which rely heavily on low-skilled labour (e.g. construction, trade).

8.2 Labour Productivity Developments in International Perspective

Increases in productivity do not stand out as a major source of non-oil economic growth in Bahrain, Oman and Qatar. The country studies in chapters 4-6 highlighted that while the overall size of non-oil economies rose considerably over the last decades, these increases in non-oil GDP levels were primarily driven by an accumulation of the factor inputs labour and physical capital.

High rates of non-oil economic growth are particularly observable for non-oil sectors which rely either on large-scale investments (e.g. capital-intensive manufacturing industries) or on a high availability of low-skilled, typically foreign, labour (e.g. construction, trade). Despite large public investments in the human and physical capital stocks, the non-oil economies in all three countries have not witnessed a structural change towards a greater relative importance of skill-intensive economic activities.

The following section puts the non-oil economic growth dynamics in Bahrain, Oman and Qatar into perspective by comparing labour productivity developments in all three countries with those in five comparator countries (Indonesia, Malaysia, Mexico, Singapore, United States). The comparator countries were chosen on the basis of similar characteristics to the GCC countries such as a high economic importance of oil exports (Indonesia, Malaysia, Mexico) or a high reliance on foreign labour (Singapore). Labour productivity levels in the United States serve as a reference value for labour productivity developments in the other countries.

In terms of productivity measures, this analysis draws on the labour productivity measure non-oil gross value added (GVA) per worker. Labour productivity measures indicate how productively economies utilise the factor input labour for generating gross value added.

Changes in labour productivity measures should not be equated with economy-wide productivity developments since an increase in the measure non-oil GVA per worker might both be driven by changes in the stock of other factor inputs (e.g. rising stock of physical capital per worker) as well as by productivity related developments (e.g. technological change).[1] Instead, labour productivity measures can rather be seen as an important indicator on whether the employment structure within an economy undergoes a structural change towards economic activities with higher levels of value added.

Time series of the labour force and of non-oil gross value added levels in all eight economies were sourced from the International Labour Organisation and from the United Nations Statistics Division, respectively. Data sources for the labour force in the GCC countries are given in the appendix.

---

[1] As laid out in section 3.3, the computation of more comprehensive multi-factor productivity indicators (e.g. total factor productivity) which aim to account for changes in the stocks of multiple factor inputs is impeded by a scarcity of data on the endowments of different factor inputs within the non-oil economies of GCC countries (e.g. total stock of non-oil physical capital).

Table 8.1 shows the average annual growth rates of non-oil GVA per worker, the total labour force as well as aggregate non-oil GVA during the period 1980-2013 for Bahrain, Oman and Qatar as well as for the five comparator countries. The cross-country comparison of average annual growth rates for aggregate non-oil gross value added (GVA) and labour productivity levels in table 8.1 highlights two important characteristics of non-oil economic growth patterns in the GCC countries.

First, the GCC countries witnessed comparatively high rates of aggregate non-oil economic growth over the last decades. Aggregate non-oil GVA levels in Qatar and in Oman grew by an annual average of 7.5% and 6.8%, respectively during the period 1980-2013 and, hence, by higher rates than in all other countries displayed in table 8.1.

Second, this rapid expansion of non-oil economic activities in the GCC countries was primarily driven by a strongly rising size of the countries' labour force and not by increasing labour productivity levels. Increases in labour productivity constitute a much less important source of non-oil economic growth in Bahrain, Oman and Qatar than in the United States and in the three Asian comparator countries (Indonesia, Malaysia, Singapore).

In contrast to the latter countries, the total labour force in Bahrain, Oman and Qatar grew by much higher rates than the labour productivity indicator non-oil GVA per worker. This factor input-driven growth dynamic is particularly pronounced in Qatar which witnessed on the one hand strong increases in the total labour force (annual average growth rate 1980-2013: 8.6%) and in aggregate non-oil GVA levels (7.5%) but on the other hand an overall decline of non-oil GVA per worker levels (-1.1%) during the period 1980-2013.

Oman is the only GCC country which witnessed a substantial increase of non-oil GVA levels per worker during the period 1980-2013. The considerable overall improvement of Omani labour productivity levels during these years might be ascribed to the fact that Oman became an oil producing country only in the year 1967. As will be discussed at greater length in the following section, the positive impact of new gained oil wealth on various drivers of labour productivity in Oman (e.g. educational level and health status of population, capital intensity of economy) started to unfold at a much later time than in Bahrain and Qatar, which had already commenced oil production by the years 1934 and 1949, respectively. Albeit

Table 8.1: CAGR Non-Oil GVA per Worker, Labour Force, and Aggregate Non-Oil GVA 1980-2013

(in per cent)

	Non-Oil GVA per Worker	Total Labour Force	Aggregate Non-Oil GVA
Bahrain	0.2	5.5	5.7
Oman	1.2	5.6	6.8
Qatar	-1.1	8.6	7.5
Indonesia	3.4	2.5	5.9
Malaysia	3.0	3.1	6.2
Mexico	0.0	2.7	2.7
Singapore	4.5	2.1	6.7
United States	1.1	1.2	2.3

Sources: United Nations Statistics Division, *National Accounts Main Aggregates Database*; International Labour Organisation, *ILOSTAT and LABORSTA Databases*; Appendix A.

Notes: Compound annual growth rates (CAGR) for the period 1980-2013 were calculated by the author. Gross value added (GVA) time series are in constant 2005 US-Dollar prices. Aggregate non-oil GVA was calculated by subtracting GVA by mining and quarrying (ISIC Rev. 3 Code C) from total GVA. Non-oil GVA does not include GVA by the production of electricity, gas and water supply (ISIC Rev. 3 Code E) since the latter economic activities are aggregated with mining and quarrying within the National Accounts Main Aggregates Database. However, this deficiency is considered to be of minor importance in view of the low sectoral shares of electricity, gas and water supply at total gross value added in Bahrain, Oman and Qatar (tables 4.6, 5.6, and 6.6).

labour productivity levels in Oman increased during the years 1980-2013, the average annual increase of the labour productivity indicator non-oil GVA per worker (1.2%) is clearly below the respective growth rate of the labour force in Oman (5.6%).

Apart from being only a minor source of non-oil economic growth, labour productivity developments in the GCC countries also appear to exhibit a less stable long-term trend than labour productivity developments in most comparator countries. Figure 8.1 shows the developments patterns of the labour productivity indicator non-oil GVA per worker during the period 1980-2013 for Bahrain, Oman and Qatar as well as for the five comparator countries relative to the initial value of this indicator in the United States.

The long-term evolution of non-oil GVA levels per worker differs considerably across the eight countries displayed in figure 8.1. While the indicator non-oil GVA per worker points to a clear long-term upward trend of labour productivity levels in the United States and in the three Asian comparator countries (Indonesia, Malaysia, Singapore), long-term labour productivity trends in the three GCC countries and in Mexico are shown to be more volatile.

Among other factors, the rather volatile development pattern of labour productivity levels in the GCC countries during the years 1980-2013 appears to be related to a high cyclicality of investment. As seen in chapter 7.4, overall investment levels in the GCC countries increased markedly during years of high oil price levels (1974-1985, 2002-2013) as public and private sectors embarked on various large-scale investment projects (e.g. wholesale ports, build-up production capacities in various industries).

The upswing of investment levels impacted labour productivity developments lastingly, albeit in a non-uniform manner. On the one hand, high public and private investments in the production capacities of different companies elevated gross value added levels per worker particularly within capital-intensive manufacturing industries (e.g. petrochemicals, aluminium).

On the other hand, implementation of various large-scale investment projects led to a strong expansion of employment in non-oil sectors which exhibit low levels of labour productivity (e.g. construction, trade). Hence, while these large-scale investment projects contributed to a strongly growing size of non-oil economies as well as to a rapid modernisation of the public infrastructure, the impact of investment on non-oil labour productivity levels in the GCC countries is ambiguous.

8.3 Public Expenditure and Human Capital

The strong expansion of non-oil economic activities in Bahrain, Oman and Qatar was accompanied by an upswing of overall employment levels over the last decades. A large fraction of this employment growth, however, took place in non-oil sectors which exhibit low levels of labour productivity (e.g. construction, trade, household services). As a result, non-oil economic growth in the GCC countries was largely driven by an increasing size of the factor input labour and not by rising levels of labour productivity.

Figure 8.1: Non-Oil GVA per Worker 1980-2013

(Index; Labour Productivity Level United States 1980=100)

(a) Bahrain

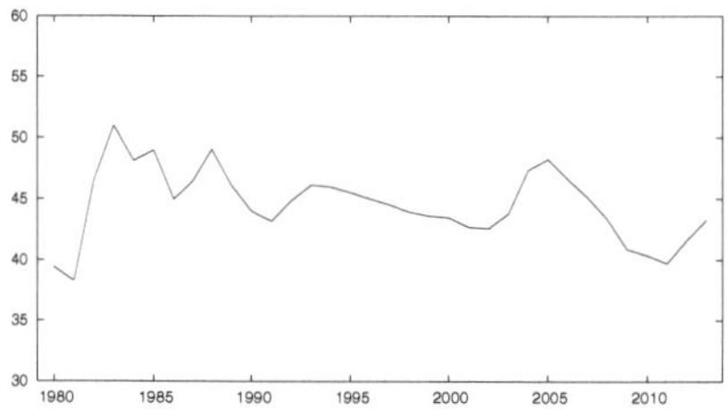

(b) Oman

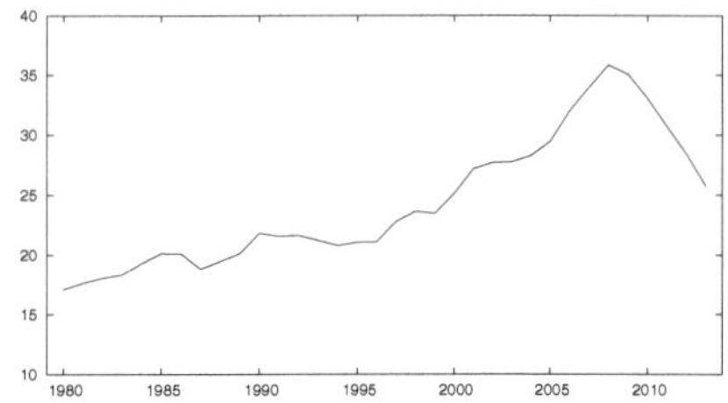

(c) Qatar

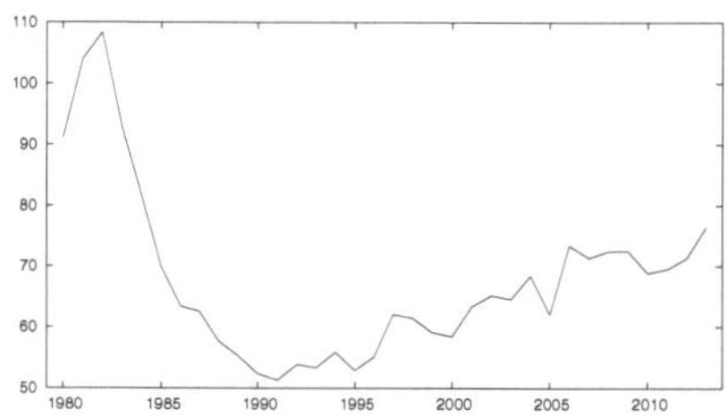

(d) Indonesia

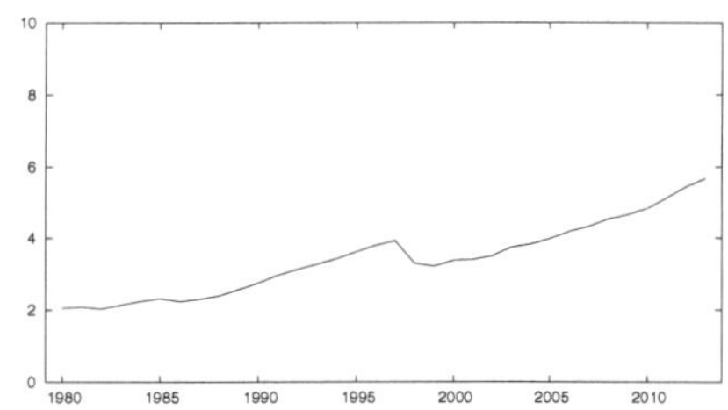

(e) Malaysia

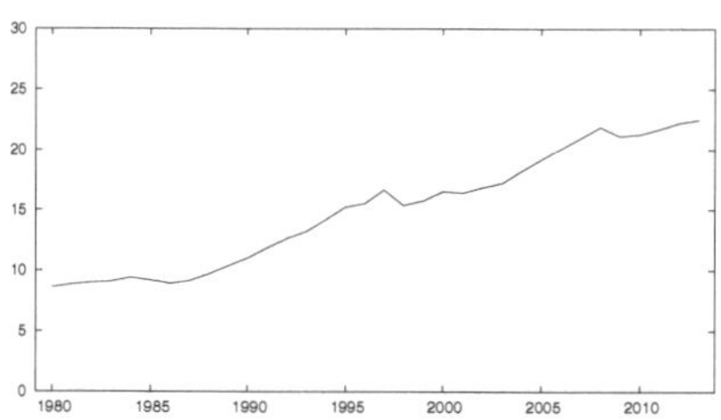

(f) Mexico

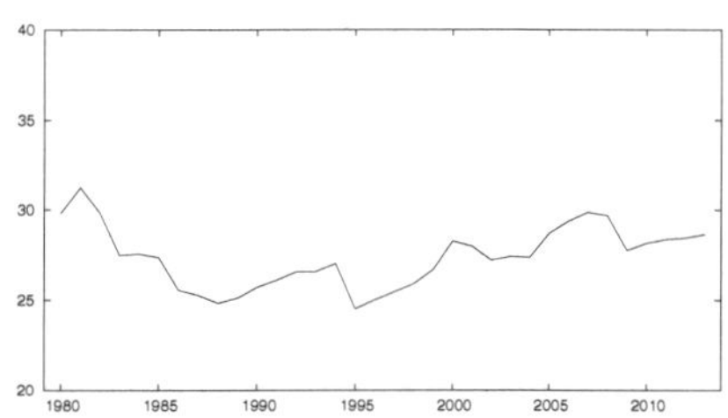

(g) Singapore

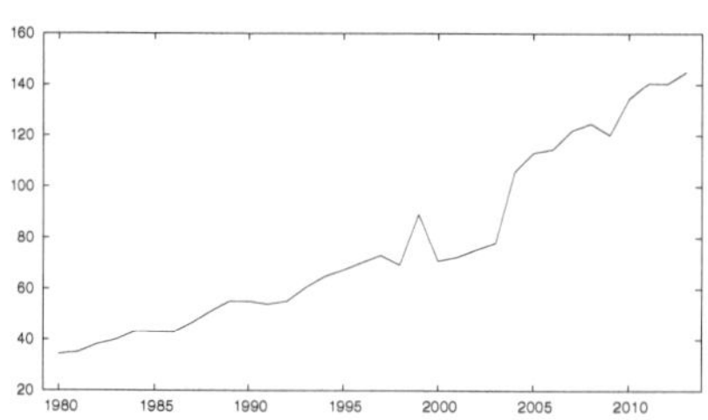

(h) United States

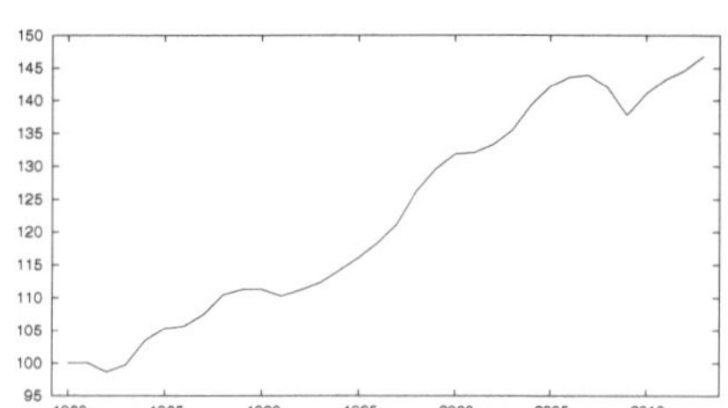

Sources and Notes: See table 8.1.

The cross-country comparison of non-oil economic growth patterns in section 8.2 between the three GCC countries Bahrain, Oman and Qatar as well as five comparator countries (Indonesia, Malaysia, Mexico, Singapore, United States) showed that increases in labour productivity levels constitute a much less important source of economic growth in the GCC countries than in most comparator countries. For getting a better grasp of non-oil economic growth dynamics in the GCC countries, the next two sections seek to elaborate which factors constrained sustained increases of labour productivity within GCC non-oil economies.

The following section examines the role of public education and health expenditures for labour productivity developments in the three GCC countries and in the five comparator countries. The main question in this regard is whether the substantial cross-country differences in labour productivity developments can partially be attributed to differing trajectories of the human capital stocks and, if so, to different public expenditure patterns on human capital formation within the GCC and the comparator countries.

In particular, this section seeks to analyse if the lack of sustained increases of labour productivity within the GCC countries was caused by insufficient public outlays on human capital formation. This analysis takes place against the background of the resource curse hypothesis. Different proponents of this line of thought such as Gylfason (2001) ascribe an underwhelming long-term economic development of resource-rich countries to comparatively low public expenditures on education within these countries (*neglect of education*).

The views on the relative importance of human capital for long-term productivity developments differ across different strands of economic growth theory. Various endogenous growth models point to human capital as a crucial determinant of long-term productivity developments (e.g. Azariadis and Drazen 1990; Caballe and Santos 1993). According to this line of thought, improvements in the educational level or in the health status of a country's workforce might raise the productivity of the factor input labour lastingly. In view of this high importance of human capital, several endogenous growth models ascribe public expenditures on education and health a potential positive impact on productivity developments (e.g. Eckstein and Zilcha 1994; Blankenau 2005).

Instead, more recent strands of economic growth theory such as the institutions view challenge the notion that human capital exerts a direct impact on productivity developments (e.g. Acemoglu et al. 2005; Acemoglu and Johnson 2007). While acknowledging a potential productivity enhancing impact of human capital, this line of thought deems the country-specific impact of human capital to be highly dependent on other factors such as the institutional characteristics of an economy. Here, the institutions view regards improvements in the economy-wide stock of human capital a necessary but not a sufficient condition for accelerating productivity growth.

As will be argued below, the economic development patterns in the GCC countries lend support to the notion that improvements in the human capital stock are not a sufficient condition for raising labour productivity levels. This assertion is based on the observation that the lack of sustained increases in labour productivity stands in stark contrast to a considerable improvement of the stocks of human capital within the GCC countries since the 1970s.

High oil and gas export revenues, most notably, during the years of the two oil price booms (1974-1985, 2002-2013) allowed GCC governments for a rapid modernisation of the public infrastructure (e.g. build-up wholesale ports and airports, expansion electricity production and road networks) and for a strong expansion of public education and health services. This was accompanied by an upswing of several indicators of the educational level and the health status of GCC populations over the last decades (e.g. adult literacy, life expectancy).

Furthermore, the relative size of public education and health expenditures in the GCC countries is on a much higher level than in most of the five comparator countries examined above (Indonesia, Malaysia, Mexico, Singapore, United States). Therefore, the scale of public education and health expenditures does not appear to be the binding constraint for sustained improvements of labour productivity within the GCC countries. Instead, as will be laid out in the next section, the lack of sustained increases in labour productivity can rather be attributed to institutional characteristics such as a high segmentation of GCC labour markets.

In the following, the roles of public education and health expenditures as well as human capital development patterns are examined in more detail against the background of the differing labour productivity trajectories in Bahrain, Oman, Qatar and in the five comparator countries (Indonesia,

Malaysia, Mexico, Singapore, United States). This cross-country analysis starts by comparing the size of public education and health expenditures in all eight economies (table 8.2). Thereupon, it examines the development patterns of the human capital stock across these countries (tables 8.3 and 8.4).

Table 8.2 shows the size of general government expenditures on education and health in Bahrain, Oman, Qatar and in the five comparator countries (Indonesia, Malaysia, Mexico, Singapore, United States) during the period 1980-2013 in relation to aggregate non-oil gross value added. Even though this cross-country comparison is complicated by a scarcity of data on general government outlays in some countries, available figures clearly show that the differing development patterns of labour productivity can hardly be explained by the scale of public education and health expenditures within the respective economies.

A missing link between the size of public education and health expenditures and labour productivity developments is particularly evident when comparing Bahrain, Oman and Qatar with the three Asian countries Indonesia, Malaysia and Singapore. While the scale of public spending on education and health in Oman, Qatar and, to a lesser extent, Bahrain was on a much higher level than in the three Asian comparator countries, the growth rates of the labour productivity indicator non-oil GVA per worker in the latter three countries clearly exceeded those of the GCC countries over the last decades (table 8.1).

Here, a comparatively low impact of public education and health expenditure on labour productivity developments is particularly apparent for Qatar. Despite ranking second in terms of the size of public expenditure on education and on health, Qatar stands out as the only country which saw an overall decline of the labour productivity indicator non-oil GVA per worker during the period 1980-2013.[2] With regard to the comparatively high levels of (budgetary) public education and health expenditures in the GCC countries, it is important to point out that these figures might even understate the total amount of public spending on education and health as large-scale projects such as Education City in Qatar were financed by off-budget public entities (Brandenburg 2012:227-244).

[2]As shown in table 8.2, the shares of public education and health expenditures at aggregate non-oil gross value added in Qatar declined since the 1990s. These declines were not caused by cutbacks in public education and health expenditures but, instead, by strongly rising levels of aggregate non-oil gross value added in Qatar since the mid-1990s.

Table 8.2: Public Education and Health Expenditures GCC and Comparator Countries 1980-2013

(in per cent of non-oil gross value added)

	1980 -1989	1990 -1999	2000 -2013	1980 -2013
Public Education Expenditure				
Bahrain	4.3	4.6	4.1	4.3
Oman	7.3	7.6	7.9	7.6
Qatar	9.2	6.9	4.5	6.6
Indonesia	na	1.4[1]	2.6[2]	2.3[3]
Malaysia	6.3	5.2	6.9	6.2
Mexico	na	4.4[4]	5.7[5]	5.2[6]
Singapore	4.8	3.9	3.6	4.0
United States	na	5.1[7]	5.6[5]	5.4[8]
Public Health Expenditure				
Bahrain	2.5	2.8	2.6	2.6
Oman	3.4	3.9	3.3	3.5
Qatar	4.9	3.9	3.7	4.1
Indonesia	na	0.7[9]	1.1	1.0[10]
Malaysia	na	1.6[9]	2.4	2.2[10]
Mexico	na	2.4	3.3	2.9[11]
Singapore	na	1.6[9]	1.3	1.4[10]
United States	4.2	5.8	7.4	6.0

Sources: United Nations Statistics Division, *National Accounts Main Aggregates Database*; OECD, *Education Database & Health Statistics*; WHO, *Global Health Expenditure Database*; IMF, *Government Finance Statistics*; Ministry of Finance Malaysia; Appendix A.

Notes: Public education and health expenditure figures of comparator countries refer to spending by general governments in order to account for cross-country differences in the fiscal roles of different tiers of government. General government expenditures in Bahrain, Oman and Qatar do not differ from central government expenditures as all (budgetary) spending power within these countries lies with central government institutions. Aggregate non-oil gross value added (GVA) does not include GVA by the production of electricity, gas and water supply since the latter economic activities are aggregated with mining and quarrying within the National Accounts Main Aggregates Database. However, this deficiency is considered to be of minor importance in view of the low sectoral shares of electricity, gas and water supply at total gross value added in Bahrain, Oman and Qatar (tables 4.6, 5.6, and 6.6).

[1] Refers to 1998-1999. [2] Refers to periods 2000-2002 and 2009-2011.
[3] Refers to periods 1998-2002 and 2009-2011. [4] Refers to 1993-1999.
[5] Refers to 2000-2011. [6] Refers to 1993-2011. [7] Refers to 1992-1999.
[8] Refers to 1992-2011. [9] Refers to 1995-1999. [10] Refers to 1995-2013.
[11] Refers to 1990-2013.

The analysis of human capital development patterns is complicated by the difficulty to measure a rather complex concept such as human capital adequately. Rosen (2008:98) defines human capital as "the stock of skills and productive knowledge embodied in people." In this sense, human capital can be seen to encompass various aspects of productive capacities such as the general educational level within an economy, industry-specific work experience or the health status of people. Due to the lack of a single comprehensive measure for human capital, the economic literature has typically utilised different education and health indicators as proxy variables for human capital such as life expectancy (Bloom et al. 2004) or the number of average schooling years in the labour force (Barro 2001).

In terms of education indicators, Hanushek and Wößmann (2007) recommend indicators on educational outcomes (e.g. results from international students performance tests) as a more accurate measure of the educational level within an economy. In their view, quantitative education indicators such as enrollment ratios or the average number of schooling years are not suitable for measuring the educational level within an economy since these measures do not account for the quality of school education.

For gaining a more comprehensive view on human capital developments, this analysis draws on different sets of variables. Table 8.3 compares the development of four education and health indicators between 1980 and 2013 for all eight economies (secondary school enrollment, adult literacy, life expectancy, infant mortality). Table 8.4 displays the test results of the trends in international mathematics and science study (TIMSS) in the year 2011, an international student performance test of mathematics and science knowledge.[3]

The education and health indicators in table 8.3 point to comparatively large improvements of the socio-economic development levels in the GCC countries both from a regional and from a global perspective. For example, secondary school enrollment rates and the health status of local populations (life expectancy, infant mortality) improved markedly in the GCC countries over the last three decades and are now on levels similar to those of the United States. Furthermore, the GCC countries ranked much higher in terms of these three socio-economic indicators than Indonesia or the re-

[3]Unfortunately, an examination of long-term trends in these educational indicators is impeded by a non-availability of TIMSS results for most of the examined countries over a sufficiently long time period.

Table 8.3: Education and Health Indicators GCC and Comparator Countries 1980-2013

	Secondary Enrollment (% of age cohort)		Adult Literacy (% of adults aged 15+)	
	1980	2012	1980	2012
Bahrain	59.0	95.5	71.2	94.6[1]
Oman	8.8	93.5	36.2	86.9[1]
Qatar	70.1	111.6[2]	69.8	96.7
Indonesia	28.7[3]	82.5	67.3	92.8[2]
Malaysia	45.6	70.8	69.5	93.1[1]
Mexico	43.6	85.7	83.0	94.2
Singapore	na	na	82.9	96.4
United States	91.1	93.7	na	na
Memo: Arab World	38.0	72.0	na	76.4[1]
	Life Expectancy at Birth (years)		**Infant Mortality (per 1,000 live births)**	
	1980	2013	1980	2013
Bahrain	69.8	76.7	26.7	5.2
Oman	59.7	76.9	79.1	9.8
Qatar	72.9	78.6	29.6	7.0
Indonesia	58.6	70.8	85.4	24.5
Malaysia	68.1	75.0	25.4	7.2
Mexico	66.6	77.4	56.0	12.5
Singapore	72.2	82.3	12.0	2.2
United States	73.7	78.8	12.6	5.9
Memo: Arab World	58.5	70.1	90.3	29.7

Sources: World Bank, *World Development Indicators*; World Bank (2008).
Notes: Secondary enrollment rates are gross enrollment ratios. Gross enrollment ratios divide the total number of students enrolled (regardless of age) by the population in the official age cohort of the respective educational level. Due to grade repetitions and the enrollment of over-aged or under-aged students, gross enrollment ratios may exceed 100%.
[1] Refers to 2010.
[2] Refers to 2011.
[3] Refers to 1981.

gional average for the Arab world in the year 2013.

In particular, the education and health indicators in table 8.3 indicate a rapid improvement of the socio-economic development level in Oman. Among all the countries examined in table 8.3, Oman witnessed the largest improvements during the period 1980-2013 in terms of secondary school enrollment, adult literacy, life expectancy as well as infant mortality. While only 8.8% of the respective age cohort in Oman were enrolled in secondary schools during the year 1980, this indicator stood at 93.5% by the year 2012. As a result of this strong increase in school enrollment levels, adult literacy rates rose from a mere 36.2% in 1980 to 86.9% in 2010. Furthermore, life expectancy in Oman increased by a very high seventeen years during the period 1980-2013.

The Omani development experience, however, also illustrates the limited impact of improvements in the human capital stock on labour productivity trajectories in the GCC countries. Even though Oman witnessed a much larger improvement in both the educational level and the health status of its population than the three Asian comparator countries (Indonesia, Malaysia, Singapore) during the years 1980 and 2013, labour productivity growth rates in the latter three countries clearly exceeded those in Oman over the same time period.

In terms of the causes for the strong improvement of human capital in Oman, public expenditure can reasonably be ascribed a very important role for elevating both the educational level and the health status of the Omani population. Until the start of oil production in the year 1967, Oman was a poor subsistence economy without hardly any modern-day infrastructure, public schools and medical facilities.

The socio-economic development level in Oman improved markedly after the launch of oil production and, even more so, during the years of the first oil price boom (1974-1985) as spiralling public export revenues allowed for a rapid expansion of public education and health services in the following decades. During the period 1970-2013, the numbers of public schools and public hospital beds in Oman increased from 16 to 1,042 and from 12 to 4,821, respectively (table 5.2).

Similar to Oman, the socio-economic development levels in Bahrain and Qatar were elevated by a strong expansion of public education and health

Table 8.4: TIMSS 2011 Test Scores GCC and Comparator Countries

	Test Score Mathematics 8th Grade	Test Score Science 8th Grade
Bahrain	394	442
Oman	359	415
Qatar	362	390
Indonesia	398	416
Malaysia	429	429
Mexico	n.a.	n.a.
Singapore	671	663
United States	519	537
Memo: Average All Countries	471	483
Memo: Average Arab Countries	400	423

Sources: Mullis et al. (2012:220), Martin et al. (2012:218).
Notes: The Trends in International Mathematics and Science Study (TIMSS) in the year 2011 encompasses eighth grade student test results for 42 different countries. This country sample includes 11 Arab countries (Bahrain, Jordan, Lebanon, Morocco, Oman, Palestine, Qatar, Saudi Arabia, Syria, Tunisia, United Arab Emirates). The TIMSS science assessment covers biology, chemistry, physics and earth science. Tests scores in the above table refer to the average achievements in schools where more than 90% of the students have the language of the test (and, hence, the language of instruction) as their native language. These test scores are deemed to be a more accurate indicator on the educational level of local GCC populations than the average achievement of all schools participating in the TIMSS assessment. Given the very high share of non-nationals working in GCC countries, the latter test score is likely to be impacted heavily by the average achievements in international schools of foreign communities. The average achievements of non-national students in international schools, however, do not appear as an adequate measure for the quality of education within the host country.

services after the start of oil production (sections 4.2 and 6.2). However, since Bahrain and Qatar already started oil production in the years 1934 and 1949, respectively, the positive impact of public expenditure on the educational level and the health status of local populations unfolded at a much earlier time than in Oman.

The large improvements in the educational level and the health status after the start of oil production, in turn, highlight the important role of resource wealth for elevating socio-economic developments levels within the GCC countries. Hence, while public education and health expenditure in the GCC countries did not contribute to a sustained upswing of labour productivity levels, the education and health indicators in table 8.3 indicate a positive impact of public expenditure on the stock of human capital within the GCC countries.

Instead, the impact of public education and health expenditure in the GCC countries is less distinct when drawing on the TIMSS student performance results in table 8.4 as a proxy for the stock of human capital. This applies particularly to Oman and Qatar. Despite spending comparatively large amounts on education, student test results in both countries are clearly below those in most comparator countries (Indonesia, Malaysia, Singapore, United States) and below the average test score of (less resource-rich) Arab countries. These test results, in turn, question the efficiency of public expenditure in raising the productive capacities of the labour force in both countries.

Overall, the lack of sustained increases in labour productivity appears not to be related to the size of public outlays on human capital formation within the GCC countries. Instead, as will be argued in the following section, the structure of GCC labour markets stands out as a much more relevant constraint for sustained increases in labour productivity.

A large share of the national workforce in the GCC countries continue to be employed in public sector activities. Instead, private sector activities are dominated by low-cost foreign employees. Furthermore, the incentives for nationals to seek employment outside the public sector are diminished by a substantial wage gap between public and private sector activities. This continued segmentation of GCC labour markets constitutes a very important factor why high public outlays on human capital formation have not translated into a structural change of employment patterns towards more skill-intensive economic activities.

8.4 Public Expenditure and Structural Change

The lack of sustained increases in labour productivity levels stands in stark contrast to a substantial improvement of socio-economic development levels in the GCC countries over the last decades. Public expenditures of GCC governments on public infrastructure and on the provision of public health and education services increased markedly since the 1970s. Although these increases in public expenditure gave rise to a rapid modernisation of the public infrastructure as well as to considerable improvements of the health status and the educational level of local populations, they did not ignite a structural change within employment patterns towards a rising importance of skill-intensive economic activities. The absence of such a structural change in employment patterns, in turn, can be singled out as a very important factor for the lack of sustained increases in labour productivity.

The following section examines in more detail why the employment structures of nationals and non-nationals in Bahrain, Oman and Qatar did not witness rising employment shares of skill-intensive economic activities. A very important question in this regard is whether structural changes in employment patterns were impeded by different categories of public expenditure in Bahrain, Oman and Qatar.

This section starts by reviewing the links between structural changes and productivity developments. Thereupon, it presents differing views from the economic literature on whether governments should actively promote structural changes in the production or employment patterns of an economy. Building on that, this section analyses the impact of public expenditure on employment patterns in Bahrain, Oman and Qatar.

The economic literature regards structural changes in the composition of employment and production as an important determinant of long-term productivity developments. In this view, economy-wide productivity levels might not only be elevated by a more efficient utilisation of factor inputs within the existing economic structure but also by a reallocation of capital and labour from low-productivity sectors to high-productivity sectors.

The link between structural change and labour productivity developments was emphasised early on by Kuznets (1966, 1973). In his comparative analysis of economic growth patterns in early industrialising countries since the 18th century, Kuznets showed that strongly rising output levels per worker in different countries were typically associated with large structural shifts in employment and production from agriculture to industry and, subsequently, to services.

In terms of more recent growth experiences, McMillan and Rodrik (2011) link the high growth rates of labour productivity in several Asian countries to structural changes in the labour markets of the respective economies. When examining labour productivity and employment patterns for a broad cross-section of Asian, Latin American and African countries during the period 1990-2005, McMillan and Rodrik (2011) find that the growth rates of labour productivity in most Asian countries clearly exceeded those in Latin American and African countries. The authors ascribe the comparatively high growth rates of labour productvity in Asian countries to structural changes in employment patterns as most Asian countries witnessed much higher labour flows from low-productivity to high-productivity sectors than the Latin American and African countries examined in their sample.

While the economic literature agrees upon the importance of structural change for long-term productivity developments, there is no such consensus on the extent to which a government should promote structural changes in the composition of employment and production. Following disappointing results of state-led industrialisation efforts under import substitution policy regimes in the 1960s and the 1970s, most economic policy recommendations during the 1980s proposed a limited role for governments as a means for raising the growth potential of an economy.

These policy recommendations which came to be known as the *Washington Consensus* do not put much faith in the capabilities of governments for steering a structural transformation of an economy. Instead, governments are advised to pave the way for a bigger role of the private sector through a liberalisation of product and factor markets and through a privatisation of state enterprises.

The responsibilities of governments are largely confined to general economic objectives such as securing property rights or macroeconomic stability. In terms of public expenditure, the Washington Consensus acknowledges a potential positive impact of certain public expenditure categories (education, health, infrastructure) on the overall productive capacity of an economy but does not recommend the promotion of selected industries through fiscal means (e.g. investment subsidies, public sector credit, tax holidays). (Williamson 1990)

The latter point is challenged by proponents of *Developmental State Theory* such as Evans (1995) or Rodrik (2004, 2008). These authors call for a more active role of governments in an economic development process than proposed by the Washington Consensus and argue that governments should facilitate structural changes in an economy by stimulating private sector investment in new sectors.

Evans (1995) and Rodrik (2004, 2008) point to the growth experiences of most Asian countries over the last decades and emphasise that the governments of these countries incentivised private sector investment in the build-up of new sectors by various economic policy measures (e.g. trade protection, public sector credit, investment subsidies).

The rationale for the provision of such government incentives is based on the assumption that private sector investment levels in the build-up of new industries tend to be below the social optimum of an economy due to large initial investment needs and to high uncertainties about these new industries' viability. In this view, governments might alleviate the shortfall of private sector investment in new industries by providing investment incentives (e.g. public sector credit, investment subsidies). The success of this interventionist economic policy, however, is seen to depend crucially on a range of important conditions (e.g. independence and high competence of government bureaucracy, allocation of public resources based on clear performance benchmarks).

The governments of GCC countries played a more dominant role within local economies than the governments of most other countries over the last decades. Yet, while large-scale public investments, most notably, during the years of the first oil price boom (1974-1985) increased non-oil production capacities lastingly, the economic policy of GCC governments at that time did not primarily aim at the promotion of a structural change within non-oil economies. In this regard, the economic policy of GCC governments during earlier decades differs substantially from the economic policy stance envisaged by Developmental State Theory.

The dominant economic role of GCC governments originates from the start of oil production and, even more so, from the strong increase of oil prices since the mid-1970s as huge inflows of public oil export revenues allowed GCC governments to exert considerable influence on economic developments. During the years of the first oil price boom (1974-1985), GCC governments invested heavily in the infrastructure of local economies (e.g. road networks, wholesale ports, airports) and in the production capacities of (partly) state-owned companies.

Even though these large-scale public investments elevated production capacities across different non-oil sectors strongly, the promotion of high productivity economic activities did not stand out as a preeminent economic policy goal of GCC governments. Instead, various economic policy measures during the years of the first oil price boom rather aimed at a distribution of oil rents among local populations. This is exemplified by a strong expansion of public sector employment and by the build-up of extensive welfare systems for GCC citizens. In view of the latter economic policies, Luciani (1990) referred to the GCC countries as "Allocation States".

The emphasis on the promotion of non-oil economic activities increased after the strong decline of world market prices for crude oil in the year 1986. Substantial budgetary pressures during much of the 1990s exposed the limits of this oil rent driven development strategy and prompted GCC governments to foster the development of non-oil economies by other economic policy measures. In this context, the private sector was increasingly assigned a bigger economic role. GCC governments implemented several liberalisation measures since the 1990s which included lifting restrictions to foreign investment in different non-oil sectors (e.g. real estate, financial sector) and ending government monopolies in sectors such as telecommunication (Gray 2013:122-130; Valeri 2009:220-224; Fasano and Iqbal 2003).

This was supplemented by large-scale public investments during the years of the second oil price boom (2002-2013). Here, GCC governments sought to stimulate private sector investment by improving the production conditions within non-oil economies through large-scale investments in the economic infrastructure and by the formation of joint ventures with private sector investors in different non-oil sectors. While the public sector continues to play a dominant, albeit more indirect, role, the prominence of private sector capital has increased markedly within GCC non-oil economies since the 1990s.

So far, however, neither the above mentioned liberalisation measures nor large-scale public investments in the economic infrastructure have ignited a structural change within non-oil economies towards a rising importance of skill-intensive economic activities. Even though these economic policies led to an increasing scale of non-oil economic activities, they did not transform the underlying growth patterns.

Instead, non-oil economic growth in the GCC countries continues to be driven by economic activities which rely on a high availability of low-skilled labour (e.g. construction, trade) or on large-scale investments in the stock of physical capital (e.g. petrochemicals, aluminium). As a result, a large portion of the employment growth during the investment boom of the 2000s falls upon non-oil sectors which exhibit low levels of labour productivity (e.g. construction, trade).

The lack of a structural change in employment patterns towards skill-intensive economic activities can be ascribed to two major factors. First, GCC labour markets continue to exhibit a high degree of segmentation as a result of the GCC governments' role as an employer of first resort for the national workforce. In this regard, the high public wage bill of GCC countries can be singled out as an important impediment for a structural change in GCC labour markets since the strong expansion of public sector employment and the payment of comparatively high public sector wages diminished the incentives of nationals for seeking employment outside the public sector.

Second, the growth promoting policies of GCC governments did not induce a structural change in investment patterns towards a higher importance of skill-intensive economic activities. While large-scale public investments in the economic infrastructure and the easing of investment restrictions for the private sector contributed to a substantial upswing of investment levels by both public and private sector companies during the 2000s, a very large part of these investments took place in non-oil sectors which do not rely on skill-intensive labour. Not least as a result of a high abundance of both capital and cheap foreign labour, most investments in GCC non-oil economies continue to flow to economic activities which exhibit either a high capital intensity or a high reliance on low-skilled labour.

A high segmentation of the labour markets in Bahrain, Oman and Qatar is evident when looking at the employment structures of nationals and non-nationals in tables 8.5 and 8.6. While a large share of the national work force is employed within public sectors activities (public administration, public education and health services), employment of non-nationals falls primarily upon non-oil sectors which exhibit low levels of labour productivity (construction, trade, household services).

The importance of public sector employment for the national labour force increased markedly during the years of the first oil price boom (1974-1985). Facilitated by spiraling public oil export revenues, GCC governments expanded employment levels within the public sector rapidly since the mid-1970s. For example, the number of ministries in Bahrain increased from 13 to 29 between the years 1973 and 1978 (Abdel-Latif 1985:99).

This rapid expansion of public sector employment did not aim primarily at the build-up of state capacity but, instead, rather served as a means for enhancing the political legitimacy of GCC governments by distributing newly gained oil wealth among local citizens. A report by the World Bank (1994:70) ascribed the public administration in Oman during the early 1990s a "low level of efficiency" in the provision of government services as well as high levels of overstaffing as exemplified by the existence of "many unnecessary departments".

Over the following decades, GCC governments continued to increase public sector employment levels in order to provide employment for a growing national labour force. Despite reform efforts, most notably, in the less resource-rich GCC countries Bahrain and Oman for raising the employment share of nationals within the private sector, public sector activities remain, by far, the most important employment sector within all GCC countries. By the census year 2010, the combined employment share of public sector activities (public administration, public education and health services) for nationals stood at around 41% in Bahrain, 55% in Oman and 75% in Qatar (table 8.5).[4]

The incentives of nationals in the GCC countries for working in the private sector are diminished by a substantial wage gap between public and

[4]Unfortunately, census figures in Bahrain and Oman do not provide breakdowns of the employment in education and health services into public and private sectors. With regard to Qatar, around 96% of the employment in education and health services during the census year 2010 falls upon the public sector (table 8.5). In view of the latter figure, it seems reasonable to assume that the public sectors in Bahrain and Oman also account for a large portion of the employment in education and health services.

Table 8.5: Sectoral Structure Employment of Nationals in Census Years

Bahrain

	1971	1981	1991	2001	2010
Bahraini Nationals:	(% of Bahraini Employees)				
Main Sectors:					
Public Administration	9.8	19.2	34.7	29.9	31.1
Wholesale and Retail Trade	11.9	9.6	7.9	9.4	13.3
Manufacturing	4.6	6.7	8.3	12.2	10.8
Education & Health Services[1]	14.1	15.0	13.7	14.5	10.7

Oman

	1975	1978	1993	2003	2010
Omani Nationals:	(% of Omani Employees)				
Main Sectors:					
Public Administration & Defence	17.5[2]	19.5[2]	55.7	46.3	42.6
Education & Health Services[1]	na	na	10.0	16.7	12.9
Retail and Wholesale Trade	na	na	4.7	6.9	9.8
Transport, Storage, Communications	na	na	4.7	5.5	7.2

Qatar

	1970	1986	1997	2004	2010
Qatari Nationals:	(% of Qatari Employees)				
Main Sectors:					
Public Administration	17.0	na	57.1	54.7	58.9
Education & Health Services[1]	na	na	22.6	23.6	16.2
Of which: Public Sector	na	na	na	23.3	15.6
Mining & Quarrying	15.4	6.9	5.7	7.7	7.1
Transport, Storage, Communication	8.0	na	2.4	2.1	4.1

Sources: BH/MFNE (1972); BH/MCA (1982); BH/CIO (2001, 2004, 2011b); World Bank (1979); OM/MoD (1994b); OM/MoNE (2004); OM/NCSI (2013c); UN-IDO (1980); QA/CSO (1987b, 1992); QA/PC (1999b, 2004b); QA/SA (2010b).
Notes: Calculations by the author.
[1] Includes employment in public and private sectors.
[2] Public Administration & Defence employment figures for the years 1975 and 1978 refer to all public sector activities (e.g. public education services).

private sector activities. As shown in tables 8.7 and 8.8, monthly average wages in the public sectors of Bahrain, Oman and Qatar are clearly above those in the countries' private sectors. Not least as a result of its high resource endowment, this wage gap is particularly pronounced in Qatar. In view of the comparatively high public sector wages, public expenditure can be singled out as a very important impediment for a structural change in the employment patterns of the national labour force in GCC countries.

Apart from high public sector wages, the segmentation of GCC labour markets is strengthened by labour market legislation which strongly discriminates between national and non-national employees. This is exemplified by the existence of minimum wages for the private sectors in GCC countries which apply only to national employees. As a result, wages for national employees within the GCC private sectors tend to be way above the wages for non-nationals.

For example, the average wage of national employees within Bahrain's private sector was around three times higher than the average wage of non-nationals during the year 2014 (table 8.7). Hence, in terms of employment policies for the national labour force the GCC countries continue to resemble strong features of oil rentier economies.

A lack of structural change towards high productivity sectors is also observable for the employment patterns of non-nationals in Bahrain, Oman and Qatar. As shown in table 8.6, the majority of non-nationals continue to be employed in private sector activities which exhibit low levels of labour productivity (e.g. construction, trade, household services).

Growth promoting policies of GCC governments such as public investments in the economic infrastructure, the formation of (partly) state-owned companies in different non-oil sectors and the easing of restrictions on private sector investors contributed to a strong increase in overall employment levels but did not lead to a reallocation of the factor input labour from low-productivity to high-productivity sectors. Instead of fostering the development of skill-intensive economic activities, most economic policies of GCC governments over the last decades rather strengthened the extensive nature of non-oil economic growth. Here, capital-intensive manufacturing industries and non-oil sectors which rely on a high availability of low-skilled labour (e.g. construction, trade) stand out as the main drivers of non-oil economic growth during the investment boom of the 2000s.

Table 8.6: Sectoral Structure Employment of Non-Nationals in Census Years

Bahrain

	1971	1981	1991	2001	2010
Non-Bahraini Nationals:	(% of Non-Bahraini Employees)				
Main Sectors:					
Construction	21.3	31.4	18.2	12.2	27.9
Wholesale and Retail Trade	9.6	11.4	12.6	13.3	16.4
Household Services	11.2	14.9	13.1	16.3	16.0
Manufacturing	10.4	9.3	15.0	20.2	12.4

Oman

	1975	1978	1993	2003	2010
Non-Omani Nationals:	(% of Non-Omani Employees)				
Main Sectors:					
Construction	na	na	24.0	25.5	40.0
Household Services	na	na	7.7	12.1	12.3
Retail and Wholesale Trade	na	na	18.0	15.4	11.7
Manufacturing	na	na	13.0	10.8	6.9

Qatar

	1970	1986	1997	2004	2010
Non-Qatari Nationals:	(% of Non-Qatari Employees)				
Main Sectors:					
Construction	18.8	22.4	22.9	30.1	42.2
Wholesale and Retail Trade	17.4	na	12.2	13.9	11.8
Household Services	na	na	18.5	13.7	11.0
Manufacturing	8.5[1]	7.5	9.6	10.2	8.3

Sources: BH/MFNE (1972); BH/MCA (1982); BH/CIO (2001, 2004, 2011b); World Bank (1979); OM/MoD (1994b); OM/MoNE (2004); OM/NCSI (2013c); UN-IDO (1980); QA/CSO (1987b, 1992); QA/PC (1999b, 2004b); QA/SA (2010b).

Notes: Calculations by the author.

[1] Includes employment in public utilities.

The continued importance of low-skilled labour in all three countries is particularly observable with regard to the countries' construction sectors which all exhibited strongly rising numbers of non-national employees during the 2000s. The share of the construction sector at total non-national employment in Bahrain, Oman and Qatar rose by about 12-16 percentage points over the course of the 2000s (table 8.6).

This strong increase of construction activity during the 2000s was primarily driven by the implementation of various large-scale real estate projects, most of which were initiated by private sector investors (e.g. Bahrain Bay, Blue City, The Pearl) and by high public investments in the economic infrastructure such as the build-up of economic cities (e.g. Bahrain Investment Wharf, Sohar Industrial Port, Salalah Free Zone, Ras Laffan Industrial City, Mesaieed Industrial City). The latter public investments projects comprised not only the construction of state-of-the-art production sites but also the building of logistics facilities within these economic zones (e.g. ports) and a substantial expansion of production capacities at public utilities (e.g. electricity).

The large-scale public investments during the 2000s improved the production conditions within non-oil economies markedly and, as a result, contributed to rising investment levels by both public and private sector companies. A large portion of these investments, however, took place in non-oil sectors which either depend on a high availability of unskilled labour (e.g. trade) or exert little spillover effects on overall employment patterns such as capital-intensive manufacturing industries (e.g. petrochemicals, aluminium, steel). Hence, while stimulating non-oil economic activity, the growth promoting policies of GCC governments did not transform the factor input-driven growth dynamics in GCC non-oil economies towards rising growth contributions by skilled labour.

Instead, several economic policy measures strengthened the importance of low-skilled labour and capital as the main factors of production within non-oil economies. For example, GCC governments fostered the build-up of production capacities in capital-intensive manufacturing industries and labour-intensive non-oil sectors (e.g. wholesale trade) through the formation of joint ventures with national or international private sector investors (e.g. Oman India Fertiliser Company, Salalah Port Services Company, Qatar Chemical Company). Apart from high public investments in the economic infrastructure and in the production facilities of different com-

Table 8.7: Wages Public and Private Sectors Bahrain and Oman (in US-Dollar)

Bahrain - Average Monthly Wages (2014)

	Public Sector	Private Sector
Bahraini Nationals	2,176	1,774
Non-Bahraini Nationals	na	566

Oman - Average Monthly Wages (2013)

	Public Sector	Private Sector
Omani Nationals	2,586[1]	986
Non-Omani Nationals	na	na

Sources: BH/SIO (2015); OM/NCSI (2015).
Notes: The average monthly public sector wage for Omani nationals and non-Omani nationals in the year 2013 was computed by drawing on disaggregated data in the Statistical Year Book 2014 on the numbers of employees and the annual wage bills for 39 ministries and public authorities in Oman. The disaggregated data covers 96.9% of total employment and 98.6% of the total wage bill in Oman's public sector (excluding defence and security).
[1] Refers to Omani nationals and non-Omani nationals.

Table 8.8: Wages and Work Hours Public and Private Sector Qatar (2013)

	Public Sector	Private Sector
Average Monthly Wage (US-Dollar)	6,494	1,891
Average Monthly Work Hours (Hours)	40	51

Sources: QA/MDPS (2014b).
Notes: No breakdown of wages and work hours for Qatari and non-Qatari nationals available.

panies, the development of capital-intensive manufacturing industries (e.g. petrochemicals, aluminium) was strongly aided by the provision of important production inputs such as electricity and oil and gas feedstocks at comparatively low prices (table 7.7).

With regard to low-skilled labour, different institutional aspects of GCC labour markets can be singled out as important reasons why GCC private sector businesses continue to figure prominently in economic activities where cheap foreign labour constitutes a very important production input (e.g. construction). In particular, the existence of sponsorship systems which give employers a strong sway over non-national employees and a substantial wage gap between national and non-national employees have contributed to a high preference of GCC private sector businesses for cheap foreign labour.

As mentioned above, this strong wage gap results from labour market legislation which restricts the eligibility of minimum wages in GCC private sector to national employees. Given an almost unlimited access of private businesses to cheap foreign labour, a high availability of the factor input low-skilled labour stands out as a very important comparative advantage of the GCC non-oil economies. As a result of the high abundance of low-skilled labour, GCC private sector businesses have had no incentive to invest in the build-up of production capacities in skill-intensive economic activities (Hertog 2013:13-19).

Conclusion

The strong fall of world market prices for oil and gas since summer 2014 poses an important economic policy challenge for the six member countries of the Gulf Cooperation Council (GCC; Bahrain, Kuwait, Oman, Qatar, Saudi Arabia, United Arab Emirates). Large decreases of public oil and gas export revenues put considerable strain on government finances in all GCC countries since the year 2014. This, in turn, highlights the long-term need for raising the economic importance of non-oil sectors.

While the fiscal and external accounts of GCC economies continue to be dominated by oil and gas export revenues, the economic policy goal of non-oil economic development is not a new one. A stronger emphasis of GCC governments on non-oil economic development already became observable after the end of the first oil price boom (1974-1985). Not least as a result of substantial budgetary pressures during much of the 1990s, most GCC governments implemented various liberalisation measures which aimed at fostering non-oil economic growth such as the lifting of restrictions to foreign investment and the end of government monopolies in certain non-oil sectors (e.g. real estate, financial sector, telecommunications).

In addition to allowing for a greater role of the private sector, GCC governments sought to advance the development of non-oil economies through large-scale public investments, most notably, during the years of the second oil price boom (2002-2013). This included large public investments in the economic infrastructure which aimed at improving the production conditions for public and private sector companies within non-oil sectors (e.g. build-up economic cities, expansion wholesale ports, increase electricity production capacities). Furthermore, GCC governments invested heavily in the business expansions of (partly) state-owned companies in different non-oil sectors (e.g. petrochemicals, aluminium, air transport, wholesale port operations, real estate).

This more active non-oil economic development stance of GCC governments since the 1990s was accompanied by a shifting perception of GCC economic policies within the academic literature. For a large part of the 1980s and 1990s, the economic policy stance of the GCC countries was largely seen through the lenses of rentier state theory (e.g. Beblawi 1990; Luciani 1990). This line of thought typically emphasised the distributive nature of GCC economic policies as exemplified by the strong expansion of public sector employment and the build-up of extensive welfare systems for local populations since the 1970s. Instead, more recent publications increasingly singled out developmental aspects of GCC economic policies such as the successful business expansions of (partly) state-owned companies in different non-oil sectors (e.g. Gray 2011; Hertog 2010).

This book took a new look at the economic diversification efforts of three GCC governments (Bahrain, Oman, Qatar). Building both on an econometric analysis and detailed country studies, it examined the impact of different categories of public expenditure (capital, education, health) on non-oil economic growth in all three countries since the 1970s. Over the last four decades, a strong upswing of public expenditure levels in Bahrain, Oman and Qatar gave rise to a substantial expansion of non-oil production capacities and to a large improvement of socio-economic development levels. The underlying question examined in this book is whether these large-scale public investments in the stocks of human and physical capital paved the way for a stronger role of self-sustaining non-oil economic growth in future.

For gaining a more comprehensive understanding of the link between public expenditure and non-oil economic growth in Bahrain, Oman and Qatar, this book analysed the impact of public expenditure on non-oil economic growth dynamics against the background of economic growth theory. In doing so, it examined not only to what extent public expenditure contributed to a rising overall size of non-oil economies but also how public expenditure impacted different sources of growth such as economy-wide productivity levels over the last decades. Therefore, this book examined the impact of different categories of public expenditure (capital, education, health) both on aggregate non-oil GDP and on labour productivity developments. By elaborating the channels through which public expenditure tends to impact non-oil economic growth, this book provides a new perspective on the efficiency of public expenditure for raising the growth potential of non-oil economies in Bahrain, Oman and Qatar lastingly.

The central argument laid out in this book is that the upswing of public expenditure levels since the 1970s contributed to a strongly growing size of non-oil economies but did not alter the structure of local economies in a developmental sense. The assertion that public expenditure has not played a developmental role within non-oil economies is based on two observations. First, high public investments in the stocks of human and physical capital did not promote a structural change in non-oil economic activities from low-productivity to high-productivity sectors. Second, while increasing the output levels of various non-oil sectors markedly, large public expenditures on non-oil economic development have not raised the relative importance of non-oil economies vis-a-vis the oil and gas sector over the last decades.

Empirical results from a cointegration and causality analysis and from country studies show that public expenditure in Bahrain, Oman and Qatar tends to stimulate non-oil economic growth in a much different way than envisaged by economic growth theory. Economic growth models typically relate a growth-enhancing impact of certain categories of public expenditure (e.g. infrastructure, education, health) to increases in economy-wide productivity levels. In this view, public spending might raise the productivity of economic activities and, hence, long-term economic growth prospects by removing infrastructure bottlenecks, promoting the development of skill-intensive industries or by improving the educational level and the health status of the country's workforce.

In contrast, public expenditure in the GCC countries fostered non-oil economic growth primarily through an accumulation of the factor inputs labour and physical capital. A growth-enhancing impact of public expenditure is particularly observable for non-oil sectors which rely either on a high availability of low-skilled, typically, foreign labour (e.g. construction, trade) or on large-scale investments for the build-up of production capacities (e.g. production of aluminium and petrochemicals, air transport).

Instead, improvements in economy-wide productivity levels do not stand out as an important source of non-oil economic growth in Bahrain, Oman and Qatar. While the upswing of public expenditure levels in the GCC countries since the 1970s contributed to a strongly growing overall size of non-oil economies, labour productivity levels witnessed either a decrease (Bahrain, Qatar) or much smaller increases than non-oil GDP levels (Oman) over the same time period.

This differing impact of public expenditure on non-oil GDP and labour productivity developments was found to be particularly pronounced in Qatar which embarked on a big push non-oil development strategy since the late 1990s. On the one hand, empirical results from cointegration and causality analysis point to a comparatively strong positive causal impact of different public expenditure categories on non-oil GDP levels in Qatar. This finding can be ascribed to the implementation of various large-scale investment projects by the Qatari government since the late 1990s. During these years, large (budgetary and off-budgetary) public investments in the economic infrastructure (e.g. Hamad International Airport, Hamad Port, Education City) and in the business expansions of (partly) state-owned companies (e.g. Qatar Airways, Qatar Steel Company, Qatar Fertilizer Company, Qatari Diar) led to strong increases of non-oil GDP levels.

On the other hand, Qatar's non-oil economy witnessed a marked overall decline of labour productivity levels during the sample period of the econometric analysis (1979-2013). Hence, while fostering a strong increase of non-oil GDP levels, the active economic policy stance of the Qatari government has so far not succeeded in igniting a structural change in non-oil economic activities towards a rising importance of high-productivity sectors.

Furthermore, public investment on non-oil economic development in Bahrain, Oman and Qatar did not reduce the dependence of non-oil economies on the oil and gas sector lastingly. Instead, non-oil economic growth in all three countries still relies heavily on a steady inflow of oil and gas export proceeds as public expenditure continues to be a very important catalyst of economic growth in most non-oil sectors.

Non-oil GDP growth typically accelerated during periods of high oil price levels (1974-1985, 2002-2013). During these years, large inflows of oil and gas export revenues allowed GCC governments for high public investments in the build-up of economic infrastructure (e.g. economic cities, wholesale ports, airports, public utilities) and in the expansion of production capacities at (partly) state-owned companies across different non-oil sectors (e.g. aluminium, petrochemicals, port operators, air transportation). These large-scale public investments, in turn, elevated the output levels of different non-oil sectors markedly.

In addition, the positive impact of large-scale public investments on non-oil

GDP levels was amplified by an upswing of private sector investment activity, most notably, during the 2000s. GCC governments stimulated private sector investment activity by different fiscal measures such as the formation of several joint ventures with private sector investors or the provision of various investment incentives to private sector businesses (e.g. build-up economic cities, provision of subsidised production inputs). As seen in section 7.3, public expenditure in the GCC countries exhibits a much stronger tendency to crowd-in than to crowd-out private investment. This can be ascribed to the fact that the strong increases of public expenditure during periods of high oil price levels were largely funded by external oil and gas proceeds and not by taxes on private businesses or higher levels of domestic borrowing.

The strong increase of public and private investment levels, however, did not ignite a more self-sustaining growth dynamic across non-oil sectors. Instead, public expenditure remains an important driver of input-driven growth in most non-oil sectors (e.g. wholesale trade, construction, energy-intensive manufacturing industries). Economic growth in the latter non-oil sectors continues to rely on high public investments in the economic infrastructure and in non-oil production capacities and on the provision of production inputs at highly subsidised prices (e.g. electricity, oil and gas feedstocks).

Given the high dependence of GCC government finances on oil and gas export proceeds, non-oil economic growth in the GCC countries can rather be seen as a complement than as a substitute of oil and gas production. In summary, the strong increases of public expenditure since the 1970s impacted the non-oil economies of Bahrain, Oman and Qatar primarily by fuelling factor input-driven growth.

The dominant role of factor accumulation in non-oil GDP growth dynamics stands out as an important country-specific characteristic of GCC non-oil economies. A cross-country comparison of non-oil economic growth patterns in section 8.2 between the three GCC countries (Bahrain, Oman, Qatar) and five comparator countries (Indonesia, Malaysia, Mexico, Singapore, United States) showed that while the GCC countries witnessed comparatively large rates of aggregate non-oil economic growth, increases in labour productivity constitute a much less important source of non-oil economic growth in the GCC countries than in most comparator countries. In contrast to the latter countries, non-oil economic growth in Bahrain,

Oman and Qatar is largely driven by a strongly rising size of the countries' labour force and not by rising productivity levels of the factor input labour.

This minor importance of increases in productivity as a source of growth can partly be ascribed to public expenditure patterns. Long-term increases in economy-wide productivity levels are typically driven by a reallocation of the factor inputs labour and physical capital from low-productivity to high-productivity sectors. Public expenditure patterns in the GCC countries inhibited such a structural change in employment and production patterns in two important aspects.

First, the high public wage bill of GCC governments impeded a structural change in the employment patterns of the national workforce since the strong expansion of public sector employment and the payment of comparatively high public sector wages diminished the incentives of nationals for seeking employment outside the public sector. Second, large-scale public investments in the economic infrastructure and in non-oil production capacities did not alter the underlying growth dynamics within GCC non-oil economies towards a higher importance of skilled labour. Instead of promoting skill-intensive economic activities, these large-scale investments rather strengthened the importance of an abundance of capital and low-skilled labour as the main comparative advantages of GCC non-oil economies.

While the overall economic policy stance adopted by most GCC governments since the 1990s was more active than postulated by rentier state theory, the employment policies of GCC governments continue to resemble strong features of a rentier state. Despite some reform efforts, most notably, in the less resource-rich GCC countries Bahrain and Oman for raising the employment shares of nationals within the private sector, the public sector still constitutes, by far, the most important employment sector for the national workforce in all GCC countries.

In addition, public sector wages for national employees in the GCC countries continue to be on a much higher level than wages for most private sector activities which serves as a means for GCC governments for distributing oil wealth among local citizens. The large wage gap between public and private sectors, however, diminishes the incentives for nationals to seek employment outside the public sector and, as a result, impedes a structural change in the employment patterns of the national workforce towards a higher importance of skill-intensive economic activities. Therefore, the strong segmentation of GCC labour markets can be singled out as an important factor why high public outlays on human capital formation did not translate into sustained improvements of labour productivity.

The continued high importance of public sector employment as a tool for political patronage again became apparent after the start of the Arab Spring in the year 2011. Here, GCC governments responded to mass demonstrations in other Arab countries against domestic governments by expanding public sector employment and by raising public sector wages for the national workforce. These measures, in turn, further aggravated the segmentation of GCC labour markets.

Apart from high public sector wage bills, the lack of structural changes in production and employment patterns can also be ascribed to the fact that the growth promoting economic policies of GCC governments did not transform the underlying non-oil growth dynamics towards a higher importance of the factor input skilled labour. Large-scale public investments in the non-oil economic infrastructure and the easing of investment restrictions for the private sector contributed to a substantial upswing of investments by both public and private sector companies, most notably, during the 2000s. Yet, a very large part of these investments took place in non-oil economic activities which either depend on a high availability of low-skilled labour (e.g. large-scale real estate projects, wholesale trade) or on high investments in production capacities (e.g. petrochemicals, aluminium, steel, air transport).

The continued dominant role of the factor inputs capital and low-skilled labour for non-oil economic growth dynamics is particularly evident when looking into the main drivers of non-oil export and employment growth during the investment boom of the 2000s. Non-oil exports were primarily elevated by strongly rising export volumes of capital-intensive manufacturing industries (e.g. petrochemicals, aluminium) and, to a lesser extent, by increasing re-export volumes from free trade zones (e.g. Salalah Free Zone). In addition, the strong increase of foreign employment levels during the investment boom of the 2000s was largely driven by non-oil sectors which exhibit low levels of labour productivity (e.g. construction, wholesale trade, household services).

GCC governments aided the input-driven growth dynamics in different aspects. For example, large-scale investments in the economic infrastructure (e.g. build-up economic cities, expansion handling capacities wholesale ports, increase electricity production capacities) benefitted primarily capital-intensive manufacturing industries or labour-intensive non-oil sectors such as wholesale trade or construction. Apart from public investments in the economic infrastructure, GCC governments fostered the development of the latter non-oil sectors through the formation of joint ventures with national or international private sector investors (e.g. Oman India Fertiliser Company, Salalah Port Services Company, Qatar Chemical Company) and through the provision of highly subsidised production inputs for capital-intensive manufacturing industries (electricity, oil and gas feedstocks).

Moreover, the growth promoting policies of GCC governments did not reduce the relative attractiveness of the factor input low-skilled foreign labour within non-oil economies. Here, a high preference of GCC non-oil businesses for cheap foreign labour results from different institutional aspects of GCC labour markets such as the existence of sponsorship systems which give employers a strong sway over non-national employees and from a substantial wage gap between national and non-national employees. Given an almost unlimited access to cheap foreign labour, non-oil sector businesses have had no incentive to invest in the build-up of production capacities in skill-intensive economic activities.

Hence, far from fostering a structural change towards a higher importance of skilled labour, the growth promoting economic policies rather strengthened the importance of existing comparative advantages of GCC non-oil economies such as an abundance of capital and a high availability of low-skilled foreign labour. Put differently, large-scale public investments in the economic infrastructure and in non-oil production capacities led to a strong increase of non-oil GDP levels but did not succeed in "constructing [a] comparative advantage" as postulated by proponents of Developmental State Theory such as Evans (1995:9).

Overall, this book showed that large public investments in the stocks of human and physical capital have not raised the growth potential of the non-oil economies in Bahrain, Oman and Qatar lastingly. While contributing to an increase of non-oil GDP levels, they did not ignite sustained increases in labour productivity levels over the last decades.

This lack of sustained increases in labour productivity cannot be related to an insufficient size of public spending on human and physical formation. Since the 1970s, the non-oil economies of all three countries witnessed strongly rising levels of public spending on the provision of education and health services and on the build-up of public infrastructure. This, in turn, led to a rapid modernisation of public infrastructure and strong improvements of the educational level and the health status of local populations. Hence, the scale of public expenditure on human and physical formation does not appear as a binding constraint for sustained increases in labour productivity.

Instead, this book singled out institutional aspects of GCC labour markets as a much more important constraint for sustained increases in labour productivity. In particular, the strong segmentation of GCC labour markets inhibited a structural change in employment and production patterns towards a rising importance of skill-intensive economic activities. In view of the latter, the non-oil growth experience of Bahrain, Oman and Qatar lends support to more recent strands of economic growth theory such as the institutions view which emphasise that a potential productivity-enhancing impact of different public expenditure categories (e.g. infrastructure, education, health) is highly dependent on other factors such as the institutional characteristics of an economy.

While this book offered an explanation why large public investments in the stocks of human and physical capital did not translate into sustained increases in labour productivity, it did not provide recommendations on how to raise the efficiency of public expenditure for fostering the development of non-oil economies. By highlighting the factors which impeded a positive impact of public expenditure on productivity developments, however, the empirical results of this book point to two important questions which deserve more academic scrutiny. First, which labour market policies are most appropriate for reducing the strong segmentation of GCC labour markets? Second, how can GCC governments induce a structural shift in the investment patterns of public and private sector companies towards the build-up of production capacities in skill-intensive economic activities?

The adverse impact of GCC employment policies on the incentives of national employees for seeking employment outside the public sector is well documented within the academic literature. In addition, most scholars agree that attempts of GCC governments for raising the employment share of nationals in the private sector through the imposition of mandatory employment quotas have largely failed (e.g. Bahrainization, Omanization). In terms of labour market reforms, containing the growth of public sector employment and public sector wages stands out as an obvious economic policy priority for GCC governments. Yet, in view of the large wage gap between public and private sector activities, raising the employment share of nationals within the private sector is likely to require substantial additional economic policy action. So far, only limited systematic research has been conducted on different measures of active labour market policies which were adopted by GCC governments over the last decades (e.g. vocational training, wage subsidies, fees on foreign wages). A more thorough understanding of the effectiveness of these labour market policies might help to devise a comprehensive economic policy strategy for reducing the segmentation of GCC labour markets.

Apart from the GCC governments' role as an employer of first resort for the national workforce, the minor importance of skill-intensive economic activities can also be attributed to a continued strong demand by public and private sector companies for low-skilled foreign labour. Therefore, inducing a structural change in non-oil investment patterns towards the build-up of production capacities in skill-intensive economic activities stands out as an important economic policy challenge of GCC governments for raising the growth potential of non-oil economies lastingly.

Promoting such a structural change in investment patterns is a daunting task as it goes beyond standard economic policy advice such as a liberalisation and deregulation of product and factor markets and public investments in the economic infrastructure. While the implementation of the latter measures since the 1990s contributed to a substantial upswing of overall investment levels in GCC non-oil economies, it did not alter the underlying investment patterns. Instead, a very large part of investments continues to fall upon either labour-intensive or capital-intensive non-oil sectors. Going forward, one option for incentivising higher investment in skill-intensive economic activities might be reducing the relative attractiveness of labour-intensive or capital-intensive non-oil sectors through changes in the prevailing factor endowments. This might be achieved, for example, by limiting the availability of cheap foreign labour for non-oil businesses or by reducing the production subsidies in capital-intensive manufacturing industries. For the time being, the suitability of such economic policy measures for raising investment in skill-intensive economic activities within GCC non-oil economies remains an important area for future research.

References

Abdel-Latif, A. (1985): Public Finance in Bahrain from 1935 to 1981 with Special Emphasis on the Allocation of Oil Revenues in the Past, Present and Future. In: Nugent, J.B. and T.H. Thomas, eds. Bahrain and the Gulf. London: Croom Helm, pp. 96-106.

Acemoglu, D. (2009): Introduction to Modern Economic Growth. Princeton: Princeton University Press.

Acemoglu, D. and S. Johnson (2007): Disease and Development: The Effect of Life Expectancy on Economic Growth. Journal of Political Economy, 115(6), 925-985.

Acemoglu, D. and F. Zilibotti (2001): Productivity Differences. Quarterly Journal of Economics, 116(2), 563-606.

Acemoglu, D., S. Johnson and J.A. Robinson (2001): The Colonial Origins of Comparative Development: An Empirical Investigation. American Economic Review, 91(5), 1369-1401.

Acemoglu, D., S. Johnson and J.A. Robinson (2002): Reversal of Fortune: Geography and Institutions in the Making of the Modern World Income Distribution. Quarterly Journal of Economics, 117(4), 1231-1294.

Acemoglu, D., S. Johnson and J.A. Robinson (2005): Institutions as a Fundamental Cause of Long-Run Growth. In: Aghion, P. and S.N. Durlauf, eds. Handbook of Economic Growth. Amsterdam: North Holland, pp. 384-473.

Acemoglu, D., S. Johnson, J.A. Robinson and Y. Thaicharoen (2003): Institutional Causes, Macroeconomic Symptoms: Volatility, Crises and Growth. Journal of Monetary Economics, 50, 49-123.

Agenor, P.-R. (2008): Health and Infrastructure in a Model of Endogenous Growth. Journal of Macroeconomics, 30(4), 1407-1422.

Agenor, P.-R. and B. Moreno-Dodson (2006): Public Infrastructure and Growth: New Channels and Policy Implications. World Bank Policy Research Working Paper No. 4064.

Aghion, P. and P. Howitt(1992): A Model of Growth Through Creative Destruction. Econometrica, 60(2), 323-351.

Aghion, P. and P. Howitt (1998): Endogenous Growth Theory. Cambridge, Massachusetts: MIT Press.

Aghion, P., C. Harris, P. Howitt and J. Vickers (2001): Competition, Imitation and Growth with Step-by-Step Innovation. Review of Economic Studies, 68, 467-492.

Alderman, H., J.R. Behrman and J. Hoddinott (2005): Nutrition, Malnutrition, and Economic Growth. In: Lopez-Casasnovas, G., B. Rivera and L. Currais, eds. Health and Economic Growth. Cambridge, Massachusetts: MIT Press, pp. 169-194.

Alesina, A., S. Özler, N. Roubini, and P. Swagel (1996): Political Instability and Economic Growth. Journal of Economic Growth, 1(2), 189-211.

Alesina, A., A. Devleeschauwer, W. Easterly, S. Kurlat and R. Wacziarg (2003): Fractionalization. Journal of Economic Growth, 8(2), 155-194.

AlHasan, H.T. (2012): Labor Market Politics in Bahrain. In: Hertog, S., ed. National Employment, Migration and Education in the GCC. The Gulf Region: Economic Development and Diversification, Vol. 4. Berlin: Gerlach Press, pp. 107-151.

Allen, C.H. (1987): Oman: The Modernization of the Sultanate. Boulder, Colorado: Westview Press.

Allen, C.H. and W.L. Rigsbee (2000): Oman under Qaboos: From Coup to Constitution, 1970-1996. London: Frank Cass.

Aly, H. and M. Strazicich (2000): Is Government Size Optimal in the Gulf

Countries of the Middle East? An Empirical Investigation. International Review of Applied Economics, 14(4), 475-483.

Al-Faris, A.F. (2002): Public Expenditure and Economic Growth in the Gulf Cooperation Council Countries. Applied Economics, 34(9), 1187-1193.

Al-Khulaifi, A.S. (2012): Government Expenditure and Economic Growth in Qatar: A Time Series Analysis. European Journal of Scientific Research, 79(3), 457-466.

Al-Kuwari, A.K. (1978): Oil Revenues in the Gulf Emirates. Epping, Essex: Bowker Publishing Company.

Al-Lamki, S.M. (1998): Barriers to Omanization in the Private Sector: The Perceptions of Omani Graduates. International Journal of Human Resource Management, 9(2), 377-400.

Al-Maawali, A. (2000): Privatisation and its Impact on the Economic Development of the Sultanate of Oman. Unpublished doctoral dissertation, Manchester Metropolitan University.

Al-Yousef, A. (1985): An Evaluation of Bahrain's Major Industries and Their Future Prospects. In: Nugent, J.B. and T.H. Thomas, eds. Bahrain and the Gulf. London: Croom Helm, pp. 123-131.

Ambinder, L.P., N. de Silva, and J. Dewar (2000): The Mirage Becomes Reality: Privatization and Project Finance Developments in the Middle East Power Market. Fordham International Law Journal, 24(4), 1029-1051.

Anderson, T.W.(1958): An Introduction to Multivariate Statistical Analysis. New York: John Wiley and Sons.

Andrews, D.W.K. (1993): Tests for Parameter Instability and Structural Change With Unknown Change Points. Econometrica, 61(4), 821-856.

Arrow, K.J. and M. Kurz (1970): Public Investment, the Rate of Return and Optimal Fiscal Policy. Baltimore: Johns Hopkins University Press.

Aschauer, D.A. (1989a): Is Public Expenditure Productive. Journal of Monetary Economics, 23(2), 177-200.

Aschauer, D.A. (1989b): Does Public Capital Crowd Out Private Capital. Journal of Monetary Economics, 24(2), 171-188.

Azariadis, C. and A. Drazen (1990): Threshold Externalities in Economic Development. Quarterly Journal of Economics, 105(2), 501-526.

Baba, R. (2007): Islamic Financial Centers, In: Hassan, M.K. and M.K. Lewis, eds. Handbook of Islamic Banking. Cheltenham: Edward Elgar, pp. 384-400.

Bahrain, Kingdom of (BH)

BH, Bahrain Monetary Agency [BMA] (1980-1986): Annual Report (various issues). Manama: BMA.

BH, Bahrain News Agency [BNA] (2005): Royal Decree to Establish Economic Development Board. 9. May 2005. [online]. Available from: http://www.bna.bh/portal/en/news/386606 [Accessed: 15 August 2013].

BH, BNA (2008): Economic Vision 2030 for Bahrain. 23. October 2008. [online]. Available from: http://www.bna.bh/portal/en/news/428203 [Accessed: 15 August 2013].

BH, Central Bank of Bahrain [CBB] (2001-2015): Statistical Bulletin (various issues). Manama: CBB.

BH, CBB (2016): CBB Register. January 2016. [online]. Available from: http://www.cbb.gov.bh/iis/register [Accessed: 30 January 2016].

BH, Central Informatics Organisation [CIO] (2001-2014): Statistical Abstract 2000-2013 (various issues). Manama: CIO.

BH, Central Informatics Organisation [CIO] (2011b): Results of Census 2010. Manama: CIO.

BH, Central Informatics Organisation [CIO] (2014b): National Accounts 2013. Manama: CIO.

BH, Central Informatics Organisation [CIO] (2014c): Manufacturing 2006-2013. Manama: CIO.

BH, Central Statistics Organisation [CSO] (1984-1996): Statistical Abstract 1983-1995 (various issues). Manama: CSO.

BH, Economic Development Board [EDB] (2004): Reforming Bahrain's Labour Market: Summary of Workshop Presentations. 23. September 2004. [online]. Available from: http://bahrainonline.org/attachment.php?attachmentid=11072&d=1101846103 [Accessed: 31 July 2013].

BH, EDB (2010): Annual Report 2009. Manama: EDB.

BH, EDB (2013): Bahrain: Healthcare Fact Sheet. March 2013. [online]. Available from: http://www.bahrain.com/DocumentsLibrary/EDB%20-%20Healthcare%20-%20March%202013.pdf [Accessed: 10 August 2013].

BH, Gulf Air [GA] (2013): History Gulf Air. August 2013. [online]. Available from: http://www.gulfair.com/English/aboutgulfair/Pages/History.aspx [Accessed: 16 August 2013].

BH, Ministry of Cabinet Affairs [MCA] (1982): Bahrain Census of Population and Housing - 1981. Manama: MCA.

BH, Ministry of Finance [MoF] (2005): Government Financial Statistics 2000-2004. Manama: MoF.

BH, MoF (2007-2014): Final Accounts 2006-2013 (various issues). Manama: MoF.

BH, Ministry of Finance and National Economy [MFNE] (1972): Statistics of the Population Census 1971. Manama: MFNE.

BH, MFNE (1991): Thirty Years of Economic and Social Development in the State of Bahrain. Manama: MFNE.

BH, MFNE (1996): The Government Financial Statistics 1990-1994. Manama: MFNE.

BH, MFNE (2000): The Government Financial Statistics 1995-1999. Manama: MFNE.

BH, Ministry of Works [MoW] (2009): Annual Report 2008. Manama: MoW.

BH, Social Insurance Organization [SIO] (2015): Statistical Report 2015 - Quarter 1: Civil and Private Sectors. Manama: SIO.

BH, University of Bahrain [UB] (2009): University of Bahrain: Brief History. [online]. Available from: http://www.uob.edu.bh/english/pages.aspx?module=pages&id=1814&SID=312 [Accessed: 10 August 2013].

Banerjee, A.V., S. Cole, E. Duflo and L. Linden (2007): Remedying Education: Evidence from Two Randomized Experiments in India. Quarterly Journal of Economics, 122(3), 1235-1264.

Barro, R.J. (1990): Government Spending in a Simple Model of Endogenous Growth. Journal of Political Economy, 98(S5), 103-125.

Barro, R.J. (1991): Economic Growth in a Cross Section of Countries. Quarterly Journal of Economics, 106(2), 407-443.

Barro, R.J. (1999): Notes on Growth Accounting. Journal of Economic Growth, 4(2), 119-137.

Barro, R.J. (2001): Human Capital and Growth. American Economic Review, 91(2), 12-17.

Barro, R.J. and R.M. McCleary (2003): Religion and Economic Growth across Countries. American Sociological Review, 68(5), 760-781.

Barro, R.J. and X. Sala-i-Martin (1992a): Convergence. Journal of Political Economy, 100(2), 223-251.

Barro, R.J. and X. Sala-i-Martin (1992b): Public Finance in Models of Economic Growth. Review of Economic Studies, 59(4), 645-661.

Barro, R.J. and X. Sala-i-Martin (1997): Technological Diffusion, Convergence, and Growth. Journal of Economic Growth, 2, 1-27.

Barro, R.J. and X. Sala-i-Martin (2004): Economic Growth. Cambridge, Massachusetts: MIT Press.

Basu, S. and D.N. Weil (1998): Appropriate Technology and Growth. Quarterly Journal of Economics, 113(4), 1025-1054.

Baumol, W.J. (1986): Productivity Growth, Convergence, and Welfare: What the Long-Run Data Show. American Economic Review, 76(5), 1072-1085.

Beblawi, H. (1990): The Rentier State in the Arab World. In: Luciani, G., ed. The Arab State. London: Routledge, pp. 85-98.

Benhabib, J. and M.M. Spiegel (1994): The Role of Human Capital in Economic Development: Evidence from Aggregate Cross-Country Data. Journal of Monetary Economics, 34, 143-173.

Benhabib, J. and M.M. Spiegel (2005): Human Capital and Technology Diffusion. In: Aghion, P. and S.N. Durlauf, eds. Handbook of Economic Growth. Amsterdam: North Holland, pp. 935-966.

Birks, J.S. and C.A. Sinclair (1979): International Labour Migration in the Arab Middle East. Third World Quarterly, 1(2), 87-99.

Birks, J.S. and C.A. Sinclair (1980): Arab Manpower: The Crisis of Development. London: Croom Helm.

Birks, J.S. and C.A. Sinclair (1987): Successful Education and Human Resource Development - The Key to Sustained Economic Growth. In: Pridham, B.R., ed. Oman: Economic, Social and Strategic Developments. London: Croom Helm, pp. 145-167.

Blankenau, W. (2005): Public Schooling, College Subsidies and Growth. Journal of Economic Dynamics and Control, 29(3), 487-507.

Bloom, D.E., D. Canning and J. Sevilla (2004): The Effect of Health on Economic Growth: A Production Function Approach. World Development, 32(1), 1-13.

Bloom, D.E., J.D. Sachs, P. Collier and C. Udry (1998): Geography, Demography, and Economic Growth in Africa. Brookings Papers on Economic Activity, 1998(2), 207-295.

Borensztein, E., J. De Gregorio and J-W. Lee (1998): How Does Foreign Direct Investment Affect Economic Growth. Journal of International Economics, 45, 115-135.

Bose, N., M.E. Haque and D.R. Osborn (2007): Public Expenditure and Economic Growth: A Disaggregated Analysis for Developing Countries. Manchester School, 75(5), 533-556.

Brandenburg, T. (2012): Bridging the Knowledge Gap: Internationalization and Privatization of Higher Education in the State of Qatar and the Sultanate of Oman. Doctoral dissertation, Universitätsbibliothek Mainz.

Breitung, J., R. Brüggemann and H. Lütkepohl (2004): Structural Vector Autoregressive Modeling and Impulse Responses. In: Lütkepohl, H. and M. Krätzig, eds. Applied Time Series Econometrics. Cambridge: Cambridge University Press, pp. 159-196.

British Petroleum [BP] (2012): BP Statistical Review of World Energy, June 2012. London: British Petroleum.

Brock, W.A. and S.N. Durlauf (2001): Growth Empirics and Reality. World Bank Economic Review, 15(2), 229-272.

Caballe, J. and M.S. Santos (1993): On Endogenous Growth with Physical and Human Capital. The Journal of Political Economy, 101(6), 1042-1067.

Cameron, A.C. and P.K. Trivedi (2009): Microeconometrics: Methods and Applications. Cambridge: Cambridge University Press.

Candelon, B. and H. Lütkepohl (2001): On the Reliability of Chow-Type Tests for Parameter Constancy in Multivariate Dynamic Models. Economics Letters, 73, 155-160.

Canning, D. and P. Pedroni (2008): Infrastructure, Long-Run Economic Growth and Causality Tests for Cointegrated Panels. Manchester School, 76(5), 504-527.

Caselli, F., G. Esquivel and F. Lefort (1996): Reopening the Convergence Debate: A New Look at Cross-Country Growth Empirics. Journal of Economic Growth, 1, 363-389.

Cheung, Y.-W. and K.S. Lai (1993): Finite-Sample Sizes of Johansen's Likelihood Ratio Tests for Cointegration. Oxford Bulletin of Economics and Statistics, 55(3), 313-328.

Cheung, Y.-W. and K.S. Lai (1995): Lag Order and Critical Values of the Augmented Dickey-Fuller Test. Journal of Business and Economic Statistics, 13(3), 277-280.

Chow, G.C. (1960): Tests of Equality Between Sets of Coefficients in Two Linear Regressions. Econometrica, 28(3), 591-605.

Coase, R.H. (1937): The Nature of the Firm. Economica, 4, 386-405.

Coe, D.T. and E. Helpman (1995): International R & D Spillovers. European Economic Review, 39, 859-887.

Crystal, J. (1995): Oil and Politics in the Gulf: Rulers and Merchants in Kuwait and Qatar. Cambridge: Cambridge University Press.

CSIS (2010): The Gulf Military Balance in 2010: An Overview. 23 April 2010. [online]. Available from: http://csis.org/publication/gulf-military-balance-2010-overview [Accessed: 23 January 2014].

De Long, J.B. and L.H. Summers (1991): Equipment Investment and Economic Growth. Quarterly Journal of Economics, 106(2), 445-502.

DeJong, D.N., J.C. Nankervis, N.E. Savin and C.H. Whiteman (1992): Integration Versus Trend Stationarity in Time Series. Econometrica, 60(2), 423-433.

Devarajan, S., V. Swaroop and H. Zou (1996): The Composition of Public Expenditure and Economic Growth. Journal of Monetary Economics,

37(2), 313-344.

Diamond, J. (1977): Wagner's "Law" and the Developing Countries. The Developing Economies, 15(1), 37-59.

Dickey, D.A. and W.A. Fuller (1979): Distribution of Estimators for Autoregressive Time Series with a Unit Root. Journal of the American Statistical Association, 74, 427-431.

Dickey, D.A. and W.A. Fuller (1981): Likelihood Ratio Tests for Autoregressive Time Series with a Unit Root. Econometrica, 49(4), 1057-1072.

Dito, M. (2007): Migration Policies and Challenges in the Kingdom of Bahrain. In: The American University in Cairo. Conference on Migration and Refugee Movements in the Middle East and North Africa. 25 October 2007. [online]. Available from: http://www.aucegypt.edu/GAPP/cmrs/Pages/meeting.aspx [Accessed: 31 July 2013].

Dolado, J.J. and H. Lütkepohl (1996): Making Wald Tests Work for Cointegrated VAR Systems. Econometric Reviews, 15(4), 369-386.

Doornik, J.A. (1998): Approximations to the Asymptotic Distributions of Cointegration Tests. Journal of Economic Surveys, 12(5), 573-593.

Durlauf, S.N., A. Kourtellos and A. Minkin (2001): The Local Solow Growth Model. European Economic Review, 45(4-6), 928-940.

Durlauf, S.N., P.A. Johnson and J. Temple (2005): Growth Econometrics. In: Aghion, P. and S.N. Durlauf, eds. Handbook of Economic Growth. Amsterdam: North Holland, pp. 555-677.

Easterly, W. and R. Levine (1997): Africa's Growth Tragedy: Policies and Ethnic Divisions. Quarterly Journal of Economics, 112(4), 1203-1250.

Easterly, W. and S. Rebelo (1993): Fiscal Policy and Economic Growth: An Empirical Investigation. Journal of Monetary Economics, 32(3), 417-458.

Eaton, J. and S. Kortum (1996): Trade in Ideas: Patenting and Productivity in the OECD. Journal of International Economics, 40, 251-278.

Eckstein, Z. and I. Zilcha (1994): The Effects of Compulsory Schooling on Growth, Income Distribution and Welfare. Journal of Public Economics, 54(3), 339-359.

El Mallakh, R. (1979): Qatar: Development of an Oil Economy. New York: St. Martin's Press.

Elliott, G., T.J. Rothenberg and J.H. Stock (1996): Efficient Tests for an Autoregressive Unit Root. Econometrica, 64(4), 813-836.

Energy Information Administration [EIA] (2014): Country Analysis Qatar, January 2014. Washington, DC: U.S. Department of Energy.

Engle, R.F. and C.W.J. Granger (1987): Co-Integration and Error Correction: Representation, Estimation, and Testing. Econometrica, 55(2), 251-276.

Ernst & Young (2011): Doing Business in Oman: An Executive's Guide to Doing Business in Oman. Muscat: Ernst & Young.

European Commission, International Monetary Fund, Organisation for Economic Co-operation and Development, United Nations and World Bank (1993): System of National Accounts, 1993. New York: United Nations Publications.

European Commission, International Monetary Fund, Organisation for Economic Co-operation and Development, United Nations and World Bank (2009): System of National Accounts, 2008. New York: United Nations Publications.

Evans, P.B. (1995): Embedded Autonomy: States and Industrial Transformation. New Jersey: Princeton University Press.

Fasano, U. and Z. Iqbal (2003): GCC Countries: From Oil Dependence to Diversification. Washington, DC: International Monetary Fund.

Fasano, U. and Q. Wang (2001): Fiscal Expenditure Policy and Non-Oil Economic Growth: Evidence from GCC Countries. IMF Working Paper 01/195.

Fasano, U. and Q. Wang (2002): Testing the Relationship Between Government Spending and Revenue: Evidence from GCC Countries. IMF Working Paper 02/201.

Fernald, J.G. (1999): Roads to Prosperity? Assessing the Link between Public Capital and Productivity. American Economic Review, 89(3), 619-638.

Fernandez, C., E. Ley and M.F.J. Steel (2001): Model Uncertainty in Cross-Country Growth Regressions. Journal of Applied Econometrics, 16(5), 563-576.

Financial Times (2014): Bahrain Land Deals Highlight Alchemy of Making Money from Sand. 10. December 2014. [online]. Available from: http://www.ft.com/intl/cms/s/0/b6d081a2-74b8-11e4-8321-00144feabdc0.html#axzz3SO5yGdf7 [Accessed: 21 February 2015].

Fischer, A.M. (1990): Cointegration and I(0) Measurement Error Bias. Economics Letters, 34(3), 255-259.

Fischer, S. (1993): The Role of Macroeconomic Factors in Growth. Journal of Monetary Economics, 32(3), 485-512.

Fosfuri, A., M. Motta and T. Ronde (2001): Foreign Direct Investment and Spillovers Through Workers' Mobility. Journal of Development Economics, 53, 205-222.

Fossey, J. (2010): Securing Salalah. Containerisation International, 43(12), 41-43.

Franklin, R. (1985): Migrant Labor and the Politics of Development. MERIP Reports, 132, 7-13.

Gallup, J.L. and J.D. Sachs (2001): The Economic Burden of Malaria. American Journal of Tropical Medicine and Hygiene, 64(1), 85-96.

Gelb, A., J.B. Knight and R.H. Sabot (1991): Public Sector Employment, Rent Seeking and Economic Growth. The Economic Journal, 101(408), 1186-1199.

Gerakis, A.S. and O. Roncesvalles (1983): Bahrain's Offshore Banking Center. Economic Development and Cultural Change, 31(2), 271-293.

Gerschenkron, A. (1962): Economic Backwardness in Historical Perspective. New York: Praeger Publishers.

Ghali, K.H. (1997): Government Spending and Economic Growth in Saudi Arabia. Journal of Economic Development, 22(2), 165-172.

Glomm, G. and B. Ravikumar (1992): Public versus Private Investment in Human Capital: Endogenous Growth and Income Equality. Journal of Political Economy, 100(4), 818-834.

Gramlich, E.M. (1994): Infrastructure Investment: A Review Essay. Journal of Economic Literature, 32(3), 1176-1196.

Granger, C.W.J. (1969): Investigating Causal Relations by Econometric Models and Cross-Spectral Methods. Econometrica, 37(3), 424-438.

Granger, C.W.J. (1981): Some Properties of Time Series Data and Their Use in Econometric Model Specification. Journal of Econometrics, 16, 121-130.

Granger, C.W.J. and P. Newbold (1974): Spurious Regressions in Econometrics. Journal of Econometrics, 2, 111-120.

Gray, M. (2011): A Theory of "Late Rentierism" in the Arab States of the Gulf. Georgetown University School of Foreign Service in Qatar, Center for International and Regional Studies, Occasional Paper No. 7.

Gray, M. (2013): Qatar: Politics and the Challenges of Development. Boulder, Colorado: Lynne Rienner Publishers.

Grossman, G.M. and E. Helpman (1991): Quality Ladders in the Theory of Growth. Review of Economic Studies, 58(1), 43-61.

Gupta, S., M. Verhoeven and E.R. Tiongson (2002): The Effectiveness of Government Spending on Education and Health Care in Developing and Transition Economies. European Journal of Political Economy, 18(4), 717-737.

Gwartney, J.D., R.G. Holocombe and R.A. Lawson (2006): Institutions and the Impact of Investment on Growth. Kyklos, 59(2), 255-273.

Gylfason, T. (2001): Natural Resources, Education, and Economic Development. European Economic Review, 45(4), 847-859.

Hancock, M. (2008): The Middle East's Rising Star. MEED, 52(41), 58-61.

Hanushek, E.A. and D.D. Kimko (2000): Schooling, Labor-Force Quality, and the Growth of Nations. American Economic Review, 90(5), 1184-1208.

Hanushek, E.A. and L. Wößmann (2007): The Role of Education Quality in Economic Growth. World Bank Policy Research Working Paper 4122.

Haque, M.E. and R.A. Kneller (2008): Public Investment and Growth: The Role of Corruption. Working Paper, Center for Growth and Business Cycle Research, University of Manchester.

Harrod, R.F. (1942): Toward a Dynamic Economics: Some Recent Developments of Economic Theory and Their Application to Policy. London: Macmillan.

Hassler, U. and V. Kuzin (2009): Cointegration Analysis under Measurement Errors. In: Binner, J.M., D.L. Edgerton and T. Elger, eds. Advances in Econometrics, Volume 24. Bingley: Emerald, pp. 131-150.

Hausmann, R. and D. Rodrik (2003): Economic Development as Self-Discovery. Journal of Development Economics, 72(2), 603-633.

Hertog, S. (2010): Defying the Resource Curse: Explaining Successful State-Owned Enterprises in Rentier States. World Politics, 62(2), 261-301.

Hertog, S. (2011): The Evolution of Rent Recycling During Two Booms in the Gulf Arab States: Business Dynamism and Societal Stagnation. In: Legrenzi, M. and B. Momani, eds. Shifting Geo-Economic Power of the Gulf: Oil, Finance and Institutions. Aldershot: Ashgate, pp. 55-74.

Hertog, S. (2012a): Public Industry as Tool of Rentier Economy Diversification: The GCC Case. In: Luciani, G., ed. Resources Blessed: Diversification and the Gulf Development Model. Berlin: Gerlach Press, pp. 115-138.

Hertog, S. (2012b): A Comparative Assessment of Labor Market Nationalization Policies in the GCC. In: Hertog, S., ed. National Employment, Migration and Education in the GCC. The Gulf Region: Economic Development and Diversification, Vol. 4. Berlin: Gerlach Press, pp. 65-106.

Hertog, S. (2013): The Private Sector and Reform in the Gulf Cooperation Council. Research Paper No. 30, Kuwait Programme on Development, Governance and Globalisation in the Gulf States, London School of Economics and Political Science.

Heston, A., R. Summers and B. Aten (2011): Penn World Table Version 7.0. Center for International Comparisons of Production, Income and Prices at the University of Pennsylvania, May 2011.

Hicks, J. (1932): The Theory of Wages. London: Macmillan.

Hindley, A. (1996): Ras Laffan: Ready for Action. MEED, 40(35), 12.

Hodson, N. (2013): Breaking Loose: Reduced Private Sector Dependence on Governments in GCC Economies. In: Hertog, S., G. Luciani and M. Valeri, eds. Business Politics in the Middle East. London: Hurst & Co., pp. 101-132.

Hosoya, K. (2003): Tax Financed Government Health Expenditure and Growth with Capital Deepening Externality. Economics Bulletin, 5(14), 1-10.

Howitt, P. (2000): Endogenous Growth and Cross-Country Income Differences. American Economic Review, 90(4), 829-846.

IBRD (1972): The Economy of Oman. Report No. EMA-55a. 12. September 1972. Washington D.C.: International Bank for Reconstruction and Development [IBRD].

IBRD (1974): Current Economic Position and Prospects of Oman. Report No. 393a-OM. 31. May 1974. Washington D.C.: IBRD.

IMF (2001): Government Finance Statistics Manual 2001. Washington D.C.: IMF.

IMF (2002): Public Information Notice No. 02/127: IMF Concludes 2002 Article IV Consultation with Oman. 6. November 2002. [online]. Available from: http://www.imf.org/external/np/sec/pn/2002/pn02127.htm [Accessed: 14 October 2013].

IMF (2003): United Arab Emirates: Selected Issues and Statistical Appendix. IMF Country Report No. 03/67. 12. March 2003. Washington D.C.: IMF.

IMF (2010): Qatar: Statistical Appendix. IMF Country Report No. 10/62. 11. March 2010. Washington D.C.: IMF.

IMF (2011): Qatar: 2010 Article IV Consultation. IMF Country Report No. 11/64. 9. March 2011. Washington D.C.: IMF.

IMF (2012): Qatar: 2012 Article IV Consultation. IMF Country Report No. 12/18. 31. January 2012. Washington D.C.: IMF.

IMF (2013a): Oman - 2013 Article IV Consultation Concluding Statement of the IMF Mission. 14. May 2013. [online]. Available from: http://www.imf.org/external/np/ms/2013/051413.htm [Accessed: 23 January 2014].

IMF (2013b): Qatar: 2012 Article IV Consultation. IMF Country Report No. 13/14. 16. January 2013. Washington D.C.: IMF.

IMF (2014a): Press Release No. 14/289: IMF Executive Board Concludes 2014 Article IV Consultation with Bahrain. 18. June 2014. [online]. Available from: http://www.imf.org/external/np/sec/pr/2014/pr14289.htm [Accessed: 6 November 2014].

IMF (2014b): Qatar: 2014 Article IV Consultation. IMF Country Report No. 14/108. 6. May 2014. Washington D.C.: IMF.

IMF (2014c): General Data Dissemination System: Qatar - Central Government Operations. June 2014. [online]. Available from: http://dsbb.imf.org/pages/gdds/DQAFViewPage.aspx?ctycode=QAT&catcode=CGO00&Type=CF [Accessed: 28 June 2014].

IMF (2014d): World Economic Outlook Database, April 2014. 8. April 2014. [online]. Available from: http://www.imf.org/external/ns/cs.aspx?id=28 [Accessed: 17 July 2014].

IMF (2015): Regional Economic Outlook: Middle East and Central Asia, October 2015. Washington D.C.: IMF.

International Bureau of Eduction (2012): World Data on Education - Seventh Edition 2010/11. 3. February 2012. [online]. Available from: http://www.ibe.unesco.org/en/services/online-materials/world-data-on
-education/seventh-edition-2010-11.html [Accessed: 24 September 2012].

Islam, N. (1995): Growth Empirics: A Panel Data Approach. Quarterly Journal of Economics, 110(4), 1127-1170.

Johansen, S. (1988): Statistical Analysis of Cointegration Vectors. Journal of Economic Dynamics and Control, 12, 231-254.

Johansen, S. (1992): Determination of Cointegration Rank in the Presence of a Linear Trend. Oxford Bulletin of Economics and Statistics, 54(3), 383-397.

Johansen, S. (1994): The Role of the Constant and Linear Terms in Cointegration Analysis of Nonstationary Time Series. Econometric Reviews, 13(2), 205-229.

Johansen, S. (2002): A Small Sample Correction for the Test of Cointegrating Rank in the Vector Autoregressive Model. Econometrica, 70(5), 1929-1961.

Johansen, S. and K. Juselius (1992): Testing Structural Hypotheses in a Multivariate Cointegration Analysis of PPP and the UIP for UK. Journal of Econometrics, 53, 211-244.

Johansen, S. and K. Juselius (1994): Identification of the Long-Run and the Short-Run Structure: An Application to the ISLM Model. Journal of Econometrics, 63, 7-36.

Juselius, K.(2006): The Cointegrated VAR Model: Methodology and Applications. Oxford: Oxford University Press.

Kamps, C. (2005): The Dynamic Effects of Public Capital: VAR Evidence for 22 OECD Countries. International Tax and Public Finance, 12(4), 533-558.

Keller, W. (1996): Absorptive Capacity: On the Creation and Acquisition of Technology in Development. Journal of Development Economics, 49, 199-227.

Keller, W. (2002): Trade and the Transmission of Technology. Journal of Economic Growth, 7, 5-24.

Krueger, A.B. and M. Lindahl (2001): Education for Growth: Why and For Whom. Journal of Economic Literature, 39(4), 1101-1136.

Kuznets, S. (1966): Modern Economic Growth: Rate, Structure, and Spread. New Haven: Yale University Press.

Kuznets, S. (1973): Modern Economic Growth: Findings and Reflections. American Economic Review, 63(3), 247-258.

Kwiatkowski, D., P.C.B. Phillips, P. Schmidt and Y. Shin (1992): Testing the Null Hypothesis of Stationarity against the Alternative of a Unit Root: How Sure Are We That Economic Time Series Have a Unit Root. Journal of Econometrics, 54, 159-178.

Kyriacou, G. (1991): Level and Growth Effects of Human Capital: A Cross-Country Study of the Convergence Hypothesis. Working Paper, C.V. Starr Center for Applied Economics, New York University.

Lai, E. (1998): International Intellectual Property Rights Protection and the Rate of Product Innovation. Journal of Development Economics, 55, 133-153.

Landau, D. (1986): Government and Economic Growth in the Less Developed Countries: An Empirical Study for 1960-1980. Economic Development and Cultural Change, 35(1), 35-75.

Lawson, F.H. (1989): Bahrain: The Modernization of Autocracy. Boulder, Colorado: Westview Press.

Leamer, E.E. (1983): Let's Take the Con Out of Econometrics. American Economic Review, 73(1), 31-43.

Leamer, E.E. (1985): Sensitivity Analyses Would Help. American Economic Review, 75(3), 308-313.

Lee, J. and M.C. Strazicich (2004): Minimum LM Unit Root Test with One Structural Break. Working Paper, Department of Economics, Appalachian State University.

Lemieux, T. (2006): The "Mincer Equation" Thirty Years After Schooling, Experience, and Earnings. In: Grossbard, S., ed. Jacob Mincer: A Pioneer of Modern Labor Economics. New York: Springer, pp. 127-145.

Levine, R. and D. Renelt (1992): A Sensitivity Analysis of Cross-Country Growth Regressions. American Economic Review, 82(4), 942-963.

Li, Q. and J.S. Racine (2006): Nonparametric Econometrics. Princeton: Princeton University Press.

Linton, O.B. and J.P. Nielsen (1995): A Kernel Method of Estimating Structured Nonparametric Regression Based on Marginal Integration. Biometrika, 82(1), 93-100.

Liu, Z. and T. Stengos (1999): Non-Linearities in Cross-Country Growth Regressions: A Semiparametric Approach. Journal of Applied Econometrics, 14(5), 527-538.

Longrigg, S.H. (1968): Oil in the Middle East. London: Oxford University Press.

Looney, R.E. (1989): An Economic Assessment of Bahrain's Attempts at Industrial Diversification. The Industrial Bank of Kuwait Papers No.

33.

Looney, R.E. (1994): Manpower Policies and Development in the Persian Gulf Region. Westport: Praeger Publishers.

Lucas, R.E. (1988): On the Mechanics of Economic Development. Journal of Monetary Economics, 22, 3-42.

Luciani, G. (1990): Allocation vs. Production States: A Theoretical Framework. In: Luciani, G., ed. The Arab State. London: Routledge, pp. 65-84.

Luciani, G. (2012): The Resource Curse and the Gulf Development Challenge. In: Luciani, G., ed. Resources Blessed: Diversification and the Gulf Development Model. Berlin: Gerlach Press, pp. 1-28.

Lumenga-Neso, O., M. Olarreaga and M. Schiff (2005): On Indirect Trade-Related R & D Spillovers. European Economic Review, 49, 1785-1798.

Lütkepohl, H. (2004): Vector Autoregressive and Vector Error Correction Models. In: Lütkepohl, H. and M. Krätzig, eds. Applied Time Series Econometrics. Cambridge: Cambridge University Press, pp. 86-158.

Lütkepohl, H., P. Saikkonen and C. Trenkler (2001): Maximum Eigenvalue versus Trace Tests for the Cointegrating Rank of a VAR Process. Econometrics Journal, 4, 287-310.

MacKinnon, J.G. (1991): Critical Values for Cointegration Tests. In: R.F. Engle and C.W.J. Granger, eds. Long-Run Economic Relationships: Readings in Cointegration. New York: Oxford University Press, pp. 266-276.

Maddison, A. (1982): Phases of Capitalist Development. New York: Oxford University Press.

Madigan, D. and J. York (1995): Bayesian Graphical Models for Discrete Data. International Statistical Review, 63(2), 215-232.

Mankiw, N.G., D. Romer and D.N. Weil (1992): A Contribution to the Empirics of Economic Growth. Quarterly Journal of Economics, 107(2),

407-437.

Martin, M.O., I.V.S. Mullis, P. Foy and G.M. Stanco (2012): TIMSS 2011 International Results in Science. Amsterdam: International Association for the Evaluation of Educational Achievement.

Mauro, P. (1995): Corruption and Growth. Quarterly Journal of Economics, 110(3), 681-712.

McMillan, M.S. and D. Rodrik (2011): Globalization, Structural Change and Productivity Growth. National Bureau of Economic Research Working Paper No. 17143.

MEED (1981): Government to Take Control of C & W. MEED, 25(26), 8-10.

Mincer, J. (1974): Schooling, Earnings, and Experience. New York: Columbia University Press.

Mirza, A. (2009): Octal Petrochemicals. MEED, 53(11), 28-29.

Mullis, Ina V.S., M.O. Martin, P. Foy and A. Arora (2012): TIMSS 2011 International Results in Mathematics. Amsterdam: International Association for the Evaluation of Educational Achievement.

Munnell, A.H. (1990): Why Has Productivity Growth Declined? Productivity and Public Investment. New England Economic Review, (January/ February), 3-22.

Murphy, K.M. and F. Welch (1990): Empirical Age-Earnings Profiles. Journal of Labor Economics, 8(2), 202-229.

Musgrave, R.A. and A.T. Peacock (1967): Classics in the Theory of Public Finance. London: Macmillan.

Nafi, Z.A. (1983): Economic and Social Development in Qatar. London: Frances Pinter.

Nehru, V. and A. Dhareshwar (1993): A New Database on Physical Capital Stock: Sources, Methodology and Results. Revista de Analisis

Economico, 8(1), 37-59.

Nelson, C.R. and C.L. Plosser (1982): Trends and Random Walks in Macroeconomic Time Series. Journal of Monetary Economics, 10, 139-162.

North, D.C. (1989): Institutions and Economic Growth: An Historical Introduction. World Development, 17(9), 1319-1332.

North, D.C. (1990): Institutions, Institutional Change and Economic Performance. Cambridge: Cambridge University Press.

North, D.C. and R. Thomas (1973): The Rise of the Western World: A New Economic History. Cambridge: Cambridge University Press.

Obaidullah, M. (2007): Securitization in Islam. In: Hassan, M.K. and M.K. Lewis, eds. Handbook of Islamic Banking. Cheltenham: Edward Elgar, pp. 191-199.

OECD (2001): Measuring Productivity: Measurement of Industry-Level and Aggregate Productivity Growth. Paris: OECD Publications.

Oman, Sultanate of (OM)

OM, Central Bank of Oman [CBO] (1986-2004): Annual Report 1985-2003 (various issues). Muscat: CBO.

OM, CBO (1980a-2015d): Quarterly Statistical Bulletin, March 1980 - December 2015 (various issues). Muscat: CBO.

OM, Development Council [DC] (1981-1993): Statistical Year Book 1980-1992 (various issues). Muscat: DC.

OM, Ministry of Development [MoD] (1994-1996): Statistical Year Book 1993-1995 (various issues). Muscat: MoD.

OM, MoD (1994b): General Census of Population, Housing and Establishments 1993: Detailed Publication of the Results of the General Census. Muscat: MoD.

OM, Ministry of Manpower [MoM] (2014): Omanisation % per Sector.

[online] Available from: http://www.manpower.gov.om/portal/en/OmanisationPerSector.aspx [Accessed: 28 February 2014].

OM, Ministry of National Economy [MoNE] (1998-2012): Statistical Year Book 1997-2011 (various issues). Muscat: MoNE.

OM, MoNE (2001b): Sixth Five-Year Development Plan 2001-2005: Basic Components and Main Indicators of the Plan. Muscat: MoNE.

OM, MoNE (2002b): The General Framework of the Sixth Five-Year Development Plan 2001-2005: Volume I. Muscat: MoNE.

OM, MoNE (2007b): Long-term Development Strategy (1996-2020): Vision for Oman's Economy (Oman 2020) (second edition). Muscat: MoNE.

OM, MoNE (2011b): Taqrīr mutābaʿa adāʾ al-iqtiṣād al-waṭani li-ʿām 2009 [Follow-Up Report on the Performance of the National Economy in the Year 2009]. Muscat: MoNE.

OM, National Center for Statistics and Information [NCSI] (2013-2016): Statistical Year Book 2012-2015 (various issues). Muscat: NCSI.

OM, NCSI (2013b): National Accounts Bulletin 2013. Muscat: NCSI.

OM, NCSI (2013c): Ḫaṣāʾiṣ al-qūwa al-ʿāmila min wāqiʿ at-taʿdādāt as-sukkānīya [Characteristics of the Labour Force from the Reality of the Population Censuses]. Muscat: NCSI.

OM, NCSI (2015b): National Accounts Bulletin 2015. Muscat: NCSI.

OM, Oman LNG [OLNG] (2010): Annual Report 2009. Mina Al Fahal: OLNG.

OM, Omar Zawawi Establishment [OMZEST] (2013): Companies: Oman Methanol Company LLC. [online]. Available from: http://www.omzest.com/companies/oman-methanol-company-llc.html [Accessed: 23 November 2013].

OM, Oman Oil Company [OOC] (2012): Oman Oil Company: Investments. [online]. Available from: http://www.oman-oil.com/Investment.html [Accessed: 13 December 2013].

OM, Oman Power and Water Procurement Company [OPWP] (2011): Annual Report 2010. Muscat: OPWP.

OM, Omantel [Otel] (2013): Annual Report 2012. Muscat: Otel.

OM, Sohar Port and Freezone [SPF] (2013): Setting Up Business: Incentives. [online]. Available from: http://www.soharportandfreezone.com/en/setting-up-business/incentives [Accessed: 27 February 2014].

OM, United Power Company [UPC] (2011): Annual Report 2010. Muscat: UPC.

Parente, S.L. and E.C. Prescott (1994): Barriers to Technology Adoption and Development. Journal of Political Development, 102(2), 298-321.

Patterson, K. (2010): A Primer for Unit Root Testing. Basingstoke: Palgrave Macmillan.

Perron, P. (1989): The Great Crash, the Oil Price Shock and the Unit Root Hypothesis. Econometrica, 57(6), 1361-1401.

Pfeiffer, J. (1991): Bahrain: Stand und Perspektiven als Offshore-Zentrum der GCC-Staaten. Munich, Cologne, London: Weltforum Verlag.

Phillips, P.C.B. (1986): Understanding Spurious Regressions in Econometrics. Journal of Econometrics, 33, 311-340.

Phillips, P.C.B. and C.C. Lee (1996): Efficiency Gains from Quasi-Differencing under Non-Stationarity. In: Robinson, P.M. and M. Rosenblatt, eds. Athens Conference on Applied Probability and Time Series: Essays in Memory of E.J. Hannan. New York: Springer, pp. 300-314.

Pritchett, L. (1996): Mind Your P's and Q's: The Cost of Public Investment is Not the Value of Public Capital. World Bank Policy Research Working Paper No. 1660.

Pritchett, L. (1997): Divergence, Big Time. Journal of Economic Perspectives, 11(3), 3-17.

Pritchett, L. (2001): Where Has All the Education Gone. World Bank Economic Review, 15(3), 367-391.

Psacharopoulos, G. (1994): Returns to Investment in Education: A Global Update. World Development, 22(9), 1325-1343.

Psacharopoulos, G. and H.A. Patrinos (2004): Returns to Investment in Education: A Further Update. Education Economics, 12(2), 111-134.

Qatar, State of (QA)

QA, Aspire Zone Foundation [AZF] (2013): Annual Report 2011/12. Doha: AFZ.

QA, Central Statistical Organization [CSO] (1981-1998): Annual Statistical Abstract 1980-1997 (various issues). Doha: CSO.

QA, CSO (1984b): Industrial Survey 1982. Doha: CSO.

QA, CSO (1987b): At-taʿdād al-ʿām li-s-sukkān wa al-masākin, Mārs 1986 [The General Census of Population and Housing, March 1986]. Doha: CSO.

QA, General Secretariat for Development Planning [GSDP] (2008): Qatar National Vision 2030. Doha: GSDP.

QA, GSDP (2011): Qatar National Development Strategy 2011-2016. Doha: GSDP.

QA, Industries Qatar [IQ] (2003): Articles of Association. 19. April 2003. [online]. Available from: http://www.iq.com.qa/IQ/IQ.nsf/en_Pages/en_InvestorAffairs_Downloads/$file/IQ%20Articles%20of%20Association.pdf [Accessed: 5 December 2014].

QA, Ministry of Development Planning and Statistics [MDPS] (2012-2015): Annual Statistical Abstract 2011-2014 (various issues). Doha: MDPS.

QA, MDPS (2014b): Annual Bulletin of Labor Force Survey 2013. Doha: MDPS.

QA, MDPS (2014c): Annual Bulletin of Industry and Energy Statistics 2013. Doha: MDPS.

QA, MDPS (2014d): Annual Bulletin of Transport and Communication Statistics 2013. Doha: MDPS.

QA, MDPS (2015b): National Accounts Bulletin 2007-2014. Doha: MDPS.

QA, Qatalum [QALU] (2013): Qatalum: About Us. [online]. Available from: https://www.qatalum.com/AboutUs/Pages/About-Us.aspx [Accessed: 19 July 2014].

QA, Qatar Airways [QAir] (2014): The Qatar Airways Story. May 2014. [online]. Available from: http://www.qatarairways.com/global/en/press-kits.page [Accessed: 7 July 2014].

QA, Qatar Central Bank [QCB] (1982a-2015d): Quarterly Statistical Bulletin, March 1982 - December 2015 (various issues). Doha: QCB.

QA, QCB (2013): Registered Banks in Qatar, 31. September 2013. [online]. Available from: http://www.qcb.gov.qa/Arabic/SupervisionApproac /LicensingAndRegistration/Documents/Registered_Banks_2013_Eng.pdf [Accessed: 28 August 2014].

QA, Qatar National Bank [QNB] (2014): Corporate Governance Report 2013. Doha: QNB.

QA, Qatar Petrochemical Company [QAPCO] (2014): QAPCO: About QAPCO. [online]. Available from: http://www.qapco.com.qa/print?page ID=1&nid=0 [Accessed: 19 July 2014].

QA, Qatar Petroleum [QP] (2005, 2010, 2011): Annual Report 2004, 2009, 2010. Doha: QP.

QA, Qatar University [QU] (2013): Qatar University: Our History. 21. February 2013. [online]. Available from: http://www.qu.edu.qa/the

university/history.php [Accessed: 21 June 2014].

QA, Qatargas [QG] (2014): Qatargas: Laffan Refinery. [online]. Available from: https://www.qatargas.com/English/QGVentures/Pages/LaffanRefinery.aspx [Accessed: 25 July 2014].

QA, Qatari Diar [QD] (2012): Qatari Diar: Company Profile. [online]. Available from: http://www.qataridiar.com/English/WhoWeAre/Pages/Company-Profile.aspx [Accessed: 30 August 2014].

QA, Qatarization Steering Committee [QSC] (2014): Strategic Qatarization Plan. [online]. Available from: http://www.qatarization.com.qa/qatarization/qat_web.nsf/web/plan_main?opendocument [Accessed: 29 August 2014].

QA, Statistics Authority [SA] (2010a, 2011): Annual Statistical Abstract 2009-2010 (various issues). Doha: SA.

QA, SA (2010b): The General Census of Population and Housing, and Establishment, April 2010. Doha: SA.

QA, SA (2011b): The Annual Bulletin of Building and Construction Statistics 2010. Doha: SA.

QA, The Planning Council [PC] (1999-2008): Annual Statistical Abstract 1998-2007 (various issues). Doha: PC.

QA, PC (1999b): At-taʿdād al-ʿām li-s-sukkān wa al-masākin, Mārs 1997 [The General Census of Population and Housing, March 1997]. Doha: PC.

QA, PC (2004b): At-taʿdād al-ʿām li-s-sukkān wa al-masākin, Mārs 2004 [The General Census of Population and Housing, March 2004]. Doha: PC.

QA, PC (2006b): National Accounts State of Qatar 1980-2004. Doha: PC.

QA, PC (2006c): Bulletin of Employment, Wages & Working Hours, June 2005. Doha: PC.

Quah, D.T. (1993): Galton's Fallacy and Tests of the Convergence Hypothesis. Scandinavian Journal of Economics, 95(4), 427-443.

Quah, D.T. (1996): Empirics for Economic Growth and Convergence. European Economic Review, 40(6), 1353-1375.

Quah, D.T. (1997): Empirics for Growth and Distribution: Stratification, Polarization, and Convergence Clubs. Journal of Economic Growth, 2(1), 27-59.

Rebelo, S. (1991): Long-Run Policy Analysis and Long-Run Growth. Journal of Political Economy, 99(3), 500-521.

Reuters (2011): In Bahrain, a Symbol at the Heart of Revolt. 16. June 2011. [online]. Available from: http://www.reuters.com/article/2011/06/16/us-bahrain-gfh-idUSTRE75F4LF20110616 [Accessed: 5 December 2014].

Reuters (2014): Qatar Takes Full Control of National Airline. 5. May 2014. [online]. Available from: http://www.reuters.com/article/2014/05/05/qatar-airlines-idUSL6N0NR1RH20140505 [Accessed: 16 July 2014].

Robinson, P.M. (1988): Root-N-Consistent Semiparametric Regression. Econometrica, 56(4), 931-954.

Rodrik, D. (2004): Industrial Policy for the Twenty-First Century. Working Paper, John F. Kennedy School of Government, Harvard University.

Rodrik, D. (2008): Normalizing Industrial Policy. Commission on Growth and Development Working Paper No. 3. Washington, D.C.: Commission on Growth and Development.

Romer, P.M. (1986): Increasing Returns and Long-Run Growth. Journal of Political Economy, 94(5), 1002-1037.

Romer, P.M. (1987): Growth Based on Increasing Returns Due to Specialization. American Economic Review, 77(2), 56-62.

Romer, P.M. (1990): Endogenous Technological Change. Journal of Political Economy, 98(5), S71-S102.

Romer, P.M. (1993): Idea Gaps and Object Gaps in Economic Development. Journal of Monetary Economics, 32(3), 543-573.

Romer, P.M. (1994): The Origins of Endogenous Growth. Journal of Economic Perspectives, 8(1), 3-22.

Romp, W. and J. de Haan (2005): Public Capital and Economic Growth: A Critical Survey. EIB Papers 2/2005. European Investment Bank: Luxembourg.

Rosen, S. (2008): Human Capital. In: Durlauf, S.N. and L. Blume, eds. The New Palgrave Dictionary of Economics (second edition, Volume 4). Basingstoke: Palgrave Macmillan, pp. 98-109.

Rumaihi, M.G. (1976): Bahrain: Social and Political Change since the First World War. London and New York: Bowker.

Sachs, J.D. and A.M. Warner (1995): Economic Reform and the Process of Economic Integration. Brookings Papers on Economic Activity, 1995(1), 1-95.

Sadik, M.T. and W.P. Snavely (1972): Bahrain, Qatar and the United Arab Emirates. Lexington, Massachusetts: D.C. Heath and Company.

Said, S.E. and D.A. Dickey (1984): Testing for Unit Roots in Autoregressive-Moving Average Models of Unknown Order. Biometrika, 71(3), 599-608.

Saikkonen, P. and H. Lütkepohl (2000a): Testing for the Cointegrating Rank of a VAR Process with an Intercept. Econometric Theory, 16, 373-406.

Saikkonen, P. and H. Lütkepohl (2000b): Trend Adjustment prior to Testing for the Cointegrating Rank of a Vector Autoregressive Process. Journal of Time Series Analysis, 21(4), 435-456.

Sala-i-Martin, X. (1997): I Just Ran Two Million Regressions. American Economic Review, 87(2), 178-183.

Sala-i-Martin, X., G. Doppelhofer and R.I. Miller (2004): Determinants of Long-Term Growth: A Bayesian Averaging of Classical Estimates (BACE) Approach. American Economic Review, 94(4), 813-835.

Salisbury, P. (2012): Oman's Industrial Hub Shapes Up. MEED, 56(40), 38-39.

Samuelson, P.A. (1954): The Pure Theory of Public Expenditure. Review of Economics and Statistics, 36(4), 387-389.

Samuelson, P.A. (1955): Diagrammatic Exposition of a Theory of Public Expenditure. Review of Economics and Statistics, 37(4), 350-356.

Schmidt, P. and P.C.B. Phillips (1992): LM Tests for a Unit Root in the Presence of Deterministic Trends. Oxford Bulletin of Economics and Statistics, 54(3), 257-287.

Scotchmer, S. (2004): Innovation and Incentives. Cambridge, Massachusetts: MIT Press.

Solow, R. (1956): A Contribution to the Theory of Economic Growth. Quarterly Journal of Economics, 70(1), 65-94.

Solow, R. (1960): Investment and Technical Progress. In: Arrow, K.J., ed. Mathematical Methods in the Social Sciences: Proceedings of the First Stanford Symposium, 1959. Stanford: Stanford University Press, pp. 89-104.

Sturm, J.E. and J. de Haan (1995): Is Public Expenditure Really Productive? New Evidence for the USA and the Netherlands. Economic Modelling, 12(1), 60-72.

Summers, R. and A. Heston (1988): A New Set of International Comparisons of Real Product and Price Levels Estimates for 130 Countries, 1950-1985. Journal of Income and Wealth, 34(1), 1-25.

Summers, R. and A. Heston (1991): The Penn World Table (Mark 5): An Expanded Set of International Comparisons, 1950-1988. Quarterly Journal of Economics, 106(2), 327-368.

Swan, T.W. (1956): Economic Growth and Capital Accumulation. Economic Record, 32(2), 334-361.

Temple, J. (1999a): The New Growth Evidence. Journal of Economic Literature, 37(1), 112-156.

Temple, J. (1999b): A Positive Effect of Human Capital on Growth. Economic Letters, 65(1), 131-134.

Thomas, D. and E. Frankenberg (2002): Health, Nutrition and Prosperity: A Microeconomic Perspective. Bulletin of the World Health Organization, 80(2), 106-113.

Thomas, K. (2009): Kingdom Takes on Gulf Shipping Giants. MEED, 53(16), 40-41.

Townsend, J. (1977): Oman: The Making of a Modern State. New York: St. Martin's Press.

Treichel, V. (1999): Stance of Fiscal Policy and Non-Oil Economic Growth. In: Mansur, A. and V. Treichel, eds. Oman Beyond the Oil Horizon: Policies Toward Sustainable Growth. IMF Occasional Paper No. 185. Washington DC: International Monetary Fund, pp. 19-30.

Trenkler, C. (2008): Determining p-values for Systems Cointegration Tests with a Prior Adjustment for Deterministic Terms. Computational Statistics, 23, 19-39.

United Nations, Economic Commission for Western Asia [UN-ECWA] (1980): The Population Situation in the ECWA Region: Qatar. Beirut: UN-ECWA.

United Nations, Industrial Development Organization [UN-IDO] (1980): Long-Term Prospects of Industrial Development in Qatar. Algiers: UN-IDO.

U.S. Geological Survey [USGS] (2013): 2012 Minerals Yearbook: Aluminium. Washington, DC: U.S. Department of the Interior.

Valeri, M. (2009): Oman: Politics and Society in the Qaboos State. London: C. Hurst.

Valeri, M. (2013): Oligarchy vs. Oligarchy: Business and Politics of Reform in Bahrain and Oman. In: Hertog, S., G. Luciani and M. Valeri, eds. Business Politics in the Middle East. London: Hurst & Co., pp. 17-41.

Velu, R.P., G.C. Reinsel and D.W. Wichern (1986): Reduced Rank Models for Multiple Time Series. Biometrika, 73(1), 105-118.

Vougas, D. (2003): Reconsidering LM Unit Root Testing. Journal of Applied Statistics, 30(7), 727-741.

Wacziarg, R. (2002): Review of Easterly's The Elusive Quest for Growth. Journal of Economic Literature, 40(3), 907-918.

Wagner, A. (1890): Finanzwissenschaft (third edition). Leipzig: CF Winter'sche Verlagshandlung.

Weber, M. (1930): The Protestant Ethic and the Spirit of Capitalism. London: Allen and Unwin.

Weil, D.N. (2007): Accounting for the Effect of Health on Economic Growth. Quarterly Journal of Economics, 122(3), 1265-1306.

Wells, M.J. (1967): Oil Production Brings Oman to an Uncertain Future. World Petroleum, 38(7), 22-24.

Williamson, J. (1990): What Washington Means by Policy Reform. In: Williamson, J., ed. Latin American Adjustment: How Much Has Happened. Washington, D.C.: Peterson Institute for International Economics, pp. 7-20

Wilson, R. (1983): Banking and Finance in the Arab Middle East. London: Macmillan.

Woolridge, J.M. (2010): Econometric Analysis of Cross Section and Panel Data. Cambridge, Massachusetts: MIT Press.

World Bank (1976): Current Economic Position and Prospects of Oman. Report No. 934a-OM. 10. February 1976. Washington D.C.: World Bank.

World Bank (1977): Oman - Transformation of an Economy, Volume I: Main Report. Report No. 1620-OM. 25. October 1977. Washington D.C.: World Bank.

World Bank (1978): Bahrain: Current Economic Position and Prospects. Report No. 2058-BH. 28. June 1978. Washington D.C.: World Bank.

World Bank (1979): Oman: Current Economic Position and Prospects. Report No. 2528-OM. 16. October 1979. Washington D.C.: World Bank.

World Bank (1985): Oman: Recent Economic Developments and Prospects. Report No. 5380-OM. July 1985. Washington D.C.: World Bank.

World Bank (1988a): Sultanate of Oman: Recent Economic Developments and Prospects, Volume I. Report No. 6899-OM. 12. September 1988. Washington D.C.: World Bank.

World Bank (1988b): Sultanate of Oman: Recent Economic Developments and Prospects, Volume II. Report No. 6899-OM. 12. September 1988. Washington D.C.: World Bank.

World Bank (1993): Bahrain: The Requirements for Economic Diversification and Sustainability. Report No. 11281-BH. March 1993. Washington D.C.: World Bank.

World Bank (1994): Sultanate of Oman: Sustainable Growth and Economic Diversification. Report No. 12199-OM. 31. May 1994. Washington D.C.: World Bank.

World Bank (2008): The Road Not Traveled: Education Reform in the Middle East and North Africa. Washington D.C.: World Bank

Xu, B. (2000): Multinational Enterprises, Technology Diffusion and Host Country Productivity Growth. Journal of Development Economics, 62, 477-493.

Zivot, E. and D.W.K. Andrews (1992): Further Evidence on the Great Crash, the Oil-Price Shock, and the Unit-Root Hypothesis. Journal of Business and Economic Statistics, 10(3), 251-270.

Appendices

Appendix A: Data Sources and Definition of Variables

Total Expenditure, Capital Expenditure, Current Expenditure:

Breakdowns of total public expenditure by economic type are published in most official publications of the GCC countries. Yet, due to differences in the extent of data coverage, expenditure figures from different national data sources within one country vary markedly at times. These discrepancies can primarily be ascribed to the fact that sensitive areas such as defence expenditure are excluded by some data sources. To ensure both consistency as well as a comprehensive coverage of public spending patterns only national data sources which include defence expenditure have been utilised. Nominal public expenditures are deflated by the CPI of the corresponding year.

Table A1: Data Sources - Total, Capital, and Current Expenditure

Country	Years	Data Source
Bahrain	1960-1989:	Bahrain, Ministry of Finance and National Economy [MFNE] (1991)
	1990-1999:	Bahrain, MFNE (1996, 2000)
	2000-2004:	Bahrain, Ministry of Finance [MoF] (2005)
	2005-2013:	Bahrain, MoF (2007-2014)
Oman	1967-1970[1]	IBRD (1972)
	1971-1989:	Oman, Development Council [DC] (1986, 1989, 1991)
	1990-1992:	Oman, Ministry of Development [MoD] (1995)
	1993-2009:	Oman, Ministry of National Economy [MoNE] (2001, 2003, 2005, 2007, 2009, 2012)
	2010-2013:	Oman, National Center for Statistics and Information [NCSI] (2013-2015)
Qatar[2]	1967-1969:	Al-Kuwari (1978)
	1970-1974:	El Mallakh (1979)
	1975-1992:	Qatar, Central Statistical Organization [CSO] (1983, 1988, 1992, 1996)
	1993-2013:	Qatar, Qatar Central Bank [QCB] (1997b, 1999b, 2001b, 2005a, 2009d, 2011a, 2014a, 2015a)

[1] The first public budget of the government of Oman was prepared only in the year 1971. Public expenditure data for the years 1967-1970 refers to estimates by IBRD (1972:7-8). [2] Prior to fiscal year 1989 (1. April 1989 - 31. March 1990) tenors of Qatari fiscal years had been aligned to the Hijri calendar, which is 11-13 days shorter than the Gregorian calendar. Public expenditure data for Hijri fiscal years has been adjusted accordingly.

Education Expenditure, Health Expenditure, Non-Education Expenditure, Non-Health Expenditure:

Breakdowns of government expenditure in the GCC countries by function are only available to a limited extent both from national sources and from multilateral organisations. Hence, for constructing consistent time series on public expenditure on education and health I utilise the total expenditures of the respective ministries and public agencies. In all GCC countries several ministries or public agencies have an educational mandate. Therefore, education expenditure includes not only expenditures by the respective ministries but also tertiary education expenditures from public universities (table A2). Non-Education Expenditure (Non-Health Expenditure) are the remainder of total expenditure after subtracting education expenditure (health expenditure). Nominal public expenditures are deflated by the CPI of the corresponding year.

Table A2: Ministries and Public Agencies included in Education and Health Expenditure

Country	Education Expenditure	Health Expenditure
Bahrain	Ministry of Education University of Bahrain Bahrain Center for Studies and Research	Ministry of Health
Oman	Ministry of Education Ministry of Higher Education Sultan Qaboos University Higher Education Council	Ministry of Health
Qatar[1]	Ministry of Education[2] Qatar University Supreme Council of Education	Ministry of Public Health[3] Supreme Council of Health

[1] Due to data unavailability Qatari education expenditure does not comprise expenditure by Qatar Foundation (QF). While QF has been established as a private organisation in 1995, the organisation exhibits close links to the Qatari government. According to Brandenburg (2012:227), QF is funded primarily through (off-budget) public oil revenues. Among other activities, QF promotes projects which aim to enhance the educational level in Qatar (e.g. Education City). Since QF does not publish any details about the level or the composition of its annual expenditure, the extent of QF's education related expenditure is unknown.

[2] The duties of the Ministry of Education have been assigned to the Supreme Council of Education (established in 2002) by Emiri Decree in April 2009. See International Bureau of Eduction (2012)

[3] The duties of the Ministry of Public Health have been assigned to the Supreme Council of Health by Emiri Decree in 2005.

Table A3: Data Sources - Education Expenditure

Country	Years	Data Source
Bahrain	1976-1994:	Bahrain, Central Statistics Organization[1] [CSO] (1991, 1996)
	1976-1994:	Bahrain, Central Informatics Organization [CIO] (2003)
	1995-1999:	Bahrain, Ministry of Finance and National Economy [MFNE] (2000)
	2000-2004:	Bahrain, Ministry of Finance [MoF] (2005)
	2005-2013:	Bahrain, MoF (2007-2014)
Oman	1979-1990:	Oman, Development Council [DC] (1986, 1989, 1991)
	1991-1994:	Oman, Ministry of Development [MoD] (1994, 1996)
	1995-2008:	Oman, Ministry of National Economy [MoNE] (1998, 2001, 2005, 2008, 2010, 2012)
	2009-2013:	Oman, National Center for Statistics and Information [NCSI] (2013, 2015)
Qatar[2]	1979-1995:	Qatar, Central Statistical Organization [CSO] (1983, 1988, 1991, 1993, 1998)
	1996-2004:	Qatar, The Planning Council [PC] (2003, 2006, 2008)
	2005-2009:	Qatar, Statistics Authority [SA] (2010a)
	2010-2013:	Qatar, Ministry of Development Planning and Statistics [MDPS] (2012-2015)

[1] Central Statistics Organization has been renamed to Central Informatics Organization in 2002. [2] Prior to fiscal year 1989 (1. April 1989 - 31. March 1990) tenors of Qatari fiscal years had been aligned to the Hijri calendar, which is 11-13 days shorter than the Gregorian calendar. Public expenditure data for Hijri fiscal years has been adjusted accordingly.

Table A4: Data Sources - Health Expenditure

Country	Years	Data Source
Bahrain	1976-1994:	Bahrain, Central Statistics Organization[1] [CSO] (1991, 1996)
	1995-2007:	Bahrain, Central Informatics Organization [CIO] (2004, 2009)
	2008-2013:	Bahrain, Ministry of Finance [MoF] (2010-2014)
Oman	1979-1990:	Oman, Development Council [DC] (1986, 1989, 1991)
	1991-1994:	Oman, Ministry of Development [MoD] (1994, 1996)
	1995-2008:	Oman, Ministry of National Economy [MoNE] (1998, 2001, 2005, 2008, 2010, 2012)
	2009-2013:	Oman, National Center for Statistics and Information [NCSI] (2013, 2015)
Qatar[2]	1979-1995:	Qatar, Central Statistical Organization [CSO] (1983, 1988, 1991, 1993, 1998)
	1996-2004:	Qatar, The Planning Council [PC] (2003, 2006, 2008)
	2005-2009:	Qatar, Statistics Authority [SA] (2010a)
	2010-2013:	Qatar, Ministry of Development Planning and Statistics [MDPS] (2012-2015)

[1] Central Statistics Organization has been renamed to Central Informatics Organization in 2002. [2] Prior to fiscal year 1989 (1. April 1989 - 31. March 1990) tenors of Qatari fiscal years had been aligned to the Hijri calendar, which is 11-13 days shorter than the Gregorian calendar. Public expenditure data for Hijri fiscal years has been adjusted accordingly.

Non-Oil GDP, CPI, and GDP Deflator:

As a result of the hydrocarbons sectors' dominant position in the economy, real GDP growth rates of the GCC states have been strongly influenced by changes in the annual output level of the oil sector and, to a lesser extent, of the gas sector. Therefore, I focus on non-oil real GDP growth as a more accurate measure for changes in non-oil economic activity. For this reason, the gross value added by the oil and the gas sectors is subtracted from total nominal GDP. Afterwards, the remaining non-oil GDP is deflated. Apart from the manufacturing sector, I deem the consumer price index (CPI) a better deflator for the nominal gross value added in non-oil sectors than the GDP deflator since the latter is strongly impacted by price changes in the oil and gas sectors. The gross value added in the manufacturing sector is deflated by the GDP deflator because the nominal gross value added in most manufacturing industries in the GCC states is strongly influenced by oil price developments (e.g. refining, petrochemicals).

Official breakdowns of nominal GDP by economic activity have been sourced from United Nations Statistics Division. CPI and GDP deflator data is taken from the International Financial Statistics and the World Economic Outlook databases of the IMF. CPI figure for Oman in the year 1979 originates from World Bank (1985). In addition, price data in IBRD (1972) and in World Bank (1979) has been utilised for calculating the Omani capital stock in table 5.7. Here, the nominal gross fixed capital formation time series for the years 1970-1978 have been deflated by an unweighted average of several food price changes in the respective years due to a lack of more comprehensive CPI data. No GDP deflator data is available for Qatar in the year 1979. Therefore, gross value added of the Qatari manufacturing sector in 1979 has been deflated by the CPI.

Non-Oil GDP per Worker:

Labour productivity developments are proxied by the measure non-oil GDP (in real terms) per worker. Unfortunately, comprehensive labour force time series for Bahrain, Oman and Qatar are not available from national or multilateral data sources on an annual basis for the entire sample period. Annual figures from national publications such as the annual "Statistical Year Book" in Oman or the quarterly "Economic Indicators" by the Central Bank of Bahrain have not been utilised since they do not comprise employment in public security and defence services and, therefore, deviate substantially from official census year results. Instead, annual figures for the years 1990-2013 are taken from labour force estimates in World Bank's World Development Indicators. These World Bank time series are supplemented by labour force figures from national census data and labour force estimates in the academic literature for the years prior to 1990. Missing values have been extrapolated.

Table A5: Data Sources - Labour Force

Country	Data Source
Bahrain	1975: Birks and Sinclair (1979)[1]
	1981 (Census Year): Bahrain, Central Informatics Organization [CIO] (2009)
	1982-1989: Bahrain, CIO (2001)
	1990-2013: World Bank: World Development Indicators
Oman	1978: World Bank (1979)
	1985: World Bank (1988a)
	1990-2013: World Bank: World Development Indicators
Qatar	1975: Birks and Sinclair (1980)
	1981, 1982: Qatar Statistics Authority: Annual Statistical Abstract 1981, 1983
	1986 (Census Year): Qatar Statistics Authority, downloaded from Qatar Information Exchange (www.qix.gov.qa)
	1990-2013: World Bank: World Development Indicators

[1] Does not include unemployed persons.

Domestic Credit to Private Sector & to Private Business

The times series domestic credit to private sector refers to the aggregate level of loans (and debt securities) which is provided to a country's private sector (private business and households) by domestic commercial banks. Instead, the time series domestic credit to private business does not comprise loans to domestic households. The time series domestic credit to private business was constructed by subtracting domestic credit to households from total domestic credit to the private sector (private business and households). The main data sources are the IMF's international financial statistics (IFS) database and publications by national authorities in Bahrain, Oman and Qatar. The latter publications contain breakdowns of commercial banks' aggregate assets. In case of Oman and Qatar, these breakdowns differentiate between various types of borrowers (e.g. general government, public enterprises, private sector companies). As a result, the time series domestic credit to private sector in Oman and Qatar does not include bank lending to companies which are (majority-)owned by the respective governments. Unfortunately, national authorities in Bahrain publish less detailed breakdowns of commercial banks' aggregate assets. Here, breakdowns do not distinguish between private and public sector companies but only between the private sector and the general government. As a result, Bahraini data on domestic credit to the private sector, which is consistent with the respective IFS data, is likely to include loans to public corporations. Furthermore, domestic credit data in Bahrain does only comprise retail banks (*formerly:* onshore commercial banks) but not wholesale banks (*formerly:* offshore banking units) since the wholesale/ offshore banking sector almost exclusively engages in lending to non-Bahrani entities.

Table A6: Data Sources - Domestic Credit to Private Sector & Households

Country	Years	Data Source
Bahrain	Domestic Credit to Private Sector:	
	1979-2013:	IMF - International Financial Statistics [IFS]
	1991-2013:	Bahrain, Central Bank of Bahrain [CBB] (2001, 2005, 2013, 2015)
	Domestic Credit to Households:	
	1979-1985:	Bahrain, Bahrain Monetary Agency [BMA] (1980-1986)
	1984-1991:	World Bank (1993)
	1991-2009:	Central Informatics Organisation [CIO] (2001, 2010)
	2010-2013:	Bahrain, CBB (2011-2014)
Oman	Domestic Credit to Private Sector:	
	1979-2013:	Oman, Central Bank of Oman [CBO] (1980d-2015d)
	Domestic Credit to Households:	
	1979-1982:	World Bank (1985)
	1981-1989:	Oman, CBO (1986, 1988, 1990)
	1989-1992:	Oman, Development Council [DC] (1992, 1993)
	1992-1995:	Oman, Ministry of Development [MoD] (1995, 1996)
	1995-2001:	Oman, Ministry of National Economy [MoNE] (2000, 2002)
	2001-2003:	Oman, CBO (2004)
	2003-2013:	Oman, CBO (2004a-2015d)
Qatar	Domestic Credit to Private Sector:	
	1979-2013:	Qatar, Qatar Central Bank [QCB] (1982d-2015b)
	Domestic Credit to Households:	
	1979-2013:	Qatar, QCB (1982d-2015b)

Gross Fixed Capital Formation Private Sector:

Unfortunately, only very limited detailed data on gross fixed capital formation (GFCF) is publicly available. This applies particularly for Qatar since official publications do not include breakdowns of GFCF into public and private sectors. Estimates by IMF (2010) for public and private sector GFCF in Qatar are available for the years 2002-2008. Yet, estimates by IMF (2010) for public sector GFCF are very similar to official capital expenditure figures in the respective years. Therefore, investments by state-owned companies in Qatar are (most likely) included in private sector GFCF and not in public sector GFCF time series. Similarly, publicly available figures on private sector GFCF in Bahrain include investments by state-owned companies (see footnotes of the respective tables in BH/CIO 2009 and BH/CIO 2011a). In contrast, data sources in Oman differentiate between GFCF by private sector companies and government enterprises. Furthermore, Oman is the only country which publishes sectoral breakdowns of GFCF. This allows for a separate analysis of GFCF in the non-oil economy. Instead, publicly available figures in Bahrain and Qatar refer to GFCF in the oil and in non-oil sectors.

Table A7: Data Sources - Gross Fixed Capital Formation Private Sector

Country	Years	Data Source
Bahrain	1979-1990:	Bahrain, Central Statistics Organisation [CSO] (1985, 1991)
	1991-2013:	Bahrain, Central Informatics Organisation [CIO] (2001, 2005, 2009, 2011, 2014b)
Oman	1979-1990:	Oman, Development Council [DC] (1986, 1989, 1990, 1992)
	1991-2002:	Oman, Ministry of National Economy [MoNE] (2001a, 2002a, 2009)
	2003-2013:	Oman, National Center for Statistics and Information [NCSI] (2013, 2015)
Qatar	2002-2008:	IMF (2010)

Appendix B: Econometric Results Chapter 3

Table B1: Unit Root Tests: ADF Test

All variables in constant prices

Variable	Test Statistic Level	Test Statistic First Difference	Order of Integration
Bahrain (1979-2013):			
Total Expenditure	-0.57 (0)	-4.80 (0)***	I(1)
Current Expenditure	-0.28 (0)	-1.88 (2)	I(2)
Capital Expenditure	-2.25 (4)	-2.18 (3)	I(2)
Education Expenditure	-2.01 (1)	-3.25 (0)**	I(1)
Non-Education Expenditure	-0.64 (0)	-4.93 (0)***	I(1)
Health Expenditure	-1.58 (1)	-4.83 (0)***	I(1)
Non-Health Expenditure	-0.63 (0)	-4.94 (0)***	I(1)
Non-Oil GDP	-2.36 (1)	-3.94 (0)***	I(1)
Non-Oil GDP per Worker	-3.70 (4)**	-4.32 (0)***	I(0)
Oman (1979-2013):			
Total Expenditure	-0.97 (2)	-4.05 (1)***	I(1)
Current Expenditure	-1.52 (0)	-4.69 (0)***	I(1)
Capital Expenditure	-1.69 (1)	-4.02 (0)***	I(1)
Education Expenditure	-5.57 (2)***	-3.35 (0)**	I(0)
Non-Education Expenditure	-0.75 (2)	-4.24 (1)***	I(1)
Health Expenditure	-3.83 (1)**	-5.98 (5)***	I(0)
Non-Health Expenditure	-1.00 (0)	-4.13 (0)***	I(1)
Non-Oil GDP	-2.88 (1)	-4.34 (0)***	I(1)
Non-Oil GDP per Worker	-1.20 (1)	-3.51 (0)**	I(1)
Qatar (1979-2013):			
Total Expenditure	0.13 (0)	-3.71 (0)***	I(1)
Current Expenditure	1.47 (5)	-4.83 (0)***	I(1)
Capital Expenditure	-1.00 (1)	-1.59 (2)	I(2)
Education Expenditure	0.00 (0)	-2.26 (2)	I(2)
Non-Education Expenditure	-0.01 (0)	-3.80 (0)***	I(1)
Health Expenditure	-0.19 (0)	-4.67 (0)***	I(1)
Non-Health Expenditure	0.04 (0)	-3.86 (0)***	I(1)
Non-Oil GDP	0.22 (0)	-1.89 (1)	I(2)
Non-Oil GDP per Worker	-1.13 (0)	-4.70 (0)***	I(1)

Notes: Test statistics denote the statistical significance of the γ coefficient estimate in the ADF test regression (3.14) in section 3.4.2. Statistical significance levels of 1%, 5%, and 10% are indicated by ***, **, and *, respectively. Following the approach of Cheung and Lai (1995) critical values have been adjusted for the small sample size of the variables. ADF test regressions include either a constant and a deterministic trend (variables in levels) or a constant (variables in first differences). The number of lags m in the ADF test regression (3.14) is given in parenthesis. The lag length has been determined by the Hannan-Quinn information criterion with the maximum lag length being set to 5.

Table B2: Unit Root Tests: KPSS Test

All variables in constant prices

Variable	Test Statistic Level	First Difference	Order of Integration
Bahrain (1979-2013):			
Total Expenditure	0.225 (3)***	0.255 (3)	I(1)
Current Expenditure	0.190 (3)**	0.277 (3)	I(1)
Capital Expenditure	0.219 (3)***	0.149 (3)	I(1)
Education Expenditure	0.157 (3)**	0.122 (3)	I(1)
Non-Education Expenditure	0.226 (3)***	0.259 (3)	I(1)
Health Expenditure	0.192 (3)**	0.168 (3)	I(1)
Non-Health Expenditure	0.225 (3)***	0.255 (3)	I(1)
Non-Oil GDP	0.182 (3)**	0.151 (3)	I(1)
Non-Oil GDP per Worker	0.094 (3)	0.103 (3)	I(0)
Oman (1979-2013):			
Total Expenditure	0.183 (3)**	0.163 (3)	I(1)
Current Expenditure	0.160 (3)**	0.177 (3)	I(1)
Capital Expenditure	0.196 (3)**	0.115 (3)	I(1)
Education Expenditure	0.086 (3)	0.226 (3)	I(0)
Non-Education Expenditure	0.190 (3)**	0.177 (3)	I(1)
Health Expenditure	0.102 (3)	0.175 (3)	I(0)
Non-Health Expenditure	0.186 (3)**	0.167 (3)	I(1)
Non-Oil GDP	0.086 (3)	0.279 (3)	I(0)
Non-Oil GDP per Worker	0.071 (3)	0.293 (3)	I(0)
Qatar (1979-2013):			
Total Expenditure	0.246 (3)***	0.615 (3)**	I(2)
Current Expenditure	0.242 (3)***	0.565 (3)**	I(2)
Capital Expenditure	0.237 (3)***	0.451 (3)*	I(2)
Education Expenditure	0.225 (3)***	0.274 (3)	I(1)
Non-Education Expenditure	0.246 (3)***	0.621 (3)**	I(2)
Health Expenditure	0.233 (3)***	0.364 (3)*	I(2)
Non-Health Expenditure	0.246 (3)***	0.618 (3)**	I(2)
Non-Oil GDP	0.226 (3)***	0.428 (3)*	I(2)
Non-Oil GDP per Worker	0.218 (3)***	0.284 (3)	I(1)

Notes: Test statistics are given by η estimates of the Lagrange Multiplier test in equation (3.17) in section 3.4.2. Here, variables in levels (first differences) are tested against the null hypothesis of trend stationarity (level stationarity). Statistical significance levels of 1%, 5%, and 10% are indicated by ***, **, and *, respectively. Critical values are taken from Kwiatkowski et al. (1992). The number of lags is given in parenthesis. As proposed by Kwiatkowski et al. (1992), the lag order has been determined as a function of the total sample size, T: number of lags = $integer[4(T/100)^{1/4}]$.

Table B3: Unit Root Tests: ADF-GLS Test

All variables in constant prices

Variable	Test Statistic Level	Test Statistic First Difference	Order of Integration
Bahrain (1979-2013):			
Total Expenditure	-1.23 (1)	-1.02 (4)	I(2)
Current Expenditure	-0.68 (1)	-1.30 (2)	I(2)
Capital Expenditure	-1.93 (4)	-1.66 (4)*	I(1)
Education Expenditure	-2.21 (1)	-1.89 (2)*	I(1)
Non-Education Expenditure	-1.24 (1)	-1.04 (4)	I(2)
Health Expenditure	-1.85 (1)	-1.20 (2)	I(2)
Non-Health Expenditure	-1.20 (1)	-1.04 (4)	I(2)
Non-Oil GDP	-2.18 (1)	-2.91 (1)***	I(1)
Non-Oil GDP per Worker	-2.99 (1)*	-4.05 (1)***	I(0)
Oman (1979-2013):			
Total Expenditure	-1.42 (2)	-1.23 (3)	I(2)
Current Expenditure	-1.37 (2)	-0.90 (4)	I(2)
Capital Expenditure	-1.83 (1)	-2.18 (2)**	I(1)
Education Expenditure	-2.43 (1)	-1.95 (1)**	I(1)
Non-Education Expenditure	-1.30 (2)	-1.22 (3)	I(2)
Health Expenditure	-2.05 (2)	-2.14 (2)**	I(1)
Non-Health Expenditure	-1.39 (2)	-1.23 (3)	I(2)
Non-Oil GDP	-1.98 (1)	-0.56 (3)	I(2)
Non-Oil GDP per Worker	-1.68 (1)	-0.20 (3)	I(2)
Qatar (1979-2013):			
Total Expenditure	-1.16 (1)	-1.44 (4)	I(2)
Current Expenditure	-1.00 (1)	-1.67 (5)*	I(1)
Capital Expenditure	-1.27 (2)	-1.62 (2)*	I(1)
Education Expenditure	-1.21 (4)	-1.25 (2)	I(2)
Non-Education Expenditure	-1.13 (1)	-1.48 (4)	I(2)
Health Expenditure	-1.22 (1)	-1.48 (3)	I(2)
Non-Health Expenditure	-1.11 (1)	-1.44 (4)	I(2)
Non-Oil GDP	-1.87 (2)	-1.75 (1)*	I(1)
Non-Oil GDP per Worker	-1.49 (1)	-1.98 (5)**	I(1)

Notes: Test statistics denote the statistical significance of the γ coefficient estimate in the ADF-GLS test regression (3.21) in section 3.4.2. Statistical significance levels of 1%, 5%, and 10% are indicated by ***, **, and *, respectively. Critical values are taken from Elliott et al. (1996). Variables in levels (first differences) exhibit a constant and a deterministic trend (only a constant). The number of lags m in (3.21) is given in parenthesis. The lag length has been determined by a general-to-specific procedure with the maximum lag length being set to 5.

Table B4: Unit Root Tests: Unit Root Test with Structural Break

All variables in constant prices

Variable	Test Statistic Level	First Difference	Order of Integration
Bahrain (1979-2013):			
Total Expenditure	-3.76 (5, 1994)	-5.03 (0, 1997)**	I(1)
Current Expenditure	-2.75 (3, 1993)	-7.21 (0, 1998)***	I(1)
Capital Expenditure	-4.36 (4, 2000)*	-3.62 (3, 2002)	I(0)
Education Expenditure	-3.11 (3, 1995)	-4.64 (5, 2000)**	I(1)
Non-Education Expendit.	-3.83 (5, 1994)	-5.03 (0, 1997)**	I(1)
Health Expenditure	-4.41 (3, 1999)*	-3.53 (0, 2001)	I(0)
Non-Health Expenditure	-3.56 (5, 1994)	-5.24 (0, 2000)***	I(1)
Non-Oil GDP	-5.83 (5, 2003)***	-5.04 (0, 2002)**	I(0)
Non-Oil GDP per Worker	-6.17 (4, 1991)***	-4.87 (0, 2007)**	I(0)
Oman (1979-2013):			
Total Expenditure	-3.07 (1, 1992)	-6.29 (1, 1990)***	I(1)
Current Expenditure	-2.96 (5, 2008)	-6.05 (2, 1990)***	I(1)
Capital Expenditure	-3.51 (1, 2003)	-5.45 (4, 2004)***	I(1)
Education Expenditure	-3.68 (2, 1993)	-5.24 (2, 1990)***	I(1)
Non-Education Expendit.	-3.01 (1, 1992)	-6.29 (1, 1990)***	I(1)
Health Expenditure	-3.35 (1, 1992)	-6.94 (5, 1992)***	I(1)
Non-Health Expenditure	-2.98 (1, 1992)	-6.20 (1, 1990)***	I(1)
Non-Oil GDP	-2.39 (1, 1988)	-4.20 (0, 1989)*	I(1)
Non-Oil GDP per Worker	-3.06 (2, 2000)	-4.13 (0, 2006)	I(2)
Qatar (1979-2013):			
Total Expenditure	-3.47 (5, 2001)	-4.85 (0, 1990)**	I(1)
Current Expenditure	-3.76 (0, 2000)	-6.01 (0, 1990)***	I(1)
Capital Expenditure	-3.59 (3, 2000)	-7.05 (0, 2000)***	I(1)
Education Expenditure	-3.20 (3, 1993)	-3.45 (4, 1989)	I(2)
Non-Education Expendit.	-3.31 (5, 2001)	-4.90 (0, 1990)**	I(1)
Health Expenditure	-4.21 (1, 1997)*	-4.73 (0, 2000)**	I(0)
Non-Health Expenditure	-3.26 (5, 2001)	-5.03 (0, 1990)**	I(1)
Non-Oil GDP	-3.17 (2, 1996)	-5.84 (0, 2002)***	I(1)
Non-Oil GDP per Worker	-4.12 (2, 1995)	-5.77 (0, 1991)***	I(1)

Notes: Test statistics denote the statistical significance of the ϕ coefficient estimate in the test regression (3.23) in section 3.4.2. Statistical significance levels of 1%, 5%, and 10% are indicated by ***, **, and *, respectively. Critical values are taken from Lee and Strazicich (2004). The number of lags and the break date are given in parenthesis. The lag length has been determined by a general-to-specific procedure with the maximum lag length being set to 5. The break date refers to a break both in the constant as well as in the deterministic trend of the respective variable.

Table B5: Cointegration Tests: Bahrain

All variables in constant prices

	Test Setup			Test Statistic	
Variables	Det. Terms	Lags	H_0	JOH	SAI
Full Sample (1979-2013):					
Total Expenditure	Unrestr. Const.	1	r=0	5.32	5.28
& Non-Oil GDP			r=1	0.24	na[1]
Current Expenditure	Restr. Trend	2	r=0	27.53	23.38
& Capital Expenditure			r=1	14.10	10.34
& Non-Oil GDP			r=2	4.90	1.85
Education Expenditure	Restr. Trend	1	r=0	40.37*	29.96**
& Non-Educat. Expendit.			r=1	14.55	7.33
& Non-Oil GDP			r=2	2.06	0.58
Health Expenditure	Restr. Trend	1	r=0	29.01	21.86
& Non-Health Expendit.			r=1	10.38	7.58
& Non-Oil GDP			r=2	2.99	0.80

Notes: Test statistics of the Johansen trace (JOH) test and the Saikkonen and Lütkepohl (SAI) test are given by the λ_{tr} estimate in equation (3.32) in section 3.4.3. In case of the SAI test, the likelihood ratio testing procedure in (3.32) is applied to detrended variables. The test statistic of the JOH test is adjusted by a Bartlett correction factor as suggested by Johansen (2002). The cointegration rank r of the variables is given under the null hypothesis, H_0. Statistical significance levels of the test statistic for rejecting H_0 are indicated by ***(1%), **(5%), and *(10%), respectively. The deterministic terms and the number of lags refer to the VAR estimates in equations (3.27) (JOH) and (3.33) (SAI) and have been determined by the Hannan-Quinn information criterion.

[1] In case of an unrestricted constant, the SAI test does not allow for testing the null hypothesis $H_0 : r = n-1$. With regard to their test framework Saikkonen and Lütkepohl (2000a:375-378) assume that at least one of the n different endogenous variables contains a deterministic linear trend which, however, is not part of the cointegration relations. Such a trend will not be generated by a VAR process exhibiting an unrestricted constant if all endogenous variables are stationary. Therefore, the alternative hypothesis $r = 0$ (stationarity) is ruled out by assumption. As a result, the null hypothesis, H_0, can be at most $r = n - 2$.

Table B6: Cointegration Tests: Oman

All variables in constant prices

	Test Setup			Test Statistic	
Variables	Det. Terms	Lags	H_0	JOH	SAI
Full Sample (1979-2013):					
Total Expenditure	Restr. Trend	3	r=0	24.50*	6.35
& Non-Oil GDP			r=1	3.79	2.57
Current Expenditure	Restr. Trend	1	r=0	47.10**	19.02
& Capital Expenditure			r=1	16.82	7.20
& Non-Oil GDP			r=2	4.13	0.69
Education Expenditure	Restr. Trend	1	r=0	48.75***	19.61
& Non-Education Expenditure			r=1	18.89	13.83
& Non-Oil GDP			r=2	8.45	2.84
Health Expenditure	Restr. Trend	1	r=0	43.50**	18.45
& Non-Health Expenditure			r=1	16.73	10.80
& Non-Oil GDP			r=2	7.39	0.20

Notes: Test statistics of the Johansen trace (JOH) test and the Saikkonen and Lütkepohl (SAI) test are given by the λ_{tr} estimate in equation (3.32) in section 3.4.3. In case of the SAI test, the likelihood ratio testing procedure in (3.32) is applied to detrended variables. The test statistic of the JOH test is adjusted by a Bartlett correction factor as suggested by Johansen (2002). The cointegration rank r of the variables is given under the null hypothesis, H_0. Statistical significance levels of the test statistic for rejecting H_0 are indicated by ***(1%), **(5%), and *(10%), respectively. The deterministic terms and the number of lags refer to the VAR estimates in equations (3.27) (JOH) and (3.33) (SAI) and have been determined by the Hannan-Quinn information criterion.

Table B7: Cointegration Tests: Qatar

All variables in constant prices

	Test Setup			Test Statistic	
Variables	Det. Terms	Lags	H_0	JOH	SAI
Full Sample (1979-2013):					
Total Expenditure	Restr. Trend	1	r=0	27.61**	12.15
& Non-Oil GDP			r=1	6.17	1.66
Total Expenditure	Restr. Trend	1	r=0	17.32	7.36
& Non-Oil GDP p. Worker			r=1	3.59	0.20
Current Expenditure	Restr. Trend	1	r=0	45.22**	35.84***
& Capital Expenditure			r=1	14.47	7.15
& Non-Oil GDP			r=1	5.41	0.96
Current Expenditure	Restr. Trend	1	r=0	39.91*	31.13**
& Capital Expenditure			r=1	18.52	9.57
& Non-Oil GDP p. Worker			r=1	3.46	0.25
Non-Education Expendit.	Restr. Trend	1	r=0	28.26**	13.05
& Non-Oil GDP			r=1	6.78	1.51
Non-Education Expendit.	Restr. Trend	1	r=0	17.12	6.84
& Non-Oil GDP p. Worker			r=1	3.59	0.21
Non-Health Expenditure	Restr. Trend	1	r=0	27.20**	12.31
& Non-Oil GDP			r=2	6.42	1.57
Non-Health Expenditure	Restr. Trend	1	r=0	17.16	7.19
& Non-Oil GDP p. Worker			r=2	3.68	0.17
Sub-Sample I (1979-1998):					
Current Expenditure	Restr. Trend	2	r=0	40.20*	13.07
& Capital Expenditure			r=1	9.70	5.56
& Non-Oil GDP p. Worker			r=1	3.89	0.89
Sub-Sample II (1999-2013):					
Current Expenditure	Restr. Trend	1	r=0	27.79	21.74
& Capital Expenditure			r=1	9.79	6.31
& Non-Oil GDP p. Worker			r=1	3.76	1.63

Notes: Test statistics of the Johansen trace (JOH) test and the Saikkonen and Lütkepohl (SAI) test are given by the λ_{tr} estimate in equation (3.32) in section 3.4.3. In case of the SAI test, the likelihood ratio testing procedure in (3.32) is applied to detrended variables. The test statistic of the JOH test is adjusted by a Bartlett correction factor as suggested by Johansen (2002). The cointegration rank r of the variables is given under the null hypothesis, H_0. Statistical significance levels of the test statistic for rejecting H_0 are indicated by ***(1%), **(5%), and *(10%), respectively. The deterministic terms and the number of lags refer to the VAR estimates in equations (3.27) (JOH) and (3.33) (SAI) and have been determined by the Hannan-Quinn information criterion.

Table B8: Zero Restriction Tests

Variables (& Trend)	VECM Det. Terms	Lags	r	β	Test Statistic
Bahrain (1979-2013):					
Education Expenditure	Restr. Trend	1	1	1.551	8.83***
& Non-Education Expenditure				-1.474	14.16***
& Non-Oil GDP				1.000	4.18**
& Trend				-0.056	10.48***
Oman (1979-2013):					
Total Expenditure	Restr. Trend	3	1	-0.400	6.66***
& Non-Oil GDP				1.000	5.70**
& Trend				-0.051	5.91**
Current Expenditure	Restr. Trend	1	1	0.098	0.28
& Capital Expenditure				-0.244	8.97***
& Non-Oil GDP				1.000	16.38***
& Trend				-0.054	12.54***
Education Expenditure	Restr. Trend	1	1	0.372	1.08
& Non-Education Expenditure				-0.526	9.02***
& Non-Oil GDP				1.000	2.31
& Trend				-0.057	6.08**
Health Expenditure	Restr. Trend	1	1	0.870	3.45*
& Non-Health Expenditure				-0.534	4.27**
& Non-Oil GDP				1.000	1.66
& Trend				-0.083	7.02***
Qatar (1979-2013):					
Total Expenditure	Restr. Trend	1	1	-0.846	8.49***
& Non-Oil GDP				1.000	8.10***
& Trend				-0.039	11.91***
Current Expenditure	Restr. Trend	1	1	-0.060	0.05
& Capital Expenditure				-0.490	13.59***
& Non-Oil GDP				1.000	10.79***
& Trend				-0.044	14.66***
Current Expenditure	Restr. Trend	1	1	0.508	5.04**
& Capital Expenditure				-0.566	7.25***
& Non-Oil GDP per Worker				1.000	5.62**
& Trend				0.023	2.82*

continued on next page

continued from previous page

	VECM				Test
Variables (& Trend)	Det. Terms	Lags	r	β	Statistic
Qatar (1979-2013) - continued:					
Non-Education Expenditure	Restr. Trend	1	1	-0.817	8.63***
& Non-Oil GDP				1.000	8.39***
& Trend				-0.038	12.26***
Non-Health Expenditure	Restr. Trend	1	1	-0.844	7.92***
& Non-Oil GDP				1.000	7.56***
& Trend				-0.039	11.36***
Qatar (1979-1998):					
Current Expenditure	Restr. Trend	2	1	-1.146	31.59***
& Capital Expenditure				-0.100	10.38***
& Non-Oil GDP per Worker				1.000	30.10***
& Trend				0.022	28.14***

Notes: Test statistics are given by the Λ estimate in a zero restriction test for the variable in the respective line (see equation (3.35) in section 3.4.3). Statistical significance levels of 1%, 5%, and 10% for rejecting the null hypothesis of variable exclusion are indicated by ***, **, and *, respectively. In case the VECM has been specified with a restricted trend the exclusion of this deterministic trend from the cointegration relations is also tested. The deterministic terms and the lag order in the VECM specifications are identical to the cointegration test setups for the respective variables. The cointegration rank r has been set to 1 for all VECM estimates. Coefficients in the β vector of the VECM have been normalised on the GDP coefficient.

Table B9: Stability Tests

All variables in constant prices

Variables	VECM Det. Terms	Lags	r	Stat. Significant Break Years T_B
Bahrain (1979-2013):				
Education Expenditure & Non-Education Expenditure & Non-Oil GDP	Restr. Trend	1	1	na
Oman (1979-2013):				
Total Expenditure & Non-Oil GDP	Restr. Trend	3	1	na
Capital Expenditure & Non-Oil GDP	Restr. Trend	1	1	na
Qatar (1979-2013):				
Total Expenditure & Non-Oil GDP	Restr. Trend	1	1	na
Capital Expenditure & Non-Oil GDP	Restr. Trend	2	1	na
Current Expenditure & Capital Expenditure & Non-Oil GDP per Worker	Restr. Trend	1	1	1999*
Non-Education Expenditure & Non-Oil GDP	Restr. Trend	1	1	na
Non-Health Expenditure & Non-Oil GDP	Restr. Trend	1	1	na

Notes: Statistically significant break years T_B have been identified through a Chow break point testing procedure as given in equation (3.36) in section 3.4.3. The time range for searching potential break points was 1993-1999. Statistical significance levels of 1%, 5%, and 10% for rejecting the null hypothesis of parameter constancy are indicated by ***, **, and *, respectively. Significance levels are based on bootstrap p-values. The number of bootstrap replications is 1000. In case no variable has been excluded from the cointegration vector through a zero restriction test, the specification of the VECM remains unaltered. Otherwise, deterministic terms and the lag order have been determined anew by the Hannan-Quinn information criterion.

Appendix C: Robustness Checks Chapter 3

Change Variable Order Orthogonalised Impulse Responses

Figure C1: Impulse Responses Bahrain & Oman (Modified Variable Order)

Bahrain: Public Expenditure and Non-Oil GDP

(a) Response Non-Oil GDP to Impulse Education Expend.

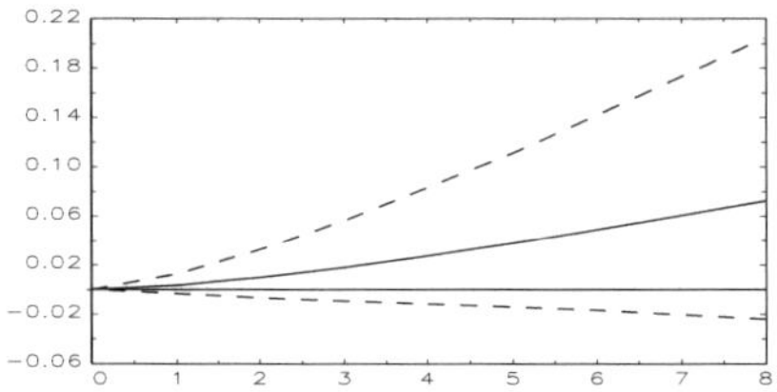

(b) Response Education Expend. to Impulse Non-Oil GDP

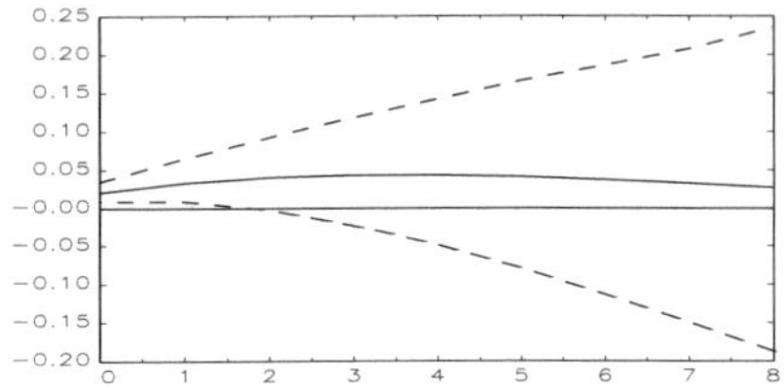

(c) Response Non-Oil GDP to Impulse Non-Education Exp.

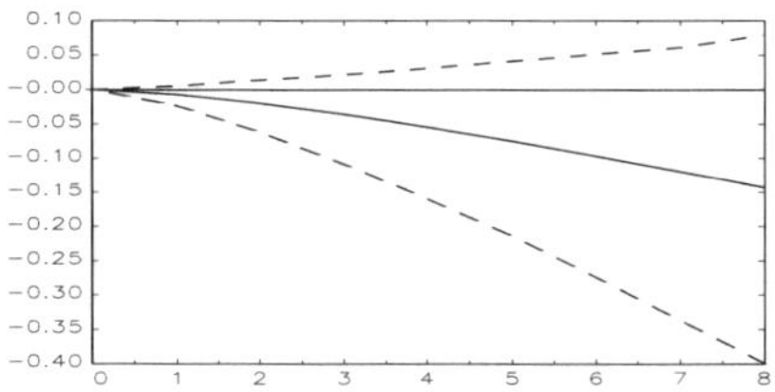

(d) Response Non-Educat. Exp. to Impulse Non-Oil GDP

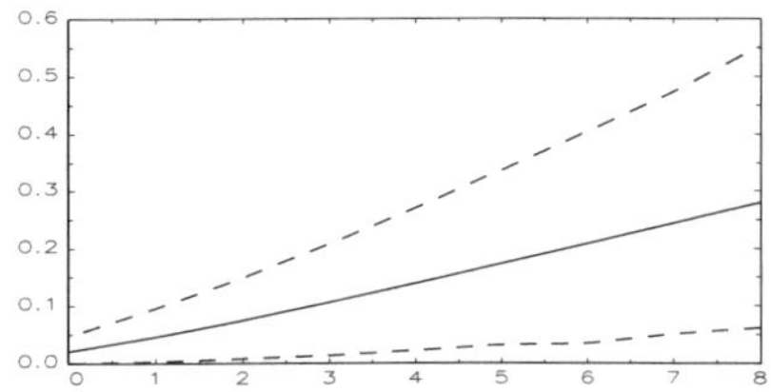

Oman: Public Expenditure and Non-Oil GDP

(e) Response Non-Oil GDP to Impulse Total Exp.

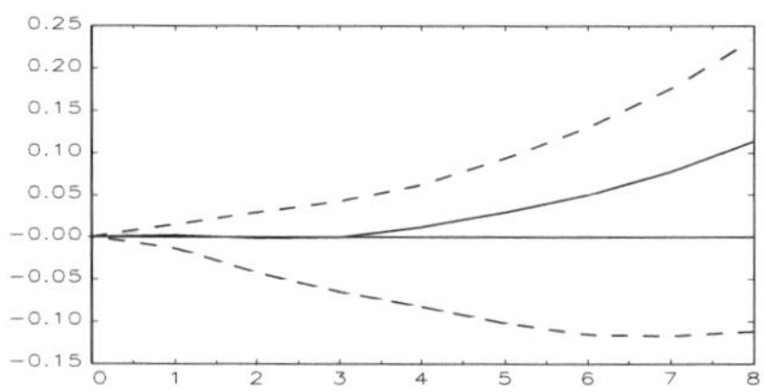

(f) Response Total Exp. to Impulse Non-Oil GDP

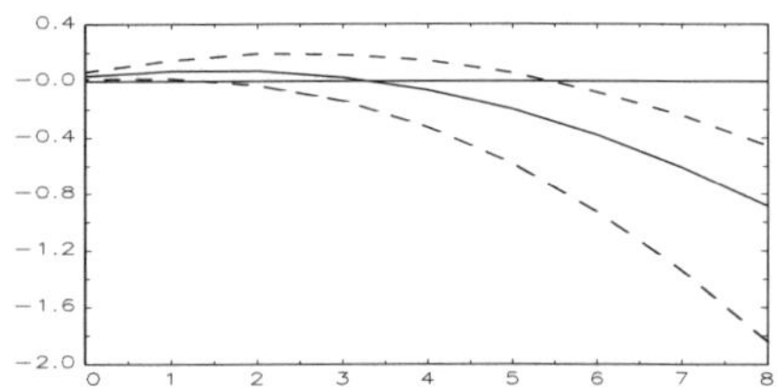

(g) Response Non-Oil GDP to Impulse Capital Exp.

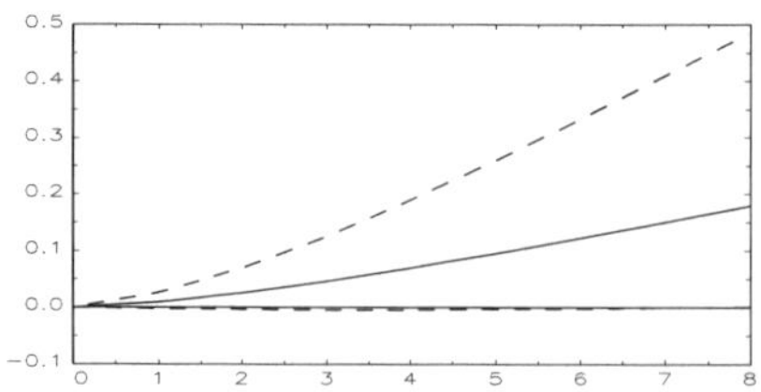

(h) Response Capital Exp. to Impulse Non-Oil GDP

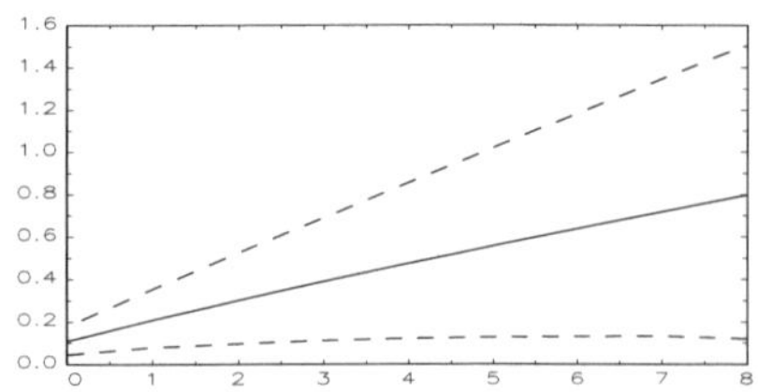

Notes: See figure C3

Figure C2: Impulse Responses Qatar I (Modified Variable Order)

Qatar: Public Expenditure and Non-Oil GDP

(a) Response Non-Oil GDP to Impulse Total Exp.

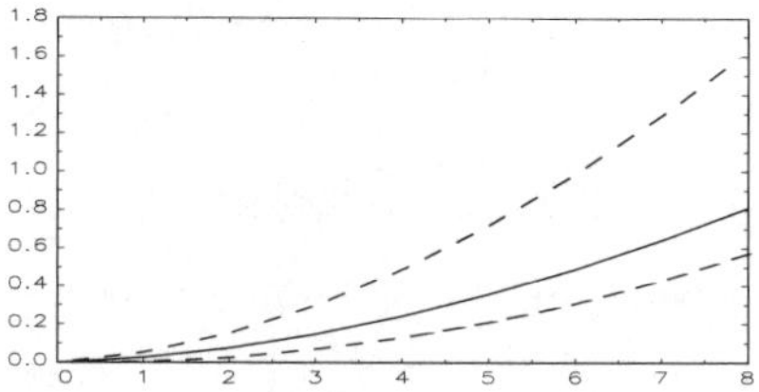

(b) Response Total Expend. to Impulse Non-Oil GDP

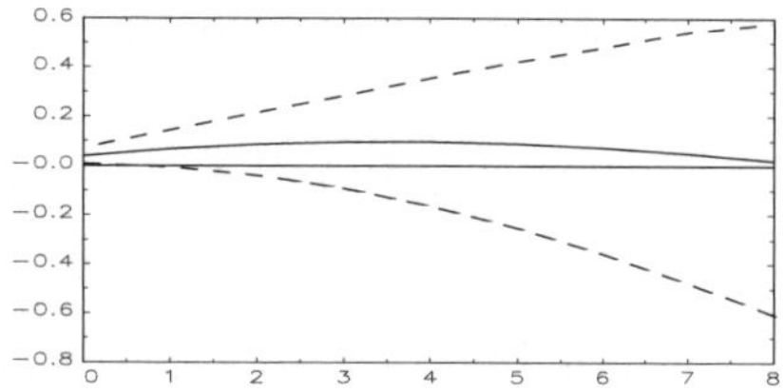

(c) Response Non-Oil GDP to Impulse Capital Exp.

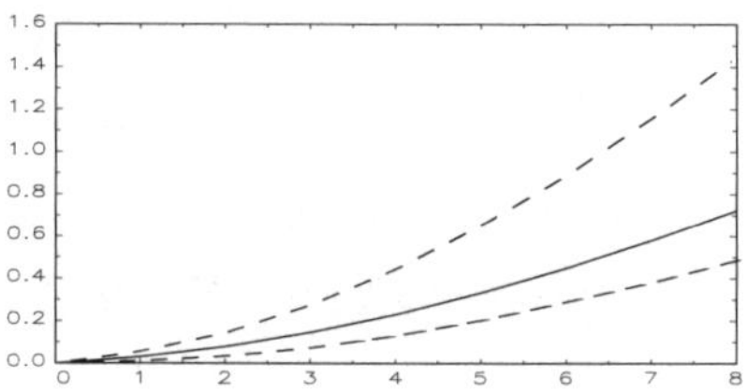

(d) Response Capital Exp. to Impulse Non-Oil GDP

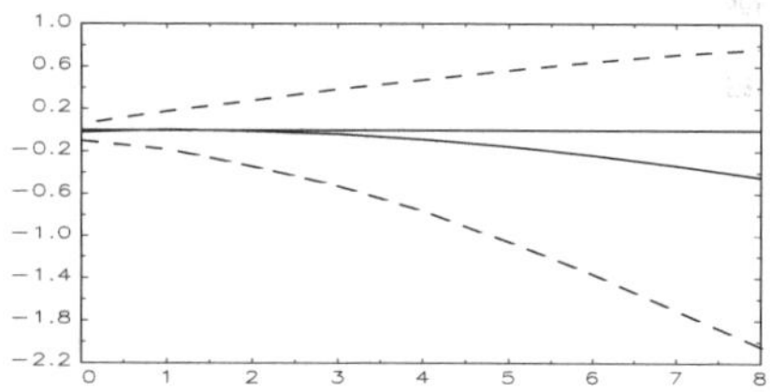

(e) Response Non-Oil GDP to Impulse Non-Education Exp.

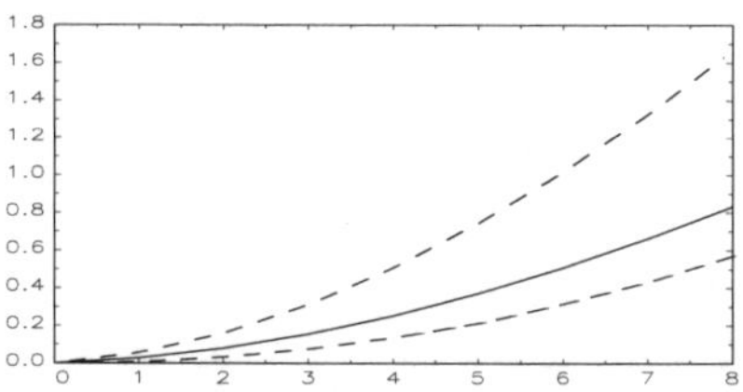

(f) Response Non-Educat. Exp. to Impulse Non-Oil GDP

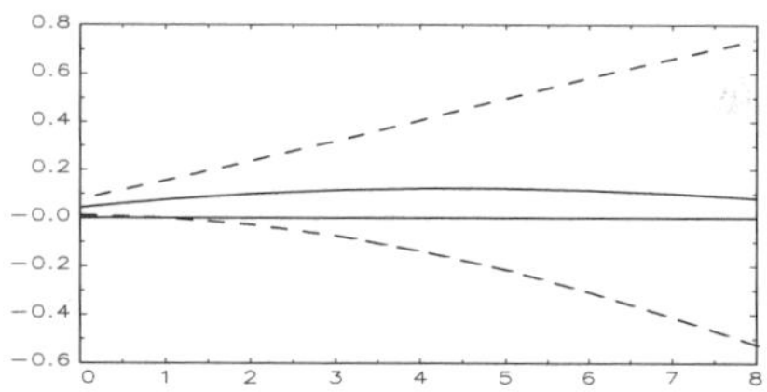

(g) Response Non-Oil GDP to Impulse Non-Health Exp.

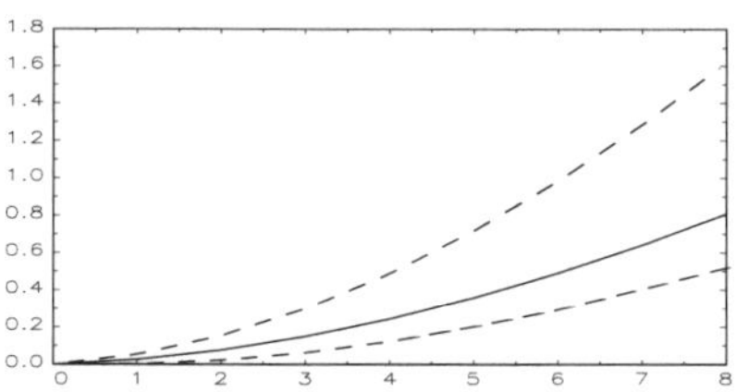

(h) Response Non-Health Exp. to Impulse Non-Oil GDP

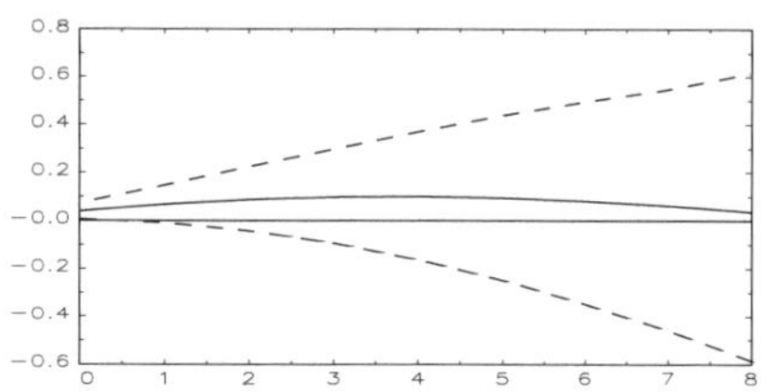

Notes: See figure C3

Figure C3: Impulse Responses Qatar II (Modified Variable Order)

Qatar: Public Expenditure and Non-Oil GDP per Worker

(a) Response GDP per Worker to Impulse Current Exp.

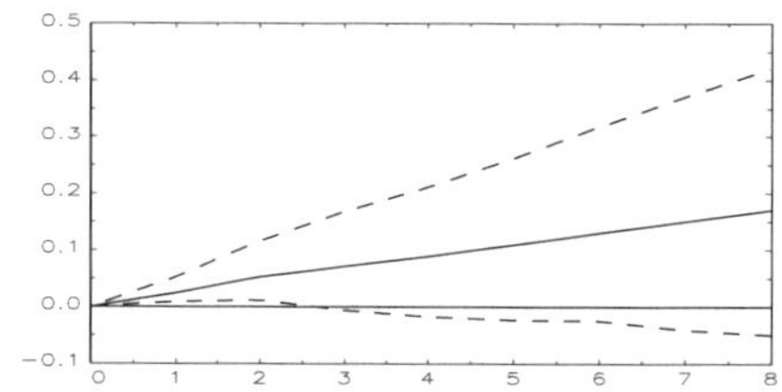

(b) Response Current Expend. to Impulse GDP per Worker

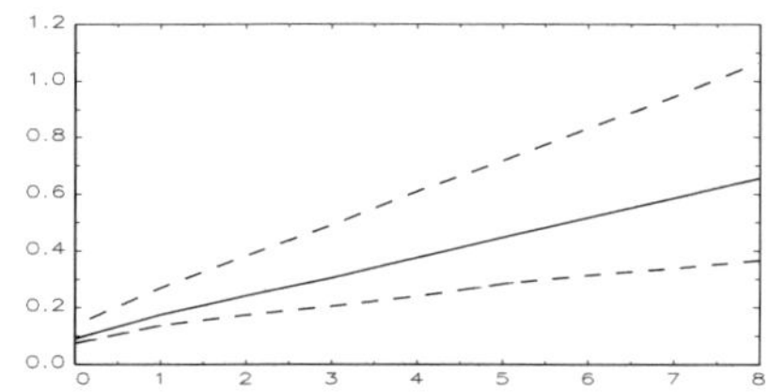

(c) Response GDP per Worker to Impulse Capital Exp.

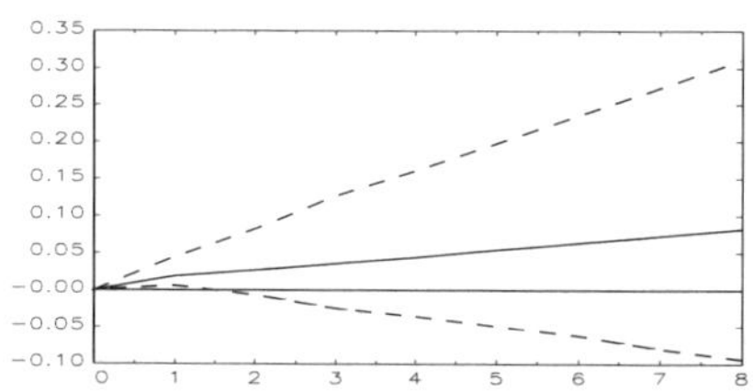

(d) Response Capital Expend. to Impulse GDP per Worker

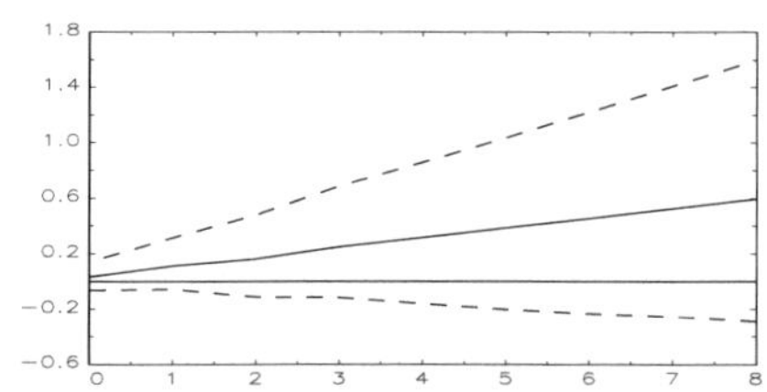

Notes: 95% Hall percentile confidence intervals (1000 bootstrap replications). VECM has been specified as shown in table 3.6. X-axis denotes number of years after initial impulse. Y-axis shows accumulated changes in the (natural log) level of responding variable. Impulse is given by one standard deviation of the orthogonalised residual of the impulse variable. In contrast to figures 3.1-3.3, non-oil GDP (per worker) has been ranked before public expenditure variables in the orthogonalised residual covariance matrix.

Robustness Check: Time Series in Current Prices

Table C1: Overview - Order of Integration (Current Prices)

All variables in current prices

	Unit Root Test Results				Overall
Variable	ADF	KPSS	ADF-GLS	Break	Evaluation
Bahrain (1979-2013):					
Total Expenditure	I(1)	I(1)	I(2)	I(1)	I(1)
Current Expenditure	I(1)	I(1)	I(2)	I(1)	I(1)
Capital Expenditure	I(2)	I(1)	I(1)	I(0)	I(1)
Education Expenditure	I(1)	I(1)	I(1)	I(1)	I(1)
Non-Education Expenditure	I(1)	I(1)	I(2)	I(1)	I(1)
Health Expenditure	I(1)	I(1)	I(2)	I(2)	I(2)
Non-Health Expenditure	I(1)	I(1)	I(2)	I(1)	I(1)
Non-Oil GDP	I(1)	I(1)	I(1)	I(0)	I(1)
Non-Oil GDP per Worker	I(1)	I(1)	I(1)	I(0)	I(1)
Oman (1979-2013):					
Total Expenditure	I(1)	I(1)	I(2)	I(2)	I(2)
Current Expenditure	I(1)	I(1)	I(2)	I(1)	I(1)
Capital Expenditure	I(1)	I(1)	I(1)	I(1)	I(1)
Education Expenditure	I(0)	I(0)	I(0)	I(0)	I(0)
Non-Education Expenditure	I(1)	I(1)	I(2)	I(2)	I(2)
Health Expenditure	I(1)	I(0)	I(1)	I(1)	I(1)
Non-Health Expenditure	I(1)	I(1)	I(2)	I(2)	I(2)
Non-Oil GDP	I(1)	I(0)	I(2)	I(2)	I(2)
Non-Oil GDP per Worker	I(1)	I(0)	I(2)	I(2)	I(2)
Qatar (1979-2013):					
Total Expenditure	I(1)	I(2)	I(2)	I(2)	I(2)
Current Expenditure	I(1)	I(2)	I(2)	I(0)	I(2)
Capital Expenditure	I(2)	I(2)	I(2)	I(1)	I(2)
Education Expenditure	I(2)	I(1)	I(2)	I(2)	I(2)
Non-Education Expenditure	I(1)	I(2)	I(2)	I(1)	I(1)
Health Expenditure	I(1)	I(2)	I(2)	I(1)	I(1)
Non-Health Expenditure	I(1)	I(2)	I(2)	I(1)	I(1)
Non-Oil GDP	I(1)	I(2)	I(1)	I(1)	I(1)
Non-Oil GDP per Worker	I(1)	I(1)	I(1)	I(1)	I(1)

Note: For detailed unit root test results of the variables please refer to tables C2-C5.

Table C2: Unit Root Tests: ADF Test

All variables in current prices

Variable	Test Statistic: Level	Test Statistic: First Difference	Order of Integration
Bahrain (1979-2013):			
Total Expenditure	-0.56 (0)	-3.93 (0)***	I(1)
Current Expenditure	-0.42 (0)	-2.65 (2)*	I(1)
Capital Expenditure	-2.25 (4)	-2.35 (3)	I(2)
Education Expenditure	-2.15 (1)	-2.91 (0)*	I(1)
Non-Education Expenditure	-0.59 (0)	-4.10 (0)***	I(1)
Health Expenditure	-1.70 (1)	-3.80 (0)***	I(1)
Non-Health Expenditure	-0.60 (0)	-4.09 (0)***	I(1)
Non-Oil GDP	-2.15 (1)	-3.22 (0)**	I(1)
Non-Oil GDP per Worker	-2.80 (1)	-3.75 (0)***	I(1)
Oman (1979-2013):			
Total Expenditure	-0.77 (0)	-4.21 (0)***	I(1)
Current Expenditure	-1.13 (0)	-4.79 (0)***	I(1)
Capital Expenditure	-0.97 (0)	-4.03 (0)***	I(1)
Education Expenditure	-4.02 (0)**	-3.59 (0)**	I(0)
Non-Education Expenditure	-0.66 (0)	-4.31 (0)***	I(1)
Health Expenditure	-2.75 (1)	-3.47 (0)**	I(1)
Non-Health Expenditure	-0.73 (0)	-4.26 (0)***	I(1)
Non-Oil GDP	-2.13 (2)	-2.93 (2)*	I(1)
Non-Oil GDP per Worker	-2.93 (2)	-2.75 (2)*	I(1)
Qatar (1979-2013):			
Total Expenditure	0.10 (0)	-3.29 (0)**	I(1)
Current Expenditure	0.02 (0)	-4.52 (0)***	I(1)
Capital Expenditure	-0.87 (0)	-1.54 (2)	I(2)
Education Expenditure	0.22 (2)	-1.24 (3)	I(2)
Non-Education Expenditure	-0.01 (0)	-3.36 (0)**	I(1)
Health Expenditure	-0.18 (0)	-4.65 (0)***	I(1)
Non-Health Expenditure	0.03 (0)	-3.41 (0)**	I(1)
Non-Oil GDP	-1.82 (2)	-2.98 (0)*	I(1)
Non-Oil GDP per Worker	-0.91 (0)	-3.97 (0)***	I(1)

Notes: Test statistics denote the statistical significance of the γ coefficient estimate in the ADF test regression (3.14) in section 3.4.2. Statistical significance levels of 1%, 5%, and 10% are indicated by ***, **, and *, respectively. Following the approach of Cheung and Lai (1995) critical values have been adjusted for the small sample size of the variables. ADF test regressions include either a constant and a deterministic trend (variables in levels) or a constant (variables in first differences). The number of lags m in the ADF test regression (3.14) is given in parenthesis. The lag length has been determined by the Hannan-Quinn information criterion with the maximum lag length being set to 5.

Table C3: Unit Root Tests: KPSS Test

All variables in current prices

Variable	Test Statistic Level	First Difference	Order of Integration
Bahrain (1979-2013):			
Total Expenditure	0.208 (3)**	0.186 (3)	I(1)
Current Expenditure	0.177 (3)**	0.217 (3)	I(1)
Capital Expenditure	0.215 (3)**	0.127 (3)	I(1)
Education Expenditure	0.161 (3)**	0.141 (3)	I(1)
Non-Education Expenditure	0.210 (3)**	0.189 (3)	I(1)
Health Expenditure	0.180 (3)**	0.136 (3)	I(1)
Non-Health Expenditure	0.208 (3)**	0.188 (3)	I(1)
Non-Oil GDP	0.196 (3)**	0.145 (3)	I(1)
Non-Oil GDP per Worker	0.155 (3)**	0.101 (3)	I(1)
Oman (1979-2013):			
Total Expenditure	0.186 (3)**	0.190 (3)	I(1)
Current Expenditure	0.166 (3)**	0.205 (3)	I(1)
Capital Expenditure	0.200 (3)**	0.129 (3)	I(1)
Education Expenditure	0.102 (3)	0.227 (3)	I(0)
Non-Education Expenditure	0.190 (3)**	0.202 (3)	I(1)
Health Expenditure	0.111 (3)	0.190 (3)	I(0)
Non-Health Expenditure	0.189 (3)**	0.194 (3)	I(1)
Non-Oil GDP	0.118 (3)	0.189 (3)	I(0)
Non-Oil GDP per Worker	0.101 (3)	0.155 (3)	I(0)
Qatar (1979-2013):			
Total Expenditure	0.241 (3)***	0.524 (3)**	I(2)
Current Expenditure	0.239 (3)***	0.505 (3)**	I(2)
Capital Expenditure	0.235 (3)***	0.418 (3)*	I(2)
Education Expenditure	0.231 (3)***	0.298 (3)	I(1)
Non-Education Expenditure	0.241 (3)***	0.529 (3)**	I(2)
Health Expenditure	0.232 (3)***	0.360 (3)*	I(2)
Non-Health Expenditure	0.241 (3)***	0.524 (3)**	I(2)
Non-Oil GDP	0.223 (3)***	0.354 (3)*	I(2)
Non-Oil GDP per Worker	0.226 (3)***	0.288 (3)	I(1)

Notes: Test statistics are given by η estimates of the Lagrange Multiplier test in equation (3.17) in section 3.4.2. Here, variables in levels (first differences) are tested against the null hypothesis of trend stationarity (level stationarity). Statistical significance levels of 1%, 5%, and 10% are indicated by ***, **, and *, respectively. Critical values are taken from Kwiatkowski et al. (1992). The number of lags is given in parenthesis. As proposed by Kwiatkowski et al. (1992), the lag order has been determined as a function of the total sample size, T: number of lags = $integer[4(T/100)^{1/4}]$.

Table C4: Unit Root Tests: ADF-GLS Test

All variables in current prices

Variable	Test Statistic Level	First Difference	Order of Integration
Bahrain (1979-2013):			
Total Expenditure	-1.53 (1)	-1.19 (4)	I(2)
Current Expenditure	-1.05 (1)	-1.54 (2)	I(2)
Capital Expenditure	-1.18 (3)	-1.80 (4)*	I(1)
Education Expenditure	-2.30 (1)	-1.85 (3)*	I(1)
Non-Education Expenditure	-1.49 (1)	-1.20 (4)	I(2)
Health Expenditure	-2.15 (1)	-1.46 (1)	I(2)
Non-Health Expenditure	-1.47 (1)	-1.21 (4)	I(2)
Non-Oil GDP	-2.23 (1)	-2.25 (2)**	I(1)
Non-Oil GDP per Worker	-2.84 (1)	-3.65 (1)***	I(1)
Oman (1979-2013):			
Total Expenditure	-1.62 (1)	-0.90 (3)	I(2)
Current Expenditure	-1.50 (1)	-0.92 (3)	I(2)
Capital Expenditure	-1.78 (1)	-1.98 (2)**	I(1)
Education Expenditure	-3.08 (3)*	-1.82 (1)*	I(0)
Non-Education Expenditure	-1.55 (1)	-0.91 (3)	I(2)
Health Expenditure	-2.14 (1)	-1.64 (2)*	I(1)
Non-Health Expenditure	-1.58 (1)	-0.91 (3)	I(2)
Non-Oil GDP	-1.85 (1)	-0.51 (3)	I(2)
Non-Oil GDP per Worker	-2.25 (1)	-0.59 (3)	I(2)
Qatar (1979-2013):			
Total Expenditure	-1.39 (1)	-1.46 (2)	I(2)
Current Expenditure	-1.50 (2)	-1.47 (3)	I(2)
Capital Expenditure	-1.37 (2)	-1.53 (2)	I(2)
Education Expenditure	-1.98 (3)	-1.14 (2)	I(2)
Non-Education Expenditure	-1.35 (1)	-1.52 (2)	I(2)
Health Expenditure	-1.15 (1)	-1.30 (3)	I(2)
Non-Health Expenditure	-1.34 (1)	-1.48 (2)	I(2)
Non-Oil GDP	-1.42 (1)	-1.86 (1)*	I(1)
Non-Oil GDP per Worker	-1.54 (1)	-1.98 (3)**	I(1)

Notes: Test statistics denote the statistical significance of the γ coefficient estimate in the ADF-GLS test regression (3.21) in section 3.4.2. Statistical significance levels of 1%, 5%, and 10% are indicated by ***, **, and *, respectively. Critical values are taken from Elliott et al. (1996). Variables in levels (first differences) exhibit a constant and a deterministic trend (only a constant). The number of lags m in (3.21) is given in parenthesis. The lag length has been determined by a general-to-specific procedure with the maximum lag length being set to 5.

Table C5: Unit Root Tests: Unit Root Test with Structural Break

All variables in current prices

Variable	Test Statistic: Level	Test Statistic: First Difference	Order of Integration
Bahrain (1979-2013):			
Total Expenditure	-3.94 (5, 1994)	-4.32 (0, 1990)*	I(1)
Current Expenditure	-3.50 (3, 1993)	-5.92 (0, 1997)***	I(1)
Capital Expenditure	-4.61 (4, 2000)**	-3.59 (3, 2002)	I(0)
Education Expenditure	-2.96 (1, 1993)	-4.40 (0, 2000)*	I(1)
Non-Education Expendit.	-4.04 (5, 1994)	-4.47 (0, 1990)*	I(1)
Health Expenditure	-4.16 (3, 1999)	-3.00 (0, 2001)	I(2)
Non-Health Expenditure	-3.90 (5, 1994)	-4.68 (0, 1990)**	I(1)
Non-Oil GDP	-5.97 (4, 2002)***	-4.15 (0, 2002)	I(0)
Non-Oil GDP per Worker	-5.82 (5, 2003)***	-4.07 (0, 2007)	I(0)
Oman (1979-2013):			
Total Expenditure	-3.53 (4, 1992)	-3.65 (0, 1990)	I(2)
Current Expenditure	-2.82 (5, 1991)	-4.89 (1, 1990)**	I(1)
Capital Expenditure	-3.39 (1, 2003)	-4.66 (0, 1989)**	I(1)
Education Expenditure	-4.54 (4, 1993)**	-3.63 (5, 1994)	I(0)
Non-Education Expendit.	-3.46 (4, 1992)	-4.10 (1, 1990)	I(2)
Health Expenditure	-2.78 (1, 1992)	-4.78 (5, 1993)**	I(1)
Non-Health Expenditure	-3.46 (4, 1992)	-3.70 (0, 1990)	I(2)
Non-Oil GDP	-3.13 (4, 1992)	-2.87 (0, 1990)	I(2)
Non-Oil GDP per Worker	-3.28 (2, 2002)	-3.78 (0, 2006)	I(2)
Qatar (1979-2013):			
Total Expenditure	-3.67 (5, 2002)	-3.95 (0, 2004)	I(2)
Current Expenditure	-4.51 (0, 2003)**	-5.66 (0, 2004)***	I(0)
Capital Expenditure	-3.79 (3, 2000)	-6.33 (0, 2000)***	I(1)
Education Expenditure	-3.31 (2, 2001)	-2.34 (2, 1989)	I(2)
Non-Education Expendit.	-3.66 (5, 2002)	-4.51 (0, 2003)**	I(1)
Health Expenditure	-3.90 (4, 1997)	-4.81 (0, 1990)**	I(1)
Non-Health Expenditure	-3.53 (5, 2002)	-4.34 (0, 2003)*	I(1)
Non-Oil GDP	-3.48 (2, 2002)	-4.82 (0, 2003)**	I(1)
Non-Oil GDP per Worker	-3.66 (2, 1995)	-4.58 (0, 1991)**	I(1)

Notes: Test statistics denote the statistical significance of the ϕ coefficient estimate in the test regression (3.23) in section 3.4.2. Statistical significance levels of 1%, 5%, and 10% are indicated by ***, **, and *, respectively. Critical values are taken from Lee and Strazicich (2004). The number of lags and the break date are given in parenthesis. The lag length has been determined by a general-to-specific procedure with the maximum lag length being set to 5. The break date refers to a break both in the constant as well as in the deterministic trend of the respective variable.

Table C6: Overview - Number of Cointegration Relations (Full Samples)

All variables in current prices

	Bahrain[1]		Oman[1]		Qatar[1]	
Variables	JOH	SAI	JOH	SAI	JOH	SAI
Total Expenditure & Non-Oil GDP	0	0	na	na	na	na
Total Expenditure & Non-Oil GDP p. Worker	1**	1***	na	na	na	na
Current Expenditure & Capital Expenditure & Non-Oil GDP	0	0	na	na	na	na
Current Expenditure & Capital Expenditure & Non-Oil GDP p. Worker	1**	2**	na	na	na	na
Education Expenditure & Non-Education Expendit. & Non-Oil GDP	0	1**	na	na	0	0
Education Expenditure & Non-Education Expendit. & Non-Oil GDP p. Worker	0	1*	na	na	0	0
Health Expenditure & Non-Health Expenditure & Non-Oil GDP	0	0	na	na	0	0
Health Expenditure & Non-Health Expenditure & Non-Oil GDP p. Worker	1**	1***	na	na	0	2**

Notes: For detailed cointegration test results of the Johansen trace test (JOH) and the Saikkonen and Lütkepohl test (SAI) please refer to tables C7-C8.

[1] The following variables have been excluded from the respective cointegration tests since they are not integrated of order one (table C1): health expenditure (Bahrain), total expenditure (Oman), education expenditure (Oman), non-education expenditure (Oman), non-health expenditure (Oman), non-oil GDP (Oman), non-oil GDP per worker (Oman), total expenditure (Qatar), current expenditure (Qatar), capital expenditure (Qatar) and education expenditure (Qatar).

Table C7: Cointegration Tests: Bahrain (Current Prices)

All variables in current prices

	Test Setup			Test Statistic	
Variables	Det. Terms	Lags	H_0	JOH	SAI
Full Sample (1979-2013):					
Total Expenditure	Restr. Trend	2	r=0	19.02	12.17
& Non-Oil GDP			r=1	4.10	0.13
Total Expenditure	Unr. Const.	2	r=0	16.47**	15.10***
& Non-Oil GDP p. Work.			r=1	0.42	na[1]
Current Expenditure	Restr. Trend	2	r=0	30.75	24.26
& Capital Expenditure			r=1	17.24	6.80
& Non-Oil GDP			r=2	4.22	1.17
Current Expenditure	Unr. Const.	2	r=0	31.38**	34.62***
& Capital Expenditure			r=1	12.18	11.87**
& Non-Oil GDP p. Work.			r=2	0.54	na[1]
Education Expenditure	Restr. Trend	2	r=0	39.28[2]	32.59**
& Non-Education Expend.			r=1	21.60	8.86
& Non-Oil GDP			r=2	5.60	0.06
Education Expenditure	Restr. Trend	2	r=0	31.83	26.31*
& Non-Education Expend.			r=1	15.62	7.51
& Non-Oil GDP p. Work.			r=2	4.99	0.32
Non-Health Expenditure	Restr. Trend	2	r=0	18.84	12.33
& Non-Oil GDP			r=1	3.91	0.18
Non-Health Expenditure	Unr. Const.	2	r=0	16.61**	15.11***
& Non-Oil GDP p. Work.			r=1	0.40	na[1]
Sub-Sample I (1979-1995):					
Total Expenditure	Unr. Const.	2	r=0	18.08**	22.46***
& Non-Oil GDP p. Work.			r=1	7.93***	na[1]
Non-Health Expenditure	Unr. Const.	2	r=0	18.20**	20.77***
& Non-Oil GDP p. Work.			r=1	8.82***	na[1]
Sub-Sample II (1979-1994):					
Capital Expenditure	Restr. Trend	2	r=0	21.47	8.48
& Non-Oil GDP p. Work.			r=1	6.38	0.06

continued on next page

continued from previous page

Variables	Test Setup Det. Terms	Lags	H_0	Test Statistic JOH	SAI
Sub-Sample III (1996-2013):					
Total Expenditure	Restr. Trend	2	r=0	20.79	12.65
& Non-Oil GDP p. Work.			r=1	6.21	0.17
Non-Health Expenditure	Restr. Trend	2	r=0	20.05	12.70
& Non-Oil GDP p. Work.			r=1	6.23	0.04
Sub-Sample IV (1995-2013):					
Capital Expenditure	Restr. Trend	1	r=0	18.11	6.31
& Non-Oil GDP p. Work.			r=1	3.38	2.17

Notes: Test statistics of the Johansen trace (JOH) test and the Saikkonen and Lütke-pohl (SAI) test are given by the λ_{tr} estimate in equation (3.32) in section 3.4.3. In case of the SAI test, the likelihood ratio testing procedure in (3.32) is applied to de-trended variables. The test statistic of the JOH test is adjusted by a Bartlett correction factor as suggested by Johansen (2002). The cointegration rank r of the variables is given under the null hypothesis, H_0. Statistical significance levels of the test statistic for rejecting H_0 are indicated by ***(1%), **(5%), and *(10%), respectively. The deterministic terms and the number of lags refer to the VAR estimates in equations (3.27) (JOH) and (3.33) (SAI) and have been determined by the Hannan-Quinn information criterion.

[1] In case of an unrestricted constant, the SAI test does not allow for testing the null hypothesis $H_0 : r = n - 1$. With regard to their test framework Saikkonen and Lütkepohl (2000a:375-378) assume that at least one of the n different endogenous variables contains a deterministic linear trend which, however, is not part of the cointegration relations. Such a trend will not be generated by a VAR process exhibiting an unrestricted constant if all endogenous variables are stationary. Therefore, the alternative hypothesis $r = 0$ (stationarity) is ruled out by assumption. As a result, the null hypothesis, H_0, can be at most $r = n - 2$.

[2] Null hypothesis rejected at 15% significance level.

Table C8: Cointegration Tests: Qatar (Current Prices)

All variables in current prices

	Test Setup			Test Statistic	
Variables	Det. Terms	Lags	H_0	JOH	SAI
Full Sample (1979-2013):					
Non-Education Expenditure	Restr. Trend	2	r=0	15.57	5.95
& Non-Oil GDP			r=1	3.26	1.14
Non-Education Expenditure	Restr. Trend	1	r=0	17.35	9.35
& Non-Oil GDP p. Worker			r=1	2.98	0.24
Health Expenditure	Restr. Trend	2	r=0	36.39	24.65
& Non-Health Expenditure			r=1	18.51	5.81
& Non-Oil GDP			r=2	3.71	0.02
Health Expenditure	Unrestr. Const.	1	r=0	26.70	18.79*
& Non-Health Expenditure			r=1	12.17	10.72**
& Non-Oil GDP p. Worker			r=2	2.58	na[1]

Notes: Test statistics of the Johansen trace (JOH) test and the Saikkonen and Lütkepohl (SAI) test are given by the λ_{tr} estimate in equation (3.32) in section 3.4.3. In case of the SAI test, the likelihood ratio testing procedure in (3.32) is applied to detrended variables. The test statistic of the JOH test is adjusted by a Bartlett correction factor as suggested by Johansen (2002). The cointegration rank r of the variables is given under the null hypothesis, H_0. Statistical significance levels of the test statistic for rejecting H_0 are indicated by ***(1%), **(5%), and *(10%), respectively. The deterministic terms and the number of lags refer to the VAR estimates in equations (3.27) (JOH) and (3.33) (SAI) and have been determined by the Hannan-Quinn information criterion.

[1] In case of an unrestricted constant, the SAI test does not allow for testing the null hypothesis $H_0 : r = n-1$. With regard to their test framework Saikkonen and Lütkepohl (2000a:375-378) assume that at least one of the n different endogenous variables contains a deterministic linear trend which, however, is not part of the cointegration relations. Such a trend will not be generated by a VAR process exhibiting an unrestricted constant if all endogenous variables are stationary. Therefore, the alternative hypothesis $r = 0$ (stationarity) is ruled out by assumption. As a result, the null hypothesis, H_0, can be at most $r = n - 2$.

Table C9: Zero Restriction Tests (Current Prices)

Variables (& Trend)	VECM Det. Terms	Lags	r	β	Test Statistic
Bahrain (1979-2013):					
Total Expenditure	Unrestr. Const.	2	1	-0.220	14.67***
& Non-Oil GDP p. Worker				1.000	18.28***
Current Expenditure	Unrestr. Const.	2	1	-0.004	0.00
& Capital Expenditure				-0.303	8.58***
& Non-Oil GDP p. Worker				1.000	8.18***
Education Expenditure	Restr. Trend	2	1	0.817	1.08
& Non-Education Expendit.				-1.231	2.91*
& Non-Oil GDP				1.000	2.26
& Trend				-0.038	2.97*
Education Expenditure	Restr. Trend	2	1	0.148	0.14
& Non-Education Expendit.				-0.250	0.90
& Non-Oil GDP p. Worker				1.000	8.28***
& Trend				-0.008	0.44
Non-Health Expenditure	Unrestr. Const.	2	1	-0.221	14.73***
& Non-Oil GDP p. Worker				1.000	18.42***
Bahrain (1979-1995):					
Total Expenditure	Unrestr. Const.	2	1	-0.131	1.02
& Non-Oil GDP p. Worker				1.000	9.34***
Non-Health Expenditure	Unrestr. Const.	2	1	-0.149	0.98
& Non-Oil GDP p. Worker				1.000	7.31***
Qatar (1979-2013):					
Health Expenditure	Unrestr. Const.	1	1	2.559	4.34**
& Non-Health Expenditure				-2.729	4.29**
& Non-Oil GDP p. Worker				1.000	1.26

Notes: Test statistics are given by the Λ estimate in a zero restriction test for the variable in the respective line (see equation (3.35) in section 3.4.3). Statistical significance levels of 1%, 5%, and 10% for rejecting the null hypothesis of variable exclusion are indicated by ***, **, and *, respectively. In case the VECM has been specified with a restricted trend the exclusion of this deterministic trend from the cointegration relations is also tested. The deterministic terms and the lag order in the VECM specifications are identical to the cointegration test setups for the respective variables. The cointegration rank r has been set to 1 for all VECM estimates. Coefficients in the β vector of the VECM have been normalised on the GDP coefficient.

Table C10: Stability Tests (Current Prices)

Variables	VECM Det. Terms	Lags	r	Stat. Significant Break Years T_B
Bahrain (1979-2013):				
Total Expenditure & Non-Oil GDP per Worker	Unrestr. Constant	2	1	1993*, 1994*, 1995*
Capital Expenditure & Non-Oil GDP per Worker	Unrestr. Constant	2	1	1993**, 1994*
Non-Health Expenditure & Non-Oil GDP per Worker	Unrestr. Constant	2	1	1994*, 1995*

Notes: Statistically significant break years T_B have been identified through a Chow break point testing procedure as given in equation (3.36) in section 3.4.3. The time range for searching potential break points was 1993-1999. Statistical significance levels of 1%, 5%, and 10% for rejecting the null hypothesis of parameter constancy are indicated by ***, **, and *, respectively. Significance levels are based on bootstrap p-values. The number of bootstrap replications is 1000. In case no variable has been excluded from the cointegration vector through a zero restriction test, the specification of the VECM remains unaltered. Otherwise, deterministic terms and the lag order have been determined anew by the Hannan-Quinn information criterion.

Robustness Check: Private Sector Non-Oil GDP

Table C11: Overview - Order of Integration (Private Sector)

All variables in constant prices

	Unit Root Test Results				Overall
Variable	ADF	KPSS	ADF-GLS	Break	Evaluation
Bahrain (1979-2013):					
Total Expenditure	I(1)	I(1)	I(2)	I(1)	I(1)
Current Expenditure	I(2)	I(1)	I(2)	I(1)	I(1)
Capital Expenditure	I(2)	I(1)	I(1)	I(0)	I(1)
Education Expenditure	I(1)	I(1)	I(1)	I(1)	I(1)
Non-Education Expendit.	I(1)	I(1)	I(2)	I(1)	I(1)
Health Expenditure	I(1)	I(1)	I(2)	I(0)	I(1)
Non-Health Expenditure	I(1)	I(1)	I(2)	I(1)	I(1)
Private Non-Oil GDP	I(1)	I(1)	I(1)	I(0)	I(1)
Oman (1979-2013):					
Total Expenditure	I(1)	I(1)	I(2)	I(1)	I(1)
Current Expenditure	I(1)	I(1)	I(2)	I(1)	I(1)
Capital Expenditure	I(1)	I(1)	I(1)	I(1)	I(1)
Education Expenditure	I(0)	I(0)	I(1)	I(1)	I(1)
Non-Education Expendit.	I(1)	I(1)	I(2)	I(1)	I(1)
Health Expenditure	I(0)	I(0)	I(1)	I(1)	I(1)
Non-Health Expenditure	I(1)	I(1)	I(2)	I(1)	I(1)
Private Non-Oil GDP	I(1)	I(0)	I(2)	I(2)	I(2)
Qatar (1979-2013):					
Total Expenditure	I(1)	I(2)	I(2)	I(1)	I(1)
Current Expenditure	I(1)	I(2)	I(1)	I(1)	I(1)
Capital Expenditure	I(2)	I(2)	I(1)	I(1)	I(1)
Education Expenditure	I(2)	I(1)	I(2)	I(2)	I(2)
Non-Education Expendit.	I(1)	I(2)	I(2)	I(1)	I(1)
Health Expenditure	I(1)	I(2)	I(2)	I(0)	I(2)
Non-Health Expenditure	I(1)	I(2)	I(2)	I(1)	I(1)
Private Non-Oil GDP	I(2)	I(2)	I(1)	I(0)	I(2)

Note: For detailed unit root test results of the variables please refer to tables C12-C15.

Table C12: Unit Root Tests: ADF Test

All variables in constant prices

Variable	Test Statistic Level	First Difference	Order of Integration
Bahrain (1979-2013):			
Total Expenditure	-0.57 (0)	-4.80 (0)***	I(1)
Current Expenditure	-0.28 (0)	-1.88 (2)	I(2)
Capital Expenditure	-2.25 (4)	-2.18 (3)	I(2)
Education Expenditure	-2.01 (1)	-3.25 (0)**	I(1)
Non-Education Expenditure	-0.64 (0)	-4.93 (0)***	I(1)
Health Expenditure	-1.58 (1)	-4.83 (0)***	I(1)
Non-Health Expenditure	-0.63 (0)	-4.94 (0)***	I(1)
Private Non-Oil GDP	-2.69 (1)	-3.66 (0)**	I(1)
Oman (1979-2013):			
Total Expenditure	-0.97 (2)	-4.05 (1)***	I(1)
Current Expenditure	-1.52 (0)	-4.69 (0)***	I(1)
Capital Expenditure	-1.69 (1)	-4.02 (0)***	I(1)
Education Expenditure	-5.57 (2)***	-3.35 (0)**	I(0)
Non-Education Expenditure	-0.75 (2)	-4.24 (1)***	I(1)
Health Expenditure	-3.83 (1)**	-5.98 (5)***	I(0)
Non-Health Expenditure	-1.00 (0)	-4.13 (0)***	I(1)
Private Non-Oil GDP	-2.62 (1)	-5.02 (0)***	I(1)
Qatar (1979-2013):			
Total Expenditure	0.13 (0)	-3.71 (0)***	I(1)
Current Expenditure	1.47 (5)	-4.83 (0)***	I(1)
Capital Expenditure	-1.00 (1)	-1.59 (2)	I(2)
Education Expenditure	0.00 (0)	-2.26 (2)	I(2)
Non-Education Expenditure	-0.01 (0)	-3.80 (0)***	I(1)
Health Expenditure	-0.19 (0)	-4.67 (0)***	I(1)
Non-Health Expenditure	0.04 (0)	-3.86 (0)***	I(1)
Private Non-Oil GDP	-0.60 (0)	-2.12 (1)	I(2)

Notes: Test statistics denote the statistical significance of the γ coefficient estimate in the ADF test regression (3.14) in section 3.4.2. Statistical significance levels of 1%, 5%, and 10% are indicated by ***, **, and *, respectively. Following the approach of Cheung and Lai (1995) critical values have been adjusted for the small sample size of the variables. ADF test regressions include either a constant and a deterministic trend (variables in levels) or a constant (variables in first differences). The number of lags m in the ADF test regression (3.14) is given in parenthesis. The lag length has been determined by the Hannan-Quinn information criterion with the maximum lag length being set to 5.

Table C13: Unit Root Tests: KPSS Test

All variables in constant prices

Variable	Test Statistic Level	First Difference	Order of Integration
Bahrain (1979-2013):			
Total Expenditure	0.225 (3)***	0.255 (3)	I(1)
Current Expenditure	0.190 (3)**	0.277 (3)	I(1)
Capital Expenditure	0.219 (3)***	0.149 (3)	I(1)
Education Expenditure	0.157 (3)**	0.122 (3)	I(1)
Non-Education Expenditure	0.226 (3)***	0.259 (3)	I(1)
Health Expenditure	0.192 (3)**	0.168 (3)	I(1)
Non-Health Expenditure	0.225 (3)***	0.255 (3)	I(1)
Private Non-Oil GDP	0.169 (3)**	0.147 (3)	I(1)
Oman (1979-2013):			
Total Expenditure	0.183 (3)**	0.163 (3)	I(1)
Current Expenditure	0.160 (3)**	0.177 (3)	I(1)
Capital Expenditure	0.196 (3)**	0.115 (3)	I(1)
Education Expenditure	0.086 (3)	0.226 (3)	I(0)
Non-Education Expenditure	0.190 (3)**	0.177 (3)	I(1)
Health Expenditure	0.102 (3)	0.175 (3)	I(0)
Non-Health Expenditure	0.186 (3)**	0.167 (3)	I(1)
Private Non-Oil GDP	0.073 (3)	0.282 (3)	I(0)
Qatar (1979-2013):			
Total Expenditure	0.246 (3)***	0.615 (3)**	I(2)
Current Expenditure	0.242 (3)***	0.565 (3)**	I(2)
Capital Expenditure	0.237 (3)***	0.451 (3)*	I(2)
Education Expenditure	0.225 (3)***	0.274 (3)	I(1)
Non-Education Expenditure	0.246 (3)***	0.621 (3)**	I(2)
Health Expenditure	0.233 (3)***	0.364 (3)*	I(2)
Non-Health Expenditure	0.246 (3)***	0.618 (3)**	I(2)
Private Non-Oil GDP	0.230 (3)***	0.465 (3)**	I(2)

Notes: Test statistics are given by η estimates of the Lagrange Multiplier test in equation (3.17) in section 3.4.2. Here, variables in levels (first differences) are tested against the null hypothesis of trend stationarity (level stationarity). Statistical significance levels of 1%, 5%, and 10% are indicated by ***, **, and *, respectively. Critical values are taken from Kwiatkowski et al. (1992). The number of lags is given in parenthesis. As proposed by Kwiatkowski et al. (1992), the lag order has been determined as a function of the total sample size, T: number of lags = $integer[4(T/100)^{1/4}]$.

Table C14: Unit Root Tests: ADF-GLS Test

All variables in constant prices

	Test Statistic		Order of
Variable	Level	First Difference	Integration
Bahrain (1979-2013):			
Total Expenditure	-1.23 (1)	-1.02 (4)	I(2)
Current Expenditure	-0.68 (1)	-1.30 (2)	I(2)
Capital Expenditure	-1.93 (4)	-1.66 (4)*	I(1)
Education Expenditure	-2.21 (1)	-1.89 (2)*	I(1)
Non-Education Expenditure	-1.24 (1)	-1.04 (4)	I(2)
Health Expenditure	-1.85 (1)	-1.20 (2)	I(2)
Non-Health Expenditure	-1.20 (1)	-1.04 (4)	I(2)
Private Non-Oil GDP	-2.39 (1)	-2.97 (1)***	I(1)
Oman (1979-2013):			
Total Expenditure	-1.42 (2)	-1.23 (3)	I(2)
Current Expenditure	-1.37 (2)	-0.90 (4)	I(2)
Capital Expenditure	-1.83 (1)	-2.18 (2)**	I(1)
Education Expenditure	-2.43 (1)	-1.95 (1)**	I(1)
Non-Education Expenditure	-1.30 (2)	-1.22 (3)	I(2)
Health Expenditure	-2.05 (2)	-2.14 (2)**	I(1)
Non-Health Expenditure	-1.39 (2)	-1.23 (3)	I(2)
Private Non-Oil GDP	-1.89 (1)	-0.74 (2)	I(2)
Qatar (1979-2013):			
Total Expenditure	-1.16 (1)	-1.44 (4)	I(2)
Current Expenditure	-1.00 (1)	-1.67 (5)*	I(1)
Capital Expenditure	-1.27 (2)	-1.62 (2)*	I(1)
Education Expenditure	-1.21 (4)	-1.25 (2)	I(2)
Non-Education Expenditure	-1.13 (1)	-1.48 (4)	I(2)
Health Expenditure	-1.22 (1)	-1.48 (3)	I(2)
Non-Health Expenditure	-1.11 (1)	-1.44 (4)	I(2)
Private Non-Oil GDP	-1.74 (2)	-2.13 (1)**	I(1)

Notes: Test statistics denote the statistical significance of the γ coefficient estimate in the ADF-GLS test regression (3.21) in section 3.4.2. Statistical significance levels of 1%, 5%, and 10% are indicated by ***, **, and *, respectively. Critical values are taken from Elliott et al. (1996). Variables in levels (first differences) exhibit a constant and a deterministic trend (only a constant). The number of lags m in (3.21) is given in parenthesis. The lag length has been determined by a general-to-specific procedure with the maximum lag length being set to 5.

Table C15: Unit Root Tests: Unit Root Test with Structural Break

All variables in constant prices

Variable	Test Statistic Level	First Difference	Order of Integratio
Bahrain (1979-2013):			
Total Expenditure	-3.76 (5, 1994)	-5.03 (0, 1997)**	I(1)
Current Expenditure	-2.75 (3, 1993)	-7.21 (0, 1998)***	I(1)
Capital Expenditure	-4.36 (4, 2000)*	-3.62 (3, 2002)	I(0)
Education Expenditure	-3.11 (3, 1995)	-4.64 (5, 2000)**	I(1)
Non-Educat. Expendit.	-3.83 (5, 1994)	-5.03 (0, 1997)**	I(1)
Health Expenditure	-4.41 (3, 1999)*	-3.53 (0, 2001)	I(0)
Non-Health Expendit.	-3.56 (5, 1994)	-5.24 (0, 2000)***	I(1)
Private Non-Oil GDP	-5.60 (4, 2004)***	-4.88 (0, 2002)**	I(0)
Oman (1979-2013):			
Total Expenditure	-3.07 (1, 1992)	-6.29 (1, 1990)***	I(1)
Current Expenditure	-2.96 (5, 2008)	-6.05 (2, 1990)***	I(1)
Capital Expenditure	-3.51 (1, 2003)	-5.45 (4, 2004)***	I(1)
Education Expenditure	-3.68 (2, 1993)	-5.24 (2, 1990)***	I(1)
Non-Educat. Expendit.	-3.01 (1, 1992)	-6.29 (1, 1990)***	I(1)
Health Expenditure	-3.35 (1, 1992)	-6.94 (5, 1992)***	I(1)
Non-Health Expendit.	-2.98 (1, 1992)	-6.20 (1, 1990)***	I(1)
Private Non-Oil GDP	-2.54 (0, 2008)	-4.13 (0, 1989)	I(2)
Qatar (1979-2013):			
Total Expenditure	-3.47 (5, 2001)	-4.85 (0, 1990)**	I(1)
Current Expenditure	-3.76 (0, 2000)	-6.01 (0, 1990)***	I(1)
Capital Expenditure	-3.59 (3, 2000)	-7.05 (0, 2000)***	I(1)
Education Expenditure	-3.20 (3, 1993)	-3.45 (4, 1989)	I(2)
Non-Educat. Expendit.	-3.31 (5, 2001)	-4.90 (0, 1990)**	I(1)
Health Expenditure	-4.21 (1, 1997)*	-4.73 (0, 2000)**	I(0)
Non-Health Expendit.	-3.26 (5, 2001)	-5.03 (0, 1990)**	I(1)
Private Non-Oil GDP	-5.12 (5, 2002)***	-5.67 (0, 2002)***	I(0)

Notes: Test statistics denote the statistical significance of the ϕ coefficient estimat in the test regression (3.23) in section 3.4.2. Statistical significance levels of 1%, 5% and 10% are indicated by ***, **, and *, respectively. Critical values are taken fror Lee and Strazicich (2004). The number of lags and the break date are given in paren thesis. The lag length has been determined by a general-to-specific procedure wit the maximum lag length being set to 5. The break date refers to a break both in th constant as well as in the deterministic trend of the respective variable.

Table C16: Overview - Number of Cointegration Relations

All variables in constant prices

	Bahrain[1]		Oman[1]		Qatar[1]	
Variables	JOH	SAI	JOH	SAI	JOH	SAI
Total Expenditure & Private Non-Oil GDP	0	0	na	na	na	na
Current Expenditure & Capital Expenditure & Private Non-Oil GDP	0	0	na	na	na	na
Education Expenditure & Non-Education Expenditure & Private Non-Oil GDP	1**	1**	na	na	na	na
Health Expenditure & Non-Health Expenditure & Private Non-Oil GDP	0	0	na	na	na	na

Notes: Statistical significance levels of cointegration relationships are indicated by ***(1%), **(5%), and *(10%), respectively. For detailed cointegration test results of the Johansen trace test (JOH) and the Saikkonen and Lütkepohl test (SAI) please refer to table C17.

[1] The following variables have been excluded from the respective cointegration tests since they are not integrated of order one (table C11): private non-oil GDP (Oman), education expenditure (Qatar), health expenditure (Qatar) and private non-oil GDP (Qatar).

Table C17: Cointegration Tests: Bahrain (Private Sector)

All variables in constant prices

	Test Setup			Test Statistic	
Variables	Det. Terms	Lags	H_0	JOH	SAI
Full Sample (1979-2013):					
Total Expenditure	Restr. Trend	2	r=0	15.26	10.40
& Private Non-Oil GDP			r=1	4.42	0.50
Current Expenditure	Restr. Trend	2	r=0	28.73	24.21
& Capital Expenditure			r=1	14.14	8.69
& Private Non-Oil GDP			r=2	4.73	1.53
Education Expenditure	Restr. Trend	1	r=0	42.84**	31.34**
& Non-Education Expendit.			r=1	13.87	6.70
& Private Non-Oil GDP			r=2	2.06	0.49
Health Expenditure	Unr. Const.	1	r=0	22.27	16.48
& Non-Health Expenditure			r=1	5.01	5.16
& Private Non-Oil GDP			r=2	0.09	na[1]

Notes: Test statistics of the Johansen trace (JOH) test and the Saikkonen and Lütkepohl (SAI) test are given by the λ_{tr} estimate in equation (3.32) in section 3.4.3. In case of the SAI test, the likelihood ratio testing procedure in (3.32) is applied to detrended variables. The test statistic of the JOH test is adjusted by a Bartlett correction factor as suggested by Johansen (2002). The cointegration rank r of the variables is given under the null hypothesis, H_0. Statistical significance levels of the test statistic for rejecting H_0 are indicated by ***(1%), **(5%), and *(10%), respectively. The deterministic terms and the number of lags refer to the VAR estimates in equations (3.27) (JOH) and (3.33) (SAI) and have been determined by the Hannan-Quinn information criterion.

[1] In case of an unrestricted constant, the SAI test does not allow for testing the null hypothesis $H_0 : r = n-1$. With regard to their test framework Saikkonen and Lütkepohl (2000a:375-378) assume that at least one of the n different endogenous variables contains a deterministic linear trend which, however, is not part of the cointegration relations. Such a trend will not be generated by a VAR process exhibiting an unrestricted constant if all endogenous variables are stationary. Therefore, the alternative hypothesis $r = 0$ (stationarity) is ruled out by assumption. As a result, the null hypothesis, H_0, can be at most $r = n - 2$.

Table C18: Zero Restriction Tests (Private Sector)

All variables in constant prices

Variables (& Trend)	VECM Det. Terms	Lags	r	β	Test Statistic
Bahrain (1979-2013):					
Education Expenditure	Restr. Trend	1	1	2.954	15.18***
& Non-Education Expenditure				-2.363	17.61***
& Private Non-Oil GDP				1.000	3.38*
& Trend				-0.085	10.18***

Notes: Test statistics are given by the Λ estimate in a zero restriction test for the variable in the respective line (see equation (3.35) in section 3.4.3). Statistical significance levels of 1%, 5%, and 10% for rejecting the null hypothesis of variable exclusion are indicated by ***, **, and *, respectively. In case the VECM has been specified with a restricted trend the exclusion of this deterministic trend from the cointegration relations is also tested. The deterministic terms and the lag order in the VECM specifications are identical to the cointegration test setups for the respective variables. The cointegration rank r has been set to 1 for all VECM estimates. Coefficients in the β vector of the VECM have been normalised on the GDP coefficient.

Table C19: Stability Tests (Private Sector)

All variables in constant prices

Variables	VECM Det. Terms	Lags	r	Stat. Significant Break Years T_B
Bahrain (1979-2013):				
Education Expenditure	Restr. Trend	1	1	na
& Non-Education Expenditure				
& Private Non-Oil GDP				
& Trend				

Notes: Statistically significant break years T_B have been identified through a Chow break point testing procedure as given in equation (3.36) in section 3.4.3. The time range for searching potential break points was 1993-1999. Statistical significance levels of 1%, 5%, and 10% for rejecting the null hypothesis of parameter constancy are indicated by ***, **, and *, respectively. Significance levels are based on bootstrap p-values. The number of bootstrap replications is 1000. In case no variable has been excluded from the cointegration vector through a zero restriction test, the specification of the VECM remains unaltered. Otherwise, deterministic terms and the lag order have been determined anew by the Hannan-Quinn information criterion.

Table C20: VECM - Final Specification (Private Sector)

All variables in constant prices

Variables (& Trend)	Det. Terms	Lags	r	β-Vector
Bahrain (1979-2013):				
Education Expenditure	Restr. Trend	1	1	2.954
& Non-Education Expenditure				-2.363
& Private Non-Oil GDP				1.000
& Trend				-0.085

Notes: Coefficients in the β vector of the VECM have been normalised on the GDP coefficient. Lag order and deterministic terms have been determined by the Hannan-Quinn information criterion.

Table C21: Granger Causality Tests (Private Sector)

All variables in constant prices

Variables	Null Hypothesis	Test Statistic
Bahrain (1979-2013):		
Education Expend.	H_0: Ed. Exp. $\nRightarrow$ Non-Ed. Exp. & GDP	2.69*
& Non-Educat. Exp.	H_0: Non-Ed. Exp. $\nRightarrow$ Ed. Exp. & GDP	4.02**
& Priv. Non-Oil GDP	H_0: GDP $\nRightarrow$ Ed. Exp. & Non-Ed. Exp.	0.03

Notes: The direction of causality between cointegrated variables has been analysed by Wald tests which examine whether the respective VECM coefficients in equation (3.38) are zero (section 3.4.5). Statistical significance levels of the test statistic for rejecting the null hypothesis, H_0, of no Granger causality are indicated by *** (1%), ** (5%), and * (10%), respectively. Here, the symbol $\nRightarrow$ denotes "does not Granger cause". The VECM have been specified as shown in table C20.

Appendix D: Econometric Results and Robustness Check Chapter 7

Econometric Results Chapter 7

Table D1: Overview - Order of Integration

All variables in constant prices

	Unit Root Test Results				Overall
Variable	ADF	KPSS	ADF-GLS	Break	Evaluation
Bahrain (1979-2013):					
Total Expenditure	I(1)	I(1)	I(2)	I(1)	I(1)
Private Sector GFCF	I(1)	I(1)	I(1)	I(1)	I(1)
Credit Private Sector	I(1)	I(2)	I(1)	I(2)	I(1)
Credit Private Business	I(1)	I(1)	I(1)	I(2)	I(1)
Oman (1979-2013):					
Total Expenditure	I(1)	I(1)	I(2)	I(1)	I(1)
Private Sector GFCF	I(1)	I(1)	I(1)	I(0)	I(1)
Credit Private Sector	I(0)	I(0)	I(0)	I(0)	I(0)
Credit Private Business	I(1)	I(0)	I(0)	I(1)	I(1)
Qatar (1979-2013):					
Total Expenditure	I(1)	I(2)	I(2)	I(1)	I(1)
Credit Private Sector	I(1)	I(2)	I(2)	I(1)	I(1)
Credit Private Business	I(1)	I(2)	I(2)	I(0)	I(2)

Note: For detailed unit root test results of the variables please refer to tables D2-D5.

Table D2: Unit Root Tests: ADF Test

All variables in constant prices

	Test Statistic		Order of
Variable	Level	First Difference	Integration
Bahrain (1979-2013):			
Total Expenditure	-0.57 (0)	-4.80 (0)***	I(1)
Private Sector GFCF	-1.33 (0)	-4.46 (0)***	I(1)
Credit Private Sector	-1.92 (1)	-3.60 (0)**	I(1)
Credit Private Business	-1.34 (0)	-3.91 (0)***	I(1)
Oman (1979-2013):			
Total Expenditure	-0.97 (2)	-4.05 (1)***	I(1)
Private Sector GFCF	-1.57 (0)	-5.79 (0)***	I(1)
Credit Private Sector	-3.46 (1)*	-3.53 (0)**	I(0)
Credit Private Business	-2.82 (1)	-3.75 (0)***	I(1)
Qatar (1979-2013):			
Total Expenditure	0.13 (0)	-3.71 (0)***	I(1)
Credit Private Sector	-1.13 (1)	-3.89 (0)***	I(1)
Credit Private Business	-1.39 (3)	-3.16 (0)**	I(1)

Notes: Test statistics denote the statistical significance of the γ coefficient estimate in the ADF test regression (3.14) in section 3.4.2. Statistical significance levels of 1%, 5%, and 10% are indicated by ***, **, and *, respectively. Following the approach of Cheung and Lai (1995) critical values have been adjusted for the small sample size of the variables. ADF test regressions include either a constant and a deterministic trend (variables in levels) or a constant (variables in first differences). The number of lags m in the ADF test regression (3.14) is given in parenthesis. The lag length has been determined by the Hannan-Quinn information criterion with the maximum lag length being set to 5.

Table D3: Unit Root Tests: KPSS Test

All variables in constant prices

	Test Statistic		Order of
Variable	Level	First Difference	Integration
Bahrain (1979-2013):			
Total Expenditure	0.225 (3)***	0.255 (3)	I(1)
Private Sector GFCF	0.190 (3)**	0.141 (3)	I(1)
Credit Private Sector	0.227 (3)***	0.356 (3)*	I(2)
Credit Private Business	0.219 (3)***	0.336 (3)	I(1)
Oman (1979-2013):			
Total Expenditure	0.183 (3)**	0.163 (3)	I(1)
Private Sector GFCF	0.209 (3)**	0.197 (3)	I(1)
Credit Private Sector	0.063 (3)	0.058 (3)	I(0)
Credit Private Business	0.077 (3)	0.054 (3)	I(0)
Qatar (1979-2013):			
Total Expenditure	0.246 (3)***	0.615 (3)**	I(2)
Credit Private Sector	0.227 (3)***	0.383 (3)*	I(2)
Credit Private Business	0.223 (3)***	0.480 (3)**	I(2)

Notes: Test statistics are given by η estimates of the Lagrange Multiplier test in equation (3.17) in section 3.4.2. Here, variables in levels (first differences) are tested against the null hypothesis of trend stationarity (level stationarity). Statistical significance levels of 1%, 5%, and 10% are indicated by ***, **, and *, respectively. Critical values are taken from Kwiatkowski et al. (1992). The number of lags is given in parenthesis. As proposed by Kwiatkowski et al. (1992), the lag order has been determined as a function of the total sample size, T: number of lags $= integer[4(T/100)^{1/4}]$.

Table D4: Unit Root Tests: ADF-GLS Test

All variables in constant prices

	Test Statistic		Order of
Variable	Level	First Difference	Integration
Bahrain (1979-2013):			
Total Expenditure	-1.23 (1)	-1.02 (4)	I(2)
Private Sector GFCF	-1.69 (1)	-1.63 (4)*	I(1)
Credit Private Sector	-1.62 (1)	-2.05 (2)**	I(1)
Credit Private Business	-1.63 (1)	-2.19 (2)**	I(1)
Oman (1979-2013):			
Total Expenditure	-1.42 (2)	-1.23 (3)	I(2)
Private Sector GFCF	-1.51 (1)	-2.28 (3)**	I(1)
Credit Private Sector	-3.45 (1)**	-3.71 (1)***	I(0)
Credit Private Business	-2.90 (1)*	-3.07 (1)***	I(0)
Qatar (1979-2013):			
Total Expenditure	-1.16 (1)	-1.44 (4)	I(2)
Credit Private Sector	-1.27 (1)	-1.10 (5)	I(2)
Credit Private Business	-1.21 (1)	-1.61 (2)	I(2)

Notes: Test statistics denote the statistical significance of the γ coefficient estimate in the ADF-GLS test regression (3.21) in section 3.4.2. Statistical significance levels of 1%, 5%, and 10% are indicated by ***, **, and *, respectively. Critical values are taken from Elliott et al. (1996). Variables in levels (first differences) exhibit a constant and a deterministic trend (only a constant). The number of lags m in (3.21) is given in parenthesis. The lag length has been determined by a general-to-specific procedure with the maximum lag length being set to 5.

Table D5: Unit Root Tests: Unit Root Test with Structural Break

All variables in constant prices

Variable	Test Statistic Level	First Difference	Order of Integration
Bahrain (1979-2013):			
Total Expenditure	-3.76 (5, 1994)	-5.03 (0, 1997)**	I(1)
Private Sector GFCF	-3.79 (4, 2001)	-5.11 (2, 2002)***	I(1)
Credit Private Sector	-4.11 (3, 1996)	-3.97 (0, 2005)	I(2)
Credit Private Business	-4.05 (3, 1996)	-4.11 (0, 2003)	I(2)
Oman (1979-2013):			
Total Expenditure	-3.07 (1, 1992)	-6.29 (1, 1990)***	I(1)
Private Sector GFCF	-4.34 (5, 2000)*	-6.78 (0, 2000)***	I(0)
Credit Private Sector	-4.80 (5, 1991)**	-5.92 (5, 1992)***	I(0)
Credit Private Business	-3.74 (3, 1990)	-5.71 (5, 2008)***	I(1)
Qatar (1979-2013):			
Total Expenditure	-3.47 (5, 2001)	-4.85 (0, 1990)**	I(1)
Credit Private Sector	-3.39 (1, 2002)	-4.67 (1, 2004)**	I(1)
Credit Private Business	-4.23 (5, 1991)*	-4.93 (1, 2004)**	I(0)

Notes: Test statistics denote the statistical significance of the ϕ coefficient estimate in the test regression (3.23) in section 3.4.2. Statistical significance levels of 1%, 5%, and 10% are indicated by ***, **, and *, respectively. Critical values are taken from Lee and Strazicich (2004). The number of lags and the break date are given in parenthesis. The lag length has been determined by a general-to-specific procedure with the maximum lag length being set to 5. The break date refers to a break both in the constant as well as in the deterministic trend of the respective variable.

Table D6: Cointegration Tests: Bahrain, Oman and Qatar

All variables in constant prices

	Test Setup			Test Statistic	
Variables	Det. Terms	Lags	H_0	JOH	SAI
Bahrain (1979-2013):					
Total Expenditure	Restr. Trend	2	r=0	16.08	12.89
& Private Sector GFCF			r=1	2.97	0.71
Total Expenditure	Restr. Trend	2	r=0	18.47	10.49
& Credit Priv. Sector			r=1	6.38	0.15
Total Expenditure	Unrestr. Const.	1	r=0	13.38*	4.36
& Credit Priv. Business			r=1	3.10*	na[1]
Oman (1979-2013):					
Total Expenditure	Restr. Trend	2	r=0	19.17	12.61
& Private Sector GFCF			r=1	7.01	0.61
Total Expenditure	Restr. Trend	2	r=0	12.59	9.28
& Credit Priv. Business			r=1	3.25	2.59
Qatar (1979-2013):					
Total Expenditure	Restr. Trend	2	r=0	23.10	14.56*
& Credit Priv. Sector			r=1	10.76*	0.83

Notes: Test statistics of the Johansen trace (JOH) test and the Saikkonen and Lütkepohl (SAI) test are given by the λ_{tr} estimate in equation (3.32) in section 3.4.3. In case of the SAI test, the likelihood ratio testing procedure in (3.32) is applied to detrended variables. The test statistic of the JOH test is adjusted by a Bartlett correction factor as suggested by Johansen (2002). The cointegration rank r of the variables is given under the null hypothesis, H_0. Statistical significance levels of the test statistic for rejecting H_0 are indicated by ***(1%), **(5%), and *(10%), respectively. The deterministic terms and the number of lags refer to the VAR estimates in equations (3.27) (JOH) and (3.33) (SAI) and have been determined by the Hannan-Quinn information criterion.

[1] In case of an unrestricted constant, the SAI test does not allow for testing the null hypothesis $H_0 : r = n - 1$. With regard to their test framework Saikkonen and Lütkepohl (2000a:375-378) assume that at least one of the n different endogenous variables contains a deterministic linear trend which, however, is not part of the cointegration relations. Such a trend will not be generated by a VAR process exhibiting an unrestricted constant if all endogenous variables are stationary. Therefore, the alternative hypothesis $r = 0$ (stationarity) is ruled out by assumption. As a result, the null hypothesis, H_0, can be at most $r = n - 2$.

Table D7: Zero Restriction Tests

All variables in constant prices

Variables (& Trend)	VECM Det. Terms	Lags	r	β	Test Statistic
Bahrain (1979-2013):					
Total Expenditure	Unrestr. Const.	1	1	1.000	7.50***
& Credit Priv. Business				-0.645	6.86***
Qatar (1979-2013):					
Total Expenditure	Restr. Trend	2	1	1.000	2.85*
& Credit Priv. Sector				-1.071	2.95*
& Trend				0.056	2.76*

Notes: Test statistics are given by the Λ estimate in a zero restriction test for the variable in the respective line (see equation (3.35) in section 3.4.3). Statistical significance levels of 1%, 5%, and 10% for rejecting the null hypothesis of variable exclusion are indicated by ***, **, and *, respectively. In case the VECM has been specified with a restricted trend the exclusion of this deterministic trend from the cointegration relations is also tested. The deterministic terms and the lag order in the VECM specifications are identical to the cointegration test setups for the respective variables. The cointegration rank r has been set to 1 for all VECM estimates. Coefficients in the β vector of the VECM have been normalised on the total expenditure coefficient.

Table D8: Stability Tests

All variables in constant prices

Variables	VECM Det. Terms	Lags	r	Stat. Significant Break Years T_B
Bahrain (1979-2013):				
Total Expenditure & Credit Priv. Business	Unrestr. Const.	1	1	na
Qatar (1979-2013):				
Total Expenditure & Credit Priv. Sector	Restr. Trend	2	1	na

Notes: Statistically significant break years T_B have been identified through a Chow break point testing procedure as given in equation (3.36) in section 3.4.3. The time range for searching potential break points was 1993-1999. Statistical significance levels of 1%, 5%, and 10% for rejecting the null hypothesis of parameter constancy are indicated by ***, **, and *, respectively. Significance levels are based on bootstrap p-values. The number of bootstrap replications is 1000. In case no variable has been excluded from the cointegration vector through a zero restriction test, the specification of the VECM remains unaltered. Otherwise, deterministic terms and the lag order have been determined anew by the Hannan-Quinn information criterion.

Table D9: VECM - Final Specification

All variables in constant prices

Variables (& Trend)	Det. Terms	Lags	r	β-Vector
Bahrain (1979-2013):				
Total Expenditure	Unrestr. Const.	1	1	1.000
& Credit Priv. Business				-0.645
Qatar (1979-2013):				
Total Expenditure	Restr. Trend	2	1	1.000
& Credit Priv. Sector				-1.071
& Trend				0.056

Notes: Coefficients in the β vector of the VECM have been normalised on the total expenditure coefficient. Lag order and deterministic terms have been determined by the Hannan-Quinn information criterion.

Table D10: Granger Causality Tests

All variables in constant prices

Variables	Null Hypothesis	Test Statistic
Bahrain (1979-2013):		
Total Expenditure	H_0: Total Exp. $\nRightarrow$ Credit	7.54***
& Credit Priv. Business	H_0: Credit $\nRightarrow$ Total Exp.	0.27
Qatar (1979-2013):		
Total Expenditure	H_0: Total Exp. $\nRightarrow$ Credit	5.41***
& Credit Priv. Sector	H_0: Credit $\nRightarrow$ Total Exp.	1.97

Notes: The direction of causality between cointegrated variables has been analysed by Wald tests which examine whether the respective VECM coefficients in equation (3.38) are zero (section 3.4.5). Statistical significance levels of the test statistic for rejecting the null hypothesis, H_0, of no Granger causality are indicated by *** (1%), ** (5%), and * (10%), respectively. Here, the symbol $\nRightarrow$ denotes "does not Granger cause". The VECM have been specified as shown in table D9.

Robustness Check: Time Series in Current Prices

Table D11: Overview - Order of Integration

All variables in current prices

Variable	Unit Root Test Results				Overall
	ADF	KPSS	ADF-GLS	Break	Evaluation
Bahrain (1979-2013):					
Total Expenditure	I(1)	I(1)	I(2)	I(1)	I(1)
Private Sector GFCF	I(1)	I(1)	I(1)	I(1)	I(1)
Credit Private Sector	I(1)	I(1)	I(1)	I(0)	I(1)
Credit Private Business	I(1)	I(1)	I(1)	I(0)	I(1)
Oman (1979-2013):					
Total Expenditure	I(1)	I(1)	I(2)	I(2)	I(2)
Private Sector GFCF	I(1)	I(1)	I(1)	I(0)	I(1)
Credit Private Sector	I(1)	I(0)	I(0)	I(1)	I(1)
Credit Private Business	I(1)	I(0)	I(1)	I(1)	I(1)
Qatar (1979-2013):					
Total Expenditure	I(1)	I(2)	I(2)	I(2)	I(2)
Credit Private Sector	I(1)	I(1)	I(1)	I(1)	I(1)
Credit Private Business	I(2)	I(2)	I(1)	I(0)	I(2)

Note: For detailed unit root test results of the variables please refer to tables D12-D15.

Table D12: Unit Root Tests: ADF Test

All variables in current prices

Variable	Test Statistic Level	First Difference	Order of Integration
Bahrain (1979-2013):			
Total Expenditure	-0.56 (0)	-3.93 (0)***	I(1)
Private Sector GFCF	-1.25 (0)	-4.39 (0)***	I(1)
Credit Private Sector	-1.69 (1)	-3.33 (0)**	I(1)
Credit Private Business	-1.67 (1)	-3.72 (0)***	I(1)
Oman (1979-2013):			
Total Expenditure	-0.77 (0)	-4.21 (0)***	I(1)
Private Sector GFCF	-1.44 (0)	-5.91 (0)***	I(1)
Credit Private Sector	-3.08 (1)	-3.60 (0)**	I(1)
Credit Private Business	-2.53 (1)	-4.00 (0)***	I(1)
Qatar (1979-2013):			
Total Expenditure	0.10 (0)	-3.29 (0)**	I(1)
Credit Private Sector	-1.30 (1)	-3.53 (0)**	I(1)
Credit Private Business	-1.66 (3)	-1.80 (2)	I(2)

Notes: Test statistics denote the statistical significance of the γ coefficient estimate in the ADF test regression (3.14) in section 3.4.2. Statistical significance levels of 1%, 5%, and 10% are indicated by ***, **, and *, respectively. Following the approach of Cheung and Lai (1995) critical values have been adjusted for the small sample size of the variables. ADF test regressions include either a constant and a deterministic trend (variables in levels) or a constant (variables in first differences). The number of lags m in the ADF test regression (3.14) is given in parenthesis. The lag length has been determined by the Hannan-Quinn information criterion with the maximum lag length being set to 5.

Table D13: Unit Root Tests: KPSS Test

All variables in current prices

Variable	Test Statistic Level	First Difference	Order of Integration
Bahrain (1979-2013):			
Total Expenditure	0.208 (3)**	0.186 (3)	I(1)
Private Sector GFCF	0.191 (3)**	0.132 (3)	I(1)
Credit Private Sector	0.218 (3)***	0.274 (3)	I(1)
Credit Private Business	0.213 (3)**	0.282 (3)	I(1)
Oman (1979-2013):			
Total Expenditure	0.186 (3)**	0.190 (3)	I(1)
Private Sector GFCF	0.213 (3)**	0.213 (3)	I(1)
Credit Private Sector	0.091 (3)	0.068 (3)	I(0)
Credit Private Business	0.101 (3)	0.066 (3)	I(0)
Qatar (1979-2013):			
Total Expenditure	0.241 (3)***	0.524 (3)**	I(2)
Credit Private Sector	0.220 (3)***	0.319 (3)	I(1)
Credit Private Business	0.218 (3)***	0.404 (3)*	I(2)

Notes: Test statistics are given by η estimates of the Lagrange Multiplier test in equation (3.17) in section 3.4.2. Here, variables in levels (first differences) are tested against the null hypothesis of trend stationarity (level stationarity). Statistical significance levels of 1%, 5%, and 10% are indicated by ***, **, and *, respectively. Critical values are taken from Kwiatkowski et al. (1992). The number of lags is given in parenthesis. As proposed by Kwiatkowski et al. (1992), the lag order has been determined as a function of the total sample size, T: number of lags = $integer[4(T/100)^{1/4}]$.

Table D14: Unit Root Tests: ADF-GLS Test

All variables in current prices

Variable	Test Statistic: Level	Test Statistic: First Difference	Order of Integration
Bahrain (1979-2013):			
Total Expenditure	-1.53 (1)	-1.19 (4)	I(2)
Private Sector GFCF	-1.69 (1)	-1.71 (4)*	I(1)
Credit Private Sector	-1.68 (1)	-2.06 (2)**	I(1)
Credit Private Business	-1.62 (1)	-2.10 (2)**	I(1)
Oman (1979-2013):			
Total Expenditure	-1.62 (1)	-0.90 (3)	I(2)
Private Sector GFCF	-1.44 (1)	-2.08 (3)**	I(1)
Credit Private Sector	-3.09 (1)*	-2.99 (1)***	I(0)
Credit Private Business	-2.65 (1)	-2.57 (1)***	I(1)
Qatar (1979-2013):			
Total Expenditure	-1.39 (1)	-1.46 (2)	I(2)
Credit Private Sector	-1.43 (1)	-1.65 (4)*	I(1)
Credit Private Business	-1.43 (1)	-1.73 (2)*	I(1)

Notes: Test statistics denote the statistical significance of the γ coefficient estimate in the ADF-GLS test regression (3.21) in section 3.4.2. Statistical significance levels of 1%, 5%, and 10% are indicated by ***, **, and *, respectively. Critical values are taken from Elliott et al. (1996). Variables in levels (first differences) exhibit a constant and a deterministic trend (only a constant). The number of lags m in (3.21) is given in parenthesis. The lag length has been determined by a general-to-specific procedure with the maximum lag length being set to 5.

Table D15: Unit Root Tests: Unit Root Test with Structural Break

All variables in current prices

Variable	Test Statistic: Level	Test Statistic: First Difference	Order of Integration
Bahrain (1979-2013):			
Total Expenditure	-3.94 (5, 1994)	-4.32 (0, 1990)*	I(1)
Private Sector GFCF	-3.63 (5, 1992)	-5.27 (2, 2002)***	I(1)
Credit Private Sector	-4.40 (3, 2005)*	-3.98 (0, 1989)	I(0)
Credit Private Business	-4.48 (3, 2005)**	-4.12 (4, 1989)	I(0)
Oman (1979-2013):			
Total Expenditure	-3.53 (4, 1992)	-3.65 (0, 1990)	I(2)
Private Sector GFCF	-4.57 (5, 2000)**	-6.82 (0, 2000)***	I(0)
Credit Private Sector	-3.36 (1, 1990)	-4.76 (5, 1992)**	I(1)
Credit Private Business	-3.69 (3, 1990)	-5.63 (5, 1992)***	I(1)
Qatar (1979-2013):			
Total Expenditure	-3.67 (5, 2002)	-3.95 (0, 2004)	I(2)
Credit Private Sector	-3.41 (1, 2003)	-4.73 (1, 2004)**	I(1)
Credit Private Business	-4.26 (3, 2003)*	-5.04 (1, 2004)**	I(0)

Notes: Test statistics denote the statistical significance of the ϕ coefficient estimate in the test regression (3.23) in section 3.4.2. Statistical significance levels of 1%, 5%, and 10% are indicated by ***, **, and *, respectively. Critical values are taken from Lee and Strazicich (2004). The number of lags and the break date are given in parenthesis. The lag length has been determined by a general-to-specific procedure with the maximum lag length being set to 5. The break date refers to a break both in the constant as well as in the deterministic trend of the respective variable.

Table D16: Cointegration Tests: Bahrain

All variables in current prices

Variables	Test Setup			Test Statistic	
	Det. Terms	Lags	H_0	JOH	SAI
Bahrain (1979-2013):					
Total Expenditure	Restr. Trend	2	r=0	17.16	12.76
& Private Sector GFCF			r=1	3.79	0.19
Total Expenditure	Restr. Trend	2	r=0	19.95	10.15
& Credit Priv. Sector			r=1	6.08	0.01
Total Expenditure	Unrestr. Const.	2	r=0	14.64*	3.75
& Credit Priv. Business			r=1	0.66	na[1]

Notes: Test statistics of the Johansen trace (JOH) test and the Saikkonen and Lütkepohl (SAI) test are given by the λ_{tr} estimate in equation (3.32) in section 3.4.3. In case of the SAI test, the likelihood ratio testing procedure in (3.32) is applied to detrended variables. The test statistic of the JOH test is adjusted by a Bartlett correction factor as suggested by Johansen (2002). The cointegration rank r of the variables is given under the null hypothesis, H_0. Statistical significance levels of the test statistic for rejecting H_0 are indicated by ***(1%), **(5%), and *(10%), respectively. The deterministic terms and the number of lags refer to the VAR estimates in equations (3.27) (JOH) and (3.33) (SAI) and have been determined by the Hannan-Quinn information criterion.

[1] In case of an unrestricted constant, the SAI test does not allow for testing the null hypothesis $H_0 : r = n - 1$. With regard to their test framework Saikkonen and Lütkepohl (2000a:375-378) assume that at least one of the n different endogenous variables contains a deterministic linear trend which, however, is not part of the cointegration relations. Such a trend will not be generated by a VAR process exhibiting an unrestricted constant if all endogenous variables are stationary. Therefore, the alternative hypothesis $r = 0$ (stationarity) is ruled out by assumption. As a result, the null hypothesis, H_0, can be at most $r = n - 2$.

Table D17: Zero Restriction Tests

All variables in current prices

	VECM				Test
Variables (& Trend)	Det. Terms	Lags	r	β	Statistic
Bahrain (1979-2013):					
Total Expenditure	Unrestr. Const.	2	1	1.000	15.50***
& Credit Priv. Business				-0.705	15.33***

Notes: Test statistics are given by the Λ estimate in a zero restriction test for the variable in the respective line (see equation (3.35) in section 3.4.3). Statistical significance levels of 1%, 5%, and 10% for rejecting the null hypothesis of variable exclusion are indicated by ***, **, and *, respectively. In case the VECM has been specified with a restricted trend the exclusion of this deterministic trend from the cointegration relations is also tested. The deterministic terms and the lag order in the VECM specifications are identical to the cointegration test setups for the respective variables. The cointegration rank r has been set to 1 for all VECM estimates. Coefficients in the β vector of the VECM have been normalised on the total expenditure coefficient.

Table D18: Stability Tests

All variables in current prices

	VECM			Stat. Significant
Variables	Det. Terms	Lags	r	Break Years T_B
Bahrain (1979-2013):				
Total Expenditure	Unrestr. Const.	2	1	na
& Credit Priv. Business				

Notes: Statistically significant break years T_B have been identified through a Chow break point testing procedure as given in equation (3.36) in section 3.4.3. The time range for searching potential break points was 1993-1999. Statistical significance levels of 1%, 5%, and 10% for rejecting the null hypothesis of parameter constancy are indicated by ***, **, and *, respectively. Significance levels are based on bootstrap p-values. The number of bootstrap replications is 1000. In case no variable has been excluded from the cointegration vector through a zero restriction test, the specification of the VECM remains unaltered. Otherwise, deterministic terms and the lag order have been determined anew by the Hannan-Quinn information criterion.

Table D19: VECM - Final Specification

All variables in current prices

Variables (& Trend)	Det. Terms	Lags	r	β-Vector
Bahrain (1979-2013):				
Total Expenditure	Unrestr. Const.	2	1	1.000
& Credit Priv. Business				-0.705

Notes: Coefficients in the β vector of the VECM have been normalised on the total expenditure coefficient. Lag order and deterministic terms have been determined by the Hannan-Quinn information criterion.

Table D20: Granger Causality Tests

All variables in current prices

Variables	Null Hypothesis	Test Statistic
Bahrain (1979-2013):		
Total Expenditure	H_0: Total Exp. $\nRightarrow$ Credit	9.72***
& Credit Priv. Business	H_0: Credit $\nRightarrow$ Total Exp.	0.75

Notes: The direction of causality between cointegrated variables has been analysed by Wald tests which examine whether the respective VECM coefficients in equation (3.38) are zero (section 3.4.5). Statistical significance levels of the test statistic for rejecting the null hypothesis, H_0, of no Granger causality are indicated by *** (1%), ** (5%), and * (10%), respectively. Here, the symbol $\nRightarrow$ denotes "does not Granger cause". The VECM have been specified as shown in table D19.